D0349511

ONE WEEK LOAN
UNIVERSITY OF GLAMORGAN
TREFOREST LEARNING RESOURCES CENTRE
Pontypridd, CF37 1DL
Telephone: (01443) 482626
Books are to be returned on or before the last date below

Women and Freedom
in Early America

Women and Freedom in Early America

EDITED BY

Larry D. Eldridge

NEW YORK UNIVERSITY PRESS
New York and London

NEW YORK UNIVERSITY PRESS
New York and London

Copyright © 1997 by New York University

All rights reserved

Library of Congress Cataloging-in-Publication Data
Women and freedom in early America / edited by Larry D. Eldridge.
p.   cm.
Includes index.
ISBN 0-8147-2193-1 (cloth : alk. paper).—ISBN 0-8147-2198-2
(pbk. : alk. paper)
1. Women—United States—History   2. United States—History—
Colonial period, ca. 1600–1775.   I. Eldridge, Larry D.
HQ1416.W65   1997
305.4'0973—dc20   96-25303
                    CIP

New York University Press books are printed on acid-free paper,
and their binding materials are chosen for strength and durability.

Manufactured in the United States of America

10 9 8 7 6 5 4 3 2 1

Learning Resources
Centre

1216628b

For my mother, Louise.
A woman close to my heart.
A woman I much admire.

Contents

Acknowledgments

A few years ago, here at Widener University, I taught for the first time an undergraduate seminar in colonial women's history. The idea for this volume came out of discussions in that class. Since then I have spoken often with those students and others about what sorts of essays to include, about what they would find interesting, challenging, enlightening. Their input shaped this volume more than they know. I thus owe a great debt to our history majors. Above all among them, though, I must thank Tina Arcidiacono. She not only helped me envision the volume, but also labored tirelessly as my editorial assistant during the two years it took to bring this project to completion. Her work has been superior, her commitment steadfast.

I also gratefully acknowledge the help and support of others here at Widener. At the beginning, Barbara Norton reviewed the publication prospectus and encouraged me to go forward with the project. David Wrobel offered advice and encouragement throughout, and I am indebted to him and to Michael Clark for helping me with some difficult editorial decisions The essays on New France are much better for the kind attention Philippe de Gain gave them. Margaret Sadoff was a godsend as my administrative assistant in the later stages of the project. Nor could this book have been completed had it not been for a generous Provost's Grant. I offer a special thanks to Lawrence Buck, who made that grant possible.

I would be remiss if I did not also acknowledge that the women in my life have, in many ways, made significant contributions. In creating this volume, I have thought much about the lives of my mother, Louise, my mother-in-law, Ella, and my sisters, Wendy, Glenda, and Sharon. Their own diverse experiences of freedom, the struggles and successes they have known, have helped shape in me a consciousness and sensitivity I would not otherwise have had. Virginia, my wife and for more than twenty years the love of my life, continues as always to be a rock of patience and support. Emily, my daughter, starts first grade this year. She is my brightest hope for the future and shows every sign of becoming the woman of uncommon grace and intelligence her mother is.

Introduction:
A Remarkable Diversity

Elisabeth de Joybert (Madame de Vaudreuil), though born in the Canadian backwoods, went on to marry a man who eventually became governor-general of New France. For decades, this lady of the French Canadian nobility worked assiduously to advance her family's interests. In 1709, when political foes attacked Governor Vaudreuil, she personally went to the court at Versailles to defend him. Her husband's enemies complained bitterly of Madame de Vaudreuil's influence, and with good reason. Through her astute efforts her husband "enjoyed a longer term of office than any of his counterparts, and six of their seven sons received coveted commissions and colonial governorships." She remained for decades a formidable force in Canadian society and politics.

Phillis Merritt Wanton struggled just to keep her children and to find a home. In 1800, this "Negro woman" appeared before the town authorities in Providence, Rhode Island. She had been called there to give an account of herself and possibly to face ejection from the town as an undesirable transient. She was, she told them, the mother of three children, the youngest a four-year-old daughter she had with her. Phillis was without her husband, a slave freed in 1791. He was in Newport, "at times insane." She herself was an emancipated slave, and she wished only to make a home and a living in the town. Unmoved, the councilmen ordered Phillis out of the town, sending her to Newport and whatever life awaited her there.[1]

The basic theme tying this volume together is women and freedom: how freedom was defined for and by women, how it was achieved or missed, how the parameters and realizations of freedom expanded or contracted over time. Yet the stories of Elisabeth de Joybert and Phillis Merritt Wanton nicely highlight what may be the most notable single contribution this volume makes—revealing the truly remarkable diversity of lives and circumstances the women of early America represent.

Women's lives are explored across a broad span, from Gretchen L. Green's discussion of the role of women in the establishment of the Iroquois Confederacy in the sixteenth century to the struggle through the 1820s of Deborah A. Rosen's New York women as they lost their traditional access to informal justice. Geographically, the essays range the vast colonial terrain from eastern Canada, where Terrence A. Crowley introduces us to a group of Montreal nuns struggling against ecclesiastical domination, down through the plantation South, where we meet the entrepreneurial female printers Martha J. King found in South Carolina. Two chapters focus on New France, one on the Iroquois nations, and one on the southeastern tribes as a group; the remaining twelve cover most of the British-American colonies (South Carolina, North Carolina, Virginia, Maryland, Pennsylvania, New York, and New England). Urban as well as rural areas are represented, too, from Karin A. Wulf's determined Philadelphia spinsters to Johanna Miller Lewis's independent women of the North Carolina backcountry. Ethnic diversity also marks the volume, from Lillian Ashcraft-Eason's nearly voiceless African slave women who came to the American colonies in the seventeenth century, to Eirlys M. Barker's Cherokee and Creek women challenging European notions of women's place in society.

Above all, perhaps, this volume presents early American women in an amazing variety of life circumstances. How very different were Merril D. Smith's deserted Pennsylvania wives from Vivian Bruce Conger's Maryland mothers, providing for their daughters in their wills. How very different were the experiences of Janet Moore Lindman's Baptist women, building their own devotional culture in the Delaware Valley, from Judith A. Ridner's frontier women, struggling to find economic independence. More extreme still, as noted above, how very different were the lives of Jan V. Noel's wealthy and influential women of the French Canadian nobility from those of Ruth Wallis Herndon's poor and beleaguered New England transients.

Such remarkable diversity necessitates the use of eclectic sources and methodologies. The chapters range from literary analysis of Puritan political writings, women's poetry, and African and Iroquois mythology, to examinations of material objects and architectural design, to more conventional historical analysis based on a wide array of sources, including church and court records, correspondence, diaries, journals, newspapers, and account books.

Given such diversity and the varying themes presented in this volume, there is no single "most logical" way to group the essays. Four of them range widely, covering religion, work, marriage, and politics. These I have placed together in part 1, "Race, Ethnicity, and Gender," because in addition to ranging widely they share a focus on the lives and experiences of women who were decidedly not Anglo-American. The remaining twelve essays are grouped into four sections. Part 2 explores women's lives and experience of freedom as those relate to religion. Part 3 focuses on women, work, and the colonial economy. Part 4 on marriage and the family, and part 5 on women, society, and the courts. These divisions are subjective, for each of the essays touches in some way on various aspects of women's lives. Karin A. Wulf's essay, to cite but one example, explores one approach to marriage, but is in the religion section because it draws heavily on Quaker theology.

Yet, the inherent difficulty of grouping the essays is but a minor matter. Much more important is what the volume as a whole offers, namely, a rare opportunity to see inside the lives of women across the span of American colonial space and time and in circumstances as varied as one can imagine. These chapters reveal much we did not know about women's lives; in the end, that is the central purpose of this volume. In some cases what we learn challenges long-held scholarly assumptions. In others, the judgments of historians are confirmed through further study. But above all, we come to know these women—to better understand the lives they led, the struggles they faced, the tragedies, triumphs, foibles, and fulfillment that made up their existence, much as they make up ours. In the end, the best hope we have of truly making women an integral part of our history lies in the kind of work done by the contributors here.

Finally, a note on dates and quotation style. Some of the essays in this volume employ dates with dual years (as in 1682/83). That is because up until 1752 officials in England and her colonies used the old style (Julian) calendar to date government documents. Under it the new year began on 25 March rather than on 1 January as is now the case under the new style (Gregorian) calendar (based on the calendar ordained by Gregory XIII in 1582). When dates are rendered old style, as they appear in the records, January 1 through March 24 dates ordinarily appear with dual years. In addition, at my urging the essays do not employ the device *sic* to indicate errors in the original when quoting sources. Spelling and punctuation were essentially arbitrary during the colonial period, and noting deviations from current norms quickly becomes tedious for the reader. Quotations are therefore rendered as they appear in the sources, without editorial interpolation.

NOTE

1. For the more complete stories of Elisabeth de Joybert and Phyllis Merritt Wanton, see the chapters by Jan V. Noel and Ruth Wallis Herndon in this volume.

I | Race, Ethnicity, and Gender

To be sure, not all women in early America were English, and not all lived in the British colonies. The essays in this section highlight the racial and ethnic diversity women represented. Two focus on Indian-White interactions, one explores perceptions of freedom among African women on the early Chesapeake, and one takes us into a culture very different from anything in Anglo-America—that of the nobility of New France.

Gretchen L. Green assesses the changes that took place in the economic, social, religious, and political lives of Iroquois women between 1600 and 1800. Contact with Europeans brought large changes in Iroquois life, altering the traditional role of women as breadwinners and family heads, but did Iroquois women suffer a loss of freedom as a result? Drawing on archeological and architectural evidence, Jesuit and other European-American eyewitness accounts and ethnographies, New York and New France colonial records, merchants' letter books, and the papers of Indian agents, Green offers an answer. The extremities of matriarchy in early Iroquois society have been overstated, she insists, and so, inevitably, have the alterations that took place in the centuries after European contact. Changes certainly occurred, some of them profound, yet reciprocity had always characterized relations between the sexes in Iroquois society, and fundamentally that remained even as log cabins replaced the longhouses.

Jan V. Noel explores the lives of women among the nobility of New France. Focusing on the experiences of three notable women from important families, Noel shows that Canadian society in general, and the noble caste in particular, placed severe restrictions on women, yet some of those women were able to exert great influence and wield significant power nonetheless. Very active in politics, in financial enterprise, and in forwarding the interests of their families, these women made a place for themselves in an environment that, while apparently opulent and enviable, severely circumscribed women's freedom.

Eirlys M. Barker explores the lives of women in the Indian tribes of the American Southeast. She shows how the women of these tribes enjoyed freedoms far beyond those of European women of the time, how European men encountering such freedom reacted, and how over time— as the Indians went from the status of valuable allies to that of hated impediments to White expansion—Indian women themselves came increasingly to be denigrated rather than respected.

Studying the lives of seventeenth-century black slave and servant women is one of the most difficult tasks in early American historical research. They appear but rarely in the extant records and left few writings of their own. Such women came from cultures in which slavery was common and found an apparently fluid servitude situation in the early Chesapeake. How did that combination of experiences affect their perception of freedom? Drawing creatively on sources ranging from African tribal mythology to legal confrontations and exchanges preserved in colonial court records, Lillian Ashcraft-Eason addresses that perplexing question.

1 Gender and the Longhouse: Iroquois Women in a Changing Culture

GRETCHEN L. GREEN

The Euroamerican concept of freedom does not translate well into native North American cultures. Rather than struggling to be free, native peoples such as the Iroquois struggle to maintain their solidarity, their interconnectedness as a people. While many Euroamerican women in the colonial period strived for greater freedom in their lives, such a notion would have seemed strange to their Iroquois counterparts. Similarly, Native American feminism today has more to do with restoring the gender balance lost when European customs and values encroached on native ones than it has to do with altering "traditional" gender relations in their own culture.[1] Women in Iroquois society two hundred to four hundred years ago needed men, but to say this alone is to say very little and is even misleading; Iroquois men also needed women. Neither men nor women in Iroquois society were independent; the interdependence and balance of male and female were socially, culturally, economically, and politically necessary. Women and men had different roles and functions, but gender differences are not necessarily gender inequalities and do not necessarily lead to them.[2] In Iroquois society the differences did not imply inequity. This sense of balance and equally valued differences varied markedly from gender relations in any European or Euroamerican society (but was similar to that in some west African cultures).

Among the Iroquois, women and men were not literal equals. Women were full social persons "with their own rights, duties, and responsibilities, which were complementary and in no way secondary to those of men."[3] This holds true for Iroquois society throughout and beyond the colonial period of American history. Despite major cultural changes, the most tangible of which was the shift from traditional dwellings to Euroamerican ones—from longhouses to log houses, gender balance remained characteristic of Iroquoia.

The extended-family household and the community were in many ways one and the same in societies such as the Iroquois nations.[4] In Iroquois culture this was manifested symbolically by the longhouse. The longhouse—made of an oblong frame of saplings covered with bark— was the dwelling used through much of the colonial period for each extended family. The village was the longhouse writ large, and the tribe was the longhouse writ larger. The union of the five Iroquois tribes— Mohawk, Oneida, Onondaga, Cayuga, and Seneca, with the sixth, Tuscarora, joining in 1720, was the highest expression of the longhouse metaphor; the Mohawks were keepers of its eastern door, the Senecas of its western door, and so on. The Iroquois Confederacy was a huge longhouse spread across what is now New York state, from Niagara Falls to the Hudson River, encompassing all of the Iroquois people in one large extended family living together.

Difficulties arise in making sense of the scanty and at times conflicting information about women's status in Iroquoia for the seventeenth and eighteenth centuries. Firsthand accounts by those trained in studying cultural differences are not available, so we must rely on the amateur and unconscious anthropologists of the 1600s and 1700s, as well as on other historical and archaeological information. We must be wary, however, of the compound bias in these sources. Virtually all who observed and recorded information were men, and men from a male-dominated (European) background. They filtered all they saw through the lens of their own culture's gender relations. To them, for example, women congregating separately from men in a village were stigmatized, whereas men meeting apart from women signified men's superiority. These outsiders interpreted the activity of male-only meetings as seminal to the workings of the community. Also, since European men of the time believed implicitly that nothing women might have to say would be important (a belief specific to European culture), they spoke almost exclusively to men. They thus learned only the male perspective on how Iroquois society operated, and they used it alone as the basis for their interpretations. There is a male reality and a female reality, and both are necessary for constructing a complete picture of a culture and its history.[5]

Yet, despite the biased sources, there is plenty of evidence that Iroquois gender relations were much more balanced than those of neighboring colonial communities. In one sense that should not be surprising. Iroquois society and culture were kin-based, tribal. In contrast to state societies and cultures, such as those of Europe, tribal societies make no distinction between the public and the private, and therefore separate, spheres for men and women. Moreover, since Iroquois society was kin-based and also matrilineal (tracing descent through the mother), a person's very identity and standing in the society was tied to a relationship with one's mother, not at all with one's father. Biological paternity was insignificant.[6] Two or more matrilineal lineages were formed into clans, some Iroquois tribes having three clans, others seven or eight. Marrying within one's clan was not allowed; clan exogamy prevailed. A father had a different clan affiliation from that of his children. Iroquois society was also generally matrilocal. A married couple lived with the wife's family, not the husband's.[7] Generally, sisters lived with their husbands, children, parents, and unmarried brothers in a longhouse headed by the sisters' mother or grandmother (an elder female relative). Twenty to forty people might live in a longhouse. In the area of disciplining children, a child's mother and the mother's relatives might have as much influence as the father, or even more. A typical figure of authority for an older boy was his maternal uncle, or his mother's cousin.[8]

Matrilineality and matrilocality gave women certain kinds of safeguards and ensured a balance of power between the sexes unlike anything in European society.[9] Matrilocality, for instance, meant that women need not fear domestic violence or marital rape, at least while at home.[10]

And divorce was easily arranged by either spouse. A husband initiated divorce by taking his personal belongings and leaving his in-laws' long-house, and a wife accomplished it by placing her husband's belongings outside the door of her family's longhouse. As Iroquois men still express it today, husbands were guests in their wives' extended-family house-holds, so that they had to behave and answer to the matron, the head of the household.[11] And women often had control over whom they would marry. An Anglican missionary among the Mohawks in 1716 noted that "the Women court the men when they design Marriage." [12] In this kin-based society the husband-wife relationship carried little of the social, legal, economic, religious, and emotional meaning that was evident among Europeans; one's relationships with one's mother's kin were much more significant than a relationship with a spouse.

Matrilocality also had the tendency to disperse related men and con-solidate related women, with notable economic consequences. Related women living together formed cooperative work groups and as a result consolidated their economic power.[13] In fact, economic roles were im-portant indicators of the reciprocity between men and women in Iroquois society at the time of contact with European outsiders. Even in hunter-gatherer societies, women contributed as much as men to the food base, perhaps more. In the agricultural society of the Iroquois, women were the farmers and so contributed an even greater share to the subsistence base.[14]

European colonists often misinterpreted the implications of this divi-sion of labor. John Bartram, a Philadelphia naturalist and traveler, con-cluded from a brief visit to Onondaga country in 1743 that Onondaga men were "lazy and indolent at home, the women continual slaves, modest, very loving, and obedient to their husbands." Bartram, unfamiliar with Iroquois culture, did not take into account that hunting, men's primary contribution to the subsistence base, was hard work. In upper-class European and American colonial culture, hunting was sport, a leisure activity. Nor did Bartram and others like him witness the men clearing fields for the women or building longhouses and palisades. This was men's work in the village, but since it did not take place on a daily basis, it was invisible to the casual outsider. Men worked routinely on making tools and tanning hides, which looked like leisure activities to Bartram.[15]

After the men had finished clearing the land, women planted, culti-vated, and harvested the crops. They turned shucking and braiding corn into festivals to which the men were invited. Of course, from a Euroamerican perspective, female farming was inappropriate; "ladies" did not work in the fields, and even if peasant or slave women did, at least they were accompanied by men who were also sweating to bring in the crops. The idea that men would sit back and allow women to perform this work without their assistance seemed barbarous. Hence the impres-sion that women were drudges and men leisured.

Yet the only woman who had firsthand experience in both societies, and whose thoughts on the subject were recorded, gave surprising testi-mony. Mary Jemison, an Irish woman, was captured in 1758 as a teenager in Pennsylvania and lived out her long life among the Senecas. Jemison had ample chance to compare the lot of women in Seneca and in early American society. She claimed that Seneca women on the whole had easier lives than did white women, with "cares . . . not half as numerous, nor as great." She pointed out that Seneca women worked in the fields without a master or overseer and that "we could work as leisurely as we pleased," with an elder woman coordinating the cooperative effort through each family's fields. Jemison chose to stay in Seneca society even when she had numerous chances to leave and return to Pennsylvania—a telling point about the attraction of Iroquois society for women.[16]

Given that women were the farmers, it made sense that the society was matrilineal and matrilocal. Fields were passed down from generation to generation of clan women. Women were said by both Iroquois men and women—from the 1700s to the present—to be the owners of the land.[17] Matrilocality went along with this. Although village locations changed every twenty years or so, women controlled their common ex-tended-family plots, and the women decided when to move a village site.[18] Within every longhouse the senior woman, the matron, distributed the food equitably once it had been harvested and processed. This applied not only to agricultural products—corn, beans, and squash, the "three sisters" triumvirate of Indian agriculture—but also to fish, gath-ered berries and nuts, harvested maple syrup, and to meat, which the men brought in.[19]

Women were entrepreneurs as well. As early as 1634 a Dutchman reported that several Iroquois women from a nation west of the Mohawks, probably Oneida, were traveling by themselves without male companions on a journey of at least six days each way between Iroquois villages. These women, on reaching the Mohawk village of Canagere, sold dried and fresh salmon and green tobacco for some Dutch currency and wampum.[20] The sums they received for the salmon and tobacco indicate that the level of trade was substantial. The traders did not sell all of their salmon, and so moved on to the next Mohawk village further east. This took place in the heavy snow cover of December and reveals much about Iroquois women. They seemed to be self-assured, entrepreneurial, and not afraid to go by themselves, as well as physically capable of travelling in harsh weather on foot for days on end. This glimpse of Iroquois women stands in stark contrast to their Euroamerican counterparts, few of whom would have enjoyed the freedom implicit in this scene.[21]

Evidence of Iroquois women trading, and traveling long distances to do so, exists for the later colonial period as well. In the 1750s Robert Sanders, an Albany, New York, merchant who did business with Montreal and Kahnawake [22] Mohawk traders, wrote to his Montreal business associates that they should soon be receiving courier packages from female traders from Kahnawake. Marie Magdelene and Agnesse were the names of the most prominent female Kahnawake traders who carried furs, wampum, other commodities, and correspondence back and forth between Montreal and Albany. At least part of the time they traveled alone. The journey took them through almost two hundred miles of geographically and geopolitically difficult terrain.[23]

One Kahnawake woman who was not only a trader-courier but was also involved in intercolonial politics and diplomacy was Susanna, wife of Thanyuchta, a prominent politician at Kahnawake. Susanna traveled back and forth from Kahnawake to Albany fairly often, meeting while in Albany with the colony of New York's commissioners of Indian affairs. On at least one occasion she negotiated with them over English prisoners that some Kahnawake warriors had taken. Conrad Weiser, the Pennsylvania Indian agent, remarked in his journal that Susanna was considered "a noted woman" and "very intelligible," adding that she was personally acquainted with many non-Indian politicians and traders in the English colonies.[24]

Susanna probably traveled alone. And there are other references to Iroquois women traveling long distances (probably on foot, or perhaps partly by canoe) by themselves to trade, to conduct incidental diplomacy, or to pursue personal desires. One Iroquois woman in 1656 "undertook a second journey of more than four hundred leagues, over the snow, the ice, and the roughest roads" to seek a dog her nephew had visualized in a dream.[25] Molly Brant, a prominent Mohawk woman, traveled to Philadelphia and other places as a diplomat-in-training in the 1750s.[26] In 1791 an American official in Seneca country mentioned a Seneca woman trader who drove a hard bargain in selling her goods.[27] Since female involvement in trade and diplomacy would have seemed foreign to colonists and therefore was not recognized (and since Native American women often were invisible or anonymous in colonial records), these few pieces of evidence that do survive are no doubt merely the tip of the iceberg. The modern-day editors of the Dutchman's 1634 account aptly note that "perhaps [Iroquois] women had always been involved at some level in trade and their participation had simply gone unreported."[28]

Iroquois women were involved not only in external trading, but inasmuch as marriage had an economic as well as a social component, women also traded with their husbands and husbands' families upon marriage. Anthropologists often assume that in tribal societies the husband or his family take a leading role in the marriage bargain and that any exchange between the husband and the wife's family is a form of "bride price" or purchase of the wife. Iroquois women, however, often took the initiative in seeking husbands for themselves, and a Jesuit missionary and student of Iroquois culture noted that women, not men, usually arranged marriages.[29] Furthermore, the economic exchange that took place at marriage ceremonies symbolized not unequal relationships between husbands and wives, but reciprocal ones, as illustrated by an Iroquois wedding custom. The marrying couple and their parents sat on a bench facing the presiders, and next to the bride's parents rested a basket of Indian-style corn bread. Next to the groom's parents a basket of venison awaited. At the close of the ceremony, the parents distributed portions of the corn bread and venison to the wedding guests to symbolize the promise of the husband and wife to provide for each other the fruits of their labors—his from the forest domain and hers from the domain of the cultivated field.[30]

This duality underscores the complementarity of roles as opposed to hierarchically based relationships. The Iroquois pattern stood in stark contrast to marriage in colonial America, in which the bride was virtually a piece of property being transferred from her father to her husband.

The complementarity of the female cultivated field and the male forest was metaphorically embedded in Iroquois culture and society. Men held strictly to the cultural mandate that they were not to till the fields once they had cleared them. After the American Revolution, when a Seneca spiritual leader and Quaker missionaries attempted to change the culture by encouraging men to farm and women to cease farming and to retire inside log houses, men and women resisted the change. Men resisted becoming farmers, not because they considered it degrading—as Euroamericans assumed—but because they knew that it was a violation of the natural order for men to be involved in the female domain of coaxing the "three sisters" from Mother Earth. Iroquois men believed that the bond between women and the crops was so intimate and sacred that only women were qualified and able to bring crops to harvest.[31]

Moreover, in the Iroquois world the agricultural fields were part of the female-oriented center of life; the traditional male activity of hunting was peripheral. In spatial and to some degree functional (as well as religious) terms, Iroquois society and culture was divided into center and periphery. The center was the village and the cleared fields nearby; these were primarily female in orientation, as the earth itself was female. The forest beyond was primarily male. There were no hard and fast rules of segregation, however. Women accompanied men on hunting trips and diplomatic forays, activities that were linked symbolically with the forest space, and men cleared fields, built longhouses, and erected palisades within the village.

Men also participated in village politics, along with women.[32] In fact, both had institutionalized roles within a political system far more democratic than that of any state society. The center of Iroquois life, the village, was both symbolically female and integral to political life—in sharp contrast to patterns of colonial American society. Clan mothers, selected from matrons by matrons (senior women of each longhouse or lineage), had the right to choose and depose league sachems (chiefs). The clan mother submitted her nomination to the other sachems, and they usually ratified her choice. She watched over the actions of the sachem she appointed, and if she felt he was not upholding the requirements of his office, she could "knock off the horns" or depose him. Each of these clan mothers also sat in the Iroquois league council meetings along with the sachems they had appointed. There were forty-nine sachems and forty-nine clan mothers, an equal balance of men and women. All of these representatives were chosen by women.[33]

Through this system women were able to moderate the influence of men and vice versa. It seems that women never served as sachems themselves, although J. N. B. Hewitt, an Iroquois student of his culture, implied that this was possible. Women did serve as *Agoianders*, or deputy chiefs, in Mohawk society in the 1700s.[34] A legend about a female chief who lived centuries ago and was a peacemaker between warring Iroquois tribes at the time of the birth of the Iroquois Confederacy hints at this possibility as well. In 1654 Marie de l'Incarnation, the French woman who observed Iroquois and other native societies, mentioned the "women of quality," or "captainesses," who played important roles in decision making at the local political level and who selected diplomatic representatives for peace initiatives.[35]

The question whether women were ever sachems may not be a significant indicator of their degree of political influence because sachems enjoyed "great prestige but had little power." A man of ambition in Iroquois society would prefer to gain achieved status through bravery in warfare than ascribed status through appointment as a sachem. Increasingly over the 1600s and 1700s, sachems were sharing influence with these "pine tree chiefs," who gained influence but never any official status through their brave deeds. Pine tree chiefs were often war chiefs, and theirs was only one of a number of groups with input into the political process in Iroquoia.[36] As Father Joseph-François Lafitau observed in the first decade of the 1700s, in Iroquois political life "[t]he women are always the first to deliberate. . . . They hold their councils apart and, as a result of their decisions, advise the [sachems] on matters on the mat, so that the latter may deliberate on them in their turn." The sachems, he continued, "on this advice, bring together the old people [elders] of their clan. . . . The warriors also have their council apart." Lafitau went on to explain that the council of elders was the most influential one of all of these separate groups, but that even the elders' council "does not work for itself," but rather "serve[s] only to represent and aid the women."[37] Even the council of elders included women, contrary to Euroamerican assumptions.[38] Another Jesuit missionary, Father Claude Dablon, observed in 1671 that Iroquois women of high rank were "much respected" in the political roles similar to those Lafitau described. Dablon also mentioned the tangible results of female political influence, noting that "one of these women of quality took the lead in persuading the [Onondaga people], and afterward the other nations, to make peace with the French."[39]

Lafitau also observed, at Kahnawake, that the women at large had orators who would speak for them in political councils or meetings. This was true at the village, nation, and confederacy levels. The men (sachems and warriors) also had orators who routinely spoke on their behalf in at-large meetings. Speakers had an obligation to press forward the opinion of the group they spoke for, regardless of their own personal feelings on the matter being considered.[40] Euroamericans misunderstood the role of speakers, an error that contributed to their portrayal of an exclusively male political system. Colonial politicians did not realize that the speaker was merely an orator, a mouthpiece, for a group of people and that no one person had decision-making power over a village or a nation or the Iroquois confederacy. But as time went on, Euroamericans' attempts to deal with speakers as legitimate sources of power resulted in the legitimation of that power, which was exclusively male. The changing role of speakers diminished female political influence.[41]

When Euroamericans held meetings with Iroquois delegates, the format was bicultural. This often meant leaving the women behind because colonial politicians and diplomats complained about the presence of women at such forums.[42] In Euroamerican culture it did not make sense for women to be present at such councils, and colonial men assumed that the same held true in any other culture, ignoring evidence to the contrary or refusing to acquiesce to prevailing norms in North America. Although the Iroquois conceded the point, their men insisted on waiting until the day following any important talks to announce their consensus-based policy, after conferring with their female counterparts in the evening following the official proceedings. Only outwardly was the Iroquois political system altered in contact with other cultures. In fact, by the 1790s the Senecas were reasserting the right of women to address Euroamerican officials. Colonel Thomas Proctor, a U.S. envoy, reported that Seneca matrons harangued him both publicly and privately regarding American efforts to purchase a large part of Seneca territory. The matrons warned Proctor that he must listen to them as well as to the sachems "for we are the owners of this land and it is ours; for it is we that plant it for our and their [the sachems'] use." Iroquois politics and gender relations had not changed completely by the 1790s.[43]

Iroquois women enjoyed considerable power over matters of peace and war. They could prevent a war party from starting out by withholding food and moccasins for the trip, and a matron could commission a war party, forcing men of a related longhouse to conduct war as a means to obtain captives (who would be potential adoptees into the matron's family and clan). Once captives were brought to the village, the matron had final authority over whether to adopt any captive as a family member. The matron would also "requicken" an ancestral name for the adoptee. This amounted to considerable prestige and genuine authority for the matron and served to counteract and to balance the importance of men's role in warfare, which grew in prominence in the 1600s and 1700s.[44]

Although the underlying bases of some of women's powers were losing significance by the end of the eighteenth century, the powers they exercised remained, indicating a cultural commitment to gender balance in Iroquois society. Well into the nineteenth century (and even to the present day within the Onondaga nation) women were still appointing sachems and being involved in the political process, and descent for land ownership was still reckoned matrilineally despite the passing of the female-oriented agricultural economy.[45] A shift away from matrilocality and extended-family longhouses toward (often) single-family, dispersed log houses, a shift that was taking place throughout the eighteenth century, did not signal the end of matrilineages. Although less often synonymous with a physical household, matrilineages, as subdivisions of clans, remained important as a way of defining one's relationship to others in the clan-based society.[46]

Even Jesuit missionaries, known for their overt attempts to introduce patriarchy into native communities,[47] did not eliminate matrilocality or matrilineality in the Mohawk mission community of Kahnawake. From the 1670s until their expulsion from Quebec in the 1760s, the Jesuits tolerated matrilocal longhouses and female agriculture, and Kahnawake women were, it appears, as active as any other Iroquois women, traveling, trading, and conducting diplomacy. In the colonial period, Catholicism does not seem to have had a significant impact on Kahnawake gender relations. Lafitau's comments about the "superiority" of women in Iroquois politics came from his observations at Kahnawake.[48]

Regarding matrilineality at Kahnawake, a dual naming practice developed. People retained their clan affiliations and their matrilineally given names (a single name in the Mohawk language) alongside Christian given names bestowed at baptism. In the parish registers both names were used, Mohawk and Christian (French). Not until 1876, with the Canadian government's interference, were the people of Kahnawake forced to use patrilineal naming practices, at least for official purposes. Only then was the matrilineal naming system at Kahnawake significantly modified and undermined.[49]

. . .

Gender relations at Catholic Iroquois communities were no less balanced than those at other Iroquois communities. A variety of factors affected gender balance in Iroquoia in the colonial period. Various groups were more or less exposed to Catholic or Protestant Christianity, some more disposed than others to hold fast to traditional spirituality. Some villages lived in much closer proximity to encroaching Euroamericans than others. And of course there were cultural as well as political differences between the various tribes of the Iroquois Confederacy. All of these factors had some effect on gender relations.

Yet, despite differing specific circumstances in a variety of communities, complementarity between women and men survived throughout the 1600s, the 1700s, and beyond. Iroquois women went about their business not as appendages or drudges of the men in their lives, but as distinct persons in a society based on interdependence and reciprocity. In striking contrast to any Euroamerican (or African American) woman who held social or political power in colonial North America, Iroquois women held such power because of their gender, not in spite of it. Changing historical circumstances, although affecting all people to some degree, had only a minor impact on the balance of center and periphery, of female and male, in Iroquois societies. The continuity of women's lives from longhouse to log house was a powerful one.

NOTES

Thanks to Carol Karlsen, Lea McChesney, Brian Deer, Alice Nash, and Cheryl Bluto-Delventhal for their assistance in the conceptualization of this essay.

1. The term *traditional* in reference to native cultures is problematic. It usually refers to the period just prior to extensive contact with outsiders (Europeans and others), but this is highly subjective and implies that subsequent cultural traits are somehow less authentic.

2. See Stephanie Coontz and Peta Henderson's introduction to *Women's Work, Men's Property: The Origins of Gender and Class*, edited by Coontz and Henderson (London: Verso, 1986), 1–2, 12. See also Eleanor Leacock, "Women, Power, and Authority," in *Visibility and Power: Essays on Women in Society and Development*, edited by Leela Dube, Eleanor Leacock, and Shirley Ardener (Delhi: Oxford University Press, 1986), 111.

3. Eleanor Leacock, "Women's Status in Egalitarian Society: Implications for Social Evolution," in *Myths of Male Dominance: Collected Articles on Women Cross-Culturally*, edited by Eleanor Leacock (New York: Monthly Review Press, 1981), 152. See also Joseph François Lafitau, *Customs of the American Indians Compared with the Customs of Primitive Times*, edited and translated by William N. Fenton and Elizabeth Moore, 2 vols. (Toronto: Champlain Society, 1974–77), 1:69–70.

4. Leacock, *Myths of Male Dominance*, 136 (for the problem of the concept of tribe, see 135); Mona Etienne and Eleanor Leacock, introduction to *Women and Colonization: Anthropological Perspectives*, edited by Etienne and Leacock (New York: Praeger, 1980), 4–5; Alice Schlegel, "Male and Female in Hopi Thought and Action," in *Sexual Stratification: A Cross-Cultural View*, edited by Alice Schlegel (New York: Columbia University Press, 1977), 252; Coontz and Henderson, introduction to *Women's Work: Men's Property*, 15–16; M. Z. Rosaldo, "The Use and Abuse of Anthropology," *Signs* 5, no. 3 (1980):397–410.

5. Mona Etienne and Eleanor Leacock, introduction to *Women and Colonization*, edited by Etienne and Leacock, 4; Rayna Reiter, introduction to *Toward an Anthropology of Women*, edited by Rayna Reiter (New York: Monthly Review Press, 1975), 12–15. Reiter suggests that male dominance in a culture may be merely a male fantasy; something that men assert but that women deny (see 15). See also Annette B. Weiner, *Women of Value, Men of Renown: New Perspectives in Trobriand*

Exchange (Austin: University of Texas Press, 1976), 15–17, 228–29; Sally Slocum, "Woman the Gatherer: Male Bias in Anthropology," in Reiter, *Toward an Anthropology of Women*, 36–50. Also, regarding present-day male bias in archaeology, see Marie Ferdais, "Matrilinéarité et/ou matrilocalité chez les Iroquoiens: Remarques critiques et méthodologiques à l'usage des archéologues," *Recherches amérindiennes au Québec* 10 (1980):181–88; Janet Spector, *What This Awl Means: Feminist Archaeology at a Wahpeton Dakota Village* (St. Paul: Minnesota Historical Society Press, 1993), chaps. 1 and 2.

6. Even in patrilineal native North American groups, often biological paternity was not important, and fathers as well as mothers took on responsibility for all children of the extended family, not only their own. See Leacock, *Myths of Male Dominance*, 239–87.

7. There were a few exceptions, such as the need for a sachem (and his wife) to live in his maternal clan lineage longhouse.

8. Cara Richards, "Huron and Iroquois Residence Patterns, 1600–1650," in *Iroquois Culture, History, and Prehistory*, edited by Elisabeth Tooker (Albany: University of the State of New York, 1967), 51–56; Daniel K. Richter, *The Ordeal of the Longhouse: The Peoples of the Iroquois League in the Era of European Colonization* (Chapel Hill: University of North Carolina Press, 1992), 20; Joan Jensen, "Native American Women and Agriculture: A Seneca Case Study," in *Unequal Sisters: A Multicultural Reader in U.S. Women's History*, edited by Ellen Carol DuBois and Vicki L. Ruiz (New York: Routledge, 1990), 63; George Hamell, letter to author, 8 March, 1994.

9. Eleanor Leacock, "Women, Power and Authority," 114; Stephanie Coontz and Peta Henderson, "Property Forms, Political Power, and Female Labor," in Coontz and Henderson, *Women's Work, Men's Property*, 36–37, 111, 115–34; Weiner, *Women of Value, Men of Renown*, 231.

10. There is virtually no evidence of rape in eastern woodlands societies anyway, an indication that men did not feel the need to dominate women. See June Namias, *White Captives: Gender and Ethnicity on the American Frontier* (Chapel Hill: University of North Carolina Press, 1993), 47–48, 89.

11. John Mohawk, comments made at panel discussion on Iroquois history, "The Great Debate," October 15, 1993, Kahnawake, Canada.

12. From Society for the Propagation of the Gospel Records, cited in Daniel K. Richter, " 'Some of Them ... Would Always Have a Minister with Them': Mohawk Protestantism, 1683–1719," *American Indian Quarterly* 16, no. 4 (Fall 1992): 478. There was also evidence of polyandry, or women taking plural husbands, and no evidence of polygyny, or men taking plural wives, in Iroquoia in the 1700s. See Lafitau, *Customs of the American Indians*, 1:336–37.

13. Barbara Nowak, "Women's Roles and Status in a Changing Iroquois Society," in *Occasional Papers in Anthropology*, vol. 1, edited by Ann McElroy and Carolyn Matthiasson (Buffalo: Department of Anthropology, State University of

New York), 105–6; Carol Ember, "An Evaluation of Alternative Theories of Matrilocal versus Patrilocal Residence," *Behavior Science Research* 9, no. 2 (1974), 135–49.

14. Anthropologists have overestimated the importance of meat and hunting in traditional societies. See Slocum, "Woman the Gatherer," 43; Rosaldo, "Use and Abuse of Anthropology," 410; Etienne and Leacock, *Women and Colonization*, 10; Spector, *What This Awl Means*, 76–77; Karen Anderson, *Chain Her by One Foot: The Subjugation of Women in Seventeenth-Century New France* (London: Routledge, 1991), 225.

15. John Bartram, *Observations on . . . His Travels from Pensilvania to Onondaga, Oswego, and the Lake Ontario (1743)* (London, 1751; reprint, Ann Arbor, Mich.: University Microfilms Fascimile Series, 1966), 77. For a similar interpretation, see Milo M. Quaife, ed., *The Indian Captivity of O. M. Spencer* (Chicago: R. R. Donnelly, 1917), 75.

16. June Namias, ed., *A Narrative of the Life of Mrs. Mary Jemison* (Norman: University of Oklahoma Press, 1992), 84; James Axtell, "The White Indians of Colonial America," in *The European and the Indian: Essays in the Ethnohistory of Colonial North America*, edited by James Axtell (New York: Oxford University Press, 1981); John Demos, *The Unredeemed Captive: A Family Story from Early America* (New York: Knopf, 1994); Lafitau, *Customs of the American Indians*, 2:54–55. Although many European men thought they saw Indian female farmers as drudges, a rare European female observer did not find this at all; she saw Iroquois women's work as not so different from her own. European men had an erroneous, mythical (and class-bound) view of the female workload in their own culture; they carried with them the fiction of women as creatures of leisure. This was true only for the aristocracy. See Natalie Zemon Davis, "Iroquois Women, European Women," in *Women, "Race," and Writing in the Early Modern Period*, edited by Margo Hendricks and Patricia Parker (London: Routledge, 1994), 245.

17. Lafitau, *Customs of the American Indians*, 1:69, 86; [Thomas Proctor], *Narrative of the Journey of Col. Thomas Proctor to the Indians of the North-West* [1791], reprinted in *Pennsylvania Archives* 4 (1876):600; Jensen, "Native American Women and Agriculture," 54; Diane Rothenberg, "Mothers of the Nation: Seneca Resistance to Quaker Intervention," in Etienne and Leacock, *Women and Colonization*, 68; Ronald Wright, *Stolen Continents* (Toronto: Penguin, 1991), 332; Ellen Gabriel in *Kahnesetake: 270 Years of Resistance*, National Film Board of Canada, 1992; Arthur C. Parker, *Parker on the Iroquois*, edited by William Fenton (Syracuse, N.Y.: Syracuse University Press, 1968), 42.

18. Martha Randle, "Iroquois Women, Then and Now," in *Symposium on Local Diversity in Iroquois Culture*, Smithsonian Institution, Bureau of American Ethnology, Bulletin 149 (Washington, D.C., 1951), 173; Richter, *Ordeal of the Longhouse*, 126; Lafitau, *Customs of the American Indians*, 2:69–70.

19. There is evidence that women also knew how to hunt (and they accompa-

nied men on winter hunts). See Lafitau, *Customs of the American Indians*, 1:305; Charles H. Torok, "Tyendinaga Acculturation," in *Iroquois Culture, History and Prehistory*, edited by Elisabeth Tooker (Albany: New York State Museum and Science Center, 1970), 32.

20. Wampum was a form of Dutch-Native intercultural currency, which also became both a medium for diplomatic protocol and a mnemonic device that the Iroquois used ceremonially. It was made from beads strung together in rows and then sewn together to form a belt of many rows of beads creating a distinctive design.

21. Charles T. Gehring and William A. Starna, eds. and trans., *A Journey into Mohawk and Oneida Country, 1634–1635: The Journal of Harmen Meyndertsz van den Bogaert* (Syracuse, N.Y.: Syracuse University Press, 1988), 6, 36. See also William Guy Spittal, ed., *Iroquois Women: An Anthology* (Ohsweken, Ont.: Iroqrafts, 1990), 116–17.

22. Kahnawake is a predominantly Mohawk (Catholic) community just south across the St. Lawrence River from Montreal. Its modern habitation dates from the 1670s.

23. [Robert Sanders], "Sanders Letter-Book 1752–1758," National Archives of Canada, 31, 44, 51, 62; Gretchen Green, " 'A Sort of Republic': The Kahnawake Iroquois and Free Trade in an Age of Imperial Competition," paper presented at the Institute of Early American History and Culture, Williamsburg, Va., February 1991.

24. Edmund B. O'Callaghan and Berthold Fernow, eds., *Documents Relative to the Colonial History of the State of New York*, 15 vols. (Albany: Weed and Parsons, 1853–87), 6:795.

25. Reuben G. Thwaites, ed., *The Jesuit Relations and Allied Documents*, 73 vols. (Cleveland: Burrows, 1896–1901), 43:273.

26. Gretchen L. Green, "Molly Brant, Catharine Brant, and Their Daughters: A Study in Colonial Acculturation," *Ontario History* 81, no. 3 (1989), 237. Pierre Charlevoix documented a 1691 female diplomatic mission in *History and General Description of New France*, edited by John G. Shea, 6 vols. (1744; New York: Harper, 1900), 4:198–99. Lewis Henry Morgan also noted women of all ages and physical conditions traveling long distances in the 1800s. See William Fenton, ed., *League of the Iroquois* (Secaucus, N.J.: Citadel Press, 1962), 117.

27. Proctor, *Narrative of the Journey*, 561.

28. Gehring and Starna, *A Journey into Mohawk and Oneida Country*, 36. This was similar to the activities of Algonkian women as outlined in Robert Grumet, "Sunksquaws, Shamans, and Tradeswomen: Middle Atlantic Coastal Algonkian Women during the 17th and 18th Centuries," in Etienne and Leacock, *Women and Colonization*, 43–62.

29. Lafitau, *Customs of the American Indians*, 1:69.

30. William Guy Spittal, note on Ann Shafer, "The Status of Iroquois

Women," in Spittal, *Iroquois Women*, 122. Also Ann Lewis, "Separate Yet Sharing," *The Conservationist* 30 (January-February 1976):17; Elisabeth Tooker, "Women in Iroquois Society," in *Extending the Rafters: Interdisciplinary Approaches to Iroquoian Studies*, edited by Michael K. Foster, Jack Campisi, and Marianne Mithun (Albany: State University of New York Press, 1984), 118; "Traditional Wedding Ceremonies," *Eastern Door* 3, no. 4 (March 25, 1994):20.

31. Merle H. Deardorff, "The Religion of Handsome Lake: Its Origins and Development," in *Symposium on Local Diversity*, 94; Anthony F. C. Wallace, *The Death and Rebirth of the Seneca* (New York: Random House, 1972), chap. 9; Nancy Shoemaker, "The Rise or Fall of Iroquois Women," *Journal of Women's History* 2 (Winter 1992):39–57.

32. William N. Fenton, "Structure, Continuity, and Change in the Process of Iroquois Treaty Making," in *The History and Culture of Iroquois Diplomacy*, edited by Francis Jennings, William N. Fenton, Mary Druke, and David R. Miller (Syracuse, N.Y.: Syracuse University Press, 1985), 9.

33. J. N. B. Hewitt, "Status of Women in Iroquois Polity Before 1784," in *Annual Report of the Board of Regents of the Smithsonian Institution for 1932*, Washington, D.C., 479, 481. Hewitt also implied that women could be chiefs (see 484). In the Iroquois Book of the Great Law, the rhetoric of "nephews and nieces," the balancing of men and women, is evident. See Parker, *Parker on the Iroquois*, 42–59, 106–13.

34. Lafitau, *Customs of the American Indians*, 1:293. This was not widely known by outsiders who witnessed only pan-Iroquois political meetings. Lafitau explained that "they are recognized in the [village level] but they are not shown before the allied nations as is the custom and practice for the chiefs" (see 294).

35. William Beauchamp, "Iroquois Women," *Journal of American Folklore* 13 (April-June 1900):89; George Hamell, "From Longhouse to Log House: At Home among the Senecas, 1790–1828," paper presented at U.S. Capitol Historical Society's "Native Americans in the Early Republic" symposium, March 1992, 23; Marie de l'Incarnation, *Correspondance*, ed. Dom Guy Oury (Solesmes: Abbaye Saint-Pierre, 1971), Sept. 24, 1654, cited in Davis, "Iroquois Women, European Women," 357n.

36. Fenton, "Structure, Continuity, and Change," 12–13. Regarding the rise of pine tree chiefs at the expense of traditional sachems and the effect on women (particularly matrons), see Green, "Molly Brant, Catharine Brant, and Their Daughters," 235–50; Morgan in Fenton, *League of the Iroquois*, 100–103.

37. Lafitau, *Customs of the American Indians*, 1:295, 69. Also Fenton, *League of the Iroquois*, 106.

38. Fenton, "Structure, Continuity, and Change," 11. Also, Sally Slocum points out the dangers of assuming that the generic pronoun refers to men only. See Slocum, "Woman the Gatherer," 38.

39. Thwaites, *Jesuit Relations*, 54:281.

40. Lafitau, *Customs of the American Indians*, 1:298–99; Beauchamp, "Iroquois Women," 86–87; William L. Stone, *The Life and Times of Red-Jacket, or Sa-go-ye-wat-ha; Being the Sequel to the History of the Six Nations* (New York: Wiley and Putnam, 1841), 56–60, 154–56.

41. Nowak, "Women's Roles and Status," 99; James Axtell, ed., *The Indian Peoples of Eastern America: A Documentary History of the Sexes* (New York: Oxford University Press, 1981), 151.

42. For example, see James Sullivan, Alexander Flick, and Milton Hamilton, eds., *The Papers of Sir William Johnson*, 14 vols. (Albany: University of the State of New York, 1921–65), 3:707–12; also Spittal's note on Ann Shafer, "The Status of Iroquois Women," 119.

43. Proctor, *Narrative of the Journey*, 600.

44. Lafitau, *Customs of the American Indians*, 2:99, 101, 154–71; [James Smith], *Scoouwa: James Smith's Captivity Narrative* (Columbus: Ohio Historical Society, 1978), 29–31; Namias, *A Narrative of the Life of Mrs. Mary Jemison*, 75–80; Hewitt, "Status of Women in Iroquois Polity," 480; James Lynch, "The Iroquois Confederacy, and the Adoption and Administration of Non-Iroquoian Individuals and Groups Prior to 1756," *Man in the Northeast* 30 (1985):83–99. Judith K. Brown emphasizes the economic basis for women's ability to prevent war parties. See Brown, "Economic Organization and the Position of Women among the Iroquois," *Ethnohistory* 17, (1970):151–67, and Brown, "Iroquois Women: An Ethnohistoric Note," in Reiter, *Toward an Anthropology of Women*, 235–51.

45. See Shoemaker, "Rise or Fall of Iroquois Women," 39–57; Cara E. Richards, "The Role of Iroquois Women: A Study of the Onondaga Reservation," (Ph.D. diss., Cornell University, 1957), 14, 55. Richards found that in the mid-twentieth century, descent reckoning for land ownership was still matrilineal at Onondaga. Present-day Iroquois expressions of the importance of women in the polity demonstrate the continuity of this cultural feature. See, for example, George Judson, "Some Indians See a Gamble with Future in Casinos," *New York Times*, May 15, 1994, E5; Aroniawenrate, "Time Track," *Eastern Door*, June 3, 1994, 3.

46. See Bartram, *Observations on His Travels*, 40; Hamell, "From Longhouse to Log House," 25; Fenton, "From Longhouse to Ranch-type House," in Tooker, *Iroquois Culture, History, and Prehistory* (1970), 12. Regarding the survival of matrilineages, see Fenton's review of *Ordeal of the Longhouse*, by Richter, in *Ethnohistory* 41 (1994): 346.

47. See Eleanor Leacock, "Montagnais Women and the Jesuit Program for Colonization," in Etienne and Leacock, *Women and Colonization*, 25–42; Anderson, *Chain Her by One Foot*; Carol Devens, *Countering Colonization: Native American Women and Great Lakes Missions, 1630–1900* (Berkeley: University of California Press, 1992). See also Nancy Shoemaker, "Kateri Tekakwitha's Tortuous Path to Sainthood," in *Negotiators of Change: Historical Perspectives on Native American*

Women, edited by Nancy Shoemaker (New York: Routledge, 1995); K. I. Koppedrayer, "The Making of the First Iroquois Virgin: Early Jesuit Biographies of the Blessed Kateri Tekakwitha," *Ethnohistory* 40 (1993): 277–306.

48. See Gretchen Green, "A New People in an Age of War: The Kahnawake Iroquois, 1667–1760" (Ph.D. diss., College of William and Mary, 1991). The shift away from matrilocal extended-family longhouses was taking place in the 1750s and 1760s at Kahnawake, but not as a result of any Jesuit policy. Female farming remained a tradition there long after the 1760s. For another example of an eighteenth-century woman from Kahnawake in a strong spiritual as well as temporal role, see Helen H. Tanner, "Coocoochee: Mohawk Medicine Woman," *American Indian Culture and Research Journal* 3, no. 3 (1979):23–42.

49. Archives Nationales de Québec à Montréal, Paroisse Mission St.-François-Xavier, Co. Laprairie, Québec, Registres des baptêmes, mariages, sepultures. Also Thwaites, *Jesuit Relations,* 54:275–79; Kathleen Jamieson, "Sex Discrimination and the Indian Act," in *Arduous Journey: Canadian Indians and Decolonization,* edited by J. Rick Ponting (Toronto: McClelland and Stewart, 1986), 117–21; Demos, *The Unredeemed Captive,* chap. 7.

2 Women of the New France Noblesse

JAN V. NOEL

New France was in many ways an archaic colony. It lacked the vigorous commercial class that had such a profound impact on the economic and political evolution of the English colonies. It also lacked a nobility invigorated, as in France, by intermarriage with dynamic entrepreneurs and financiers. Ironically, though, New France's rather backward social structure allowed certain French Canadian women some surprising liberties. A number of women found freedom to engage in business, travel, and political activity. Here we shall examine three families with generations of mothers and daughters who engaged in bold public action, and the conditions that permitted such unusual conduct.

Rather than forerunners of some future more "liberated" feminine condition, the women discussed here were inhabitants of a backwater—one that was slow to adopt the new rigidities of gender that were beginning to supplant the rigidities of caste in Europe. They were in some ways throwbacks to an earlier age of medieval fortresses and walled towns. Such strongholds offered women their own forms of freedom, but it was the rather stiff freedom not of ambitious, free-wheeling individuals, but of players in a pageant: dressed in costume, they were able to ad lib their script, to speak and act dynamically, only to the extent that they remained within the codes of their aristocratic order. In their public enterprises they were not stepping outside of established roles; rather, they were fulfilling their well-accepted duties as members of a military noblesse. Here in brief are their stories.

Agathe St. Père (Madame de Repentigny) is considered the founder of French Canada's textile industry. She must have developed certain managerial skills early; the death of her mother when Agathe was barely fifteen left her to raise ten siblings, including a newborn baby. At age twenty-eight she married Pierre Legardeur de Repentigny, a warrior from one of Montreal's most distinguished families. The couple had one son and seven daughters. In her middle age, Agathe went into business. In 1705 she ransomed nine New England weavers who had been captured by the Indians and hired them to work for her. She had copies made of the town's one loom and arranged for Canadian men and women to serve as apprentices to the skilled New Englanders. The strong, coarse cloth her factory produced provided working-class Montreallers, who could not afford imported woolens, with warm, heavy capes to wear over their other garments. When the weavers later returned to Boston, the apprentices continued the operation. Some remained at St. Père's workshop; others used looms she distributed to their homes. Agathe St. Père also experimented with Indian dyeing and tanning techniques using local plants and minerals. The king was sufficiently impressed to grant royal subsidies for several years.[1]

Another outstanding Montrealler was Louise de Ramezay.[2] She was raised in a sylvan riverside chateau, and her father was the town governor. Upon his death in 1724 Louise's mother, Charlotte de la Ronde (Madame de Ramezay), carried on the family timber and sawmill operation located in the Richelieu Valley near their seigneurial lands. Many vicissitudes befell the business. A flood carried away the mill; a legal dispute with neighboring landowners dragged on ruinously; a careless ship captain let the timber rot in Quebec rather than transporting it to France. But the daughter, Louise, succeeded where her mother had failed. Managing to settle the land question amicably, she secured additional timber reserves and restored the business. Going into partnership with another woman, she opened a second sawmill. Later she purchased a Montreal tannery, bringing a master tanner into the partnership. Sometimes managing matters herself and sometimes employing foremen, Louise de Ramezay traveled frequently between Montreal, Chambly, and Quebec to oversee the various operations. In acquiring additional properties and making them profitable, Louise is credited with restoring the family's flagging fortunes. Her colonial operations were sufficiently flourishing that she did not go along when her brother and other friends and relatives fled to France at the time the British conquered New France in 1760. She remained in business until her death in 1776.

The women of a third powerful family exercised control that was political as well as economic. Born in the Acadian backwoods, Elisabeth de Joybert (Madame de Vaudreuil) provides an aristocratic variant of the rags to riches story. Though she lost her father at age five, Elisabeth received government assistance to attend the Ursuline convent school in Quebec City, where her teachers described her as pretty and refined.[3] She married a man who was eventually appointed governor-general of New France. The family fortunes were advanced by two guardians at the French court: initially by Madame de Marson, Elisabeth's mother, who managed to secure audiences with French officials to advance her daughter's Canadian family. Madame de Marson was reported to have been responsible for Vaudreuil's appointment as governor. In 1709, when political enemies were undermining the position of Governor Vaudreuil (a man described by the intendant as one ignorant of all subjects except military ones),[4] Elisabeth herself sailed to defend her husband's interests at Versailles. There, no doubt, her mother coached her in the ways of the court and introduced her to the right people. Elisabeth won the ear of the colonial minister Jérome Pontchartrain to such an extent that he permitted her to read the complaints of her husband's enemies—which they naturally thought they were making in confidence. Her correspondence and audiences with two different ministers extended over a period of thirty years. Although the minister did not always support her proposals, his comments in the margins of her letters, and a number of favorable results, indicate that they were taken seriously. The bonds with the crown grew even closer when Madame de Maintenon and several others highly placed at court recommended Elisabeth for the position of under-governess to the family of the Duke de Berry, a grandson of King Louis XIV.

Madame de Vaudreuil built a network of supporters for the governor, making "clever use of her influence by recommending various Canadians for appointment and advancement."[5] During the time she was in France, cries of outrage emanated from her husband's enemies back in Quebec. "She controls all the positions in Canada," wrote the attorney general. "She writes magnificent letters from all sorts of places to the seaports about the power she can exert over him [Pontchartrain]. . . . She offers her protection, she threatens to use her influence." He added that "she causes great fear and imposes silence on most of those who could speak against her husband."[6] Another Quebec official wrote that "everything is in a wretched state; a mere woman is in control, to the same extent when she is absent as when she is here."[7] He also claimed that Vaudreuil was entirely governed by his wife. Be that as it may, her "somewhat phlegmatic"[8] husband enjoyed a longer term of office than any of his counterparts, and six of their seven sons received coveted commissions and colonial governorships. For two decades a range of highly placed colonials spoke of Madame de Vaudreuil, "La Gouvernante," as a formidable force.

In a sense the women of the Repentigny, Ramezay, and Vaudreuil families are only the most successful and dramatic of the long list of publicly active women in New France.[9] In another sense, though, they are quite exceptional. These three families were members of a small ruling caste, some 3 percent of the population. Their status was sufficiently high that it outweighed gender restrictions other women may have faced. They belonged to the Second Estate, the nobility, which was considered so far above the common people as to have different blood (hence "bluebloods") from the ordinary villeins or "vile persons." Of particular interest is the way in which rules of caste took precedence over rules of gender—at a time when patriarchal authority was on the rise in France.[10] In Canada the notion that men and women had strictly separate natures and roles would await the arrival of a new elite after the British conquest in 1760.

. . .

This chapter focuses on the losers in the battle for empire in North America. New France was the neglected colony of a top-heavy absolute monarchy in France that was inefficient in finance and intemperate in war, destined to come crashing down in 1789. Although New France was less burdened with palaces and courtiers, it was in some ways an even clearer case of a too-grand edifice built on shaky foundations. As early as 1701 New France claimed territory stretching from Acadia on the Atlantic, westward past the Great Lakes, and down the Mississippi River Valley to the Gulf of Mexico. But upon this vast ground there were few French settlers: about 14,000 in 1700, compared to some 225,000 in the American colonies. Given this disparity and the enmity between the two empires, it is surprising that New France endured until 1760, by which time the triumphant American colonies had some 1,500,000 and the losers only 70,000.

This underpopulated colony could only sustain itself with swords drawn and cannons roaring. In the mother country rich bourgeoisie and educated administrators of the *noblesse de la robe* were intermarrying with the old military noblesse, taming them for a courtly role, but the more archaic variant continued to predominate in New France. Well over three-quarters of the Canadian nobility sprang from military families.[11] The Canadian was reported to "love war more than any other thing." [12] Another French visitor wrote that in Canada most military officers were nobles and that New France possessed more of the ancient (that is, military) nobility than any other French colony, perhaps more than all the others put together.[13] Visitors to the colony noted the Canadian officers' valor, hardihood, and willingness to campaign, as well as their patience in waiting long years for promotions.[14]

For the women of this elite a central fact of life was the loss of fathers, husbands, brothers, sons—their departure for overseas service, their absence on summer campaigns in the interior, their arrival home with wounds, or their failure to return at all. Agathe St. Père's life was certainly shaped by war. Her father, grandfather, uncle, and son were all killed by Indians. The Norman clan of Legardeur de Repentignys and Legardeur de Tillys into which she married boasted some nineteen of these "*chevaliers de St. Louis*" who served their government not only at Saratoga, Michilimackinac, and Labrador, but under the exotic skies of Martinique and Pondicherri in India. Louise de Ramezay's father campaigned against the Iroquois and defended Quebec City from a fleet sent up from Boston in 1690. As for Louise's four brothers, the eldest, Claude, died at age nineteen fighting with the French navy at Rio de Janeiro. Louis died at age twenty-one leading thirty Frenchmen into battle against the Cherokees. Charles-Hector perished at age thirty-six in a shipwreck. The sole surviving one, Jean-Baptiste-Nicolas Roch, was already an ensign in the colonial troops at age eleven.

These families were part of what historian William Eccles has described as a military caste system.[15] Such a system is "characterized by hereditary status, endogamy, and social barriers rigidly sanctioned by custom, law, or religion."[16] Status passed from father to son. The founding pool of 181 nobles intermarried to the extent that within a few generations they were nearly all related to one another.[17] Nobles had a distinctive demographic profile that included slightly longer life, much higher celibacy rates, and bigger families for those who did marry. Although commoners typically conceived in spring, nobles conceived in the autumn, when summer campaigns were over.[18] Male and female nobles occupied separate pews at the front of the church, and generally they laid claim to bishoprics and to the administrative positions in convents.

There were other caste signifiers, too. Manual labor was forbidden. Though prohibitions on commerce among the nobility had been abolished in the colony, trade was an adjunct to military or administrative service and was not to interfere with "living nobly." Nobles alone could duel. They had distinctive forms of dress: not only the warrior's armor and sword but also the powdered wigs; floral brocades; satin and velvet garments; trimmings of lace, braid, and ribbons; silk stockings; and silver-buckled shoes that nobles of both sexes wore by prerogative while entertaining, paying court, or attending state functions.

• • •

In 1705, when Montreal was still a small town of about two hundred houses, mostly wooden, there began to take shape on Notre Dame Street near the waterfront a massive stone mansion with four chimneys and walls about three feet thick. The proud owner, Claude de Ramezay, described it as "unquestionably the most beautiful in Canada."[19] The great pile was in chaste Norman style. From the windows could be seen gardens, orchards, and fields stretching down toward the St. Lawrence. Not long after the foundations were laid, Claude began imploring the Crown for subsidies, the governorship requiring "much expense to sustain . . . with honour." [20] Honor meant providing not only for the couple's ten children but also for frequent visits from Madame de Ramezay's kin and allies, the governor's military cronies, and frequent official visitors to Montreal.

Opening the stately door of the Ramezays' chateau in Montreal or the Vaudreuils' in Quebec, one would immediately be struck by the coats of arms that signified noble rank, discernible on stained glass windows, furniture, and knickknacks around the room. On the wall were tapestries and tableaux of various members of the noble family and of the royals. Typical trappings included gold-framed mirrors, armoires, chess and other board games, and copper-trimmed bellows to assure a blazing fire. There was also the rare sight—in a colony where most were illiterate and no newspaper ever saw publication—of a few books and a writing desk. At mealtime one sat down to fine china and silver tableware. [21]

One luxury conspicuously absent was privacy. The interconnected rooms were thoroughfares. Beds of assorted size were scattered about in most of the rooms, even kitchens and vestibules. These were the days when servants—sometimes of a different sex—still slept close by their masters or mistresses; when royal weddings included public dressings for bed and royal newlyweds holding court receptions from their beds. Colonials followed suit. A lady of the Vaudreuil family entertained distinguished visitors from her sickbed, for example, and a visiting military engineer shared a bedroom with a married couple. [22] Agathe St. Père and her husband shared their Montreal home with the textile factory, retaining the right to use the courtyard door to reach the upstairs apartments of their own large family. A little convent of Ursulines shared the Ramezays' stone house in Trois-Rivières before the family was transferred to Montreal. The Chateau St. Louis, Quebec home of the Vaudreuils and successive governors-general, was full of all sorts of live-in guests—adopted Indian children, New England captives, envoys who stayed so long suspicions arose that they were spies, children's boarding school friends and others from France, and of course servants, including the cook, the carpenter, and the wine steward. In the 1720s some forty people lived in the chateau during the busy autumn and winter season, most of them sitting down to breakfast and dinner every day.[23]

One person *not* necessarily at home was the mother. Elisabeth de Joybert left for France to look after family legal affairs in 1696/97 when her husband was too involved with military concerns to go himself. She left again in the autumn of 1709, turning over to a nursemaid baby Marie-Elisabeth, about two months old. She did not return home until 1721 (though the governor came to France for a long visit). After two years in the colony she was off to France again because she wanted to secure family favor with the new minister. Returning only briefly in 1724, she departed shortly after her husband died in 1725. At that time she left the now teenage Marie-Elisabeth and her sister for another half year before bringing them to France. Every spring the governor, with or without his wife, would decamp from the Chateau to spend the summer in Montreal. The chateau's furnishings suggested the parents' peripatetic existence: clothes were stored in portable chests rather than dressers, and the governor kept his old camp bed.[24]

Noble families experienced very little of what would today be considered private life. The limited space to which they were confined is well symbolized by the elaborate curtained beds of the period, which doubled as bedrooms. Even when the bed curtains were drawn, the intimacy of the conjugal couple would have been rather limited by modern standards. How much empathy existed between forty-seven-year-old veteran officer Philippe de Vaudreuil and his seventeen-year-old bride Elisabeth de Joybert? Even with Agathe St. Père and Charlotte de la Ronde, more typical in being a decade younger than their mates,[25] how much meeting of the minds was there between seasoned officers and fresh graduates of convent schools?

Wives did not compensate for the emotional or physical absence of their husbands by clinging to their children. In the towns noble infants a few months after birth were typically ejected not only from the bed but from their home and were sent out to nursemaids in the countryside until the age of two. There were no cooing and crawling infants to humanize the great halls. These and other child-rearing practices were not healthful. Infant mortality rates among the eighteenth-century colonial noblesse climbed toward 50 percent around 1750—double the rate for the rest of the population.[26] Montreal children who survived nursing came home for a few years before going off a several days' journey to board at the elite Ursuline convent in Quebec, where future businesswoman Louise de Ramezay was packed off with her older sisters at the age of five;[27] or for regimental training, sometimes at the military academies in France; or to another household to begin the lifelong cultivation of relationships with other "people of quality."

The evidence is not that their mothers tried to keep them at home, but quite the contrary. Lest there be an interval between schooling and career, Madame de Vaudreuil and other mothers besieged the Crown with letters begging that their sons be admitted into the army at lower ages. When the king reduced the age to fifteen in the 1720s, they implored that their fourteen-year-olds at least be placed at the top of the waiting list.[28] So hot was this deadly quest that Madame de Ramezay, who had lost her three eldest sons to war, responded to the shipwreck death of the fourth with a letter to France, praying for an army commission for the sole surviving son.[29] Maintenance of caste seemed to take precedence over mere physical survival, or even what might be thought of today as prudent financial planning by sending some sons to a safer career. Perhaps six-year-old ensign Pierre de Vaudreuil was still playing with the little toy cannons given to children when he began to move among the deadly originals.

The careers and marriages of such children were as much matters of parental strategy as they were of youthful taste. Historian John Bosher has pointed to the necessity for parental consent (for women to age twenty-five, men to thirty) and the signatures on marriage contracts by diverse cousins, aunts, and uncles as indicators that a good marriage was a step up for the whole family.[30] Such concerns were even stronger in the case of aristocrats, whose daughters would lose noble status unless they married nobles, and whose sons had to marry a sufficiently wealthy bride to continue to "live nobly." Foreign military service, which often resulted in settlement abroad, meant that there were not enough noble grooms to go around. The number of noblewomen who took the veil while still nubile may have indicated piety, but it also reflected parental decisions and pressures to prevent marriage to commoners.[31] The child-rearing and marriage practices of these people suggest that they, like their houses, lacked private interiors.

. . .

A further peculiarity of chateau families is that the paterfamilias cannot be portrayed as a breadwinner. From the 1670s requests began to multiply for government support for Canadian nobles unable to support their large families.[32] La Potherie wrote that Canada was a poor country, heavily dependent on Crown gratifications. The lack of commercial agriculture prevented seigneuries from approaching the levels of prosperity attained by many noble landowners in France. In the seventeenth century Pierre St. Ours's daughters had even been reduced to tilling the fields.[33] More commonly, officers relied on fur trading to supplement their incomes. But it remained true that "the officers who are married have only their appointments to sustain their families; their wives are in distress when they die."[34]

Dispatch after dispatch from the governor and intendant solicited pensions, fur-trading licenses, and the king's "graces" or gratifications for impecunious widows and their children.[35] When Elisabeth de Vaudreuil's father died, the intendant wrote in 1685 to supplicate the Crown on behalf of the mother and two children who were "so reduced in fortune as to be without bread."[36] When Claude de Ramezay died in 1724, Governor Vaudreuil commented that he had served "with honour . . . and lived very comfortably, having always spent more than his salary, which is the reason he has left only a very small estate to his widow and children."[37] Sitting down at the writing desk to pen supplications, the widow secured a pension for herself and a captaincy for her son.[38] Under these circumstances it was necessary for nobles of both sexes to make very active efforts to secure Crown favors, good marriages, and whatever revenues would allow them to "live nobly"—or at least to keep the wolf from the door.

It was well within French custom for women, whether noble or not, to supervise the management of family resources. With colonial men so frequently away for war or trade, it was quite common for them to delegate powers of attorney to their wives or female relatives. Both Agathe St. Père and her daughter received them from male relatives heading west. After the War of Austrian Succession broke out in 1744, there was a widespread transfer of these business powers to wives.[39] Louise de Ramezay used such powers to supervise the family properties on behalf of her sisters and her last surviving brother, who was preoccupied with his military command. When he yielded Quebec City up to General Wolfe's army in the winter of 1759–60 and followed the defeated army to France, Louise remained in the colony. She looked after family interests by selling a good part of the now productive property to her widowed sister, whose children would continue the line in Canada. Thus Louise de Ramezay served her dynasty well. So too did Agathe de Repentigny, who added to the wealth of the family not only through her industry but through aggressive land purchases. The result seems to have been plenty of money for dowries for the seven daughters, who married noblemen or entered convents. All in all, there were a number of ways our chateau families lacked gender specialization. The money-making châtelaines seem to have been quite unreliable as nurturers; the fathers were equally inadequate as breadwinners.

• • •

Let us turn to one final way in which both men and women answered the call of caste: the duty to serve the king. Although eighteenth-century noblewomen no longer emulated their men in strapping on armor to ward off enemy attacks, they performed other public service to the Crown. This sometimes took the form of participation in state functions, such as military reviews or accompanying the intendant (with or without their husbands) as part of his entourage when he traveled.[40] It could also involve direct wielding of political power, such as we have seen in the case of Elisabeth de Joybert. Noblewomen appear to have been informed about statecraft and to have assumed themselves appropriate practitioners. In addition they were willing to make sacrifices as part of public duty.

The Ramezay women appeared as starry-eyed, though somewhat star-crossed, idealists in service of the Crown. Louise de Ramezay and her siblings grew up in the public eye. Despite the magnificence of their Montreal mansion, they present a picture not of self-indulgent luxury, but rather of the stress of royal service. Their mother, herself raised in a noble family, knew the requirements of "living nobly." They included hosting lavish banquets and all-night balls, being present at military and civil ceremonies, and in her particular case, smoothing over the quarrels of her irascible husband, who had an unfortunate habit of attacking superiors. Perhaps at the banquets Charlotte de la Ronde gazed longingly at the pattern on her china—sheep grazing on a quiet meadow. A family story recounts a rather mournful sense of duty, as well as her daughters' reaction to life at the head of a pageant. Two of her daughters expressed surprise at seeing her up early on the morning after a very late ball at the chateau.

> "It's as it should be, my children," responded Madame de Ramezay, "your father has to go before nine to the Champ-de-Mars to review the new regiment, whose principal officers we had here last evening."
>
> "But you are as pale this morning, dear mother, as if you'd been in bed a whole month. It's this wretched ball that's wrecked you. As for us, we've slept from eleven until eight in the morning, we're going to sleep some more in the carriage, and it was with great difficulty that we attended mass; . . . Tell us, dear mother, doesn't this noisy and dissipated life vex you?"
>
> "It vexes me a great deal," replied their mother.
>
> "Why then," replied Catherine, "put on these big dinners?"
>
> "Oh, my child," answered the mother with a sigh, "I must admit we'd have more happiness and peace if we could live retired on our seigneurie; but what would people think of us, if we refused to associate with his Majesty's officers, with high-ranking citizens?"
>
> Grasping from these last words the troublesome position of her family, Catherine hugged her mother and cried out: "You have more cares than pleasures! . . . permit your daughters to embrace a state which never offers such vexations."[41]

Continuing this tradition of service, Louise and two of her sisters as young women offered to take the place of nuns who had died caring for the sick during a 1724 smallpox epidemic, requesting in return only burial in the nuns' chapel, should they perish.[42]

Elisabeth de Joybert's service in France perhaps also qualifies as heroism in service of the Crown, though the circumstances were scarcely edifying. Troubles began when she first rushed over to France during time of war to counter the charges against her husband; the ship was captured by the English. Eventually arriving at Versailles, she was, as we have seen, exceedingly successful in ingratiating herself both to the royal family and to the colonial minister. However, it may have been her discretion and the fact that she would one day return to a distant colony that helped qualify her for service to the king's grandson, the Duke of Berry. It was a disordered and scandal-ridden household. The duke, so poorly educated that his courtiers had to script even the shortest of his speeches, disgraced himself at the time of the Treaty of Utrecht by becoming too tongue-tied to say a word to those gathered in state to hear him. His wife was an imperious woman who became drunk at table and grew so bold in infidelity that she tried to persuade one of her courtiers to elope with her. Although personal duties in the royal household were an honor for the nobility, this particular assignment must have had a tortuous side. Those in attendance needed to avoid taint from the scandals and to be discreet in managing and concealing their employers' follies.[43] The Duchess of St. Simon, who also served there, wrote that the position was beneath Madame de Vaudreuil, a woman of considerable talent, who had accepted it in order to advance the interests of her large family—as indeed it did. Madame de Vaudreuil's court service and influence gave her a stature that even the top Canadian administrators— respected in the colony but considered nonentities at Versailles—sometimes lacked.[44] When she finally sailed back to Quebec in 1721 after her twelve-year absence, ensconced in the captain's quarters and surrounded by servants, the former pauper from Acadia held her head high. Landing in Canada, the Ursuline's former "modest" student was reported to have acquired the air of a great and proud noblewoman.[45]

Both Elisabeth de Vaudreuil and Agathe St. Père considered politics their realm. Madame de Vaudreuil wrote an urgent letter to the minister in 1710 outlining recent intelligence she had received from an English ship regarding a planned attack on Acadia. She implored the minister to ship arms to the colony and outlined the differing strategy and equipment needed if the campaign were in winter or in summer. In another letter she clearly outlined the various supplies needed to secure Indian alliances.[46] Agathe St. Père also showed familiarity with governmental concerns. A letter she wrote to the minister and the king in 1705 about her textile factory proposed a number of projects such as buffalo wool clothing and a form of rot-resistant material for ships' rigging. Cloth production and development of colonial resources were precisely the concerns that had appeared in colonial dispatches for the previous fifteen years.[47] These women lived in mansions that housed the administrative offices and banquet tables where business was done; the seat of government was also their family home. Like "living nobly" and breadwinning, crown service was a birthright of noblewomen as well as noblemen.

. . .

The enterprising noblewomen we have examined here, if more dynamic or successful than others of their caste, were not so much stepping outside an established role as fulfilling one. Their "place" was not in the bosom of a small private family of modern conception. A very different family life is suggested by the curtained beds spread around the manors, the sending away of infants and children, and the frequent absences of father, mother, or both.

The fate of Madame de Ramezay, burning the candle at both ends with her public duties, losing four sons, and left widowed with a large debt, shows that this demanding role did not necessarily reward its practitioners with either happiness or security. Her own attempts to restore the family fortunes were only partially successful. Her single daughter, Louise, however, became a long-term entrepreneur of considerable wealth and range of holdings. She may have had a taste for business, and evidently had a talent for it, but surely it was the duty to safeguard the family property and pay off its debts while her male kin were busy defending the colony that propelled her into enterprise, just as it had propelled her mother before her. Agathe St. Père, who raised ten of her mother's children and then eight of her own, probably seldom called an hour her own. Providing food and clothing for all those youngsters and developing colonial resources do not fall neatly into public and private categories, but all were part of her duties toward her "own"—a circle that included her immediate kin, the nobility as a whole, and as her statesmanlike letter of 1705 suggests, the colonial minister and the king. Elisabeth de Vaudreuil and her mother both carried service to their own to the highest court, Versailles; and the daughter acquired such importance that she did not hesitate to mix general political advice with appeals on behalf of family and protégés. It is indicative of the "normal" nature of such activities that in both the Ramezay and Vaudreuil families, mothers and daughters pursued similar public careers.

Despite a certain arrogance, these people had very little sense of themselves as unique individuals. That awaited the later, romantic awareness of self and valorization of private emotions. Death struck too often and too early for them to imagine that they were singular or irreplaceable. They thought of themselves as part of their family and caste. If in their business journeys, their willingness to delegate child care to others, and their economic and political power, they resemble some modern career women, there is little evidence that they were personally ambitious. It was rather the family honor they wished to enhance. Indeed, some of their public activity was clearly an ordeal rather than an advantage.

These figures are so different from their modern counterparts that they are perhaps best remembered by analogy to chess, a game of theirs that has come down to modern times, and one that evokes an archaic sense of fulfilling a part within an entrenched, highly ritualized order. In chess one can move only along well-established lines, but by moving deftly within the rules of the game one can outmaneuver opponents and outrun adversity. And chess reflects their concern with maintaining family, caste, and religion in service of the Crown. All pieces on the board strive to protect their king and defeat his opponents. The knights can make short, devastating charges. The rooks or castles—those of landed wealth such as Louise de Ramezay—can use it to move energetically across the board and prevent disaster. The bishops have their own considerable, if oblique, power as representatives of a hierarchical church that placed high-born daughters well. The queen—even though this was an age in which monarchs desperately desired male heirs—is the most powerful piece in the game. The king, who must not be taken, is of course the most important, but he is too stately for maneuver. The queen's might lies in the fact that she can strike suddenly from across the board and win the game. Certainly it was not often the case in real life that women were allowed such power. But, as Madame de Vaudreuil might tell you, the rules of the game did open up the possibility.

NOTES

1. The New France colonial correspondence at the National Archives of Canada (hereafter cited as NAC), series CIIA, contains the letters from and about Madame de Repentigny. Some of the relevant documents are printed in *Rapport de l'archiviste de la province de Québec*, Quebec (hereafter cited as RAPQ), 1939–40. See also *Dictionary of Canadian Biography* (Toronto: University of Toronto Press, 1966–) (hereafter cited as DCB), 3:580–81; Jean B. A. Ferland, *Cours d'histoire du Canada* (Quebec, 1865), 2:392; E. Z. Massicotte, "Agathe de St. Père," *Bulletin des recherches historiques* (hereafter cited as BRH) 1944:202–7; Marine Leland, "Madame de Repentigny," BRH 1954:75–77; Joseph-Noël Fauteux, *Essai sur l'industrie au Canada sous le régime français*, vol. 1 (Quebec: Proulx, 1927); Pierre-Georges Roy, "La famille Le Gardeur de Repentigny," BRH 1947:195–216; *Collection des manuscrits . . . relatifs à la Nouvelle France* (Quebec: Côte, 1883–84).

2. The key primary sources on the Ramezay women are NAC, Colonial series CIIA, and NAC Manuscript Group 18 H54. There are biographies of various members of the Ramezay family in the DCB, volumes 2–4; that of Louise appears in 4:653–55. See also Victor Morin, "Les Ramezay et leur château," *Cahiers de Dix*, vol. 3 (Montreal: Publication des Dix, 1938); Pierre-Georges Roy, *La famille Ramezay* (Levis, 1910); Ovide Lapalice, *Histoire de la seigneurie Massue* (Montreal: Société historique, 1930).

3. A. Cimon, *Les Ursulines de Québec* (Quebec, 1863), 1:484.

4. Cited in DCB 2:566.

5. DCB 2:301–2, a text containing an excellent compilation of sources of Madame de Vaudreuil. See also Yves Zoltvany, *Philippe de Rigaud de Vaudreuil* (Toronto: McClelland and Stewart, 1974), esp. 110 and 215. The key colonial correspondence for Madame de Vaudreuil is NAC, CIIA, vols. 21–49, some of which is printed in RAPQ 1942–43, 1946–47, and *Collection des manuscrits*, vol. 1.

6. See Ruette d'Auteuil, "Mémoire sur l'état présent du Canada," RAPQ 1922–23, 50; and DCB 2:302.

7. NAC, CIIA, vol. 36, Riverin à Toulouse, April 9, 1716; DCB 2:302.

8. The term is Yves Zoltvany's. See Zoltvany, *Vaudreuil*, 217.

9. For examples see Jan V. Noel, "New France: Les femmes favorisées," in *Rethinking Canada*, edited by Veronca Strong-Boag and Anita Fellman (Toronto: Copp Clark, 1991).

10. See for example Bonnie S. Anderson and Judith P. Zinsser, *A History of Their Own* (New York: Harper and Row, 1988), 2:96–99, 112–22; Roland Mousnier, *La famille, l'enfant et l'éducation en France et en Grande-Bretagne du XVIe au XVIIe siècle* (Paris: Centre de documentation universitaire, 1975), 319–31; Richard Vann, "Women in Pre-Industrial Capitalism," in *Becoming Visible*, edited by Renate Bridenthal and Claudia Koonz (Boston: Houghton Mifflin, 1977).

11. Lorraine Gadoury, *La noblesse de Nouvelle France* (Montreal: Hurtubise, 1991), 51.

12. Charles Le Roy Bacqueville de la Potherie, *Histoire de l'Amérique septrentrionale*, 3d ed. (Paris: Nyon, 1753), 1:279, 366.

13. Pierre-François-Xavier de Charlevoix, *Histoire et description générale de la Nouvelle-France* (Montreal, 1976), 1:399.

14. Louis Franquet, *Voyages et mémoires sur le Canada* (Montreal: Editions Elysée, 1974), 56; La Potherie, *Histoire de l'Amérique septrentrionale*, 1:366–68. See also W. J. Eccles, "The Social, Economic, and Political Significance of the Military Establishment in New France," in *Essays on New France*, by William Eccles (Toronto: Oxford, 1987).

15. Eccles, "Military Establishment in New France," 115–16.

16. *Webster's New International Dictionary*, 3d ed. On caste, see also David Sills, ed., *International Encyclopedia of the Social Sciences* (New York: Macmillan, 1968), 2:334–35.

17. Franquet, *Voyages et mémoires sur le Canada*, 148.

18. Gadoury, *La noblesse de Nouvelle France*, 57–58, 63, 124, 140, 146, 149.

19. DCB 2:546.

20. NAC, C11A, vol. 22, Oct. 12, 1705, Ramezay au ministre.

21. See, for example, the inventory of the Chateau St. Louis, RAPQ 1921–22, 238–61.

22. Franquet, *Voyages et mémoires sur le Canada*, 134–35, 140.

23. NAC, C11A, vol. 46, Mme de Vaudreuil à Maurepas, Oct. 29, 1724.

24. See the governor's inventory in RAPQ 1922, 237ff.

25. Lorraine Gadoury found a nine-year gap among the noblesse. See Gadoury, *La noblesse de Nouvelle France*, 76.

26. Gadoury, *La noblesse de Nouvelle France*, 146–51.

27. NAC, C11A, vol. 22, C. Ramezay au ministre, Oct. 12, 1705; Lapalice, *Histoire de la seigneurie Massue*, 30.

28. NAC, C11A, vol. 51, Hocquart à Maurepas, Oct. 25, 1729; RAPQ 1946–47, 409; Eccles, "Military Establishment in New France," 116.

29. NAC, C11A, vol. 50, Mme de Ramezay à Maurepas, Oct. 8, 1728.

30. John Bosher, "The Family in New France," in *In Search of the Visible Past*, edited by Barry Gough (Waterloo, Ont.: Wilfrid Laurier University Press, 1975).

31. Pehr Kalm, *Voyage de Pehr Kalm au Canada* (Montreal: Tisseyre, 1977), 230; Gadoury, *La noblesse de Nouvelle France*, 62–78. Nobles (particularly females) had a rate of vocation five to ten times higher than commoners.

32. RAPQ 1926–27, 111–31.

33. Cited in Allan Greer, *Peasant, Lord, and Merchant* (Toronto: University of Toronto Press, 1985), 10.

34. La Potherie, *Histoire de l'Amérique septrentrionale*, 367–68. See also Franquet, *Voyages et mémoires sur le Canada*, 56.

35. See NAC, C11A, vols. 52–58 for a rich sampling.

36. Cited in Guy Fregault, "Un cadet de Gascogne: Philippe de Rigaud de Vaudreuil," *Revue d'histoire de l'Amérique française* 5 (1951–52):21.

37. NAC, C11A, vol. 46, Vaudreuil et Beauharnois à Maurepas, Oct. 2, 1724; DCB 2:548; Morin, "Les Ramezay," 43.

38. NAC, C11A, vol. 50, May 24, 1728; vol. 50, Mme de Ramezay à Maurepas, Oct. 8, 1728; vol. 56, Mme de Ramezay à Maurepas, Aug. 25, 1731; vol. 58, Hocquart à Maurepas, Oct. 15, 1732.

39. NAC, Baby Collection, Correspondence, 2, Havy et Lefebve à Mme Guy, Quebec, Aug. 3, 1745, 664–65.

40. Franquet, *Voyages et mémoires sur le Canada*, 129–30.

41. Abbé A. Daniel, *Histoire des grandes familles françaises du Canada* (Montreal: Senécal, 1867), 438–40.

42. Daniel, *Histoire des grandes familles françaises du Canada*, 440.

43. Duke of Saint Simon, *Memoirs of Louis XIV and the Regency* (Washington: Dunne, 1901), vol. 2, chaps. 16–28; vol. 3, chap. 6.

44. Elisabeth Begon, *Lettres au cher fils: Correspondance d'Elisabeth Begon avec son gendre* (Montreal: Hurtubise, 1972), 177.

45. This according to the Bishop of Quebec. See NAC, C11A, vol. 47, Bishop à Maurepas, Oct. 4, 1725; and DCB 3302.

46. NAC, C11A, vols. 30, 31, Mme de Vaudreuil à Pontchartrain, Feb. 15, 1710, May 1, 1710, Mémoire 1710, *Collection des manuscrits*, 2:511–13; RAPQ 1947–48, 186–88.

47. Fauteux, *Essai sur l'industrie*, 455–65; Massicotte, "Agathe de St. Père," 204. St. Père's letter appears in NAC, C11A, Oct. 13, 1705.

Princesses, Wives, and Wenches: White Perceptions of Southeastern Indian Women to 1770

EIRLYS M. BARKER

By the eighteenth century white males in North America and Europe knew exactly what the status of women was, both in the home and in the world at large. Women of European origin were born into a patriarchal society. They were reared from birth to be obedient to their fathers and submissive helpmeets for their future husbands. This was not so in Native American society. Many of the earliest colonists commented on what seemed to them a woman's high degree of freedom over personal matters, including choosing a husband and even, in some instances, making the decision to end a marital relationship. In the southeastern tribes women exercised control over their personal lives and bodies to a greater extent than did contemporary women of European descent. The structure of native society led to the high degree of respect and freedom that Native American women experienced.

The area of the American Southeast is vast, extending from the Atlantic coast west to the Mississippi River and from the Ohio River to the Gulf of Mexico. It is an area containing many Indian tribes—more properly referred to as nations—descended from peoples of varied traditions and language groups. These included the Creeks, the Cherokees, the Catawbas, the Yamasees, the Choctaws, the Chickasaws, and the Natchez. By the beginning of the seventeenth century these nations had experienced times of great upheaval and change. Throughout the Americas the native inhabitants suffered a dramatic decline in population as a result of European contact.[1] The consequences of this disaster forced remnants of nations that were once numerous to seek an existence as part of new units or federations that European invaders called, for example, Creek and Catawba, by the eighteenth century.[2] Yet, the old clan and family structures remained in place. Most of the southeastern tribes maintained a traditional matrilinear system of inheritance. They were not matriarchies, and the division of labor was gender-based; however, outsiders often believed Indian women had more personal freedom and wielded more influence over the lives of their families and villages than their European peers did.

Among the cultural baggage that the first European settlers brought with them to North America was the concept of patriarchy, one at odds with Indian ideas of an orderly society. Historian Lawrence Stone has argued that the "despotic authority of husband and father" in England was reinforced from the 1500s onward by both church and state. The growth of Protestantism destroyed the female cult of the Virgin Mary and instead emphasized a literal interpretation of the Bible.[3] That approach institutionalized the perception of woman as Eve, responsible for the expulsion from the Garden of Eden. Small wonder that she needed to be guarded by her menfolk and that a woman's legal and social status suffered as a consequence.[4]

Under English law a wife's position was clear: she had no independent legal status. In the eighteenth century Sir William Blackstone explained that "by marriage, the husband and wife are one person in law, that is, the very being or legal existence of a woman is suspended during the marriage, or at least it is incorporated and consolidated into that of the husband: under whose wing, protection, and *cover* she performs everything, and is therefore called in our law-french a *feme-covert*."[5] Although unmarried women and widows had a measure of protection under the law, a wife could not own property. Any she brought into the marriage was her dowry and became the property of her spouse. She could not easily escape from an unhappy, even abusive, marriage.[6]

The composition of the English family had changed by the seventeenth century, undermining traditional female authority within the household. During the middle ages the family was an extended one, often with three generations living under the same roof. The Protestant emphasis on the sanctification of marriage and on the nuclear family as a little commonwealth lessened the old bonds of kinship. Women were taught that their husbands were the heads of their households with authority over all matters. A wife could expect obedience from servants, from her minor male children, and from her daughters until their own marriages, but she owed the same complete deference and loyalty to her husband. The trend toward a nuclear family composed of husband, wife, young children, and perhaps some servants was accelerating, along with an increase in the wish for privacy. This removed influential female role models, such as grandmothers or mothers-in-law, from the household.[7] In contrast, Native American society in the Southeast at the time of contact was based on extended families living together in dwellings headed by an older female member.

The southeastern Indians lived in settled villages where a woman's clan built huts closely clustered together.[8] The women were in charge of providing food for their extended households, from planting seeds of corn, squash, and beans, to gathering berries and nuts. They also dried meat into jerky and turned deerskins and furs into clothing. Older women taught the children to fish and to trap small animals such as rabbits and directed all such daily operations for their extended family network. The men were often absent for long periods of time pursuing their primary economic function, hunting to provide their kin with meat. With the presence of Europeans came a new market demand for furs and skins—deerskins became the major commodity and currency of the area. It became necessary to go farther afield to acquire enough skins to exchange for essential trade goods. This also led to an increase in warfare when Indians roamed into and poached on their neighboring tribes' traditional hunting grounds. The longer men are absent, the more women exercise effective control in any situation.

Outsiders sometimes depicted Indian women as embodying the savagery of the "New World," as being too free, too close to nature, and too apt to follow their own whims and desires. The earliest European accounts often commented on the minimal clothing worn by the natives, and this was reflected in the popular engravings made of Caribbean and Florida Indians and those based on John White's 1580s watercolors of the Carolina tribes closest to the Roanoke colony.[9] They especially dwelt on the scant nature of women's dress—a contrast to the European woman, who, humble or noble, hid most of her body under layers of heavy fabrics. Indian women had to be licentious if they did not follow the basic Christian rules of dress and decorum. According to Amerigo Vespucci at the turn of the sixteenth century, the "women go about naked and are very libidinous. . . . Urged by excessive lust, they defiled and prostituted themselves." The perceived "lusty" and libertine nature of Indian women was often used as an excuse for rape by the "Christian" soldiers.[10]

Some of the early English writers, such as Robert Beverley in Virginia, tried to dispel the idea that the women were "Incontinent" in their affections. They were merely "inspir'd with Mirth and good Humor," he said. Beverley was also unusual in promoting the idea of intermarriage with the Indians as a means of gaining and keeping their friendship.[11] By the mid-eighteenth century most writers stressed the "mild, amiable, soft disposition" of the women and the modesty of their clothing.[12]

During the seventeenth century an increasing number of Europeans moved into the interior of the continent. Some were soldiers, others prospective planters. Among the first wave who both observed and cohabited with Indian women for lengthy periods of time were those men who risked much in the lucrative but dangerous Indian trade. The Europeans active in the southeastern deerskin trade—confusingly called Indian traders—realized that to be accepted, the best tactic was to marry Indian women and thus have a fixed place in native society. Many of these traders and the agents and soldiers who policed Indian-White relations and trade have given us the most accurate glimpses of the status and expectations of Indian women in their own societies, although the observers imposed their Eurocentric interpretations on much of what they saw and did not dwell on the minute details of everyday life.

The master traders always boasted that their consorts were important leaders in their tribes who had freely entered into lucrative relations with the newcomers. James Adair declared that he wrote his *History of the American Indians* while enjoying the company of a "Chikkasah female, as great a princess as ever lived among the ancient Peruvians, or Mexicans."[13] In the early years of the trade, even humble traders wielded great power in their native villages. They came with desirable goods that enhanced the quality of life, so that tribal leaders encouraged marriage with their relatives. The marriage of the Powhatan "princess" Pocahontas to the Virginia planter John Rolfe was merely one of the first and most famous of such alliances. One of the most prominent Native Americans in the early eighteenth century was the Creek leader Coosaponakeesa, the much-married Mary Musgrove Mathews Bosomworth. She was Georgia's counterpart to Pocahontas in the "Indian Princess" mystique.[14] Despite her prominence, her lineage is obscure and much debated. She was probably closely related through her mother to the Lower Creek "Emperor" Brims and thus exerted influence over his successor, Chigelly. Mary's father was a British trader named Griffin, but it was her Creek connections that gave her authority among the Indians. By her later years she acquired the status of "Beloved Woman," which enabled her to be an effective interpreter of culture and language to the early Georgia colonists.

The Indian women who were leaders in their tribes insisted on receiving privileges such as their share of the presents the colonial governments issued. When influential Indians visited Charles Town, the center of government in South Carolina, for formal conferences with the governors, their wives and other female relatives expected to receive gifts and often took part in the ceremonies.[15] Senawki, wife of Tomochichi, the Yamacraw chief who welcomed the first Georgia colonists, not only visited London and attended the royal court with her husband in 1734, but two years later took the initiative in talks with John Wesley, one-time Indian agent for Georgia.[16]

Most Indian women had a freer choice of marriage partners than most European women of this time, for "a marriage is settled by the agreement of both people," meaning those directly involved, not their parents.[17] It was the woman's freely-given acceptance that sealed an alliance. There were no essential religious ceremonies or vows, merely an acknowledgment by the couple and their town that an acceptable union was taking place. Surveyor Bernard Romans in the 1760s was struck with the simplicity of Creek marriage. It was "without much ceremony, seldom any more than to make some presents to the parents, and to have a feast." [18] A 1683 description of Louisiana's Indians mentioned that "very frequently they marry without any noise," although there would often be "feasts with pomp and rejoicing." [19] Sexual relationships with unattached Indian women were acceptable to most of the southern tribes as long as the women consented, for young girls "are the mistresses of their own bodies," as related to a young Frenchman in the 1720s.[20]

Because these clans were exogamous—it was necessary to marry outside the clans—Indian women were free to marry any foreigners.[21] Although a new husband moved to live with his wife's clan, he did not become a member of that clan. Even so, the union gave him a whole new group of relatives.[22] Initially, it was probably not much more exotic for a Creek woman to cohabit with a white Carolinian than for her to marry a Chickasaw or a Cherokee. According to South Carolina's first Indian agent, Thomas Nairne, the southeastern Indians believed that marriage within one's own clan or one's father's clan was "an unclean thing . . . the greatest crime in the world," comparable to the "worst sort of Incest" in European society. This, combined with the catastrophic decline in population, underscored the need for new sources of strangers to serve as marriage partners. As early as 1708 Nairne had commented on the "break up of their Townships . . . since the use of fire armes the fatell small pox and other European distempers." [23] There were possibly ten times as many women as men among the tribes by the mid-eighteenth century, indicating another practical reason for accepting European husbands, whatever qualities particular individuals might bring with them.[24]

The wives of Indian traders chose a lavish and exotic way of life, compared with most of their peers. The traders came with goods that made lives easier for all, but especially for the women. Many Europeans had commented that the women were "the Chief, if not the only manufacturers." Some, such as William Byrd II of Virginia, thought they did "the little Work" that was done in native society, regarding them as mere beasts of burden. As the women's primary economic function was to be in charge of the food, the trader wives gained status by being the first to acquire metal hoes, axes, and knives, sturdy but lightweight copper kettles to cook the food instead of having to fashion earthenware pots that were brittle and heavy, and metal fishhooks and needles. Such items freed them from much of the drudgery of their lives, as did manufactured cloth. Byrd seemed particularly incensed that the men were "at most employ'd only in the Gentlemanly Diversions of Hunting and Fishing." He neither understood the men's role in helping to clear the land for farming nor realized their role in providing meat for their communities. John Brickell, who in the 1730s updated Lawson's work on North Carolina, noted that the "Industry of Wives" produced crops without the use of plows, with the "Men's minds being wholly taken up in Hunting." Adair, however, that long-term resident in Indian country, knew that Creek men would not go to war until they had "helped the women to plant a sufficient plenty of provisions."[25] Still, the women's crucial economic role gave them influence over clan or village decisions. If they were against a war sortie, they could refuse to parch corn, dry jerky, or make the moccasins that were needed for such a venture.[26]

The social ties that came through marrying Indian women were crucially important to the newcomers. All the nations were subdivided into totemic clans, which were the most meaningful social element for the southeastern Indians. Within Cherokee society, "to be without a clan ... was to be without any rights, even the right to live."[27] It was fellow clansmen who avenged a murder.[28] Nairne described the Chickasaws' clan system and its usefulness to Europeans: "It is the easyest thing in the world, for an English Traveller to procure kindred among the Indians, It's but taking a mistress of such a name, and he has at once relations in each Village, from Charles Town to the Missisipi."[29] This was illustrated many times; for example, in 1758 some Indians refused to surrender to South Carolina authorities Samuel Jarron, who had "escaped the Watch" at Keowee, a Cherokee town. The Indians' leader explained, "We look upon him ... as one of our Brothers. He has lived among us several Years; he has had some of our Women, and has got Children by them. He is our Relation, and shan't be taken up."[30] Adair also recounted some instances of wives saving their husbands' lives with the help of their families. One trader was told by his wife to run away when foreign Indians raided his storehouse, and he had few qualms about leaving her because "her family was her protection." [31]

One of the most confusing differences observed by Europeans was the Indian system of matrilineal inheritance. Inheritance in societies derived from Germanic antecedents came through the male line; primogeniture had become the norm in Western Europe, with the oldest son claiming his father's property, or, if there were no direct male heirs, the closest legitimate male relative. For Native Americans, because inheritance was matrilineal, a foreign father did not disrupt their society. Nairne understood that "the Chiefs sisters son alwaies succeeds and never his own." [32] A Frenchman in Louisiana in 1703 had asked why this was so and was told that "nobility can come only from the woman, because the woman is more certain than the man about whom the children belong to." Alien blood would not therefore confuse issues of clan, town, or tribal status, so it was not essential to police the personal aspect of women's lives. [33]

The Indian conception of property was also very different, again benefiting females. Under English law a married woman owned nothing "without the license of her husband. For all her personal chattels are absolutely his own." [34] Indians in North America owned what they used every day or what they fashioned themselves. Males, therefore, traditionally owned the weapons they used, as well as their clothes and what Europeans regarded as personal possessions. Dwellings and agricultural tools, used mostly by women, were owned by the women. [35] Thus, the gender-based division of labor gave women ownership over the products from, and the implements used in, those tasks. Because husbands lived in their wives' dwellings, it was easy for a man to remove his possessions from his wife's home if the relationship ended, for everything he owned was portable. [36]

Divorce for most of the southeastern tribes was "at the choice of either of the parties," another shock to Europeans, whose women enjoyed no such inherent right. [37] Among the Creeks the man could remarry immediately, but the wife had to wait until the end of the annual harvest festival, the Busk, with its purification ceremonies and significance. [38] Divorce for the Native Americans, as compared with Europeans, was a matter with more religious than civic significance. Widows, as in Europe, were free to marry after a set period of mourning and purification. This varied from "the tedious space of four years" among the Creeks, to three years among the Chickasaws.[39]

Europeans were startled by the disposition of children from dissolved Indian unions, for the children stayed with the mother. John Lawson, raised in the English patriarchal system at the turn of the eighteenth century, commented with surprise on both the ease of divorce and how "all the Children go along with the Mother."[40] William Bartram, the Quaker naturalist, mentioned that Indians seldom separated once they had children, but if they did, "the mother takes the children under her own protection."[41] This was in stark contrast to English law; before 1837 mothers in Britain had no guardianship rights at all.[42]

As many European fathers would find to their astonishment, they had little control over the education of any *metis* (half-Indian) children—even teaching sons the arts of war and hunting was a role for the mother's brother or another close male relative within the mother's clan.[43] Indian wives and their clan kin expected to remain in charge of the children's education and upbringing. It came as a shock to traders even toward the end of the eighteenth century when their wives refused to let them send their sons to be educated in Charleston or Savannah. A Creek trader, James Germany, had married a Creek women "of a very amiable and worthy character and disposition industrious, prudent, and affectionate." But even this paragon to British eyes refused to be parted from her children.[44] It was her and her clan's responsibility to educate them. Access to European ideas and customs was not regarded as necessary for the children—in fact, devoted mothers who had experienced Eurocentric attitudes within their households might believe that the children would lose, not gain, freedom if exposed to Charleston or Savannah and racial prejudice. A woman's traditional role gave her the freedom to dictate how her offspring should be educated.

Although divorce was a common occurrence, and marriages often resembled serial monogamy, adultery was a heinous crime in all the southeastern nations except, perhaps, the Cherokees. In some nations it was punished merely by cutting off a woman's hair. In others the penalty could be death. The Chickasaws were "very jealous of their wives," and adultery was punished by "the loss of the tip of the [male adulterer's] nose, which they sometimes cut, but more generally bite off." The

Creeks tended to punish both parties equally by "severe Flagellations"; a trader named Cockran lost his ears in the 1730s for this crime.[45] The Cherokees did not punish either, believing that adultery was a meaningless concept, given either marriage partner's freedom to separate at any time.[46]

Polygyny was allowable, but most Indian marriages were probably monogamous.[47] A few chiefs might have more than one wife, but this became less prevalent with time among the nations closest to the Europeans. An observer of the Yuchis of Georgia in the 1730s, a tribe close to the settlers, remarked that "among them no one knows of polygamy."[48] Sororal polygyny, however, remained common: a man might take a wife's unmarried or widowed sister as a second wife, but only with the first wife's consent.[49] William Bartram believed that the Creeks continued to allow polygyny, but even if "every man" could take as many wives as he pleased, "the first is queen, and the others her handmaids and associates."[50]

Most accounts stress the amiability of Indian women, but one trader has left a different view. Alexander Long, a well-educated but rather disreputable fellow who had been in the Indian trade since before 1710, wrote an account of Cherokee society in 1725. He said, perhaps from bitter experience, that in Cherokee society "the women rules the roost and wears the breeches and sometimes will beat their husbands within an inch of their lives."[51] Long may have exaggerated, but one thing is clear: women reigned supreme within their households.

Native women who made it into the official record were often those complaining about trader or other abuse and those who figure posthumously as "murdered" by hostile Indians or enslaved by Europeans. This problem results from the sources, which often reinforce the idea of the women—especially of minority groups—as victims. Ironically, Indian women, so often designated as victims, had the freedom to decide the fate of captives taken in war. Women who had lost family members and partners could opt to save captives from death, to take the place of the deceased family members through adoption. Adoption was never automatic, although it became more common with the depopulation of the eighteenth century and especially after the devastating 1738 smallpox epidemic. If the captive's fate was death, women made it a long, drawn-

out affair, inflicting pains and mutilations as the fiery torture was pro-
longed over several days. It was they who scalped and dismembered the
victim, all the while singing "with religious joy."[52] In 1750 South Carolina's governor James Glen referred to the Indians as "Cruel & Barbarous.
... Even their Women, those who in all other Nations are called the
Soft & tender Sex, with them are Nursed up in Blood, & taught to
delight in Murders & Torturing."[53]

While it is tempting to view trader wives as persons used by the
foreign participants in the trade, this is a gross oversimplification. In the
Southeast no Indian woman could be forced into a marriage against her
will, and divorce, or at least an informal end to a relationship, was possible
on either side without stigma or punishment. The Indian wives of the
European traders freely chose that role. It gave them an enviable position,
providing the latest technical innovations and luxuries and allowing them
an easier and more comfortable existence than that enjoyed by many of
their peers. This element of choice sometimes led wives to act against
their own village, as during the outbreak of the Cherokee War in 1760,
when some women tried to sneak provisions to the soldiers in Fort
Loudoun during the Cherokee siege of that fort. To the chroniclers, their
actions stemmed from their appreciation of the ribbons and other baubles
the soldiers had given them; a better explanation, however, is their loyalty
to men considered their lawful partners in their society. Interestingly, the
Cherokees did not regard these actions as treasonable but understood
that the women were acting on behalf of family members.[54]

Whatever the official colonial policy on interracial unions, such liaisons
were inevitable, given the lack of European women on the frontier. As
early as 1737 an agent for Georgia commented on the huge number of
mixed offspring: "All the Indian Traders had wives among the Indians
... and he believed there were 400 children So begotten."[55] Unfortunately, we know few of these wives or offspring by name except for those
who were extraordinary in one way or another, perhaps through their
talents as interpreters or for being victimized in some way.[56]

Indian women had the liberty of choosing a nontraditional career
without being ridiculed. A feature of native society that struck nearly all
European visitors was their hospitality toward strangers. One common

custom in the South was to offer a stranger an unmarried woman as a "She-Bed Fellow" for the length of his stay. John Lawson and William Byrd II early in the eighteenth century had noted this custom among the North Carolina nations. There, the trading girls sported a haircut that set them apart from the other, unavailable women. These women were not outcasts in their villages. They could retire from their profession to marry a man of their choice without loss of status and with a dowry.[57] Nor was this a localized custom. Emperor Brims unsuccessfully offered "Bedfellows" to a royal official and his clerical cotraveler on their official 1729–31 visit to Creek country.[58] In Louisiana Father Hennepin remarked that a trading girl's parents found nothing to "censure in this; very far from that, they are glad to have their daughters earn some clothes or some furs."[59]

Other women volunteered to take part in the hunting expeditions that became an integral part of village life with the increasing demand for deerskins and other furs. This was an extension of their food-preparation function; women ground the corn for making bread.[60] In March 1740 the Indians attacking St. Augustine with General George Oglethorpe of Georgia had to be given "rice . . . having no women with them to parch or pound their Corn."[61] Women also began the work of preparing the skins for market, including scraping away excess meat and fur, soaking them in a solution of brains, and finally smoking the prepared skins. If this process was not begun in a timely fashion, these valuable trading items would rot. On those occasions when a hunting band was attacked by enemy Indians, the women would "sing their enlivening war song," which spurred their men to "become as fierce as lions."[62]

Among the Chickasaws, women on expeditions did more than such household-type chores—they had the choice to go into combat if they wished. Nairne had himself seen Chickasaw women in battle, and Bernard Romans mentioned that he had "several times seen armed women . . . going in pursuit of the invading enemy."[63] Accounts of women warriors typically mix admiration for their bravery with condemnation of the "savagery," or primitiveness, of their actions. When summoned to fight against Hernando de Soto's men in a life-and-death situation, the women of Mauvila "attacked with utter rage and determination, thus showing well that the desperation and courage of women in whatever they are determined to do is greater and more unbridled than that of men."[64] Women were usually treated more leniently when captured by native enemies, but some were killed and scalped.[65]

By the 1760s Indians were regarded increasingly as a barrier to expansion, rather than as allies against the French and Spanish or as partners in a lucrative trade. Paralleling this, Indian women in the official records are increasingly disparaged as "wenches," a word reserved in the British Empire for women of the lowest ranks, including prostitutes, servants, and slaves. The women described in early accounts were usually called "wives." By 1751 even women who warned their trader husbands that their lives were in danger from a roving band of enemy Indians are officially dismissed as the "Wenches kept by the white Men."[66] There were no more accounts of Indian "princesses" and their virtues. Mary Bosomworth's Indian ancestry was used increasingly to explain her deficiencies—her frequent temper tantrums, her obesity, and her occasional drunkenness were examples of an excess of freedom and her failure to control herself—even by her last, very proper English husband.

Freedom clearly meant very different things to Native American women and to European males. To most native women it meant a continuation of their traditional way of life, one that had struck so many early European observers as a free, if not libertine, existence. Whatever the actual status of the women within their own societies, most colonial venturers initially responded to the women in two ways. One response came from the men who for trade or diplomatic reasons were destined to live in the interior of the colony for at least part of the year. They might rationalize that an Indian consort's status in her society would help him, but, as many noted, such aid was forthcoming only if the woman saw advantages to her and her possible offspring from such an alliance. Initially, such unions were of great benefit to both parties, and the Europeans wrote in terms of Indian princesses and leaders of their nations helping them in their common economic venture. The other response was the one that, with time, became the norm. As the European peddlers of trade goods within the nations became increasingly smaller cogs in the great machine of the British Empire, they minimized the part played by their Native American wives. By the 1770s women were regarded merely as personal sexual perks and sources of comfort in an increasingly hostile environment.

By the 1770s the decline in status of the Indian trade and Indian diplomacy was reflected in a return to the original perception of Indian women as wantons. Trade and a desire for peace were no longer the prime motivations for Indian policy. As settlers advanced into "Indian country," the old way of life changed for those at the edges. Over time, changes affected all Indian women, even in remote villages, as their society was modified by the goods, diseases, and doctrines imported by traders and missionaries. The new doctrines of Christianity and patriarchy stripped women of their age-old control over their homes and the means of production, as well as their freedom to enter into and leave marital arrangements.

NOTES

1. See Henry F. Dobyns, *Their Numbers Became Thinned: Population Dynamics in Eastern North America* (Knoxville: University of Tennessee Press, 1983); Ann F. Ramenofsky, *Vectors of Death: The Archaeology of European Contact* (Albuquerque: University of New Mexico Press, 1987).

2. J. Leitch Wright, *Creeks and Seminoles: The Destruction and Regeneration of the Muscogulge People* (Lincoln: University of Nebraska Press, 1986), 1–15; James H. Merrell, *The Indians' New World: Catawbas and Their Neighbors from European Contact through the Era of Removal* (Chapel Hill: University of North Carolina Press, 1989), 92–98.

3. Lawrence Stone, *The Family, Sex, and Marriage in England 1500–1800,* abridged ed. (New York: Harper Torchbooks, 1977), chap. 5, esp. 136, 139, 141.

4. Bonnie S. Anderson and Judith P. Zinsser, *A History of Their Own: Women in Europe from Prehistory to the Present,* vol. 1. (New York: Harper and Row, 1988), 393–405, 438–44.

5. William Blackstone, *Commentaries on the Laws of England,* 4 vols. (Oxford: Clarendon Press, 1765–69), 1:430.

6. Blackstone (*Commentaries,* 3:94) shows that although divorce or annulment was possible for men, it was hard if not impossible for most women, even from influential families. Under English law there was a theoretical possibility for women to get a divorce through an act of Parliament, but before the 1857 Marriage and Divorce Act, this was only granted in two cases. See Ray Strachey,

The Cause: A Short History of the Women's Movement in Great Britain (Port Washington, N.Y.: Kennikat Press, 1928), 15, 76.

7. For a short analysis and bibliography on this theme, see Barry Coward, *Social Change and Continuity in Early Modern Europe 1550–1750*, Seminar Studies in History (London: Longman Group UK, 1988), 18–22. He does not altogether agree with Stone's analysis, but, as Stone himself indicates, there were always women and families who did not fit the norm, especially in rural and Celtic areas of Britain.

8. Kathryn E. Holland Braund, "Guardians of Traditions and Handmaidens to Change: Women's Roles in Creek Economic and Social Life during the Eighteenth Century," *American Indian Quarterly* 14 (1990):241.

9. Theodor de Bry's engravings, some based on White's paintings, gave a classical European pose to the naked-breasted females; Paul Hutton, *America 1585: The Complete Drawings of John White* (Chapel Hill: University of North Carolina Press, 1984), esp. plates 33, 35, 37, and figures 8, 10, 12, 20. For more on this theme, see Robert F. Berkhofer, Jr., *The White Man's Indian: Images of the American Indian from Columbus to the Present* (New York: Vintage Books, 1979), esp. 71–85 and plates between 138 and 140.

10. For the quotation and more on this theme, see Kirkpatrick Sale, *The Conquest of Paradise: Christopher Columbus and the Columbian Legacy* (New York: Knopf, 1990), 140–41.

11. Robert Beverley, *The History and Present State of Virginia, 1705*, Louis B. Wright, ed. (Chapel Hill: University of North Carolina Press, 1947), xxv, 38, 171.

12. James Adair, *History of the Indians*, Samuel Cole Williams, ed. (reprint, New York: Promontory Press, 1986), 6.

13. Adair, *History of the Indians*, 447–48.

14. For a perceptive discussion of the impact on Europeans of the "Noble Indian Princess myth," see Rayna Green, "The Pocahontas Perplex: The Image of Indian Women in American Culture," *Massachusetts Review* 13 (1975):698–714. See also J. Frederick Fausz, "Opechancanough: Indian Resistance Leader," in *Struggle and Survival in Colonial America*, edited by Gary B. Nash and David G. Sweet (Berkeley: University of California Press, 1981), 21–37. His conclusion is also that the only "good" Indian woman in the eyes of English colonists could be regarded as a traitor to her culture and religion. The most recent—and most accurate—attempt to set the record straight about Coosaponakeesa is Rodney M. Baine, "Myths of Mary Musgrove," *Georgia Historical Quarterly* 76 (1992):428–35.

15. For example, the Creek chief, Allic's wife, daughter, and sister attended and received lavish presents. See South Carolina Council Journal, November 22, 1746, photostat no. 2, Columbia, South Carolina, Archives.

16. February 14, 1736, John Perceval Egmont, *The Journal of the Earl of Egmont: Abstract of the Trustees' Proceedings for Establishing the Colony of Georgia, 1732–1738*, Robert G. McPherson, ed. (Athens: University of Georgia Press, 1962), 131–32.

17. Philip Georg Friedrich Von Reck, *Von Reck's Voyage: Drawings and Journal of Philip Georg Friedrich Von Reck*, Kristian Hvidt, ed. (Savannah, Ga.: Beehive Press, 1980), 48.

18. Bernard Romans, *Bernard Romans's A Concise Natural History of East and West Florida*, Rembert W. Patrick, ed. (Gainesville: University of Florida Press, 1962), 97.

19. Father Louis Hennepin, *A Description of Louisiana*, John Gilamary Shea, ed. (New York: J. G. Shea, 1880), 283.

20. Diron D'Artaguiette, "Journal of Diron D'Artaguiette, 1722–1723," in *Travels in the American Colonies: 1690–1774*, edited by Newton D. Mereness (New York: Macmillan, 1910), 73.

21. Kathryn E. Holland Braund, *Deerskin and Duffels: The Creek Indian Trade with Anglo-America, 1685–1815* (Lincoln: University of Nebraska Press, 1993), 11–12.

22. Wright, *Creeks and Seminoles*, 18–19.

23. Thomas Nairne, *Nairne's Muskhogean Journals: The 1708 Expedition to the Mississippi River*, Alexander Moore, ed. (Jackson: University Press of Mississippi, 1988), 63.

24. Adair, *History of the Indians*, 241.

25. William Byrd II, *William Byrd's Histories of the Dividing Line betwixt Virginia and North Carolina*, William K. Boyd, ed. (1728; reprint, New York: Dover, 1967), 116; John Brickell, *The Natural History of North-Carolina*, Carol Urness, ed. (1737; reprint, New York; Johnson Reprint Corp., 1969), 289; Adair, *History of the Indians*, 276, 456.

26. Among the Cherokees, women traditionally took an active role in tribal councils. Charles Hudson, *The Southeastern Indians* (Knoxville: University of Tennessee Press, 1969), 269.

27. Theda Perdue, *Slavery and the Evolution of Cherokee Society, 1540–1866* (Knoxville: University of Tennessee Press, 1979), 11–12. Hudson indicated the similarities of Southeastern Indian social patterns, and Adair commented that their "customs" were "so nearly alike." See Adair, *History of the Indians*, xxxvi; Hudson, *Southeastern Indians*, 5.

28. For an excellent account of the *lex talionis* among the Cherokees in the eighteenth century, see John Phillip Reid, *A Law of Blood: The Primitive Law of the Cherokee Nation* (New York: New York University Press, 1979).

29. Nairne, *Muskhogean Journeys*, 60–61.

30. Letter of Captain Paul Demere to Governor Glen, April 2, 1758, in *Documents Relating to Indian Affairs, 1754–1765*, edited by William L. McDowell, Colonial Documents of South Carolina (Columbia: South Carolina Department of Archives and History, 1970), 456.

31. Adair, *History of the Indians*, 282.

32. Nairne, *Muskhogean Journals*, 33, 39, 61.

33. Richebourg G. McWilliams, ed., *Fleur de Lys and Calumet: Being the Penicaut Narrative of French Adventure in Louisiana* (Baton Rouge: Louisiana State University Press, 1953), 90.

34. Blackstone, *Commentaries*, 2:497–98.

35. Reid, *Law of Blood*, 126–29.

36. On separation, the woman sometimes "carries off all the goods," including all the furs. See Hennepin, *Description of Louisiana*, 292.

37. William Bartram, "Observations on the Creek and Cherokee Indians, 1789," E. G. Squire, ed., *Transactions of the American Ethnological Society* 3 (1853):65.

38. Edward J. Cashin, *Lachlan McGillivray, Indian Trader: The Shaping of the Southern Colonial Frontier* (Athens: University of Georgia Press, 1992), 71.

39. Adair, *History of the Indians*, 195.

40. John Lawson, *A New Voyage to Carolina, 1709*, Hugh Talmadge Lefler, ed. (Chapel Hill: University of North Carolina Press, 1967), 192–93.

41. William Bartrum, *Travels of William Bartrum* (1791; reprint, edited by William Van Doren, New York: Dover, 1955), 402–3 (page references are to the reprint edition).

42. Strachey, *The Cause*, 15.

43. Wright, *Creeks and Seminoles*, 19; Braund, *Deerskin and Duffels*, 132.

44. Bartrum, *Travels*, 356–57.

45. Romans, *Natural History of Florida*, 64, 98; James Sutherland, "Letter of James Sutherland to My Lord," *South Carolina Historical Magazine* 68 (1969):83.

46. Reid, *Law of Blood*, 116–19.

47. Reid, *Law of Blood*, 97, comment on the Creeks in the 1770s.

48. Von Reck, *Voyage*, 42.

49. George Stiggins, "A Historical Narration of the Genealogy, Traditions, and Downfall of the Creek Tribe of Indians," in *A Creek Sourcebook*, edited by William C. Sturtevant (New York: Garland, 1987), 38. See also William S. Willis, "Colonial Conflict and the Cherokee Indians, 1710–1760" (Ph.D. diss., Columbia University, 1955), 135–42, for a detailed account of Cherokee marriage customs.

50. Bartrum, *Travels*, 403.

51. Alexander Long, "Alexander Long's A Small Postscript of the Ways and Manners of the Indians Called Charikees," David H. Corkran, ed., *Southern Indian Studies* 21 (1969):30.

52. Adair, *History of the Indians*, 418–19.

53. A speech (c. 1750) by Governor James Glen, "Our Situation with Regard to the Indians," James Glen Papers 1738–1777, no. 7, 4. Caroliniana Library, Columbia, S.C.

54. See John R. Alden, *John Stuart and the Southern Colonial Frontier: A Study of Indian Relations, Trade, and Land, 1754–1775* (Ann Arbor: University of Michigan Press, 1944), 114–18.

55. The agent's report is in Egmont, *Journal, 1732–1738*, 272–73.

56. "Bartlet's Wife" was a Creek interpreter in the 1730s. K. Coleman and Milton Read, eds., *Colonial Records of Georgia* (Athens: University of Georgia Press, 1982), 20:185.

57. Lawson, *New Voyage*, 177–78; John Lawson, *Lawson's History of North Carolina, 1714*, Frances Latham Harriss, ed., 2d ed. (Richmond, Va: Garrett and Massie, 1952), 150–58; Byrd, *Histories of the Dividing Line*, 116.

58. Sutherland, "Letter to My Lord," 82.

59. Hennepin, *Description of Louisiana*, 293.

60. Lawson, *New Voyage*, 216.

61. J. H. Easterby, ed., *Colonial Records of South Carolina: Journal of the Commons House of Assembly May 18, 1741 to July 10, 1742* (Columbia: Historical Commission of South Carolina, 1953), 179.

62. Adair, *History of the Indians*, 343.

63. Romans, *Natural History of Florida*, 71.

64. Garciliaso De la Vega, *The Florida of the Inca, 1605*, John G. Varner and Jeannette J. Varner, trans. and eds. (Austin: University of Texas Press, 1951), 369. De Soto's men explored and pillaged the Southeast from 1539 to 1543. De la Vega was known as the "Inca" because of his half-Indian descent. Mauvila was probably located between the Alabama and Tombigbe rivers.

65. McDowell, *Documents Relating to Indian Affairs 1754–1765*, 131.

66. McDowell, *Documents Relating to Indian Affairs 1754–1765*, 117. Two Indian women acted as spies for the commander of a frontier fort in the 1750s. Both are termed "wenches," despite the fact that one had an English name and was probably a trader's daughter. See McDowell, *Documents Relating to Indian Affairs 1754–1765*, 281, 362–63, 410–12.

4 Freedom among African Women Servants and Slaves in the Seventeenth-Century British Colonies

LILLIAN ASHCRAFT-EASON

Many women who arrived in the seventeenth-century British colonies were African born. They were most likely to have come from Upper Guinea, Gold Coast, and Angola.[1] In spite of cultural and class differences among these women, they shared cosmological perspectives that ordered their social world and gave meaning and purpose to their individual and collective lives. Adult females arrived in the colonies with these perspectives and with the memories of their diverse traditions cradled within them.[2] Because slavery was widespread in Africa,[3] there is no doubt that at the time of their capture some of the women were slaves and others owned or knew slaves. How women from these situations perceived freedom had to do with their individual experiences and social status, as well as with the ideological parameters of their African societies.

THEORETICAL PARAMETER OF FREEDOM

In African traditional societies, the inverse of slavery was not personal freedom in the sense of doing as one pleased. Having freedom meant being without restraint and restriction from a master. Principally it meant having a personal autonomy that was denied to slaves, whether they had been enslaved as captives of war, as criminals, or as pawns. To be free was to be in one's ancestral homeland among kin. This made one feel secure by belonging to and having protection of the community of birth, having access to communal resources, and having opportunities to participate in matters of governance and inherited ceremonial and ritualistic activities. To be enslaved was to be divested of identity with one's family lineage and gods. However, African slaves expected to begin new families, though not lineages, to own property (including slaves), and to be socialized into the master's family and society without fear of being sold or traded away in the second or third generation. Slave status generally was inherited matrilineally, except when the father was free and in a position to bestow his status upon the newborn.[4]

To the British, among whom many African women would be servants and slaves in the seventeenth century, freedom equated with being British, Christian, and endowed with material resources that could yield an adequate income. That is, one had to have enough resources to avoid having to sell her or his labor for self and family maintenance, as serfs on the manor or apprentices in the crafts did. The free person had a voice in governance and had both the responsibility to protect and the privilege of being protected by the Crown and associates. The unfree were those who sold their labor and tended not to be landed. They were locked in servant-master relationships, had few rights or privileges in governance, and their offspring inherited the status and social condition of their paternity.[5]

Servitude or slavery, the inverse of freedom, was the condition of African women and their progeny in the British colonies. How did they imagine freedom, and how did they think it could benefit them? In order to reconstruct their probable thinking, this chapter treats freedom as an idea with cosmological and social underpinnings as it pertained to African women and their offspring in three periods, 1619–40, 1641–70, and 1671–1700.

1619–1640

When they disembarked at Point Comfort in the Virginia colony on that fateful day in 1619, Isabell, Angelo, and Margaret could not have known that they were the first in a long stream of African women who would arrive on these shores. They had an awareness of themselves, however, as a transplanted people, servants and aliens in a foreign land, for they were captives surrounded by a white people and a culture that bore only strange resemblance to what the African women had left behind. Probably one of the curiosities alerting the first African women to the possibilities of their attaining freedom and its corresponding privileges was the presence of European coworkers. They continually flowed into the colonies, were received and treated like outsiders, worked for a period of years while being socialized into the society, and were freed after a term of service.

Depending on their ingenuity, these white outsiders to the ruling planter class were accepted by the community as citizens and were permitted to acquire real estate and generally benefit, however grudgingly, from the resources and activities of the community.[6] Observing behavior so different from the conventions of their traditional societies, which rarely made insiders of slaves, gave rise to expectations among African women that they would have such opportunities, too. From their vantage point, servitude in the colonies initially must have seemed to be based on economic indigence and religious orientation rather than on nonkinship. Some of the first African women imported into the colonies, therefore, held high aspirations of freedom, socialization into the community, and opportunities for achievement.

Finding no established, nucleated community practicing African communal traditions, these women would seek place in the new social environment by participating in Christian rituals such as baptism. The earliest recorded baptism of an African centered on family members of one of the first women, Isabell. The 1624/25 document recording that event cryptically states, "Antoney Negro: Isabell Negro: and William Theire

Child Baptized." [7] This baptism most assuredly had the support or indulgence of Isabell, if indeed she herself was not baptized, no matter who initiated the affair. The memory of African gatherings to introduce infants to the community would have been incentive enough to make an African mother feel privileged to cooperate in baptismal rituals, for she was likely to see in baptisms and child christenings substitutes for those cherished native ceremonies. [8] Curiously, however, there are few records of such events for African infants in annals of the eleven seventeenth-century colonies. This indicates (1) that the African women had no reliable forums for publicly celebrating births of their children and other important events in their lives, or (2) that the Christian rituals failed to satisfy their needs and interests, so that the women ceased to participate in them, or (3) that the ceremonies occurred and were not recorded.

Each possibility suggests its own consequential scenario, one of them being that servitude in the colonies limited the nurturing relationship between mother and child. As a result, the mother was not assured the privilege of nurturing her children so as to insure personal development keyed by proper communal ceremonies and rituals central to African traditional culture. For the mother of a newborn child, then, freedom translated into being empowered to celebrate ritualistically her infant's birth and to give the child proper launching onto life's course.

Isabell's association with the rite of baptism suggests that her family had a modicum of recognition among the British settlers as humans with spiritual needs. Although the census of 1624 lists all of the first Africans in the colony as servants, that is, as nonfree persons, there is evidence that Africans who converted to Christianity, "[particularly those who converted before coming to the Virginia colony] held a higher status than other blacks and eventually obtained their freedom." In fact, an African man who had converted to Christianity in England was residing in Virginia in the year of William's baptism. His civil status as a free person with the right to testify in court against a white person was recognized by authorities because of his 1612 conversion. [9]

Considering these realities, baptism is sure to have had political significance for Isabell and Anthony. A mother who was eager to find social acceptability for her family and herself would be likely to hope that to become a Christian was to acquire acceptance and near equality in the colonial society. For a time signs in this direction were encouraging. In 1632 the Virginia Assembly required that all masters and mistresses send their children to be catechized. Surely such legislation inspired hope in Isabell—if she learned of it—that William, then eight or nine years old, would have a formal opportunity to prepare for a place inside the society.[10]

To African women without spouses in the area, the possibilities of a dignified freedom could seem less promising as they encountered personal affronts to themselves as women. These compounded the reality of their servile status and social alienation so much that an occasional woman reacted vehemently to retain her personal freedom and autonomy against boorish encroachments. One of these was an African-born woman on Noddle's Island in Massachusetts. She was at the center of an incident that occurred in 1639, when slave owner Samuel Maverick attempted to have her breed with an African male. Each time the man was sent to lie with her, the woman disdainfully kicked him out with impertinence and resolve.[11] The most important point to be gained from this scenario is that the woman resisted mating with the man because she did not want to; to that extent she asserted her personal freedom.

If the episode stemmed from her being an African queen, as one claim holds, the woman most likely was making more than a sexual rebuff or a mere class distinction. Analysis of the scarce data suggests that she might have come from an area where there were castes and strict hierarchical order. This was true of the region influenced by Mande traditions, where marriage between royalty and commoners was virtually taboo. The Wolof, in particular, were a group with such a background; they were transported to the colonies in large numbers in the seventeenth century. The slave owner's silence regarding reactions of the African male, who was not identified as being of either royal or noble lineage, is interesting. Although the woman appeared to be reacting to the man's approaches, he might have been making them only halfheartedly. Depending on his own cultural provenance, the "spurned" man was as likely to be opposed to transcaste mating as the woman was. Beneath the socially trite excuses, an astute observer would discern a well of metaphysical reasoning.

A number of African cosmologies held that royalty was sacred and derived from reserved lineages. Awe and privilege surrounding those lineages allowed the rulers, following rituals of installation, to be regarded as partly divine and in alignment with benevolent forces of nature. To this extent royalty was conjugally untouchable, except by the noble families from which it derived.[12] Those in agreement with such metaphysical notions would be inclined not to cohabit outside their castes for fear of upsetting the balance in forces where nature and society intersected. Two aggrieved persons (as this recently captured African-born queen and man were) of this mind would take caution against compounding their already miserable plight of being enslaved by perpetrating an offence against forces of nature.[13]

Another African woman who has not been identified as having a spouse in the colonies would seem to have been held up to public scorn because of her lack of constraint over sexual impulses, in contrast to the behavior of the African queen. This servant, named Susan, gained notoriety and a footnote in history when she was discovered to be pregnant by Robert Sweatt, who probably was white since his race was not designated. The Virginia parish court ruled in 1640 that Susan was to be whipped and Sweatt was "to do public penance for his offense at James city church in the time of devine service[, which was] the usual [British] punishment for an unwed father."[14]

Whipping was a common form of punishment in the colonial period, but local church parishes seemed less reluctant to whip (African) women than white men for sexual offenses. However much race influenced the nature of the sentences, Susan is likely to have been punished in accordance with patriarchal notions of what was proper behavior for a female servant of whatever color. There is significance, nevertheless, in this parish court action. It was a marked departure from the decision rendered in the 1630 case of Hugh Davis, who was whipped before Africans and Whites for lying with an African, presumably because the person with whom he lay was designated a heathen woman.[15] One only can wonder, What was the plight of the woman? The decision in the Sweatt case suggests that colonial officials were beginning to favor men, in terms of the severity of the punishment, over (African) women in such cases.

The Sweatt case occurred about three months after John Punch, an African man, was enslaved for life as a punishment for running away, and Susan might have considered herself fortunate not to have suffered a similar fate.[16] How Susan thought about her whipping, per se, depended on how her life might have proceeded had she been in Africa, and that depended on several variables. If she had been kidnapped from a husband—whether enslaved or free and traded away, she is likely to have felt misunderstood and mistreated by colonial authorities. Their reactions to her offence certainly would indicate to her the cultural contrasts between British and most African traditional responses.

In many parts of Africa there were pragmatic approaches to human sexuality, particularly for women whose husbands were dead or otherwise absent. Some patrilineal groups adhered to a system of levirate, for example, in which a widow was inherited by her brother-in-law and so brought into a marriage that often was polygynous.[17] This permitted the widow to fulfill her sexual needs (and also to secure her children's inheritance) without disrupting the civil order that regulated sexual and other behavior. The absence of such institutional arrangements for meeting basic human urges must have seemed curious, if not sadistic, to women separated from their spouses.

Hearing that levirate, polygyny, and other non-Western conjugal arrangements existed in Africa offended British monogamous sensibilities. The British tended to disdain sexuality that did not approximate European traditions or that betrayed economic needs of the master by accumulating nonproductive bodies to be cared for. If Susan was from one of the pragmatically oriented African societies and had been married, she would resent being whipped whether Sweatt was or not, as well as not being free to satisfy a natural urge. Whether meaning to protest her captivity or to satisfy sexual urges without regard for civil codes regulating the system of servitude, Susan certainly asserted her will to use her own body as she saw fit. At any rate the ruling in this case signaled the further degradation and alienation of African women by the British colonial authority.

1641–1670

New arrivals had no knowledge of what previously had transpired relative to controlling African women in the colonies. Even when they did become aware of colonial policy and individual attitudes, African women were likely to have knowledge that was local and regional, except for possible hearsay picked up if they were "seasoned" in Barbados or the West Indies. Therefore, as the third decade of African servitude in the British colonies got under way, because the African presence was sparse, new African women arrivals would focus mostly on the in-migrations of white servants among whom they worked. They would witness those servants' upward mobility or release from servitude and derive hope that they themselves would experience a similar future of freedom and opportunity for achievement.

Because heathenism often had been the significant distinction made by the British between Africans and white servants, African women attempted to overcome that bias by converting to Christianity. A Christian conversion is noted in an African-born woman who arrived in the Massachusetts Bay colony in 1638 with thirty-nine other Africans. Three years after her arrival, she had proved her "true godliness" and was baptized and communed into the Puritan (Congregational) Church at Dorchester, Massachusetts.[18] John Winthrop's brief observation does not tell us much, but it does indicate that the woman was impelled to distinguish herself and that she was not repelled by the strictures and discipline of the theocracy-like community. There was much to remind her of African traditional environments. She would after all have been accustomed to social strictures, deference for hierarchy, and conformity to communal tradition.[19] Observing the discipline of the church bore at least a contextual resemblance to the process associated with induction into women's societies in Africa. This African convert lived outside Boston, somewhat remote from other Africans, perhaps, so membership in the church could, in her mind, have simulated belonging to the insiders' community and might have offered relief from alienation and isolation.

Other African women, like Mary Johnson, wife of Anthony, accommodated themselves to the alien situation by cooperating with their spouses to accumulate real estate and servants, as Whites often did when released from servitude or apprenticeships. To purchase and own servants (slaves?) approximated a familiar African tradition that provided a sense of self-worth and authority through accomplishment. Mary and Anthony Johnson would proceed through each of these paces. In 1651 the first headright grant given to an African was awarded to Mary's husband. The Johnsons received 250 acres of land in Accomack County, Virginia, for importing five persons. They were joined by others of African descent with the Johnson surname. Obviously the Johnsons had completed whatever tenures they were required to serve, and presumably they were married legally, had children, and were preparing to better their future.[20]

Several ominous signs flashed on the horizon, however. As these Africans were about to gain opportunities for self-fulfillment and accomplishment, they found doors shutting, showing that release from servitude or slavery did not lead to personal or even civic freedom. The first omen was the Virginia Act of 1658, which declared that African female and Native American servants were to be taxed as males already had been since 1649. Next was the Virginia code of 1662, which established that all children born in the colony would be bond or free based on the status of the mother. It is generally assumed that following the latter act the majority of Africans in the colonies were enslaved.[21]

The irony was that the 1662 code is presumed to have evolved out of the case in which a mulatto woman, Elizabeth Key, sued for her freedom because she was Christian and, although her mother was of African descent, her father was white. The plaintiff had argued successfully in 1656 that "under British common law a child followed the status of the father." [22] The new colonial code removed any hope that mulattoes would be allowed to continue to claim their freedom on the basis of European paternity.

Although it paralleled African traditions, by which children inherited the social status of the slave mother, this action in the British colonies was unfortunate, for it demeaned the black mother because of her race and set her apart from white women. In many places in the motherland, free mothers were special and assumed to be vessels through whom revered ancestors returned to earth and children derived a lineage. Even prior to passage of the fated code, such women as the African queen on Noddle's Island had assessed the cost of having children. Their conclusions often inhibited their fertility and caused them to have fewer children than their descendants, their ancestors, or their contemporaries in Africa. The fact is that African women did not sustain their population through natural growth in the seventeenth century, although 86 percent of the females transported to the colonies before 1700 were in their fertile years.

Apart from conscious determination by some to protest against their servility and enslavement by remaining childless through abstinence, by practicing African nursing traditions, or even through infanticide, other factors beyond their control also militated to keep birthrates low. The larger number of men than women, the distances between plantations, and the limited opportunities for visitation proved to be crucial. These factors, along with strictures peculiar to the monogamous European colonial setting, deprived many women of opportunities to mate.[23]

Opportunities for family life and procreation, then, were limited. Yet, wherever they did form, the bonds between children and parents and between husbands and wives were so intense that it was said to be common for Africans to walk thirty or forty miles to visit. The conditions of servitude or slavery made it virtually impossible, however, for them to enjoy a family lifestyle that even remotely approximated the traditions left behind.[24] If the decision made by the Noddle's Island woman meant that she elected not to give birth to any children, in light of the 1662 legislation she must have felt absolved of any guilt or blame. On the other hand, mothers looking down upon the faces of their adoring children might find consolation in the belief that "destiny" was the ultimate source of the children's tragic heritage.

Destiny in the African traditional sense was the cornerstone of self-knowledge. It alluded to one's awareness of the God-Force and designated course of life within one. To this extent the meaning of destiny was similar to Western concepts of luck and predestination as related to the quality of one's life and its anticipated outcome in the hereafter. It was a concept subscribed to by nearly all Africans in precolonial times. Whether assigned (as in Islamic thought) or chosen (as in African traditional thought), one's destiny was unchangeable, for it was locked in the will of God.

Even with its predestinarian, immutable bent, the African understanding of destiny was not fatalistic in the classical Greek sense. People were expected to strive to do everything within their power to have good fortune, to maintain harmony in their lives, to make sure that they had not contributed to bringing about the adversities that befell them. Following the discernment of his or her destiny, the individual was challenged to remain constantly centered in that destiny throughout the passages of life by acquiring periodic priestly divinations (both traditional and Islamic) and making the prescribed propitiative sacrifices.[25]

Before arriving in the British colonies, African women had known what they came to earth to do and the parameters of their potential. An individual's ultimate destiny was linked to her social roles and achievements. The parameters of destiny were thus influenced by societal expectations, and at the time of the Atlantic slave trade these expectations were generally gender specific. Among the Yoruba, for example, expectations that women provide social wealth (i.e., children) and material wealth were dispersed throughout Yoruba divination verses. The local marketplace that was by then closely identified with women traders was designated the abode (Ile) of the goddess of wealth (Aje).[26]

Where women as well as men could be expected to acquire wealth, female examples of achievement historically were consistent with this expectation. Wolof-, Mende-, and Mande-speaking women of Senegal, Gambia, and Guinea-Bissau, for example, were successful traders in the seventeenth century. In those locations there was a long-standing tradition of female commercial entrepreneurship and female influence among kings and chiefs.[27] This trading impulse was continued or paralleled in the colonies. The impulse to trade was said to be so great among African women and men that to many it seemed insuppressible. On the British island of Barbados, it was alleged that "nothing could keep the blacks from their markets short of locking them up." Because of these markets, black women and men could maintain a semblance of their trading traditions in the face of discouragement from settlers, who constantly complained about their "Negro" markets.[28]

African women's trading in the colonies generally was inspired by the intention to purchase their own or someone else's release from the fetters of bondage and by the desire to have a destiny-oriented identity and to survive within the alien environment. African women thereby transposed their trading traditions into a mechanism that was psychologically, if not physically, freeing. Just to survive and avoid regression into servitude, "free" African women were compelled to be enterprising. Frequently living in cities and being titheable, socially disinherited, and vulnerable to poverty, they found a work ethic of near-marketwoman proportions to be imperative. In fact, the tithe was oppressive enough to cause families to petition for relief from the tax that discriminated against "free" women of African ancestry.[29] The Virginia Assembly reiterated in 1668 that African women had been permitted to breathe too easily in the atmosphere of free enterprise. Therefore, assemblymen reemphasized the tithing code by declaring, "Negro women, though permitted to enjoy their freedome, yet ought not in all respects to be admitted to a full fruition of the exemptions and impunities of the English." This was intended to restrict possibilities for business enterprise among African women.[30]

1671–1700

After the 1660s the importation of African-born women increased, and their enslavement for life was institutionalized. Their opportunities for manumission and maintenance of family and personal welfare decreased simultaneously. The acquisitive experiences of Mary Johnson, wife of Anthony, which spanned at least two decades, may be typical of the shifting fortunes of free Africans in the colonies as opportunities became increasingly constricted. Imagine her bitter anguish when a jury of white men in Accomack County, Virginia, assembled in August 1670 and determined that widow Mary Johnson and family would have their hard-earned property taken from them. The jury's reasoning was that because "he [Anthony] was a Negroe and by consequence an alien," the land originally held by Johnson should revert to the Crown rather than descend to Johnson's heirs. This exacerbated any economic hardships that Mary already had.[31]

These decisions probably came as no great surprise to the black community, though, in light of the deteriorating racial climate. Freedom to participate fully in trading and other business enterprises and to pass property on to their heirs generally evaded Africans from the seventies on. In this sense racism now posed a threat to the very souls of cosmically oriented African women in the colonies because they were denied opportunities to maximize their potential for achievement.

It is unlikely that Ginney Bess, the woman who sponsored her child for baptism in 1683, proceeded under the optimistic assumption of early seventeenth-century Africans that she or the child would ever enjoy the freedom of white folk. Her action indicated that she had been baptized at a time previous to presenting her child for this ritual, inasmuch as this normally was prerequisite for sponsors in Congregational assemblies.[32] Until the mid-seventeenth century, baptism and membership in the church had held out to African women (or to their descendants, such as Elizabeth Key) a probable escape from slavery. Conversion had offered them the semblance of belonging to the colonial society. Even these benefits of religion were beginning to be eroded by the 1680s, when the African and African American populations and their aggregate value as laborers were climbing substantially through slave imports and slave births for the first time in colonial history.

By this time large numbers of female descendants of African-born women were entering their midteens in the Chesapeake colonies, where Africans had lived longest, and they were marrying and giving birth to increasing numbers of children fathered by African and African American males. These offspring were the first sizable generation of African Americans. The quality of their lives, however, was depressed tremendously by codes of 1690, 1691, and 1696 that restricted African-oriented worship, purchase of land by African Americans, and manumission.[33]

The suspicion is that as the African populace increased, Africans were left more to themselves and given less introduction to Christianity and less exposure to practicing Christians when the colonists began segregating racially. Or perhaps the racial biases as practiced by parish courts and church deacons were so great, and the hypocrisy and immorality of British settlers so disconcerting, that African women turned their backs on that faith. They may have become increasingly preoccupied with their cultural past, tending to relate more to African traditional thought. At any rate, evidence suggests that by the turn of the century African women spoke more frequently of their native traditions, indicating that those helped them sustain hope in the midst of depression and heartache.

Throughout their servitude and enslavement, there were women who never surrendered the vision that they would return to the motherland and recover full membership in the communities of their nativity. This African thought induced some women to long for, and even to seek, death, which was expected to launch them on that journey.[34] Expressions like the following from an African-born woman in Saybrook, Connecticut, reflect the changing views of ultimate freedom among Africans in the colonies. Unlike those who expected to return to their homelands after death, this woman, whose name was Ginney, mused in this way about her hereafter:

> When I die I shall go right to heaven, and knock at de door, and inquire for Massa Worthington. . . . Massa Worthington will come right to me; and I will say, Ginney's come. I want you to tell God that Ginney was always a good servant. She never lie, never steal, never use bad language. And then he will come back to the door and say, "Ginney, you may come in." And I will go right in, and sit in the kitchen.[35]

This signification only thinly disguises Ginney's will to void Worthington's power over her and to recover from her social alienation. After death she no longer would be an outcast in an alien land but a full-fledged citizen with privileges. In heaven she would send for Worthington and he would come to her; he would give the testimony she wanted; and she would take her place in the kitchen under her own will.

At most the comment infers that she believed only her earthly vocation would continue in heaven. She would be in the kitchen by choice. Even if she were in the kitchen, there would be a revolutionary shift in her power status, for then she would go to the kitchen only if Worthington pleased her. It is the emphasis on heaven, however, that indicated a transformation in thought regarding the hereafter. The new thought showed a shift from aspiring to return to Africa to anticipating that Africans would be transported to full membership in a multiethnic community in the sky. Ginney's statement was racially inclusive and perhaps for that reason also somewhat self-effacing.

Ginney anticipated a life beyond the grave that was as characteristic of African traditional thought as of European Christian thought. Ensconced in that anticipation was the realization that it no longer was satisfactory to localize heaven (ultimate liberation) in either Africa or the colonies. That the "righteous" as a group retired to heaven to be recipients of eternal bliss was Western and extrinsic to most systems of African thought. However, the concept of God as the supreme and everlasting being was as intrinsically African as it was Christian.[36]

As much as I would like to end this chapter with Ginney's turn-of-the-century musings, a more suitable concluding metaphor is found in the life of Frances Driggus. Frances was daughter of Sarah King Driggus, whose life as a second-generation free woman and wife of an enslaved man spanned the last half of the century. Always living on the margins of society and in poverty, Sarah bound out her daughter to John Brewer, a white local blacksmith. Brewer took sexual advantage of Frances several times and followed up his behavior by filing fornication charges against her, causing her to suffer dozens of lashes. But when she was charged by him with having a child out of wedlock, instead of quietly accepting thirty lashes and two years additional service with Brewer, Frances identified him as father of the child and received an appeal.

Striking back at her for targeting him, Brewer transferred Frances to his brother-in-law, Thomas Mills, in Accomack County. She went grudgingly, but upon discovering that he intended to send her further south in 1695, Frances petitioned the court to be discharged from servitude. The justices found for Frances. Without a financial legacy from either parent, she was so impoverished that around 1700 Frances had to bind out herself for ten years and her children for twenty. In exchange for their labor they were promised an "adequate maintenance" but no wages or freedom dues with which to get a fresh start in the event of their manumission.[37]

The moral of this narrative is that the offspring of even second-generation free women could not expect to end their lives outside servitude. Children, who in Africa had represented wealth and the recycling of life before the holocaust of slave raiding and trading, were equated with economic challenge and servitude in the colonies.

• • •

African women had come to the colonies before the women on the Mayflower, but unlike their European counterparts, on the whole their social condition and hopes steadily deteriorated throughout the seventeenth century. As the alienation became more entrenched, the meaning of freedom increasingly became associated with life after death. Freedom in the colonies increasingly took on racial overtones of caste. By the end of the century the white poor who did not have land and who had to sell their labor enjoyed protections, benefits, and privileges of which even "free," land-holding Africans were then being deprived. *Free* became synonymous with *white*, whereas *African* or *black* increasingly signified *slave* and *servant,* meaning one who had no right to breathe free and achieve because of one's color.[38]

NOTES

1. Philip Curtin, *The Atlantic Slave Trade: A Census* (Madison: University of Wisconsin, 1969), 106–7, 113; Herbert S. Klein, *The Middle Passage: Comparative Studies in the Atlantic Slave Trade* (Princeton, N.J.: Princeton University Press, 1978), 238.

2. On cultural thought consult Mechal Sobel, *Trabelin' On: The Slave Journey to an Afro-Baptist Faith* (Westport, Conn.: Greenwood Press, 1979), 3–6; D. T. Niane, "Conclusion," in *General History of Africa from the Twelfth to the Sixteenth Century,* edited by D. T. Niane (Berkeley: University of California Press, 1984), 4:674–78, 681; William D. Piersen, *Black Yankees: The Development of an Afro-American Subculture in Eighteenth-Century New England* (Amherst: University of Massachusetts Press, 1988), 75.

3. K. Nwachukwu-Ogedengbe, "Slavery in Nineteenth Century Aboh (Nigeria)," in *Slavery in Africa: Historical and Anthropological Perspectives,* edited by Suzanne Miers and Igor Kopytoff (Madison: University of Wisconsin Press, 1977), 141.

4. Miers and Kopytoff, *Slavery in Africa*; Claire C. Robertson and Martin A. Klein, eds., *Women and Slavery in Africa* (Madison: University of Wisconsin Press, 1983); Orlando Patterson, *Freedom: Freedom in the Making of Western Culture* (New York: BasicBooks, 1991), 1:135–37, 146–47.

5. Based on Edmund S. Morgan, *American Slavery, American Freedom: The Ordeal of Colonial Virginia* (New York: W. W. Norton, 1975), particularly parts 1 and 2; R. H. Tawney, "Rise of the Gentry, 1558–1640," *Economic History Review* 11 (1941):1–38.

6. Morgan, *American Slavery, American Freedom*, part 3.

7. Alden T. Vaughan, "Blacks in Virginia: A Note on the First Decade," in *Colonial Southern Slavery,* edited by Paul Finkelman (New York: Garland, 1989), 431.

8. John S. Mbiti, *African Religions and Philosophies* (Garden City, N.Y.: Anchor Books, 1970), chaps. 11 and 12.

9. Vaughan, "Blacks in Virginia," 432, and for the quoted passage, see 434; Helen T. Catterall, *Judicial Cases concerning American Slavery and the Negro* (New York: Negro Universities Press, 1968), 1:76.

10. William W. Hening, ed., *Statutes at Large: Being a Collection of All the Laws of Virginia . . .* (Richmond: Samuel Pleasants, 1819–23), 1:181; Jerome W. Jones,

"The Established Virginia Church and the Conversion of Negroes and Indians, 1620–1760," *Journal of Negro History* 66 (1961): 21.

11. Winthrop D. Jordan, *White over Black: American Attitudes toward the Negro, 1550–1812* (Baltimore: Penguin Books, 1969), 71; Piersen, *Black Yankees*, 37.

12. J. Suret-Canale, "The Western Atlantic Coast, 1600–1800," in *History of West Africa*, edited by J. F. A. Ajayi and Michael Crowder (New York: Columbia University Press, 1972), 1:387, 392–97.

13. Suret-Canale, "The Western Atlantic Coast, 1600–1800," 452–63; John Ralph Willis, "The Western Sudan from the Moroccan Invasion (1591) to the Death of Al-Mukhtar Al-Kunti (1811)," in Ajayi and Crowder, *History of West Africa*, 1:452–63.

14. William W. Hening, ed., *Statutes at Large: Being a Collection of All the Laws of Virginia* . . . (New York: Bartow, 1832), 1:552.

15. A. Leon Higginbotham, Jr., *In the Matter of Color: Race and the American Legal Process* (New York: Oxford University Press, 1978), 1:23.

16. Helen T. Catterall, ed., *Judicial Cases concerning American Slavery and the Negro* (New York: Negro Universities Press, 1968), 1:77.

17. Mbiti, *African Religions and Philosophies*, 188–89; Michael C. Kirwen, *African Widows* (Maryknoll, N.Y.: Orbis Books, 1979); Jasper Gerhard, "Polygamy in the Old Testament," *African Theological Journal* 2 (February 1969):27–57.

18. John Winthrop, *History of New England, 1630–1649*, James Savage, ed. (Boston: Little, Brown, 1852), 2:31.

19. Refer to Mbiti, *African Religions and Philosophies*, and to most standard works on African traditional religions, rituals, culture.

20. Chester W. Gregory, "Black Women in Pre-Federal America," in *Clio Was a Woman: Studies in the History of American Women*, edited by Mabel E. Deutrich and Virginia C. Purdy (Washington, D.C.: Howard University Press, 1980), 53; Virginia Easley DeMarce, " 'Verry Slitly Mixt': Tri-Racial Isolate Families of the Upper South—A Genealogical Study," *National Genealogical Society Quarterly* 80 (March 1992):19.

21. On the 1658 tax, see Gregory, "Black Women in Pre-Federal America," 53, 54. For the text of the 1662 code, see Hening, *Statutes at Large* (1832), 2:170.

22. Warren M. Billings, "The Cases of Fernando and Elizabeth Key: A Note on the Status of Blacks in Seventeenth-Century Virginia," *William and Mary Quarterly*, 3d ser., 30, no. 4 (1973):467–74.

23. Darrett B. Rutman and Anita H. Rutman, *A Place in Time: Explicatus* (New York: W. W. Norton, 1984), 182; Nancy Woloch, *Women and the American Experience* (New York: Knopf, 1984), 33; Robert V. Wells, *The Population of the British Colonies in America before 1776* (Princeton, N.J.: Princeton University Press, 1975), 162–63.

24. Refer to Russell R. Menard, "The Maryland Slave Population, 1658–1730," in *Colonial Southern Slavery*, edited by Paul Finkelman (New York: Garland, 1989), 3:209; Mbiti, *African Religions and Philosophies*, 174–76, 212–16; Ulli Beier,

ed., *Origin of Life and Death: African Creation Myths* (Ibadan: Heinemann, 1970), 121; William Bascom, *Ifa Divination: Communication between Gods and Men in West Africa* (Bloomington: Indiana University Press, 1991), 115.

25. As among the Yoruba, Ijo, Ibo, Fon, Ewe, and other West Africans. E. O. Oyelade, "The Doctrine of Predestination: A Study of Religio-Cultural Interactions in Nigeria," *Ife: Annals of the Institute of Cultural Studies*, no. 4 (1993):98–110; Mbiti, *African Religions and Philosophies*, chap. 14, "Death and the Hereafter."

26. Bascom, *Ifa Divination*, 110, 157; William Bascom, *Sixteen Cowries: Yoruba Divination from Africa to the New World* (Bloomington: Indiana University Press, 1980), 143, 117, 127, 115–17; refer to Bernard I. Belasco, *The Entrepreneur as Culture Hero: Preadaptations in Nigerian Economic Development* (New York: Praeger, 1980), chaps. 6, 7, 8.

27. Nancy J. Hafkin and Edna G. Bay, eds., *Women in Africa: Studies in Social and Economic Change* (Stanford, Calif.: Stanford University Press, 1976), 6, 114; Robertson and Klein, *Women and Slavery in Africa*, 13; E. Francis White, "Women, Work, and Ethnicity: The Sierra Leone Case," in *Women and Work in Africa*, edited by Edna Bay (Boulder, Colo.: Westview Press, 1982), 276; Bascom, *Sixteen Cowries*, 115–19, 131, 443–46, 469; Bascom, *Ifa Divination*, 73.

28. Piersen, *Black Yankees*, 31–32; DeMarce, " 'Verry Slitly Mixt'," 17–22.

29. DeMarce, " 'Verry Slitly Mixt'," 17–22; Douglas Deal, "A Constricted World: Free Blacks on Virginia's Eastern Shore, 1680–1750," in *Colonial Chesapeake Society*, edited by Lois Green Carr, Philip D. Morgan, and Jean B. Russo (Chapel Hill: University of North Carolina Press, 1988), 283.

30. Hening, *Statutes at Large* (1832), 2:267.

31. For the decision refer to Loren Schweninger, *Black Property Owners in the South, 1790–1915* (Urbana: University of Illinois Press, 1990), 15; and DeMarce, " 'Verry Slitly Mixt'," 20–21.

32. Joseph B. Earnest, Jr., *Religious Development of the Negro in Virginia* (Charlottesville, Va.: Michie Company, 1914), 21–22.

33. Allan Kulikoff, *Tobacco and Slaves: The Development of Southern Cultures in the Chesapeake, 1680–1800* (Chapel Hill: University of North Carolina Press, 1986), 353–58; Jones, "The Established Virginia Church and the Conversion of Negroes and Indians, 1620–1760," 18.

34. See Piersen, *Black Yankees*, 74–76.

35. For the quotation, see Piersen, *Black Yankees*, 76.

36. Mbiti, *African Religions and Philosophies*, chaps. 4–7.

37. Deal, "A Constricted World," 285–88.

38. A point also made by Edmund Morgan. See Morgan, *American Slavery, American Freedom*, part 4.

III | Religion

Among the most important aspects of many women's lives in early America was religion. In some respects religion could, in theory at least, be a freeing experience, one that brought spiritual equality. On the other hand, institutional religion tended inevitably to be tied to the social norms of the times, and tension between spiritual parity and social inequality gave many women pause. The three chapters in this section explore the relationship between freedom and religion for early American women of three prominent faiths: Quaker, Catholic, and Baptist.

Karin A. Wulf explores the dynamics of Quaker belief, showing how it laid the foundation for some Quaker women to challenge prevailing notions of marriage. Women could experience freedom, she reveals, not only outside of marriage, but by deliberately avoiding it. Drawing on a wide range of sources, including women's poetry, tax records, wills, estate inventories, account books, Quaker meeting records, family letters, commonplace books, and diaries, Wulf argues that a conception of spinsterhood as a form of autonomy developed among these women, and she shows that Quaker theology was central to these notions.

Since the days of Francis Parkman, the relative freedom enjoyed by colonists in New France has been painted darkly in comparison to that experienced by British colonials. From then to now, historians—focusing on men's thinking and men's experiences—have emphasized the arbitrary nature of French government and the absence of a natural rights tradition. Terrence A. Crowley challenges those distortions by focusing on women's religion rather than men's politics. He takes us inside a group of exclusively female religious orders that sprouted in eighteenth-century New France. The nuns and sisters in these communities made a critical contribution to life and society in New France by providing education, medical attention, and social services. Eschewing the inferior status of women in French colonial society at large, they established their independence from male domination by building for themselves nurturing enclaves of autonomy and respect, developing in the process a forceful conception of freedom based in communal effort rather than individual accomplishment.

Janet Moore Lindman explores the expansion of freedom among Baptist women in Pennsylvania during the half century following the establishment of the first Baptist Association there in 1707. That association, combined with strong male leadership, ensured men's domination of Pennsylvania's Baptist denominations. Thus, although the sexes enjoyed spiritual equality, the church and the wider society together limited women's freedom. As a result Baptist women developed their own spiritual community outside the meetinghouses. Using church books, wills, diaries, and correspondence, Lindman shows that Baptist women came to express their spirituality corporately in private households and women's meetings and individually through family ties, journaling, reading, and letter writing. Over time, she demonstrates, a separate female devotional culture developed, within which women found distinctive expressions of the freedom otherwise denied to them.

5

"My Dear Liberty": Quaker Spinsterhood and Female Autonomy in Eighteenth-Century Pennsylvania

KARIN A. WULF

Historians of early American women often conflate the experiences of married women with those of all women.[1] This chapter looks instead at a group of Quaker women in eighteenth-century Pennsylvania who never married. It examines in particular the poetry of Susanna Wright, who expressed ideas about spinsterhood based both on Quaker theology and on contemporary appeals to reason and rationality. Wright espoused resistance to marriage as adherence to the Quaker ideals of gender equality and partnership, which she argued were being subverted by hierarchical marriages. Wright's ideas, and those of a group of women with whom she corresponded, including Hannah Griffitts and Elizabeth Norris, represent an important strain of thinking about Quakerism, marriage, and female autonomy.

Philadelphia spinster Hannah Griffitts explained to a woman friend in 1769 that she chose to "remain single" simply "to Keep my dear Liberty Long as I can."[2] She loved men "[only] as well as I ought," she continued. Urging her friend to "Leave me to enjoy the sweet Freedom I love," Griffitts's spirited defense of her single status was written as a poetical exchange with "Sophronia," the moniker of a friend who was obviously more inclined toward matrimony than Griffitts herself. In the verses, "Sophronia" teased Griffitts about her single status, and Griffitts defended that status in like manner. But within this playful exchange was, only lightly veiled, a more profound divergence of views. Hannah Griffitts asserted that spinsterhood was "liberty" and that as a spinster she only loved men as well as any woman "ought." This might suggest that Griffitts was reminding Sophronia that women, like men, should love God above all others. In a letter to a cousin, she expanded on the theme of spinsterhood as liberty. "There are many of you weded ones who I believe are Placed in your Proper Sphere," she wrote, and "I sincerely wish you encrease of Hapiness in it—without envying you one atom." But, she continued, "Everyone is not fitted for the single life—nor was I ever moulded for The weded one."[3]

Was Hannah Griffitts unusual? Although Griffitts celebrated and defended her single status, the usual story of spinsterhood in the early modern period is a bleak one. Women who never married, we are told, spent their lives regretting that they had missed the essential female experiences of marriage and motherhood. Without a family "of their own," their lives often were focused on aging parents or nieces and nephews. They faced old age, "their status as 'spinsters' reaffirmed with each passing year," with an extraordinary "depth of sorrow."[4] Rebecca Dickinson, an oft-quoted spinster from Hatfield, Massachusetts, mourned "that others and all the world was in Possession of children and friends and a hous[e] and homes while I was so od[d] as to sit here alone."[5] No doubt many men and women who never married missed the comforts and company of a spouse, yet we should remember that many were as unhappy in marriage as Dickinson considered herself to be without it.[6] Rather than viewing "Aunt Bek's" oddity as typical of colonial spinsters, we might consider her typical only in her geographic region. Living in Hatfield, Massachusetts, Dickinson was far more likely to feel "od[d]" than was Hannah Griffitts, living in an urban environment like Philadelphia where spinsters were more common.

The rural or urban nature of their situations may have affected Griffitts's and Dickinson's respective feelings about spinsterhood, but aspects of regional culture—including religion—affected attitudes toward spinsterhood in general. Religious belief profoundly affected the way early Americans understood women's place in society and within households. New England Puritans, for example, embraced a sexual and spiritual hierarchy that emphasized women's subservience to both God and their husbands. Marriage was the fundamental social unit, and wife and mother were the most important social roles for women. Women who fell outside the norm in this regard were viewed as not simply "od[d]," but deviant.[7]

Philadelphia Quakers like Hannah Griffitts rejected these notions, basing their views in part on the teachings of their religion. Quaker theology expressly celebrated spiritual equality between men and women.[8] The workings of an "inner light" of salvation, leading to conversion, had no gendered prerequisite. Rather than seeing humankind as predestined for either salvation or doom, Quakers gave people more and God less responsibility for sinning and redemption. Behavior, control, and personal responsibility were essential for the attainment of salvation.[9] Seeking salvation was to be unmediated, either by ministers (whose role was to encourage, to give testimonial, but not to intercede) or by anyone else. Sexual hierarchy could impose on, for example, a woman's relationship with God. Quaker founder George Fox had written, "For man and woman were helpsmeet, in the image of God and in Righteousness and holiness, in the dominion before they fell; but, after the Fall, in the transgression, the man was to rule over his wife. But in the restoration by Christ into the image of God and His righteousness and holiness again, in that they are helpsmeet, man and woman, as they were before the Fall."[10] Salvation, attained through the spontaneous action of the inner light, therefore rescued men and women from the debased state of their sin. Quakers interpreted redemption not only as immortality, but also as a release from the bonds of sexual hierarchy. Thus, "in the restoration" men and women were again "helpsmeet." Without the explicit gender hierarchy of the other Protestant faiths, Quaker women became not only true coreligionists, but also ministers, whose exhortations were designed to encourage both good behavior and conversion.

Because Quakerism seemed so amenable to women's spiritual authority, and in fact depended on it, scholars have vigorously debated the implications of Quakerism's egalitarian impulses for women. Were those consequences significant for women, either inside or outside of households? The answer is complicated. Historians have suggested that Quakers who settled in Pennsylvania held more conservative views about women's role than their religious antecedents might have indicated. If that was the case, this conservatism would mirror a pattern in other radical sects, in which women were initially welcomed as virtual equals and then increasingly marginalized as church governance and even theology developed along more conservative and hierarchically gendered lines.[11] But the high proportion of women ministers, including traveling "Public Friends," and the lack of controversy around the establishment of the women's meeting in the colonies suggests that Quakers held a very positive view of women's spiritual authority and by extension perhaps household and familial authority.[12]

But did Quakerism distinguish between married and unmarried women? Women's authority in the meeting and at home, as Barry Levy and others have described it, was largely dependent on their position as wives and mothers.[13] Early Quaker leader Margaret Fell, however, was among the first to point out that not all women married, and indeed that it was perfectly acceptable for women to remain unmarried.[14] As it turns out, the household on which Levy predicated his case for Quaker domesticity, in which women were both wives and mothers and men were both husbands and fathers, had a tenuous existence. Husbands and wives often died, leaving a spouse to remarry or remain single. Some men and women married late or not at all. These and other situations inspired a household organization more like an extended kin arrangement than the nuclear family.[15] Such homes welcomed and needed spinsters. In a household headed by a widower with children, for example, a spinster sister might provide some motherly care for nieces and nephews. Through such arrangements, spinsters appropriated the available roles for women without marrying or having children. As Margaret Fell had pointed out, to be both a single woman and a Quaker was not unusual, because these were not mutually exclusive identities.

In addition to their access to a variety of female activities outside of marriage, Quaker spinsters could articulate their spinsterhood as theologically based resistance to gendered hierarchy. Because George Fox described Eden before the Fall as a place of equality between men and women, the goal of Quakers was to achieve that prelapserian state, not to mimic the sexual hierarchy that was the legacy of Eve's seduction and transgression. Marriage was to be companionate, self-selected but guided by God, and devoted in all things to "holy love."[16] If marriage was not guided by those Quakerly ideals, then perhaps women should avoid it altogether.

One of the most compelling contemporary arguments along these lines was made by Susanna Wright. Wright, called the "bluestocking of the Susquehana," thought the Quaker marriage ideal could not be realized. Men were inveterate dominators, and women were chronically subordinate. As long as that was the case, remaining unmarried was the only way for women to resist the kind of sexual hierarchy of which Quakerism expressly disapproved. Wright articulated these sentiments in a poem to a friend and fellow spinster, Elizabeth Norris of Philadelphia and Fairhill. Norris was also Hannah Griffitts's aunt. The poem and the convictions Wright expressed in it have profound implications for our understanding of the way Quakers could interpret their faith. Moreover, Susanna Wright's depiction of gender and marital relations provides an alternative to the Quaker domesticity view of family and marriage that Barry Levy has described.

Wright was part of a committed Quaker family. Her parents, John and Patience Wright, had left Lancashire, England, in 1714 and presented their "certificates" to the Chester Meeting in December of that same year. They traveled to the colonies with three of their children, James, Elizabeth, and Patience, leaving the fourth, ten-year-old Susanna, in England to continue her schooling. Sometime in the next eight years she joined the family. After a long illness, Patience, Sr., died in 1722, leaving Susanna to head her father's household. Susanna's two sisters married within a year of each other and soon, after more than twelve years in Chester, John, James, and Susanna made their way to the frontier, the newly surveyed Lancaster County. They settled just a few miles north of the Maryland border along the banks of the Susquehanna River, eventually establishing a ferry across the river. John had been a Quaker minister before the family emigrated to the colonies, and he continued to be active in both local and monthly meetings, as did his children. He was a magistrate for Chester and later Lancaster County and was first elected to the Assembly in 1718. Frontier fighting with Indians and border battles with Marylanders drew the Wrights into the center of disputes about Quaker obligations to peace and political willingness to protect private property, and James and Susanna subsequently became heavily involved in local politics. After their father's death in 1749, James took over his assembly seat, while Susanna worked through conversation, correspondence, and some direct politicking.[17]

Susanna Wright never married, although she may have had an early affair with another Quaker and Lancaster County magistrate, Samuel Blunston. Blunston married a wealthy widow. But when his wife died after only a few years of marriage, he and Susanna resumed their relationship. She acted as his secretary, and when he became ill she handled most of his substantial affairs. When he died in 1745, Blunston left her a life interest in his entire estate. Susanna and her father moved to Blunston's estate, where John Wright died in 1749 and Susanna died in 1785.

During the forty years that she was mistress of the home at Wright's Ferry, Susanna Wright entertained friends from near and far. When Mary James was captured and taken to Canada by Indians, her children stayed with Susanna Wright. Benjamin Franklin, James Logan, and various members of the Norris family were among her closest friends and most frequent correspondents. She acted as a prothonotary, sitting "for hours each day, by a little square window put together by wooden pegs and guarded by a hand-wrought iron bar," giving legal advice and dispensing herbal medicines to Indians and other neighbors.[18] She served as a scrivener throughout the county, probably in the same capacity as she had when she was handling Blunston's business. She kept a large library, experimented with horticulture, and wrote poetry. All of these activities, as well as her facility with classical and modern languages, earned her a widespread reputation. Upon meeting her in 1784, just a year before her death at age eighty-nine, Benjamin Rush called her "the famous Suzey Wright, a lady who has been celebrated above half a century for her wit, good sense and valuable improvement of mind."[19]

Susanna was also intensely spiritual and, like her parents and theirs before them, a committed Quaker.[20] The most compelling evidence of Susanna's religiosity is expressed in her poetry. An avid correspondent, Susanna was apparently an equally avid and talented poet. Although few of her poems are extant, one memoir noted that her verse was of "a deeply religious character." [21] Those poems that do remain confirm this assessment. In two poems written thirty-two years apart to commemorate the deaths of young friends, she expressed the same sense of anguish over their early deaths but prescribed resignation to the mourners (herself included). She considered the nature of heaven and the company a soul would find there, trusting that God as well as other friends would be in the "mansions of Bliss beyond . . . Azure Skyes." [22]

The most significant expression of Susanna Wright's conception of her own religiosity and its direct applicability to her singleness is in a poem she wrote to Elizabeth Norris. This poem described the Quaker vision of gender equality in stark terms. Wright depicted spinsterhood, her own and Elizabeth Norris's, as a form of resistance to the sexual hierarchy inherent in marriage. She celebrated the example that Norris set by refusing to "yield obedience" either to individual men or to a conception of marriage that was anathema to her interpretation of Quaker theology.

Before analyzing the poem in detail, it is important to understand the connections among Susanna Wright, Elizabeth Norris, and their families. Their fathers—John Wright and Isaac Norris, Sr.—served together in the Pennsylvania Assembly, and the families probably became friendly during the worst years of the Maryland-Pennsylvania border disputes, when Lancastrians were in the midst of the battleground. [23] Following their fathers, Isaac Norris, Jr., and James Wright subsequently served in the Assembly together, and Charles Norris and James conducted business together. Sisters Deborah and Elizabeth Norris, as well as later generations of Norris women, became particularly attached to Susanna ("Susee" to these friends), as did Charles and Isaac.

The two families were remarkably similar in some important respects. Both were Quaker, wealthy, politically active, and supporters of the proprietor. Both families also included strong, independent, unmarried young women. These similarities may have accounted for the rapport enjoyed by many of the families' members over a large part of the eighteenth century, and particularly among the generation that included Charles, Isaac, James, Deborah, Elizabeth and Susanna. Susanna's relationship with her brother was as close as those of Deborah and Charles, Elizabeth and Isaac. The joint nature of their undertakings implicitly acknowledged her influence with James in many of their dealings, and

Charles Norris explicitly recognized her role in a 1761 letter. In this instance James Wright had failed to attend to Assembly business, and many were criticizing his conduct. When Charles gently attempted to call James's attention to the problem, James rebuffed him. Charles then approached Susanna, because he "Shrewdly Expected" she had "Strong Influence on [her brother's] Publick Conduct." Charles did not couch this appeal in terms of domestic moral suasion. Norris knew that Susanna understood the political implications of James's neglect of duty. He noted the grumblings of those who felt that James was only elected "in Gratitude to the memory of his Father," an acknowledgment of her "observations" on the same point.[24]

Both families were accustomed to women who were conversant with politics. Charles Norris's letters to Susanna Wright in the late 1750s detailing "Foreign, or other Publick news" resemble Debby Norris's letters to Isaac in the early 1730s. Elections, Indian settlements, wars, and political gossip were featured prominently. In 1758 he related the foibles and travails of various politicians, including the "Poor Little G[overno]r," who almost received "a Drubing, on the High Way, by a Rude Carter, who would not turn out of a Deep Shallow Road" to let the distinguished gentleman, who was no favorite of the Norrises and Wrights, pass. Susanna's political instincts and enthusiasms in particular were well known.[25] A failed candidate for the Assembly from Lancaster groused about her role in his defeat: "Could any one believe that Susy culd act so unbecoming and unfemale a part as to be employ'd in copying such infamous stuff and to take her stand as she did at Lancaster in an Upper Room in a publick House and to have a Ladder erected to the window and there distribute Lies and Tickets all the day of the election[?]"[26]

Susanna Wright's unabashed politicking provides a clue to her ideas about women's appropriate spheres and functions. Like all colonials, she had specific notions about what men and women could and should do, about what was masculine and what was feminine. She considered both political and scholarly activity to be legitimately feminine (although clearly the candidate she opposed did not agree). Possibly she regretted that she and Samuel Blunston had never married, although their partnership was clearly enormously important to both of them. But whatever her feelings for Blunston, she did not extol marriage, and by extension motherhood, as a necessary female experience. In fact, she argued the reverse. In her poem to Elizabeth Norris, Wright explicitly celebrated spinsterhood.

There are three distinct parts to Wright's poem, "To Eliza Norris—at fairhill." The first (lines 1–26) describes in general terms her interpretation of male-female relationships, what she believed to be the Quaker view of the appropriate nature of those relationships, and the subversion of that Quaker ideal. The second part (lines 27–52) depicts Norris's (and probably Wright's) specific response to the general dilemma of romantic heterosexual relationships. Norris had created an independent life for herself in a rural retreat. The third portion of the poem (lines 53–61) approaches a call to arms, with Wright suggesting that if women would "forbear" marrying, men's abuse of power would be punished on the Day of Judgment.

Wright intimated that women gained some measure of control over their lives through resistance to marriage. Specifically, she posited that women could define themselves outside of marriage and in conscious resistance to prescriptive notions about male-female interactions. Women could only develop a "self" by resisting the hierarchy of gender relations.[27]

To Eliza Norris—at fairhill

Siner Adam, by our first fair mother won
To share her fate—to Taste, & be undone
And that great Law, whence no appeal must Lye
Pronounced a Doom, That He should Rule—& Die
The Patial Race, rejoycing to fulfill
This Pleasing Dictate of almighty Will,
(With no Superior virtue in Their Mind)
Assert Their Right to Govern womankind
But Womankind, call Reason to Their aid
And Question, when or where, that Law was made,
That Law Divine,—(A Plausible pretense)
oft urg'd, with none, & oft with Little Sense
from wisdom's source, no origin could draw
That form'd the Men, to keep The Sex in awe,
Say, Reason Govern, all the mighty frame

> And Reason rules, in every one, the same
> No Right, has man, his Equal, to controul,
> Since, all agree, There is no Sex in soul;
> weak woman, thus, in agreement grown strong,
> shakes off the yoke, her Parents wore too long;
> But He, who arguments, in vain, had tryed
> Hopes still for Conquest, from ye yielding side
> Soft Soothing flattery & Persuasion Tries,
> And by a Feigned submission, seeks to rise,
> steals, unperceived,—to the unguarded heart,
> And There Reigns TYRANT,—

The version of Quakerism that Susanna Wright presented was in reasonable proximity to George Fox's and Margaret Fell's views on gendered hierarchy. She began the poem with a reference to the Garden of Eden: "Siner Adam, by our first fair mother won / To share her fate—to taste, & be undone." The "fate" of Adam and Eve was "That He should Rule—& Die." Mortality and hierarchy were the twin components of Eden's "Doom." Most Christians interpreted the fall of mankind as the basis of women's inferiority and subordinate position. Quakers, however, saw the fall in another way entirely. The sin in Eden produced a corruption of God's original intention that man and woman should be "helpsmeet." Man's "Rule," as Wright put it, was then the second product of sin.

Most men were all too happy to interpret their authority over women as divinely sanctioned. They were "rejoycing to fulfill" a "Pleasing Dictate of almighty Will." Thus, rather than to think or pray about this arrangement, men simply accepted with enthusiasm what they found to be "Pleasing" and then peddled it as "almighty Will." Wright made two related comments on the uses of this interpretation of the fall as a male license to dominate. First, she cast their willingness in terms of the innate attractiveness of the arrangement and a base desire to dominate women. "(With no Superior virtue in Their Mind)" they would "Assert Their Right to Govern womankind." Her second point was that women's subordination had no theological foundation. It was a "*Pleasing* Dictate," based only on a "Plausible pretense" of divine law. The implication was that, as Fox agreed, hierarchy among men and women was a corruption of God's intent.

The men to whom Wright referred were Quakers. Both her family and Norris's family were Quaker, and the likelihood that either would marry outside the faith, which was grounds for disownment, was slim to none. So the men she wrote of were Quakers who subverted their own beliefs with their attempts to "Govern womankind." Their "assertions" of authority were not only subversive but demonstrated the seductiveness of other religious beliefs. Quakers were virtually alone in their adherence to gender equality. Puritans, for instance, believed that women had spiritual capacities equivalent to men, but the emphasis on sin, the curse of birth, and exclusion of women from church governance and the ministry all created a very different environment for women's spirituality. Wright's complaints suggest both that some Quaker women were dissatisfied with the devotion of Quaker men to real equality and perhaps even that they viewed that lack of a commitment as a sign of apostasy.

After illustrating the context of male claims to superiority, Wright explained the dialogue that followed. First, women's response to men's declaration was to question the source of its authority. They would "Question, when or where, that Law was made." She had already dismissed its "origin" "from wisdom's source." In seeking some other credible source, women would "call Reason to Their aid."

This is the first point on which Wright parted company with earlier Quaker writings, but she was probably only representative of a wider phenomenon among eighteenth-century Quakers. She insisted that an appeal to reason would reveal the dubious nature of men's "Right to Govern womankind." Reason was supposed to "[rule] in every one, the same," and reason suggested that "No Right, has man, his Equal, to controul / Since, all agree, There is no Sex in soul." The equivalence of male and female souls was part of many Protestants' beliefs, but the place of reason in determining what Wright had already depicted as a theological matter was not clear. Quakers generally questioned the role of reason in any spiritual matters, believing that reason and logic were part of the secular world, quite apart from the sacred and consequently subject to corruption.[28] Wright's reliance on reason placed her firmly among the Enlightenment generation. Of course, her interest in horticulture and her warm friendship and intellectual kinship with Enlightenment men of Philadelphia like James Logan and Benjamin Franklin are further evidence of this. Her insistence on the importance of reason in a religious context suggests a willingness to harness Enlightenment rhetoric to Quaker doctrine. Wright wryly observed that even "weak woman" would "in agreement [grow] strong," once reason exposed the fallacy of male domination. Reason armed her; she would "[shake] off the yoke, her Parents wore too long." The implication was that women of Wright's (and Norris's) own generation had a duty to challenge traditional gender norms.

The contest for authority did not end with the appeal to reason. After a pretended acquiescence to equality, men tricked women into a romantic submission. If a man could not triumph in the "arguments" of reason, "He . . . Hopes still for Conquest, from ye yielding side." Men appealed to women with "Soft Soothing flattery & Persuasion," a mockery of the language of courtship. By "a Feigned submission" to women's triumph of reason and with their agenda intact, men would "[steal], unperceived, — to the unguarded heart." Wright predicted dire consequences. Once a man had stolen into a woman's heart under false pretenses, he would "[reign] TYRANT."

Susanna Wright's analysis of romantic heterosexual relationships was bleak. Her analysis of the male strategy for dominion, carried out with a total disregard for both religion and reason, betrayed a pessimism about the power of the original Quaker vision of gendered equality. The parameters of that vision were never entirely clear. For example, the extent of the authority exercised by the women's meetings came under fire in several different Quaker communities.[29] But the relationship between individual men and women, which, as the basis for families was the heart of Quaker society, was never directly challenged. The example of George Fox and Margaret Fell Fox's own marriage was testimony to the power of partnership and the model of "helpsmeet." What Susanna Wright elucidated was the potential and relative weakness of that model in the face of what she saw as driving forces stemming from natural predispositions.

It is possible, of course, that she based this pessimistic view on her own experience and observations of other relationships. Wright had numerous male correspondents, but there is only scant evidence of her involvement with anyone other than Samuel Blunston. Charles Norris wrote to her regularly but usually addressed his correspondence to both her and her brother, James. He once joked that his own brother Isaac had bought her a diamond in England, but the relationship between Wright and the Norris brothers seems never to have been anything other than an extension of mutual intellectual and family interests. Although she and Samuel Blunston were intimate, none of their letters survive. The only evidence of the status of their relationship is that he married another woman but then left all of his property to Susanna. This poem might have reflected her ambiguities about their relationship. Her conclusion that women, held hostage by the emotions of their "unguarded heart," could and probably would be duped by men, suggests that the resumption of her affair with Blunston after his wife died was more problematic for her than for him. In her emphatic conclusion to the first part of the poem, Wright declared that men would "[reign] TYRANT" in the hearts of women. If she believed herself tyrannized by Blunston (or any other man), it was against her best efforts to employ reason and religion. It also implied a conflict of self in which she was both attracted to and repelled by the model of male domination and female submission. Everything we know of Susanna Wright suggests that she was a strong and commanding personality, who would have found this conflict painfully frustrating.

> But you, whom no Seducing Tales Can gain
> To yield obedience, — or to wear the Chain
> But set a Queen & in your freedom reign,
> O'er your own Thoughts, of your own heart Secure,
> You see, what Toys, Each Erring sex allure,
> Look round the most Intelligent, how few,
> But Passions Sway, or Childish joys pursue,
> Then Bless that Choice, which led your bloom of youth,
> from forms, & shadows, — to Enlightning truth,
> Best found, where Leisure & Retirement reign
> far, from the Proud, — The Busy — & the vain
> where Rural views, — soft gentle Joys impart
> Enlarge The thought, & Elevate the heart,
> Each Changing Scene, adorns gay Nature's face
> Ev'n winter wants not, its Peculiar grace
> Hoar frosts & dews, & Pale, & summer suns,
> Paint each Revolving season as it runs,
> The Showery Bow, delights your wond'ring Eyes
> Its Spacious Arch, & Variegated dyes,

> You watch the Transient Colours, as They fade,
> Till, by degrees,—they settle into shade
> Then Calm Reflect,—so Regular & fine
> Now seen no more,—a fate will soon be mine,
> When life's warm streams, Chill'd by deaths Fey hand
> Within these veins, a frozen Current Stands,
> Tho Conscious of Desert superior far

After an exquisite description of heterosexual relationships, in the second part of "To Eliza Norris," Susanna Wright celebrated celibacy. That, she proposed, was the solution to the conundrum of hierarchy versus equality. Neither reason nor religion could alter the course of relationships between men and women. Thus, in order to save themselves from domination, women's only recourse was to avoid marriage altogether. As written, a small space separates the first and second parts of the poem. Where the first part ends with the word "tyrant" in capital letters, the second immediately introduces Elizabeth Norris into the text as the honoree. Wright launches into her depiction of how Norris's experience is so different from that which she just described by distinguishing the two with "But you, whom no Seducing Tales Can gain / To yield obedience,—or to wear the Chain."

Whereas in her description of the process of courtship Wright concluded that men's seduction of women sealed their fate as inferiors, she portrayed Norris as an active resister. By resisting seduction and thus avoiding a life of obedience, Norris "set a Queen & in your freedom reign / O'er your own Thoughts, of your own heart Secure." Freedom allowed a woman to possess her own mind as well as to guarantee that her heart would remain "Secure." This behavior contrasted with that of the woman whose "unguarded heart" was vulnerable to "Seducing tales." The first implication was that women had to be vigilant in protecting themselves. The other implication was that women first had to recognize seductive behavior. Women who were seduced not only had left their hearts unguarded, but also had failed to identify the "Feigned submission" of men and their use of "Tales" to gain advantage for the ruses they were perpetrating. "You see," wrote Wright, "what Toys, Each Erring sex allure." To resist, women had to identify the instruments of their oppression.

Wright described Norris's willingness to defy marriage as a choice made in the "bloom of youth." Seeing the problematic nature of matrimony early in her life, Norris had been led "from forms, & shadows,—to Enlightening truth." The suggestion earlier in the poem that most of their generation had succumbed to traditional relationships was also reiterated. Most women had been either swayed by passion or captivated by men's "Seducing Tales." Among the "most Intelligent" only a "few" could claim the distinction of having made Norris's perceptive—and early—choice against marriage.

Those other women could only pursue "Childish joys," but Norris herself had pursued intellectual and spiritual interests "far, from the Proud,—The Busy—& the vain." The last part of the poem's title, indicating that it was written to Norris "at fairhill" represented part of Wright's vision of celibate independence. This independent life required, or at the least was greatly enhanced by, an intimate relationship with nature and the leisure to appreciate nature's beauty. Observation of seasonal vegetation and coloring would "Enlarge The thought, & Elevate the heart," while such natural phenomena as rainbows were "delights" to "wond'ring Eyes." Wright reveled in her own rural home, where she pursued horticultural interests, including silkworm experiments, and indulged her penchant for quiet study. Norris's home at Fairhill afforded the same opportunities, and its "Rural views" imparted "soft gentle Joys."

Wright also equated an intimacy with nature with a consciousness of mortality and aging. The passage of seasons and the transforming hand of winter reminded the perceptive mind of human death. She wrote that her own fate would mimic nature in winter and that the flow of her blood would be as icy as a river in winter, "When life's warm streams, Chill'd by deaths Fey hand / Within these veins, a frozen Current Stands." The connection between the contemplative life, resistance, and spinsterhood was explicit. Wright wrote that when facing death, both she and Norris could reflect on their "righteous" conduct. The "righteous" Christian could expect a heavenly afterlife. Wright not only argued that a hierarchy of gender was not divine intention; she also implied that it was contrary to God's will. Those who preserved God's intention of equality not only demonstrated their regeneracy, but secured their heavenly reward. All that separated them from immortality was their behavior on earth.

Till Then, my friend, the righteous claim forbear
Indulge Man in his darling vice of sway
He only Rules Those, who of Choice obey;
When strip'd of Power, & Plac'd in equal light
Angels shall Judge who had the Better right
All you can do,—is but to Let him see,
That woman still, shall sure his equal be,
By your Example, shake his ancient law,
And shine your self, the finish'd Peice you draw;

Once their lives had ended, men and women would be "Plac'd in equal light" and then "Angels . . . [would] Judge" them. "Till Then, my friend," Wright advised Norris, all either one of them could do was to maintain their resistant stance. She wrote that "All you can do,—is but to Let him see / That woman still, shall sure his equal be." During her lifetime, it was only by her "Example" of spinsterhood that any woman could "shake his ancient law" of hierarchy.

Wright reiterated two crucial convictions in the final lines of her encomium to Elizabeth Norris and spinsterhood. The first was that a hierarchy of gender was not only contrary to Quaker doctrine, but also a purely social construction. "When strip'd of Power," she wrote, men would be seen in an "equal light" with women. The "Power" that men held was tenable only on earth and was conferred by themselves. Wright did not locate the source of male "Power" other than to suggest that men based their assertions of authority over women on a fallacious reading of biblical passages. But her certainty that they would be "strip'd" of this power in heaven, as well as her analysis of women's response to seduction, at least implied a foundation in earthly social norms. The only effective resistance to male power was the rejection of a specific normative social institution—marriage.

Wright also articulated a belief in women's ability to create themselves. She encouraged Norris to "shine your self, the finish'd Peice you draw." Wright presumed that women could act independently, describing Norris's spinsterhood as a "choice." She also praised the pedagogical value of Norris's self-determined "Example," suggesting that women could produce the circumstances of their existence as well as its defining characteristics.

This interest in creating, evaluating, and displaying a "self" contrasts sharply with the way historians have thought and written about both early modern women and Quakers. An older historiography challenged the legitimacy of writing women's history in the early modern period, based on the argument that before the nineteenth century women had no collective self-consciousness. Women's experiences, these historians argued, could be accurately reflected only within the context of family history. Women were part of a collective unit, rather than individuals. In addition, Quakers were supposed to subordinate the individual entirely. Once the light of Christ had acted in and through them, they were simply vessels of the light. This view allowed women prophets, for example, to assume masculine behaviors and all Quakers to justify ecstatic behavior (such as "quaking") on the ground that the light was responsible for their conduct. Susanna Wright's claims about the obligation of women to shape their own lives and their own "selves," then, challenge the notions that women did not think of themselves as autonomous individuals and that Quakers were insensitive to individualism.

Wright's celebration of Elizabeth Norris's spinsterhood and, by implication, her own, demonstrates the elasticity of Quakerism in eighteenth-century Pennsylvania. Quaker women had access to a theology that could support an attack on traditional gender roles and marriage. By emphasizing the authority of the individual and the ability of women to create themselves in the process of resistance, Susanna Wright took full advantage of both Quaker doctrine and Enlightenment ideas. Her stance suggests that women had a range of possibilities open to them and that they could, if they wished, choose not to marry and justify their decision on theological grounds.

Exactly when or under what circumstances Susanna Wright wrote "To Eliza Norris—at fairhill" is unclear. She must have written it before 1773, when Elizabeth Norris moved from Fairhill into Philadelphia. Because the subject of the poem is marriage and its implications, she may have written it when Norris was much younger (she died in 1779 at age 74), healthier (she endured quite a long bout of illness before her death), and possibly either considering marriage or contemplating her life as a spinster. Norris lived at Fairhill most of her life, sharing the home for more than twenty years with her widowed elder brother and his daughters. To think that Wright's references to domineering men are meant to implicate

Norris's brother is intriguing, but it seems more likely that she was referring to a specific suitor. The important relationship in the poem, however, was not between women and men. Susanna Wright privileged women's relationship with knowledge, reason, nature, God, and themselves above any heterosocial or heterosexual union.

Although the personal relationship between Wright and Norris was not the subject of the poem, the intensity with which Wright wrote of their mutual spinsterhood as well as her obvious veneration of Norris's life and "Example" conveys the importance of their friendship. Other evidence suggests that unmarried women felt a special kinship with one other. This was true of both widows and spinsters. Single women were likely to give special attention in their wills and the disposition of their property to other women without spouses. This was especially true of spinster sisters, who very often left their entire estate to the other sister, and of widowed mothers, who left substantial legacies to their spinster daughters.[30] Family and friends recognized that a spinster's condition was distinctive. Perhaps only a very few described the special nature of spinsterhood as Susanna Wright did, but acknowledgment that marital status played a fundamental role in women's lives was part of a wider cultural phenomenon.

Both Susanna Wright and Elizabeth Norris were wealthy enough to afford the contemplative life of a marital resister, but a great many unmarried women lived in poverty. Often, no husband meant no money. For spinsters the need for income was paramount. Although in large, wealthy households and families spinsters could act as caretakers and housekeepers who filled gaps left by the deaths of wives and mothers, less well-off families could not support unmarried women in this way. These women were forced to seek employment and housing outside their family home. Domestic servitude was a reasonable prospect. If they could find work that would support them outside of servitude, women often paired up. Sisters or friends created their own households supported by their own labor.[31]

Although unmarried women could maintain their own households and work to support themselves, the relationship of economic and marital status to independence was less clear for women than for men. Ambiguity about women's independence derived primarily from popular and political notions of the meaning of marriage itself. Young men reached their majority at the age of twenty-one. At that point they came into any inherited property, became eligible for political participation, and could marry without the consent of their parents. Acquisition of land or completion of an apprenticeship were traditional marks of male independence. In the commercial urban seaport, where wage labor was common, the completion of an indenture probably was a similarly enfranchising experience. In either context men refrained from marriage until they achieved independence.[32] Until they could support a family themselves, either on their land or by their labor, most men remained single. Thus, the achievement of male independence often was accompanied by or marked by marriage. Women also achieved a particular social and economic status when they married, but they experienced the connection between maturity and marriage quite differently.[33] Ideally, men married once they achieved maturity and independence. For a woman, however, marriage marked both her maturity and her lack of independence.[34]

The connections between masculinity and independence, and between femininity and dependence, were reinforced by the rhetoric of the American Revolution.[35] While Susanna Wright connected marriage with a loss of self-control, describing women's subordination as the "fate," the "Doom," and the "yoke" of marriage, she did not pose this plight in political terms. But popular conceptions of the marital union as a hierarchical arrangement carried political as well as emotional weight. Writers in sixteenth- and seventeenth-century England equated familial order, particularly the maintenance of a wife's subordination to her husband, with the broader social order.[36] In Revolutionary America marriage was again used to express ideas about political relationships.[37] Jan Lewis has argued that in the postrevolutionary period a wife became a republican symbol of the consensual union between government and governed. She points out that writers acknowledged and even emphasized women's subordinate role, making the analogy quite apt in that they urged acquiescence by the masses as well as by wives. In this equation mutual affection depended on a willingness to be controlled. This is the same impulse that defined women primarily in terms of their relationship to the polity as educators and nurturers of young republicans.[38] These prescriptions were based on the near universality of marriage. An appeal to the roles of wife and mother was expected to resonate widely. In considering the importance of this phenomenon, historians have not generally considered the reaction of women like Wright. Seeing marriage and gender hierarchy as against both reason and religion, Wright also saw subordination as a denial of a woman's ability to have an individual identity. Wright was quite elderly by the time of the Revolution, dying only a year after the war's conclusion. Nonetheless, her explicit resistance to marriage and her denigration of hierarchy placed her both in sympathy with and at odds with contradictory Revolutionary rhetoric—rhetoric that espoused equality and freedom, yet often expressed freedom for men through the subordination of women within families.

Without the poem that Susanna Wright wrote for Elizabeth Norris, we might never know how she viewed her singleness. We might consider her achievements and ambitions as well as her marital status so extraordinary that they were entirely irrelevant to the ways in which "average" colonials interpreted and fashioned ideas about gender. Her synthesis of ideas about gender, Quaker theology, and marriage, however, suggests that concepts of gender systems in the colonial period generally must account for marital status as well as other differences among women, including race, freedom, ethnicity, and socioeconomic status. Historians must recognize what was clear to Susanna Wright more than two centuries ago: women knew that marriage could fundamentally perpetuate inequalities between men and women.

NOTES

The author wishes to thank Catherine La Courreye Blecki, Toby Ditz, Mary Maples Dunn, Susan Klepp, and Lorrette Treese. Fellowship assistance for this project was provided by the American Historical Association, the Quaker Collection at Haverford College, and Old Dominion University.

1. For example, see Laurel Thatcher Ulrich, *Good Wives: Image and Reality in the Lives of Women in Northern New England, 1650–1750* (New York: Knopf, 1982). Exceptions include Lee Virginia Chambers-Schiller, *Liberty, a Better Husband: Single Women in America: The Generations of 1780–1840* (New Haven, Conn.: Yale University Press, 1984); and Lisa Wilson, *Life after Death: Widows in Pennsylvania, 1750–1850* (Philadelphia: Temple University Press, 1992).

2. Hannah Griffitts, "To Sophronia. In answer to some Lines she directed to be wrote on my Fan," 1769, in the Commonplace Book of Milcah Martha Moore, Quaker Collection, Haverford College.

3. Hannah Griffitts to "My Dear Cousin," undated. Edward Wanton Smith Collection, Quaker Collection, Haverford College.

4. Terri L. Premo, *Winter Friends: Women Growing Old in the New Republic, 1785–1835* (Urbana: University of Illinois Press, 1990), 38, 45. Premo's work is a recent example of this representation of spinsters' lives. For a comparative treatment of spinsters, see Micaela di Leonardo, "Warrior Virgins and Boston Marriages: Spinsterhood in History and Culture," *Feminist Issues* 5 (Fall 1985):46–68.

5. Diary of Rebecca Dickinson, quoted in Daniel White Wells and Rueben Field Wells, *A History of Hatfield Massachusetts* (Springfield, Mass., 1910), 206–7. Dickinson is quoted in Chambers-Schiller, *Liberty, a Better Husband*, 14; Premo, *Winter Friends*, 38, 43–44, 111, 135, 162, 168; Mary Beth Norton, *Liberty's Daughters: The Revolutionary Experience of American Women, 1750–1800* (Boston: Little, Brown, 1980) 42, 142; and June Sprigg, *Domestick Beings* (New York: Knopf, 1984), 8, passim.

6. Merril D. Smith, *Breaking the Bonds: Marital Discord in Pennsylvania, 1730–1830* (New York: New York University Press, 1991), details the types of problems that led couples to seek divorce or separation. Not surprisingly, these included spousal battery and alcohol abuse, as well as unfulfilled expectations.

7. For an important analysis of the implications of Puritan theology, see Amanda Porterfield, *Female Piety in Puritan New England: The Emergence of Religious Humanism* (New York: Oxford University Press, 1992), esp. 3–39. See also Ulrich, *Good Wives*, 6–7. Puritan communities subjected an unmarried woman living alone, whether widowed or never married, to censure or worse. Carol F. Karlsen has provocatively argued in *The Devil in the Shape of a Woman: Witchcraft in Colonial New England* (New York: Norton, 1987) that the threat of female power attracted charges of witchcraft and devilry.

8. The equality of relations implied in Quaker theology notwithstanding, Quakers, like other colonials, subscribed to a hierarchical set of social relations. Colonial society was vertically arranged, though less hierarchy might be implied, for example, by alliances among people of differing socioeconomic status based on religious affiliations or kinship. All Protestants espoused an "equality of souls," but the theological and social implications of this idea varied widely. For a thoughtful analysis of the ways that gender, Puritan theology, and patriarchal social practice interacted and informed one another, see Diane Willen, "Godly Women in Early Modern England: Puritanism and Gender," *Journal of Ecclesiastical History* 43, no. 4 (October 1992):561–80. For a recent appraisal of gender equality among the Shakers, arguably the most consistently egalitarian religious group in early America, see Priscilla J. Brewer, " 'Tho' of the Weaker Sex': A Reassessment of Gender Equality among the Shakers," *Signs* 17 (1992):609–35.

9. See J. William Frost, *The Quaker Family in Colonial America* (New York: St. Martin's, 1973), chap. 1, "The Dry Bones of Quaker Theology."

10. Quoted in Mary Maples Dunn, "Saints and Sisters: Congregational and Quaker Women in the Early Colonial Period," in *Women in American Religion*, edited by Janet Wilson James (Philadelphia: University of Pennsylvania Press, 1980), 596.

11. Mary Maples Dunn, "Latest Light on Women of Light," in *Witness for Change: Quaker Women over Three Centuries*, edited by Elisabeth Potts Brown and Susan Mosher Stuard (New Brunswick, N.J.: Rutgers University Press, 1989), 73. Janet Lindman's recent work on Baptists in Pennsylvania and Virginia suggests that the same process occurred in that developing denomination. Even as church membership became "feminized," church governance became masculinized. See Janet Lindman, "A World of Baptists: Gender, Race, and Religious Community in Pennsylvania and Virginia, 1689–1825" (Ph.D. diss., University of Minnesota, 1993). On the feminization of churches in the eighteenth century, and on women in colonial religions generally, see Patricia Bonomi, *Under the Cope of Heaven: Religion, Society, and Politics in Colonial America* (New York: Oxford University Press, 1986), 105–15.

12. Dunn, "Latest Light," 73–74. The importance of traveling ministers for keeping the larger community of Quakers in contact and for providing a means of intellectual exchange among Quakers in North America and across the Atlantic is explained in Frost, *The Quaker Family*, 5–6. See also Mary Maples Dunn, "Saints and Sisters" and "Women of Light," in James, *Women in American Religion*, 27–46. In a subtle reading of Quakerism's appeal and Quakers' public presentation of their beliefs, Phyllis Mack argues that Quakers attracted so many converts precisely because they combined ecstatic moments of suspended social status (including traditional gender roles) with an organizational and social structure that reinforced and constantly referenced the stable social order (including traditional gender roles, in particular women's positions as wives and mothers.) See Phyllis Mack, *Visionary Women: Ecstatic Prophecy in Seventeenth-Century England* (Berkeley: University of California Press, 1992), 236–61.

13. Examining the women's meeting in Philadelphia and New Jersey, Jean Soderlund has argued that the usual path to leadership in the women's meeting followed a woman's marriage to an equally active or at least participatory Quaker husband. See Jean R. Soderlund, "Women's Authority in Pennsylvania and New Jersey Quaker Meetings, 1680–1760," *William and Mary Quarterly*, 3d ser., 44, no. 4 (1987):728. This does not mean, however, that single women were excluded from the meeting or from positions of leadership and authority, as evidenced by the number of unmarried women ministers. Those included perhaps the most powerful in the Philadelphia Meeting, Sarah Morris.

14. Dunn, "Saints and Sisters," 596. Based on Margaret Fell, *A Brief Collection of Remarkable Passages and Occurrances Relating to . . . Margaret Fell* (London, 1710).

Phyllis Mack noted that marriage was often an impediment for women prophets in early modern England, and many of the women (across denominations) whom she studied were spinsters or widows. Anna Trapnel, a Baptist, told a magistrate who questioned her about her marital status, "having no hindrance, why may not I go as I please, if the Lord so will?" Quoted in Mack, *Visionary Women*, 94–96.

15. See Karin Wulf, "A Marginal Independence: Unmarried Women in Colonial Philadelphia," (Ph.D. diss., Johns Hopkins University, 1993), chap. 1, on women heads of household.

16. Barry Levy, *Quakers and the American Family: British Settlement in the Delaware Valley* (New York: Oxford University Press, 1988), 70–75.

17. Susanna was also spelled Susannah. I have chosen the former spelling because it was used in her will. The few of her letters and other writings that survive are usually signed only "S Wright." Information on the Wright family came from the following sources: Minutes of the Chester, New Garden, and Sadbury Monthly Meetings, Friends Historical Library, Swarthmore College; Hempfield, Lancaster County, tax assessments for 1751, 1756–59, 1763, 1769, 1770–75, Lancaster County Historical Society, Lancaster, Pa.; will of Susanna Wright "of Hempfield in Lancaster County Single Woman," book E, 160, Historical Society of Pennsylvania, Philadelphia (hereafter cited as HSP); "Biographical Sketch of John Wright," *The Friend* 31 (September 1857–September 1858):67–68; Mrs. Henry Heistand, "I 'Samuel Blunston,' the Man and the Family," *Lancaster County Historical Society Papers* 26 (1922):191–204; Marion Wallace Reninger, "Susannah Wright," *Journal of the Lancaster County Historical Society* 63 (October 1959):183–89; "Benjamin Franklin in Lancaster County," *Journal of the Lancaster County Historical Society* 61 (1957):3–6; Franklin Ellis and Samuel Evans, *History of Lancaster County* (Philadelphia: Everts and Peck, 1883), 4:539–41; Joshua Frances Fisher, "Some Account of the Early Poets and Poetry of Pennsylvania," *Hazard's Register of Pennsylvania*, edited by Samuel Hazard, vol. 8 (July 1831–July 1832):177–78.

18. The source of this information, a descendant of James Wright, still owned the "quaint little window" in the 1950s. The Blunston house had been razed to build a bridge over the river. Reninger, "Susannah Wright," n. 186.

19. Journal of Benjamin Rush, entry for April 7, 1784, as reprinted in "Benjamin Franklin in Lancaster County," 6.

20. No evidence of her participation in the women's meeting exists, but Susanna's male relatives were active in the monthly meetings. Biographies of John Wright note that, although he became a minister at a young age and was "esteemed in his native country among Friends 'for the simplicity of his doctrine and peaceable life,' " he curtailed his ministerial activities once he became active in politics. Nonetheless, he viewed his religious and political views as inseparable. Upon leaving office, he warned against the "abuse[s] of power" that he had battled on such issues as military entanglements, contrary to Quaker passivity.

See "Biographical Sketch of John Wright," 68. Wright was removed from office for disputing with Governor Thomas on the issue of allowing indentured servants to enlist. James Wright remained active in the monthly meeting, serving as a recorder and appointed as an overseer. See Minutes of the New Garden Monthly Meeting, July 10, 1721; April 10, 1725.

21. Fisher, "Some Account of the Early Poets," 178. The largest extant collection of Wright's poetry is found in *Milcah Martha Moore's Book: The Commonplace Book of an Eighteenth-Century American,* edited by Catherine L. Blecki and Karin Wulf (Pennsylvania State University Press, forthcoming).

22. Susanna Wright, "To Polly Norris In Memory of her Amiable Sister," 1769, and "on the Death of a Young Girl—1737," Library Company of Philadelphia.

23. See Alan Tully, *William Penn's Legacy: Politics and Social Structure in Provincial Pennsylvania, 1726–1755* (Baltimore: Johns Hopkins University Press, 1977), 7–15, for specifics of the political maneuvering surrounding the settlement of the dispute, and on the violence associated with the dispute—led in part by John Wright and Samuel Blunston, respectively Susanna's father and her sometime paramour.

24. Charles Norris to Susanna Wright, Philadelphia, April 16, 1761, Logan Papers, HSP.

25. Susanna Wright's active political involvement and interests were chronicled in letters to her large circle of correspondents, including James Logan and Benjamin Franklin. See Reninger, "Susannah Wright"; and Samuel Knapp, *Female Biography; Containing Some Notices of Distinguished Women in Different Nations and Ages* (Philadelphia, 1836), 484–87.

26. Quoted in Edmund Morgan, *Inventing the People: The Rise of Popular Sovereignty in England and America* (New York: Norton, 1988), 193.

27. Scholars have paid increasing attention to the development of individualism and notions of the "self" in the early modern period, often linking changing notions of self with changing relationships within households and in families. For example, see Philip Greven, *The Protestant Temperament: Patterns of Child-Rearing, Religious Experience, and the Self in Early America* (Chicago: University of Chicago Press, 1977). Cathy N. Davidson linked fiction with gendered notions of the self and authority in *Revolution and the Word: The Rise of the Novel in America* (New York: Oxford University Press, 1986). In her analysis *The Coquette* suggests some of the same themes as Wright's poem. See especially 188–89. Pattie Cowell published Wright's poem in " 'Womankind Call Reason to Their Aid': Susannah Wright's Verse Epistle on the Status of Women in Eighteenth Century America," *Signs* 6 (1981):795–800. She called Wright "among the earliest American supporters of women's equality" but did not connect Wright's views about marriage, Quakerism, and hierarchical relationships.

28. Frost, *The Quaker Family,* 12.

29. See H. Larry Ingle, "A Quaker Woman on Women's Roles: Mary Pening-

ton to Friends, 1678," *Signs* 16 (1991): 589; and Dunn, "Women of Light," 122.

30. For typical examples of women who left property only to other women, see the wills of Elizabeth Rawle and Ann Canby. Both left their entire estates to their spinster sisters and named those sisters as executors. Book Q, no. 169, 1758, book N, no. 90, 1763, Philadelphia Wills, HSP. For mothers leaving legacies to spinster daughters, see the wills of Rachel Clague (book P, no. 14, 1770), Mary Coates (book P, no. 13, 1770), Jane Donaldson (book P, no. 2, 1770), Martha Green (book P, no. 66, 1771), and Catherine Bullock (book P, no. 311, 1773), Philadelphia Wills, HSP. Suzanne Lebsock noted something of the same phenomenon. See Lebsock, *The Free Women of Petersburg: Status and Culture in a Southern Town, 1784–1860* (New York: Norton, 1984), 135–36.

31. In Philadelphia's North Ward, for example, three pairs of spinster sisters—the Hudson, Hart, and Roberts sisters—lived and kept shop together in the late 1770s. See Wulf, "A Marginal Independence," 80–81.

32. See Alan MacFarlane, *Marriage and Love in England: Modes of Reproduction, 1300–1840* (Oxford: Basil Blackwell, 1986).

33. Whereas inherited property was often held for men until the age of twenty-one, women usually inherited earlier. Mary Cook's will, for example, written in 1726, directed that her grandchildren receive £6 apiece, "as they shall come of age respectively viz the Sons their ages of twenty-one years; the Daughters Their ages of Eighteen years or day of Marriage." Mary Cook's will, book E, no. 54, 1727, Philadelphia Wills, HSP.

34. Once women married, all their property became legally subsumed under their husband's ownership. As a *feme covert*, a married woman could not own property, make a will or devise property, or make contracts, even for her own labor. For more on the laws of coverture, see Marylynn Salmon, *Women and the Law of Property in Early America* (Chapel Hill: University of North Carolina Press, 1986), 81–140; and Susan Staves, *Married Women's Separate Property in England, 1660–1833* (Cambridge, Mass.: Harvard University Press, 1990).

35. Two compelling discussions of the complexity of gender and the American Revolution are Linda Kerber's "The Paradox of Female Citizenship in the Early Republic: The Case of *Matin vs. Massachusetts*," *American Historical Review* 97 (1992):349–78; and Carroll Smith-Rosenberg's "Dis-Covering the Subject of the 'Great Constitutional Discussion' 1786–1789," *Journal of American History* 79 (1992):841–73.

36. See for example Susan Amussen, "Gender, Family, and the Social Order," in *Order and Disorder in Early Modern England*, edited by Anthony Fletcher and John Stevenson (Cambridge: Cambridge University Press, 1985).

37. Various historians have argued both that the companionate ideal of marriage emerged in the eighteenth century and that antipatriarchal spirit ran high. For example, see Jay Fliegelman, *Prodigals and Pilgrims: The American Revolution*

against Patriarchal Authority, 1750–1800 (Cambridge: Cambridge University Press, 1982), esp. 123–44; Jan Lewis, *The Pursuit of Happiness: Family and Values in Jefferson's Virginia* (Cambridge: Cambridge University Press, 1983), 187–203; Jan Lewis, "The Republican Wife: Virtue and Seduction in the Early Republic," *William and Mary Quarterly*, 3d ser., 44 (October 1987):689–721; Daniel Blake Smith, *Inside the Great House: Planter Family Life in Eighteenth-Century Chesapeake Society* (Ithaca, N.Y.: Cornell University Press, 1980), chap. 4; Daniel Scott Smith, "Parental Power and Marriage Patterns: An Analysis of Historical Trends in Hingham, Massachusetts," *Journal of Marriage and the Family* 35 (1973):419–28; Lawrence Stone, *The Family, Sex, and Marriage in England, 1500–1800*, abridged ed. (New York: Harper Torchbooks, 1979), chaps. 7 and 8; Randolph Trumbach, *The Rise of the Egalitarian Family: Aristocratic Kinship and Domestic Relations in Eighteenth-Century England* (New York: Academic Press, 1978).

38. See Linda K. Kerber, *Women of the Republic: Intellect and Ideology in Revolutionary America* (Chapel Hill: University of North Carolina Press, 1980).

6 Women, Religion, and Freedom in New France

TERRENCE A. CROWLEY

Because corporate rather than individual rights were acknowledged in French North America before 1760, in historical writing New France has compared unfavorably with the English colonies. Monarchical sovereignty brooked no opposition in the French possessions overseas. State authority flowed into the undivided hands of governors, responsible for military affairs, and intendants or commissaries charged with overseeing finance, justice, and public order. Petitions were prohibited, public assemblies were illegal without government approval, and habeas corpus was not part of judicial criminal proceedings, although merchants in Quebec and Montreal were allowed to elect syndics to represent their position before the authorities. There was no printing press in Canada, and publications arriving from France had been subject to government censorship before printing.

New France therefore struck nineteenth-century American historian Francis Parkman as a repressive, tyrannical environment that stood in marked contrast to British America, where greater freedom prevailed. Writing about the British victory of 1760, Parkman concluded that "England imposed by the sword on reluctant Canada the boon of rational and ordered liberty. . . . A happier calamity never befell a people than the conquest of Canada by British arms." [1] Since most English-speaking historians of New France have been men who share similar liberal values, variations on this critique remained prominent. Recent historical inquiries concerning the end of the French regime have reinforced this unflattering portrait by exposing the political machinations of the French government attending the defeat by British arms in the Seven Years' War. [2]

Women's historians have come to different conclusions because they have based their assessments on criteria other than those of the liberal tradition. Women's history has been more positive in its portrayal of New France because its primary concern has been the examination of private lives within the comparative framework of women elsewhere. Oblivious to the liberal critique of ancien régime institutions, one historian has written that "with respect to their education, their range and freedom of action, women in New France seem in many ways to compare favourably with their contemporaries in France and New England." [3] But such an approach is too general. It does not sufficiently take into account the different conditions of women's lives. While most women in New France lived in families on farms along the riverways, or in the towns, others found a measure of freedom in collective institutions.

The prominent role played by Roman Catholic women in French colonial life contrasted sharply with the situation in British possessions to the south. Roman Catholicism constituted the state church in the French colonies. Although Protestants lived in New France, they were subject to various disabilities and were not permitted to conduct religious services. Counter-Reformation revivalism in France early in the seventeenth century, during the period when New France and Acadia were established, brought larger numbers of women into the Roman Catholic church. Expanded missionary efforts were integral to a reinvigorated sense of evangelism. Beginning in 1639, Roman Catholic nuns arrived in Canada to convert the country's indigenous peoples. As the colonies grew, the number of women's religious communities increased from two to seven. More religious orders were founded for women than for men in New France. A higher proportion of Canadian women assumed a religious life, and the female religious orders recruited more native-born people than their male counterparts did. The number of women in religious life surpassed the combined totals of priests and members of the male religious communities during the 1680s and continued to grow. By 1725 there were more than 260 nuns in a colony whose population totaled only some 25,000 people, a high proportion of whom were young.[4] Religious life afforded these women the opportunity to serve humanity and to attain a measure of independence in regulating their individual and collective lives largely away from male control. Such freedoms were primarily collective and involved the sublimation of individual desires in the interests of community, but they were hard won and required constant vigilance to maintain. The freedoms that religious life afforded women in New France allowed them to make a vital contribution to colonial development.

THE EARLY WOMEN'S RELIGIOUS ORDERS

The first female missionary efforts in New France were sponsored by wealthy French noblewomen. Marie-Madeleine de Chauvigny de la Peltrie read in the Jesuits' published report for 1635, the *Relation*, of the need for women to evangelize native children. A young widow stricken with a serious illness that had brought her close to death, la Peltrie made a vow that if her health was restored, she would build a house in New France and dedicate her life to teaching Indian children. When she recovered, she journeyed to Tours, where she interested Marie Guyart in her plan. Guyart was also a widow and was her own age; following the death of her husband she had entrusted the care of her son to a sister and entered the Ursuline order. Assuming the name Marie de l'Incarnation, she became assistant mistress of novices and instructor in Christian doctrine. Deeply mystical in her religious practices, Marie de l'Incarnation's mind was consumed by thoughts of the personal sacrifices that such a venture required. She arrived at Quebec in 1639 in the company of two other Ursulines, Madame de la Peltrie, and a young companion, and the Ursulines threw themselves into their mission with joyful enthusiasm. Within a few months they were teaching eighteen Indian girls and a few

French offspring. They set upon learning Indian languages. Because the Ursulines had been drawn from two different areas of France, there were internal disputes that were finally settled when the nuns from Tours accepted an additional vow to teach children and those from Paris adopted the habit worn by the nuns from the Bordeaux region. In 1646 the Ursulines opened a novitiate, although they initially remained dependent on France for recruitment. When fire destroyed their convent in 1650, they rebuilt it.

Three Augustinian nursing nuns from Dieppe arrived in Canada in the same year as the Ursulines. Although they also belonged to a cloistered order, a smallpox epidemic raging when they landed called for immediate attention. Supported by Marie-Madeleine Vignerot (duchesse d'Aiguillon), the Hospitallers constructed a two-story stone building at Sillery, outside Quebec, where the Jesuits in 1637 had begun the first reserve for native converts to Christianity. The "women in white," as the Indians called the nursing sisters, cared for some three hundred people in 1642, but they also opened a small school to provide religious instruction to young girls. Iroquois incursions forced them to seek refuge in Quebec in 1644. Two years later they constructed a hospital designated as Hôtel-Dieu because their constitution noted that they served "Jesus Christ in the person of those afflicted with illness. For this reason the House where they render these divine services of charity is called *Hôtel-Dieu*." [5] They received Marie-Françoise Giffard as their initial postulate in 1646, and Giffard became the first Canadian-born nun.

The first hospital in the mission of Ville-Marie at Montreal was begun in 1644 by a woman who also had a powerful patroness in France. Jeanne Mance was not a nun, but before departing France she had secured an endowment of forty-two thousand livres from Angélique de Faure, the widow of Claude de Bullion, a former superintendent of finance. To carry on her work, she made arrangements with the Hospitallers of Saint Joseph. This nursing community had begun in 1634 with Jérôme Le Royer de la Dauversière, who had participated in the establishment of the original Montreal mission, as its cofounder. In 1659 three nursing sisters, Judith Moreau de Brésoles, Catherine Macé, and Marie Maillet, accompanied Jeanne Mance from France to assume responsibility for the hospital that she had begun.

CONTENDING WITH RELIGIOUS PATRIARCHY

Although Christianity preached the spiritual equality of men and women, as well as of all peoples, women labored under particular liabilities within the Roman Catholic church in the early modern era.[6] A papal constitution of 1566 required that female religious orders be cloistered and that nuns take solemn, rather than simple, vows.[7] Unlike male communities, which might be grouped together under a superior general drawn from among their number, the Council of Trent (1545–63) had ruled that women's orders be placed under a bishop. Constitutions for women's communities had to receive episcopal approval. Within these confines, nuns directed their own daily lives and collective interests when they assembled in a body known as the chapter. It was in the chapter that the orders elected the priests who served as spiritual directors.

Although sometimes rent by internal divisions, the female communities closed ranks in contending with religious patriarchy. The struggles of the Ursulines and the Hospitallers of Saint Joseph are illustrative. The first constitution of the Quebec Ursulines had been written by Jérôme Lalemant, the Jesuit superior at Quebec, after careful consultation with the members of the order and their final approval through secret ballot. After François de Laval became bishop in 1659, he visited the monastery and found that some of the nuns wanted a more simplified rule. When he proposed changes, Superior Marie de l'Incarnation headed a campaign to stop him. She disliked episcopal authority over religious communities and argued for a more centralized system involving the Holy See to excise local variations. "We are subject to bishops," Marie de l'Incarnation wrote, "and that is troublesome."[8] She interpreted the changes that Laval proposed as having the potential to turn the Ursulines into a contemplative order such as the Carmelites. The concerted opposition she mounted against the bishop's plans led Laval to delay a year and then to abandon his proposals by approving their original constitution in 1662. Later, in 1681, Laval did secure the agreement of the Quebec community to bring their practices in line with those observed by the order in Paris.

The Quebec Ursulines were successful in defending themselves against unwelcome episcopal intrusions, but the Hospitallers of Saint Joseph were forced into a compromise. Clerical authorities were unhappy with their presence in Montreal. Bishop Laval, the town's parish priests, and the Jesuits wanted the Augustinian nuns of the Quebec Hôtel-Dieu to extend their services into Montreal in order to merge the two communities. Like the Ursulines, the Augustinians conformed more closely to church regulations because they were a cloistered order, unlike the Hospitallers when they had departed France. Strictly opposed to losing their separate identity, the Montreal sisters engaged in a decade-long battle with male church officials to insure their survival. To end years of acrimony, they finally yielded to episcopal insistence that they accept solemn vows and be cloistered, as their mother house in France had become since their arrival in Canada. The continuity of their community was secured at a considerable price.

SECULAR SISTERS AND THE INTRICATE INTERPLAY OF CHURCH AND STATE

After royal government superseded company rule at Quebec in 1663, the state became a larger player in colonial religious life. The king claimed temporal powers over the church. Courts such as the Conseil souverain at Quebec or the king's council in France might, upon appeal, overturn ecclesiastical decisions considered contrary to laws and customs of the kingdom. Further, the government employed church resources to provide educational, medical, and social services for colonists. In return for the subsidies that they received from the state, the various components of the institutional church needed to secure the monarchy's approval, most often through royal letters patent. Because the government also served as arbiter when wings of the church conflicted, women learned to use to their advantage the internal divisions within the church and the state.

The beginnings in Montreal of the Congregation of Our Lady revealed the ways in which religious women were able to circumvent ecclesiastical restraints by carefully navigating the dual lanes of church and state. This order had been established in France in 1598 as a noncloistered teaching community, but after 1632 when *clausura* had been accepted, the Congregation of Our Lady resorted to a device that would not restrict its activities. Within their convent the nuns created a so-called external congregation of laywomen who received religious instruction and pedagogical training. Under the pretext that they were secular sisters rather than cloistered nuns, these women were able to teach in parish schools.

Marguerite Bourgeoys was an external member of the Congregation of Our Lady at Troyes, France, where the sister of the governor of Montreal, Paul de Chomedey (sieur de Maisonneuve) was also part of the community. Maisonneuve was opposed to sending cloistered nuns to the Montreal mission, but because Bourgeoys did not labor under such constraints, she joined the immigrants who headed for the St. Lawrence River island in 1653. At first she assisted with nursing, but in 1658 she was given a stone stable where she began teaching young children. The following year Bourgeoys recruited three more young laywomen in France to assist her. As their numbers grew to more than a dozen, Marguerite Bourgeoys contemplated the creation of a community of secular sisters free to move about for instructional purposes. From her spiritual director in France, she picked up the idea that the Gospels provided a variety of examples for religious women to follow. Bourgeoys was particularly taken with the idea that the Virgin Mary had herself traveled about. François de Laval did not agree; church policies were more important than biblical precedents to the prelate. He therefore advocated that all orders of religious women be cloistered, take solemn vows, assume a veil upon becoming nuns, and wear the wimple to hide part of their heads. For this reason the bishop preferred that the Ursulines extend their instructional work to Montreal rather than relying on the secular sisters gathered around Marguerite Bourgeoys. The Sulpicians, who were the town's parish priests as well as seigneurs after 1663, sided with Bourgeoys because they saw benefits from having nuns capable of teaching in outlying areas. Governor Remy de Courcelles and Intendant Jean Talon concurred that the Congregation of Our Lady served Montreal very well. Talon permitted the town's residents to assemble to petition the king to grant the sisters official recognition. Bourgeoys traveled to the French court in 1670, and the following year royal letters patent recognizing her community were issued. Laval waited another five years, until 1676, to acknowledge the order according to canon law. When he did so, the community was acknowledged as one of secular sisters rather than of nuns.

Laval's successor as bishop, Jean-Baptiste La Croix de Chevrières de Saint-Vallier, attempted to achieve uniformity among the women's religious orders by imparting a rule to the Congregation of Our Lady akin to that of the Ursulines. Solidly opposed, the sisters managed to get Saint-Vallier to put off the matter for a year while they discussed the new constitution. Delay was what the sisters needed. Particularly contentious was the question of dowries. In cloistered orders, women's families paid a dowry for young women upon admission, in the same manner that the middle and upper classes did for their offspring at the time of marriage. The secular communities tried to avoid this practice because it reinforced class differences between those who could pay and those who could not. Although the church hierarchy and state officials wanted dowries as a means of regulating entry into religious communities, they were generally ineffective in controlling admissions. The orders often found benefactors to assume the charge on behalf of young women, or they simply circumvented official decrees by requiring less money.

The sisters of the congregation were nevertheless opposed to the imposition of this cumbersome system that was part of all cloistered communities. They made their opposition known to the superior general of the Sulpicians in Paris, who altered the bishop's text to conform more exactly to their wishes, although a system of dowries was retained because it could be circumvented in various ways. Bishop Saint-Vallier agreed to the revisions even though they did not conform to his original idea. The new rule was accepted by the Congregation of Our Lady in 1698. Like the Ursulines, the Montreal group had managed to play various male authorities against each other in order to make their views prevail, even though they paid a price by accepting the dowry system, albeit at a lower monetary level than obtained in the cloistered orders.

Because the Congregation of Our Lady allowed women greater freedom and because its dowries for admission were lower, the order grew to be the largest community of women in New France, counting 70 of the 204 religious women in the colony by 1759.[9] Initially they served in the Montreal region, including the Sulpician-sponsored Indian settlement at La Montaigne, where, in 1685, they taught forty native children in cabins made of bark. In that year one sister traveled to Port-Royal to undertake the instruction of young girls in Acadia. Marguerite Bourgeoys insisted on moral rigor and training in pedagogy. Members of the community were told that they were to perform their duties "with purity of intention, without distinction of poor or rich, relatives or friends, pretty or de-formed."[10] Instruction was provided free to the young girls, but fees might be charged for books, supplies, and firewood. The sisters followed the Ursulines in opening a boarding school that catered to wealthier colonists, but the congregation also began a House of Providence for poor adolescent girls age twelve to eighteen on the farm they began in 1668 at Point St. Charles outside the town.[11] By 1685 the House of Providence offered twenty young women instruction in religion and domestic skills. Although this work was extended temporarily to the town of Quebec in 1686, both enterprises closed within a few years because of lack of money. The sisters nevertheless fanned out into the smaller communities of the St. Lawrence Valley, opened a school in Quebec's lower town in 1691, and moved in 1727 to Louisbourg, the walled city that France had constructed on Cape Breton Island as the bulwark of its North American possessions. The Sisters of the Congregation of Our Lady helped to erode the near monopoly of men over the written word. In addition to religion, they taught reading, spelling, writing, and domestic skills. Wher-ever they went, there were beneficial results for female literacy.[12]

CONSTRAINT: THE FOUNDING OF QUEBEC'S HOSPICE

Events leading up to the creation of a new cloistered community of nuns to run Quebec's hospice (Hôpital Général) in 1701 revealed how the women's religious orders might score occasional triumphs without achiev-ing ultimate victory when the forces of church and state combined. The idea for an asylum in the colonial capital originated with Bishop Saint-Vallier. He purchased a house outside the town and secured royal ap-proval for a governing board in 1692. Although the Augustinian Hospital-lers entertained reservations about departing from a strictly medical role, they accepted the administration of the hospice for the aged, the desti-tute, and the insane. Reluctance turned into outright opposition in 1699, when the bishop announced that he wanted the Augustinians to supply twelve of their members and an annual annuity to the hospice. Fearing depletion of their human and material resources, the nuns refused the bishop's request. Saint-Vallier then manipulated elections within the order to deny office to its superior, Jeanne-Françoise Juchereau de la Ferté.[13] In the following month, when he formally separated the two orders, the nuns mounted a dual-pronged attack. They got government officials to annul his decision and secured François de Laval to serve as mediator. When word arrived from France in 1700 that the monarchy confirmed the decision of its local officials, the bishop was mortified. Saint-Vallier sought out the nuns of the Hôtel-Dieu, where "he cried with such profusion" that the nuns "were unable to hold back their tears."[14] Despite this display, neither side softened. Saint-Vallier departed for France. At the royal court he was able to use his powers of persuasion and the money that he personally contributed to the hospice as levers to secure a new decision in his favor. In 1701 the Council of State created a new cloistered religious order specifically for the Quebec hospice. The bishop provided financial guarantees, and the order was limited to twelve members.

Although the Augustinian Hospitallers were forced to comply in the face of episcopal and royal resolution, the circumstances surrounding the founding of the Quebec hospice were exceptional. Having established such an asylum in France early in his career, Bishop Saint-Vallier identified emotionally with the project. He accorded a sixth of his large personal givings to the Hôpital General, and late in life he lived there prior to his death.[15] Relations with the other women's religious communities were more dispassionate. Saint-Vallier secured the agreement of the Ursulines in 1697 to extend their teaching activities into Trois-Rivières, but because the settlement was too small to support an instructional order alone, they agreed to add a nursing role. The house in Trois-Rivières became independent of the Quebec mother house in 1732. The Ursuline convent established in New Orleans, Louisiana, was begun in 1727 with nuns from France rather than Quebec.

WHY WOMEN JOINED RELIGIOUS ORDERS

What attracted women to this expanding network of religious communities? In examining this question, it is important to remember that the family, rather than the individual, constituted the basic social unit in the West during the early modern era. In Canada during the French regime, children remained legally dependent until the age of twenty-five, and they needed parental consent to marry.[16] Because women entering a religious order exchanged the protection and support of one family for a larger one governed by a written constitution, dowries were involved in admission to most religious orders. While patriarchy prevailed in society and in the Roman Catholic church as a whole, nuns led largely self-directed lives: women were in charge on a daily basis, although the structures of the cloistered communities mirrored the hierarchy apparent in all walks of life. Choir nuns formed the elite. They came from families with more prestige, and they brought larger dowries into the community. Choir nuns were allowed to sing during the Mass, but they did not have to bother with the menial tasks accorded to the nuns called lay sisters. These women were from humbler social backgrounds, seldom knew how to read or write, and brought smaller amounts as dowries or none at all. Although their numbers constituted approximately a third of cloistered nuns by the eighteenth century, the lay sisters labored under other disabilities. In the chapter of the Quebec hospice, for instance, they had no vote except in the matter of choosing a priest to be spiritual director.[17] The Congregation of Our Lady did not observe such distinctions; there, both nuns and lay sisters voted on all matters.

Religious life offered women a variety of opportunities to employ personal talents. Despite their goal of service, business affairs figured prominently in the women's religious communities. Revenue flowing into the Hôtel-Dieu in Quebec, for instance, was so diverse that it can be divided into twelve categories.[18] The orders received gifts and endowments from private benefactors that were invested both in the mother country and in Canada. Fees, such as those that pensioners paid at the Quebec hospice, provided additional income. So did state subsidies. Dowries, whose amounts varied according to the orders' circumstances, produced 9 percent of revenue.[19] Some communities owned seigneuries, farms, or grist mills that had to be operated as well as managed; others raised livestock and ran market gardens. Craft work such as needlepoint and making brocades constituted an important part of revenue for several of the communities. Such a wide variety of economic activity provided religious women with various prospects for employment, not the least of which was the supervision of domestic servants and workers employed by the orders. Finances remained precarious, however. The Quebec hospital showed operating deficits in fifty-four of the years between 1663 and 1763, as did the town's hospice for forty-two years between 1701 and 1759. Similarly, the Sisters of the Congregation of Our Lady at Louisbourg eked out a bare existence for many years because of a poor investment made when they moved there.[20]

Noblewomen and women drawn from what might be loosely called the middle classes were attracted disproportionately into the religious life. Only a third of the nuns in the cloistered orders emanated from the farmers, laborers, and artisans, who constituted three-quarters of the colony's population, although communities of secular sisters such as the Congregation of Our Lady appealed more broadly.[21] A life of service dedicated to the poor and disabled clearly attracted women to enter the Quebec hospice, the most aristocratic of the orders. Although the Quebec hospital relied less on noble families, caring for the sick made life expectancy shorter, and the community came to draw more heavily on rural parishes to augment their ranks in the eighteenth century.[22] Both the Montreal hospital and the Sisters of the Congregation of Our Lady relied more fully on the merchant class in that town. Teaching careers would have been impossible for many women without the training and support provided by the religious communities.

Girls entered the religious life as postulates at the age of fourteen or fifteen. On average they took their vows four or five years later, at an age that was only slightly earlier than that when women married in the colony. Attrition was not high: less than a quarter of the women accepted left their orders. Those remaining in the cloistered communities lived the religious life for thirty-five years on average.[23] No aboriginal men were accepted as clerics in New France, but the women's religious orders were more receptive to the native born. Geneviève-Agnes Skanudaroua, a Huron, took vows as an Augustinian nun at Quebec in 1657, and Marie-Thérèse Gannensagouas (an Algonquin) and Marie-Barbe Atontinon (an Iroquois) were accepted as sisters of the Congregation of Our Lady. Similarly, British colonials captured in war occasionally joined the women's orders. Esther Wheelwright, whose father and grandfather had been Congregational ministers in Massachusetts, chose to remain in Quebec following her capture by Abenakis in 1703 despite concerted efforts by her family to secure her return. As Soeur de l'Enfant-Jésus, she joined the Ursulines and became superior of the order in 1760.

Many more Canadian women than men were attracted to a religious life in New France. Because the numbers entering such communities was highest during the episcopacies of Saint-Vallier (1688–1727) and of Debreil de Pontbriand (1741–60), there was a strong correlation between the disruptive influences accompanying the Anglo-French wars (1689–98, 1702–13, 1744–48, 1754–63) and the decisions by women to seek a religious life. By 1700 there were 140 nuns in New France. Montreal, a town of 1,500 people in 1715, was home to 100 sisters, although some were dispersed in the countryside attending to schools. While religious devotion began to wane in New France during the first quarter of the eighteenth century, women in religious orders nearly doubled.[24] In order to arrest this rapid expansion, the Crown raised the dowries required for entry to the cloistered orders from 3,000 to 5,000 livres in 1722, but when the effects of this measure proved too drastic, they were reduced to the former sum ten years later.[25] By the end of the French regime, the women's communities were composed almost entirely of Canadians while the majority of the male clergy remained French.

WOMEN AND RELIGIOUS ADHERENCE IN NEW FRANCE

The attractiveness of the women's religious communities in New France was paralleled in the larger society by greater devotion to institutional religion on the part of women than of men. Pious religious associations, called confraternities, made their first appearance in the colony in 1652 and continued to be formed until early in the eighteenth century. Most were open to both sexes, but some, including the Confraternity of the Holy Family, restricted their memberships to women alone. Under the watchful eye of parish priests at the local level, the confraternities encouraged regular observance of the sacraments, participation in religious services, private prayer, the upkeep of chapels, and visiting the sick or those in prison.[26] While overzealous priests who sometimes enrolled entire parishes make membership rolls suspect, women clearly predominated in the confraternities. Their lives were more sedentary than those of men, many of whom left farms to roam farther afield as fur traders and fishers. Men were thus more likely to make declarations about miraculous interventions, but women provided stronger continuing support for local churches.

Although neither of the two male religious orders founded in the Quebec colony during the seventeenth century survived the French regime, a new community of secular sisters emerged in Montreal and remains active even today. In 1737 Marguerite Dufrost de Lajemmerais, the wealthy widow of François-Madeleine d'Youville, joined with three companions to begin the Sisters of Charity. "We the undersigned," their agreement read, "to the greater glory of God, for the salvation of our souls and the relief of the poor, sincerely desire to quit the world and to renounce all that we own, in order to consecrate ourselves to the poor." [27] Popular opinion considered the women to be so foolish as to be *grises*—tipsy—and in time they adopted a gray habit in direct reference to the sobriquet, becoming known as *Soeurs grises,* or "Grey Nuns." In 1747 they assumed responsibility for Montreal's hospice, which had been established by François Charon, even though the bishop, the governor, and the intendant wanted the institution joined to its counterpart in Quebec. Marguerite d'Youville maneuvered adroitly through complicated proceedings to secure royal recognition of her order in 1753.[28]

CONCLUSION

The continuing growth of women's religious orders in New France suggests that freedom in community remained a viable option for at least one segment of the female population. The active participation of women in church life during the French regime served as the basis for the prominence that such organizations achieved. A religious life afforded not only protection and service to others; it also provided an ordered existence where daily lives were self-directed. Written constitutions served as a rudder to direct the course, while deliberations in the chapters of the communities provided direction to collective life. Although the decision to enter a religious community represented an act of individual liberty, the advantages of communal life were derived ultimately through the sublimation of self in the interests of the group. Obedience was one of the vows that all nuns were required to take. A constant mediation between individual will and collective interest was integral to the way the women's religious orders operated. Attrition from the communities, although admittedly low, was probably related to this issue, but the records are silent. Nevertheless, freedom within this context came to assume a different meaning from that predicated on the individual will alone.

The women's religious orders interpreted their freedoms more in terms of the collectivity than on an individual basis. The Ursulines and the Sisters of the Congregation of Our Lady successfully thwarted plans by bishops to alter their rules in a manner that they opposed. The Sisters of Saint Joseph and the Augustinian nuns of Quebec's hospital fought but were forced to capitulate, the latter in unusual circumstances and the former in order to bring their practices in line with their community in France. Circumventing ecclesiastical decrees through the creation of communities of secular sisters represented a major achievement since communities such as the Sisters of the Congregation and the Grey Nuns were able to work outside the confines of the cloister demanded by clerical authorities.

Religious orders flourished in New France partially because the monarchy chose to subsidize the Roman Catholic church rather than create secular institutions to provide educational, medical, and social services.[29] Women who wanted to be teachers, nurses, or social workers had few alternatives to exercising their ambitions through joining religious communities. Although this situation suggests obvious constraints, it should not detract from the positive achievements of religious women in this period of history.

The experience of the New World expanded women's evangelical role beyond that acknowledged in Europe. Because the first nuns in New France were missionaries, they received religious instruction in order to convert native peoples. Even nursing sisters ministered to the soul as well as to the body. Religious services for the sick were held daily with all the nuns in attendance. As the presence of these women was felt, public virtue was no longer conceived of as a male preserve, even though men monopolized positions of authority within the Roman Catholic church. The women's religious orders also developed a form of pedagogy that differed from that of their male colleagues by de-emphasizing physical punishments in favor of the promotion of learning.[30] Although freedoms in New France were constrained by law and patriarchy, the religious orders provided a means for women to make a contribution to human development. Freedom not only assumes different forms; it is also relative to time and place.

NOTES

1. Francis Parkman, *The Old Regime in Canada*, 2 vols. (Toronto: Morang, 1900), 2:204.

2. John F. Bosher, "The French Government's Motives in the Affaire du Canada, 1761–1763," *English Historical Review* 96 (1981):59–78; *Dictionary of Canadian Biography*, s.v. "François Bigot," by J. F. Bosher and Jean-Claude Dubé.

3. Jan Noel, "New France: Les femmes favorisées," in *The Neglected Majority*, edited by Alison Prentice and Susan M. Trofimenkoff (Toronto: McClelland and Stewart, 1985), 2:18–40. See also Naomi Elizabeth Saunders Griffiths, *Penelope's Web: Some Perceptions of Women in European and Canadian Society* (Toronto: Oxford University Press, 1976), 31–51; and Leslie Choquette, " 'Ces Amazones du Grand Dieu': Women and Mission in Seventeenth-Century Canada," *French Historical Studies* 17 (1992):627–55. See also Micheline Dumont, "Une perspective féministe dans l'histoire des congrégations des femmes," in *Sessions d'études, 1990*, by La Société canadienne d'histoire de l'Eglise catholique (SCHEC) (Ottawa, 1990), 29–35.

4. Louis Pelletier, *Le clergé en Nouvelle-France: Etude démographique et répertoire biographique* (Montreal: Presses de l'Université de Montréal, 1993), 28. Marcel Trudel, *L'Eglise canadienne sous le régime militaire, 1759–1764* (Quebec: Presses de l'Université Laval, 1957), 1:89, 109, 2:222.

5. Quoted in François Rousseau, *La croix et le scalpel: Histoire des Augustines de l'Hôtel-Dieu de Québec (1639–1989)*, vol. 1, *1639–1892* (Sillery, Quebec: Septentrion, 1989), 125.

6. Outside of spiritual equality, the scriptures chosen by the early Christian church were sometimes explicit in advocating the subordination of women to men. See, for example, 1 Cor. 14:34 and 1 Tim. 2:11–12. The gnostic gospels rejected by the ancient church had sometimes accorded women a prominent role. See Elaine Pagels, *The Gnostic Gospels* (New York: Random House, 1979).

7. Elizabeth Rapley, *The Dévotes: Women and Church in Seventeenth-Century France* (Montreal: McGill-Queen's Press, 1990), 56. Solemn vows entailed cloistering, while simple vows allowed involvement with the larger community.

8. Marie de l'Incarnation to her son, October 3, 1645, in *Marie de l'Incarnation:*

Ecrits spirituels et historiques, edited by Albert Jamet, 4 vols. (Paris: Desclée de Brouwer, 1929), 4:57.

9. Trudel, *L'Eglise canadienne*, 2:222.

10. [Marguerite Bourgeoys], *Les écrits de Mère Bourgeoys* (Montreal: Congrégation de Notre-Dame, 1964), 284.

11. See Emilia Chicoine, *Le métairie de Marguerite Bourgeoys à la Pointe-Saint-Charles* (Montreal: Fides, 1986).

12. Roger Magnuson, *Education in New France* (Montreal: McGill-Queen's Press, 1992), 134–38. Louise Dechêne, *Habitants et marchands de Montréal au 17e siècle* (Paris: Plon, 1974), 467–68. A. J. B. Johnston, *Religion and Life at Louisbourg, 1713–1758* (Montreal: McGill-Queen's Press, 1984), 86–108.

13. *Dictionary of Canadian Biography*, s.v. "Jeanne-Françoise Juchereau de la Ferté," by Cornelius J. Jaenen.

14. Albert Jamet, ed., *Les annales de l'Hôtel-Dieu de Québec, 1636–1716* (Quebec: Hôtel-Dieu, 1939), 296–97.

15. Henri Têtu, *Les Evêques de Québec: Notices biographiques* (Quebec: N. S. Hardy, 1889), 149.

16. See John F. Bosher, "The Family in New France," in *In Search of the Visible Past*, edited by Barry Gough (Waterloo, Ont.: Wilfrid Laurier University Press, 1975), 1–13.

17. Micheline D'Allaire, *Les dots des religieuses au Canada français, 1639–1800* (Montreal: Hurtubise HMH, 1986), 43; Micheline D'Allaire, *L'Hôpital Général de Québec, 1692–1764* (Montreal: Fides, 1986).

18. Trudel, *L'Eglise canadienne*, provides the most complete inventory of church property and income. For the women's religious orders, see 2:231–39, 274–79, 302–7, 322–27, 339–43, 356–61. See also Jacques Ducharme, "Les revenus des Hospitalières de Montréal au 18e siècle," in *L'Hôtel-Dieu de Montréal (1642–1973)* (Montreal: Hurtubise HMH, 1973), 209–44.

19. D'Allaire, *Les dots*, 98.

20. D'Allaire, *L'Hôpital Général*, 231–32; Rousseau, *La croix et le scalpel*, 117; Johnston, *Religion and Life at Louisbourg*, 86–108.

21. D'Allaire, *Les dots*, 181–82; Trudel, *L'Eglise canadienne*, 2:339. Pierre Hurtubise, "Origine sociale des vocations canadiennes en Nouvelle-France," in *Sessions d'études 1978*, by La Société canadienne d'histoire de l'Eglise catholique (Ottawa, 1978), 41–56.

22. Rousseau, *La croix et le scalpel*, 139.

23. D'Allaire, *Les Dots*, 57–59; D'Allaire, *L'Hôpital Général*, 131–38.

24. Pelletier, *Le clergé en Nouvelle-France*, 28; Dechêne, *Habitants et marchands de Montréal*, 467, 478.

25. Province of Canada, *Edits, ordonnances royaux, déclarations et arrêts du conseil d'Etat du roi concernant le Canada* (Quebec: Assemblée législative, 1854), 1:464, 529–30.

26. See Marie-Aimée Cliche, *Les Pratiques de dévotion en Nouvelle-France: Comportements populaires et encadrement ecclésial dans le gouvernement de Québec* (Quebec: Presses de l'Université Laval, 1988), 182–232; and Brigette Caulier, "Les confréries de dévotion à Montréal du 17e au 19e siècle," (Ph.D diss., University of Montreal, 1986).

27. Quoted in *L'Evolution des communautés religieuses de femmes au Canada de 1639 à nos jours*, by Marguerite Jean (Montreal: Fides, 1977), 54.

28. Canada, *Edits, ordonnances royaux*, 616.

29. On church finances, see Guy Frégault, *Le 18e siècle canadien: Etudes* (Montreal: Hurtubise HMH, 1968), 104–11.

30. See Rapley, *The Dévotes*, 150.

7 Wise Virgins and Pious Mothers: Spiritual Community among Baptist Women of the Delaware Valley

JANET MOORE LINDMAN

The Delaware Valley became a haven for believers of all denominations with the onset of white settlement in the 1680s. The establishment of religious tolerance attracted Europeans of various traditions, and by the eighteenth century Pennsylvania and New Jersey would become known for their ethnic and religious diversity. Notable among these religious groups were the Quakers, whose dominance of local society and politics has been extensively studied by colonial scholars.[1] The Quakers stood apart from other Protestants for their conception of the family, their stance on social issues such as slavery, and a tradition of female religious activism and leadership. The extent of Quaker women's participation in the meeting distinguished women of the Delaware Valley from those in other parts of British North America. As Jean Soderlund has noted, however, it is a mistake to assume that "the Quakers are exemplars of mid-Atlantic women."[2] The distinctiveness of the Quakers was one ingredient in a polyglot mixture of female experience in Pennsylvania and New Jersey during the eighteenth century.

Women's activity in a less prominent but no less important religious denomination of the Delaware Valley, the Baptists, was also a component in this diverse religious experience. Sectarian Protestants with origins similar to those of the Quakers, the Baptists did not challenge traditional society in the same way the Friends did.[3] Nor were Baptists known for female preaching and leadership. Set against the radicalism of the Quakers and within the religiously diverse context of the Delaware Valley, Baptists did not provide the same opportunity for female activism as found among the Quakers. Instead, the Baptists trudged a middle road in their congregational development, with female members being peripheral to church governance. This experience embodied a less extreme but more common response to the question of women's position in the church—one shared by other Protestants. Though women participated in religious and social activities of their congregations, their role in the church was marginal to the male clergy and laity. Baptist meetings were male-dominated.

As wise virgins and pious mothers, Baptist women constructed a devotional culture outside the church, based on women's traditional roles in secular society. The gendered nature of church participation caused female spirituality to flourish in the household and family. Furthermore, the female religious network developed by Baptist women in the eighteenth century laid the groundwork for the later emergence of female religious organizations. The proliferation of women's groups during the nineteenth century—including Sunday School programs, female Bible societies, and female missionary societies—had their roots in the religious activism of eighteenth-century women. Gender separation in the church and the lower status and limited participation of Baptist women made the creation of separate female organizations a logical outcome. In addition, the intermixing of women's social roles and religious activism, and the conjoining of domesticity with piety, would bring to fruition a familial and sentimentalized female spirituality in the antebellum era. The experience of women in the Baptist church fueled the establishment of this female devotional culture, which, in turn, set a pattern of gender solidarity and female institution-building that would flourish in women's religious organizations of the nineteenth century.[4]

The religious freedom enjoyed by Baptists in the Delaware Valley spurred denominational growth and affected the role of women in the church.[5] A dispersed collection of believers, stretching from Chester County, Pennsylvania, to Middlesex County in East Jersey, constituted Delaware Valley Baptists during the early stages of settlement. This informal network quickly grew into a denominational association. By the first decade of the eighteenth century, Pennsylvania and New Jersey Baptists had established the Philadelphia Baptist Association, an organization that oversaw congregational development, ministerial appointments, and orthodox practice. The formation of this denominational order enabled the male leadership of these fledgling congregations, both clerical and lay, to consolidate and institutionalize their dominance of the governing and policy making of the Baptist church.[6]

As full members of the church, Baptist women were entitled to spiritual parity with the male members, but as women they were denied access to equal participation in church government. This had been a long-standing struggle for Baptists, as they faced the dilemma of spiritual equality of women in the church versus women's dependent status in secular society.[7] Since its inception, the Baptist church had strained to replicate the structures and rituals of the "primitive church" of first-century Christians, who had expanded roles for lay men and women alike. While male members served as ministers, elders, and deacons, female members acted as preachers, eldresses, and teachers in the early church.[8] According to this tradition, female communicants of the church ostensibly enjoyed the same rights to office holding as male members. The eighteenth-century version of the church, however, developed within a cultural milieu in which full and equal participation by women was untenable. The role of Baptist women within Delaware Valley churches was thus ambivalent and circumscribed.[9]

This quandary over female status was complicated by the congregational autonomy typical of Baptists, in which individual congregations decided on their own the extent of female participation. Some churches carefully limited women to involvement in specific tasks, such as calling a minister or offering their opinions on the admission of new members. In others, female members voted on church matters but had no say in financial decisions and no access to leadership roles. In addition, voting on secular matters was rarely accessible to Baptist women. Women, it should be noted, were not entirely left out. At times female members served as witnesses in cases of church discipline, and occasionally women were sent by church leaders to notify church members when to attend meeting, or to cite female members for wrongdoing. The majority of these cases involved adultery, fornication, and illegitimacy, issues about which women allegedly possessed special knowledge. Whatever the specific task, congregations carefully distinguished between episodic exercises of power by women, such as the selection of a new minister, and the ongoing, structured authority that came with office holding and participation in church policy formulation. Female members could not join in the standard lay practices open to male members of their religious community, particularly in leadership roles as church officers. No women members served as moderators, elders, deacons, or clerks in Baptist congregations of the Delaware Valley.[10] Consequently, women posed a conundrum for the Baptist church. As sisters in the faith they qualified for full membership in the religious community. Yet, as women, they could not participate fully in church business. Unlike the Quakers, the Regular Baptist conception of spiritual equality did not extend to separate women's meetings or to female preaching.[11] Delaware Valley Baptists failed to institute the structures of the early church, thereby eliminating women from any official capacity in ecclesiastical government.

A Baptist woman first entered the religious community when applying for admission as a member. The potential communicant had to relate her conversion experience in front of the assembled members before acceptance for baptism. Once baptized, the newly reborn believer became part of the church, sharing the obligations and privileges of full membership. The process of becoming a member of a Baptist church was the same for men and women, Whites and Blacks. No separate procedure existed for female candidates, nor were they given special treatment in the conversion process or when baptized. Becoming a Baptist was a singular and individual experience, and a woman's acceptance into (or rejection from) a church did not depend upon her status in the secular world, whether married, single, free, or enslaved. Nor was her relationship to a male member relevant to her spiritual rank in the congregation. Because their secular status in the world was disassociated from their spiritual role in the church, Baptist women entered fellowship as individuals and on an equal basis with the other members. This conception of women and men as religious equals had powerful implications for the ways in which female piety was shaped and experienced. It was precisely this spiritual freedom in membership that made the exclusion of female members from leadership positions a source of conflict and inspired Baptist women to seek other forms of spiritual community.[12]

In general, female members enjoyed their individual rights within the church as full communicants, partaking of communion, participating in Sunday worship, and attending business meetings. Once part of the church, however, women came into a power structure that put them under the jurisdiction and authority of male leaders and offered them few outlets of activity comparable to the participation of laymen. In addition, the church privileges of female members were linked to a temporal society in which the ability of women to act as individuals was profoundly affected by their marital, familial, and free or enslaved status. White women's primary secular role as wives and mothers interacted with the exercise of female power in the religious community. Further, although the evolving idealization of the white female character as synonymous with the traits of a good Christian may have elevated women's status, it did not enhance their practical power.[13] For black women, their place in the black community as mothers and wives was secondary to their economic service to Whites as slaves or free laborers. Their infrequent attendance at meetings, evident in the church records, attests to the priority of their social and economic functions over their spiritual aspirations.[14] Whether black or white, the social roles of Baptist women were meshed with their spiritual status as female members of a religious community.

Baptist women supported their congregations and religious institutions in numerous ways. They opened their homes for religious meetings to accommodate itinerant preachers, or when their own churches had no meetinghouses. Widow Watts of Southampton, Pennsylvania, for example, invited the minister, David Jones, to hold services at her residence in 1786. Jones also preached in the homes of other Baptist women throughout Chester County, Pennsylvania. Baptist women traveled for their religion as well. Usually as minister's wives or female relations, women journeyed with itinerant preachers on their rounds and combined

religious activity with social visiting.[15] Baptist women assiduously supported itinerant preaching as part of their devotion to the church and
participation in their religious community. At the same time, by their
activity they maintained kin and friendship ties within that community.
Women also exerted influence in the appointment of ministers. When the
Philadelphia church needed a new clergyman in 1759, Elizabeth Biles
wrote to the Reverend Samuel Stillman, urging him to answer the call to
her congregation. When she learned that he had accepted the pastorate
at a Boston church, Biles lamented Stillman's absence in Philadelphia: "I
should [have] esteem'd it a blessing of providence to have set under your
ministry in this place." [16]

Female members also sustained the church through monetary contributions, and the financial assistance of women provided subsistence to
struggling congregations. These contributions helped in various areas,
including building costs, minister's salaries, education funds, repair bills,
and pew fees. In 1774 four female members of the Lower Dublin church
in Philadelphia County pledged money to enlarge the meetinghouse;
among them was Eleanor Northrop, who gave £6—one of the largest
donations of all the members who subscribed. These same women contributed to the minister's salary and paid for pews in the church, including
Northrop and Jane Denice, who between them paid £1.15 to share a
pew in the Lower Dublin meetinghouse. Such donations, though not as
plentiful from women as from men, contributed to the church's sustained
growth. In Montgomery County, Pennsylvania, twenty female members
gave money to help build a new meetinghouse. Contributions ranged
from the one hundred dollars presented Lydia Roberts to Jane Tennis's
five-dollar donation.[17]

Even in death Baptist women supported their congregations. In a will
dated 1760, Mary James of Chester County left her large English Bible
to the minister of the Great Valley church. Similarly, Lettice Evans, who
died in 1786, willed five pounds to the deacon of the Vincent Baptist
Church of Chester County to repair the graveyard fence. Other women
left larger bequests, which encompassed Baptists outside their home
congregations. When Elizabeth Hobbs of Hopewell, New Jersey, died in
1763, she left a large portion of her estate to the Baptist church. To her
congregation in Hopewell, she gave six pounds and two volumes of Pool's

Annotations for the ministers' use. In addition she ordered three hundred copies of Cotton Mather's *The Gospel of Justification* to be reprinted and given out to clergy and laity in New Jersey and New York. The remainder of Hobbs's estate went toward the "education of promising and pious young men of the Baptist churches," as supervised by the Philadelphia Baptist Association.[18]

Baptist women intervened to maintain their churches in the face of division and heresy. As stalwart defenders of the faith, female members of the Pittsgrove meetinghouse in Salem County, New Jersey, saved their church from the heretical snare of Universalism. Originally part of the Pennepek church of Philadelphia County, the Pittsgrove meeting was founded in 1743 as a branch of the Cohansey church, also of Salem County. An independent congregation by 1771, the Pittsgrove church flourished until the late 1780s, when the minister, William Worth, introduced Universalism into the meeting: "The aged pastor was insidiously instilling the poison of his own corrupt faith into his hearers and blindly leading them into skepticism [and] heresy." In response, some members left Pittsgrove to attend the Cohansey church, while others joined the local Presbyterian congregation. The remaining male membership embraced Universalism and supported Worth by "imbibing his spirit and sentiments [and] sustained him in holding the meetinghouse, to the entire exclusion of all Baptists for many years."[19]

Among the members who neither deserted the church nor embraced Universalism were thirteen women who met faithfully for worship during this period of division, occasionally enjoying the services of a neighboring preacher. Initially, the women were allowed to use the meetinghouse for their services when a Baptist minister was in attendance. Reverend Worth, however, made it a point to occupy the church any time a Baptist itinerant visited. The women were thus forced "to hold worship in private homes or some contigerous grove." On one occasion the sisters heard a Baptist minister preach from an open wagon. After ten years of controversy, Worth and his deacons were excluded for heresy and the church was reconstituted as Baptist. The first members inducted into the resurrected congregation were the women who had kept the faith alive in their community despite the Universalist coup.

Baptist women who engaged in pious pursuits not only supported their religion but also forged relationships with other female members. Such connections were reinforced when women attended local and regional associational meetings and made these assemblies into sites of female activity. Associational meetings encompassed a wide variety of activities, from formal business conferences attended only by male clergy and laity to all-day sessions of worship and prayer, which attracted both women and men. While male leaders gathered in official business meetings to debate issues and make policy, women attended sermons, met with friends, and heard the latest news. Large numbers of Baptist women attended associational meetings for spiritual and social interaction.[20] This official religious activity provided women the opportunity to form networks with others to build their devotional community.

The gendering of church participation did not limit Baptist women's access to, or exercise of, piety. They engaged in religious endeavors that were not confined to the meetinghouse, to the communion table, or to the male-dominated church meeting. Through the development of their own spiritual community, Baptist women of the Delaware Valley maintained their religious faith outside the church. Female piety encompassed a myriad of religious practices, which established a female devotional culture. These practices—attending association meetings, providing financial assistance, soliciting ministerial candidates, opening their homes to itinerants, defending the church from doctrinal disputes—went beyond those narrowly associated with support of the church. Such activities occurred within the confines of a male-dominated institution in which female subordination was the rule even when women's support of the church was essential to its survival, and this female devotionalism was based upon women's traditional place within the family and household. Through family relations and friendships, Baptist women devised a devotional culture that provided channels of religious activism not available to them within the meetinghouse. Female piety was maintained within social structures that emphasized women's role as nurturer and caretaker. As confessing members of the church, Baptist women came to their faith as individual believers and as part of a religious community. Nonetheless, the spiritual identity and practice of Baptist women relied on contemporary gender relations for expression, which, in turn, assisted the creation of a separate devotional culture.

Female piety occurred away from the view of male leaders and outside of formally scheduled times of religious interaction. Like other Protestants, literate Baptist women pursued their spirituality through activities such as copying sermons and Bible passages into personal journals. Others read pious literature as a means of spiritual support. Women at the Pennepek church had the use of a library of over fifty volumes of religious works in the early 1710s. By the 1760s, female members of the same church enjoyed access to the personal library of their minister, Samuel Jones. For example, Elizabeth Powell examined the first volume of Harvey's *Meditations,* and Mrs. Cunnegan borrowed a catechism and a copy of *The Philadelphia Confession of Faith.*[21] Literate women also wrote letters to family and friends counseling them about their faith. Elizabeth Biles, a member of the Philadelphia church, regularly inquired after the spiritual health of her correspondents. To one friend, Anne Potts, Biles quoted Scripture and wrote religious poetry. Biles used letter writing to exhort others about their souls as much as to maintain contact with female friends and family members. As activities conducive to spiritual interaction with other women, reading and writing enhanced female devotionalism.[22]

Whether literate or not, Baptist women took part in religious conversations as a way to affirm their own beliefs and those of others. Women counseled one another in their spiritual journeys. Margaret Macay, for example, told a group of young women about what Christ had done for her: "Jesus Christ is sweet, he is so precious, had I known his sweetness I would not have liv'd so long without him." Religious conversation between men and women as well as within female relationships was part of this network. Sylvia Spicer of Cape May, New Jersey, confided to Samuel Jones, her future husband, the happiness she had found in "obeying the Savior's commands." Mrs. Leet of Kingwood, New Jersey, discussed "vital religion" with the Reverend Hezekiah Smith during his visit to her home in November 1762.[23]

The pious practices of Baptist women centered around the household. Women's familial role necessitated and was conducive to a domestic framework for religious faith and practice.[24] Often confined to the home by work and child-care responsibilities, Baptist women molded the household into a center of female devotionalism. Religious activity in the home fell to women as much as to men, for churches admonished both to be vigilant in their practice of family worship and in the spiritual education of household members. In song and prayer, Baptist women joined their relatives and dependents in household worship. As a traditional domain of women, the household became a place for spiritual as well as temporal concerns.

Women's role in the family also shaped female piety. As mothers and sisters, Baptist women used their influence to bring others to the faith. Social expectations about the role of women put them in a position to support and encourage others' spirituality. The women of the Jones family of Montgomery County, Pennsylvania, took on this religious role. Martha Jones, mother of Samuel, the future minister of the Pennepek church, advised her son in his pursuit of "a saving knowledge of the truth." Bess, Samuel's sister, also bolstered his search for redemption in an October 1758 letter: "My heart has been exercised about you, and daily have I gone to my room as the shades of evening come, to pray for your conversion. Don't put off any longer the giving of your heart to God. If you do, you may sin away your day of grace." [25]

Female intervention in the spiritual life of male relations was well within the boundaries of women's traditional role in the family. But Baptist women went further, expanding their religious activity in the household by forming their own religious gatherings, called women's societies or women's meetings. These meetings became another locus of female piety. Though such meetings were not officially sanctioned, Baptist women organized them for spiritual support. Usually held on Sunday nights after a day of worship, the meetings, at times, were attended by clergymen, who sang, prayed, and preached for the women. With the onset of women's meetings, female piety in the household took on a more intense and focused purpose. [26]

A Baptist women's meeting was founded in Philadelphia in the 1740s; it grew out of the religious enthusiasm of this period known as the Great Awakening. Emboldened by the surge in revivalism, Pennsylvania women initiated their own religious practices. [27] In 1741, for example, black and white women alike flocked to the home of George Whitefield for spontaneous meetings during his stay in Philadelphia. Before leaving the city in May of that year, the great evangelist helped to organize "a society of young women," who he hoped would "prove to be wise virgins" in their spiritual pursuits.[28] Little is known about how long these meetings lasted, or about the women who participated in them. The women's meetings are, however, evidence of Baptist women's diligent pursuit of spiritual activity. Meeting for prayer and worship in each other's homes affirmed the role of the household as a site of female devotionalism. At the same time it maintained the segregation of female piety from the church and its male leaders.

Through household religious activities, women's meetings, friendships, and family relationships, Baptist women created a "domesticated spirituality."[29] Female piety occurred within and was structured by the family and the household. Whether in a women's meeting, family worship, or individual prayer, female spirituality was shaped by the existing gender ideology and by male dominance of religious institutions. The gendered nature of church leadership and governance left Baptist women free to develop their own religious community as they established an arena of spiritual activity outside the reach of male leaders but within women's traditional domain. This network of female devotionalism, practiced in the household and maintained through interpersonal relations, emerged in response to the restrictions placed on Baptist women by their religious institutions, as well as to women's desire to develop a meaningful and relevant spirituality. The early maturation of church institutions in the Delaware Valley and the rapid growth of male dominance in congregations encouraged the development of this female devotional culture. In addition, female activism during the Great Awakening led to greater autonomy and assertiveness on the part of Baptist women to create and sustain a gender-specific religious community. This pious network of women combined Baptist religious identity and contemporary gender relations. As true believers, Baptist women came to their faith individually; as dependents within a gendered society, women collectively developed a female devotional culture that was consistent with the familial and societal demands placed upon them in eighteenth-century America.

NOTES

1. See Gary Nash, *Quakers and Politics: Pennsylvania, 1681–1726* (Princeton, N.J.: Princeton University Press, 1968); Jean Soderlund, *Quakers and Slavery: A Divided Spirit* (Princeton, N.J.: Princeton University Press, 1988); Barry Levy, *Quakers and the American Family: British Settlement in the Delaware Valley* (New York: Oxford University Press, 1988); J. William Frost, *The Quaker Origins of Antislavery* (New York: Norwood Editions, 1980); Jack D. Marietta, *The Reformation of American Quakerism, 1748–1783* (Philadelphia: University of Pennsylvania Press, 1984); Terri L. Premo, *Winter Friends: Women Growing Old in the New Republic, 1785–1835* (Urbana: University of Illinois Press, 1990).

2. Jean R. Soderlund, "Women in Eighteenth-Century Pennsylvania: Toward a Model of Diversity," *Pennsylvania Magazine of History and Biography* 115 (April 1991):168–69.

3. There is little recent scholarship on Baptists in Pennsylvania and New Jersey in the eighteenth century. Most of what exists is general and outdated. See David Spencer, *Early Baptists in Philadelphia* (Philadelphia: William Sycklemoore, 1877); Richard Cook, *The Early and Later Delaware Baptists* (Philadelphia: American Baptist Publication Society, 1880); Henry C. Vedder, *A History of Baptists in the Middle States* (Philadelphia: American Baptist Publication Society, 1889); Norman H. Maring, *Baptists in New Jersey: A Study in Transition* (Valley Forge: American Baptist Publication Society, 1964). One exception is Jon Butler's thesis, "The Christian Experience of the Delaware Valley: The English Churches on the Eve of the Great Awakening," (Ph.D. diss., University of Minnesota, 1972). See also chapter 4 in his book *Awash in a Sea of Faith: Christianizing the American People* (Cambridge, Mass.: Harvard University Press, 1990).

4. For women's religious organizations, see Mary P. Ryan, *Cradle of the Middle Class: The Family in Oneida County, New York, 1790–1865* (Cambridge: Cambridge University Press, 1981); Nancy Hewett, *Women's Activism and Social Change: Rochester, New York, 1820–1870* (Ithaca, N.Y.: Cornell University Press, 1984); Barbara Leslie Epstein, *The Politics of Domesticity: Women, Evangelism, and Temperance in Nineteenth-Century America* (Middletown, Conn.: Wesleyan University Press, 1981); Jean E. Friedman, *The Enclosed Garden: Women and Community in the Evangelical South, 1830–1900* (Chapel Hill: University of North Carolina Press, 1985). For home-based spirituality among Protestant and Catholic women, see Colleen McDannell, *The Christian Home in Victorian America, 1840–1900* (Bloomington: Indiana University Press, 1994).

5. Pennsylvania Baptists emigrated from Wales and England in the 1680s and 1690s. In the 1660s, a group of Baptists journeyed from New England to settle in the Jerseys. They did not set up congregations, however, until the 1680s and the more widespread arrival of Baptists in Pennsylvania. Pennsylvania and New Jersey Baptists were Regular or Calvinist Baptists. See Morgan Edwards, *Materials to-*

ward a History of Baptists in Pennsylvania (Philadelphia: Joseph Crunkshank and Isaac Collins, 1770); Morgan Edwards, *Materials toward a History of Baptists in New Jersey* (Philadelphia: Thomas Dobron, 1792); Library Company of Philadelphia (hereafter cited as LCP); A. D. Gillette, ed., *Minutes of the Philadelphia Baptist Association, 1707–1807* (Philadelphia, 1851).

6. The Philadelphia Baptist Association was founded by three churches from Jersey (Middletown, Piscataway, and Cohansey) and two from Pennsylvania (Pennepek and Welsh Tract) in 1704. The association was modeled after English and Welsh organizations of the seventeenth century. The Philadelphia Baptist Association, as one of the earliest Baptist associations founded in British North America, became a central authority for the development of Baptist denominationalism in the Delaware Valley and beyond. See Jon Butler, "Power, Authority, and the Origins of American Denominational Order," *Transactions of the American Philosophical Society* 68, part 2 (1978); Robert G. Torbet, *A Social History of the Philadelphia Baptist Association, 1704–1840* (Philadelphia: American Baptist Publication Society, 1944); Gillette, *Minutes*; Francis Sacks, *The Philadelphia Baptist Tradition of Church and Church Authority, 1707–1814: An Ecumenical Analysis and Theological Interpretation*, Series in American Religion, vol. 48 (New York: Edwin Mellen Press, 1989).

7. Since the Reformation, Protestant women have embraced the spiritual equality promised by New Testament theology to justify and extend the bounds of their religious activism. At the same time, Protestant ministers have labored to convince women, with varying success, that spiritual parity did not translate into temporal equality. See Allison S. Coudert, "The Myth of the Improved Status of Protestant Women: The Case of the Witchcraze," in *The Politics of Gender in Early Modern Europe*, edited by Jean R. Brink, Allison P. Coudert, and Maryanne C. Horowitz (Kirksville, Mo.: Sixteenth Century Journal, 1989), 76–77; Mirjam De Barr, " 'Let Your Women Keep Silence in the Churches': How Women in the Dutch Reformed Church Evaded Paul's Admonition, 1650–1700," in *Studies in Church History*, vol. 27, *Women in the Church*, edited by W. T. Shiels and Diana Wood (Oxford: Basil Blackwell, 1990):389–401; Diane Willen, "Godly Women in Early Modern England: Puritanism and Gender," *Journal of Ecclesiastical History* 43, no. 4 (October 1992):561–80; Debra Parish, "The Power of Female Pietism: Women as Spiritual Authorities and Religious Role Models in Seventeenth-Century England," *Journal of Religious History* 17, no. 1 (June 1992):33–46; Marilyn Westerkamp, "Puritan Patriarchy and the Problem of Revelation," *Journal of Interdisciplinary History* 23, no. 3 (Winter 1993):571–95.

8. For more on women in the early church, see Elisabeth Schussler Fiorenza, *In Memory of Her: A Feminist Theological Reconstruction of Church Origins* (New York: Crossroad, 1985); Ross Shephard Kraemer, *Her Share of the Blessings: Women's Religions among Pagans, Jews, and Christians in the Greco-Roman World* (New York: Oxford University Press, 1992).

9. The extent of female participation in the church was a recurring issue for Philadelphia Baptists from the 1740s into the 1760s. See Janet Moore Lindman, "A World of Baptists: Gender, Race, and Religious Community in Pennsylvania and Virginia, 1689–1825," (Ph.D. diss., University of Minnesota, 1994), chap. 5.

10. Unlike the Separate Baptists of Virginia, Regular Baptists of the mid-Atlantic did not allow female preaching or prayer in the church, nor did they institute the office of deaconess. For examples of women preaching in the South, see Morgan Edwards, "Materials toward a History of Baptists in Virginia, 1772," Furman Manuscript (hereafter cited as FM), Virginia Baptist Historical Society, Richmond, Va. (hereafter cited as VBHS); Morgan Edwards, "Materials toward a History of Baptists in North Carolina, 1772," FM, VBHS; David Benedict, *A General History of the Baptist Denomination in America*, 2 vols. (New York, 1848), 2:39–40; David B. Semple, *The Rise and Progress of the Baptists in Virginia* (Richmond: Pitt and Dickinson, 1894). On deaconesses, see Charles W. DeWeese, "Deaconesses in Baptist History: A Preliminary Study," *Baptist History and Heritage* 12, no. 1 (January 1977):52–57. For more on the radicalism of Separate Baptists, see Wesley M. Gewehr, *The Great Awakening in Virginia, 1740–1790* (Gloucester, Mass.: Peter Smith, 1965); Rhys Isaac, *The Transformation of Virginia, 1740–1790* (Chapel Hill: University of North Carolina Press, 1982).

11. For a discussion of the centrality of women in the maintenance of the Quaker religion, see Jean R. Soderlund, "Women's Authority in Pennsylvania and New Jersey Quaker Meetings, 1680–1760," *William and Mary Quarterly*, 3d ser., 44, no. 4 (1987):722–49; Mary Maples Dunn, "Saints and Sisters: Congregational and Quaker Women in the Early Colonial Period," *American Quarterly* 30 (1978):582–601; Elisabeth Potts Brown and Susan Mosher Stuard, eds., *Witness for Change: Quaker Women over Three Centuries* (New Brunswick, N.J.: Rutgers University Press, 1989); Phyllis Mack, *Visionary Women: Ecstatic Prophecy in Seventeenth-Century England* (Berkeley: University of California Press, 1992). See also Margaret Morris Haviland, "Beyond Women's Sphere: Young Quaker Women and the Veil of Charity in Philadelphia, 1790–1810," *William and Mary Quarterly*, 3d ser., 50, no. 3 (July 1994):419–46. Even the complementary nature of Quakerism, however, did not constitute a direct challenge to the male dominance of secular society. See Ruth L. Smith, "Moral Transcendence and Moral Space in the Historical Experiences of Women," *Journal of Feminist Studies in Religion* 4, no. 2 (1988):21–37.

12. Female subordination in the church was also exacerbated by the Protestant tradition of a strong male leader, whether preacher, teacher, or elder. This, combined with the eventual disappearance of the offices of eldress and deaconess in the eighteenth century, circumscribed women's role in church government. See Morgan Edwards, *The Customs of the Primitive Church, Or a Set of Propositions Relative to the Name, Materials, Constitution, Power, Officers, Ordinances, Rite, Business, Worship, Discipline, Government, Etc., of a Church to Which are Added Their Proofs from*

Scripture, and Historical Narrative of the Manner in Which Most of Them Have Been Reduced to Practice (Philadelphia, 1768), LCP.

13. Margaret Masson has argued that equating traditional feminine virtues such as purity and submissiveness with an ideal Christian character developed in New England as early as the 1690s. Margaret T. Masson, "The Typology of the Female as a Model for the Regenerate: Puritan Preaching, 1690–1740," *Signs* 2 (Winter 1976):304–15. Amanda Porterfield agrees with this thesis and argues that women were "exemplars of the virtue and submissiveness associated with sainthood." She takes the premise one step further to aver that female piety reinforced "the patriarchal structures of Puritan culture," while at the same time it provided "emotional stability in both men and women." Therefore, female submissiveness became an essential ingredient in the Puritan "psychic economy." Amanda Porterfield, "Beames of Wrath and Brides of Christ: Anger and Female Piety in Puritan New England," *Connecticut Review* 11, no. 2 (Summer 1989):1–12. For more on the difference between men's and women's religious character, see Laurel Thatcher Ulrich, "Vertuous Women Found: New England Ministerial Literature, 1668–1735," in *Women in American Religion*, edited by Janet Wilson James, 67–87 (Philadelphia: University of Pennsylvania Press, 1980).

14. The number of black Baptists in the Delaware Valley remained small until the late eighteenth century. By 1813 black Baptists were numerous enough in Philadelphia to separate from the original congregation and organize their own church. See Charles S. Brooks, *Official History of the First African Church, Philadelphia, Pennsylvania* (Philadelphia, 1922).

15. Register and Diary of David Jones, 1786–1819, Historical Society of Pennsylvania, Philadelphia (hereafter cited as HSP). For itinerant visiting, see Papers of Hezekiah Smith, 1762–1777, American Baptist Historical Society of New York, Rochester (hereafter cited as ABHS-NY).

16. Dec. 2, 1759, Elizabeth Biles to Samuel Stillman, Elizabeth Biles Letterbook, Ball Estate, Dupuy Papers, HSP.

17. Church and Religious Items, Jones Section, Mrs. Irving F. McKesson Collection (hereafter cited as MIFMC), HSP; Account Book of Peter Evans, 1767–1778, HSP.

18. Papers of Samuel Jones, MIFMC, HSP; "Records of the Great Valley Baptist Church," *Collections of the Genealogical Society of Pennsylvania*, vol. 23 (Philadelphia, 1896), Genealogical Society of Pennsylvania, Philadelphia (hereafter cited as GSP); Will of Lettice Evans, Aug. 26, 1786, Chester County Archives, West Chester, Pa.; Edwards Correspondence, 1761–1786, MIFMC, HSP.

19. "History of the Pittsgrove Church by E. L. Shephard, Esq.," Fragmentary Records, 1771–1842, Pittsgrove Baptist Church, Salem County, New Jersey, GSP. By 1788 the Pittsgrove church had forty-three female members and thirty-six male members.

20. These official meetings were attended only by appointed representatives

of particular congregations, usually the minister or ruling elders. David Benedict recalled such gatherings from his youth. Benedict, *Fifty Years among the Baptists* (New York: Sheldon, 1860).

21. Pennepek Baptist Register, American Baptist Historical Society, Valley Forge, Pa.; Miscellaneous Church Papers, MIFMC, HSP.

22. Biles Letterbook, HSP.

23. "Diary of S. J.," *Baptist Family Magazine* 2, no. 13 (1881); Nov. 4, 1762, Journal 1, Papers of Hezekiah Smith; Aug. 26, 1754, A Fragment of the Oliver Hart Diary, Aug. 4, 1754 to Oct. 27, 1754, ABHS-NY.

24. Religious dissenters of the seventeenth and eighteenth centuries traditionally used the household as a safe haven and place of worship. This tradition continued among Baptist women as they made the household not only a locus of female power in the family but also a stronghold of women's religious activism. Laurel Thatcher Ulrich argues that a woman's culture existed in New England based on religious and economic networks. See her "Daughters of Liberty: Religious Women in Revolutionary New England," in *Women in the Age of the American Revolution*, edited by Ronald Hoffman and Peter J. Albert (Charlottesville: University Press of Virginia, 1989), 214.

25. "Diary of S. J.," *Baptist Family Magazine* 1, no. 2 (1880); 2, no. 8 (1881); and 2, no. 13 (1881). See Ryan, *Cradle of the Middle Class*, for more on the role of women in bringing family members into the church.

26. Such meetings were commonplace among Anglo-American Protestants. English Baptist women formed such separate meetings in the seventeenth century. See Richard L. Greaves, "Foundation Builders: The Role of Women in Early English Nonconformity," in *Triumph over Silence: Women in Protestant History*, edited by Richard L. Greaves (New York: Greenwood Press, 1985), 96, 107. Women's meetings were also present in New England by the late seventeenth century. See Dunn, "Saints and Sisters." The number of lay meetings increased dramatically during the Great Awakening in New England. See Gerald Moran, " 'The Hidden Ones': Women and Religion in Puritan New England," in Greaves, *Triumph over Silence*, 142. Mary Ramsbottom argues that the use of lay meetings among young men served as an alternative to household devotional activity where women directed religious duties. See Mary MacManus Ramsbottom, "Religious Society and the Family in Charlestown, Massachusetts, 1630–1740," (Ph.D. diss., Yale University, 1987).

27. The number of women's meetings among Delaware Valley Baptists is unknown, and little evidence has survived to document their existence. Ramsbottom found evidence of only one such meeting in Massachusetts, compared to the large number of separate meetings for men. Her conclusion that the women's meetings were at once rare and less independent than the men's, however, is questionable. See Ramsbottom, "Religious Society and the Family in Charlestown, Massachusetts, 1630–1740," 21. Charles Hambrick-Stowe, on the other

hand, argues that in the seventeenth century, leadership in women's societies was controlled by women and that, despite the increase in clerical authority after the Antinomian crisis, lay meetings continued to be popular in New England. See Charles E. Hambrick-Stowe, *The Practice of Piety: Puritan Devotional Disciplines in Seventeenth-Century New England* (Chapel Hill: University of North Carolina Press, 1986), 141. Such lay meetings of Baptist women did exist in Boston in the 1740s and in Newport in the 1760s. See Journal 2, June 10, 1764, Journal 3, Mar. 13, 1765, and Journal 4, Oct. 9 and Nov. 8, 1767, Papers of Hezekiah Smith.

28. Though not stated, this women's society was most likely Baptist. The day before, Whitefield had organized a society of young men at the Baptist church in Lower Dublin Township in Philadelphia County. Whitefield also had plans to found a society for black men and women upon his return to Philadelphia. See George Whitefield, "A Continuation of the Reverend George Whitefield's Journal, From His Embarking After the Embargo to His Arrival at Savannah, Georgia," 2d ed. (London: W. Strahan and James Hutton, 1740), 32, 38, 40, LCP. For the formal organization of women's meetings by the Quakers, see Mack, *Visionary Women*.

29. The phrase is from Laurel Thatcher Ulrich, *Good Wives: Image and Reality in the Lives of Women in Northern New England, 1650–1750* (New York: Knopf, 1982), 113–17.

III | Work and the Colonial Economy

Few aspects of colonial women's lives were as pervasive, or as important, as their work. That work has been historically underrated because so much of it, then as now, was focused in the home. Yet, as the three chapters in this section show, women's work in early America took diverse forms, and by no means was it all "housework." Moreover, the work women did had a direct relationship to their practical experience of freedom, of control over their own lives.

Martha J. King examines the lives of two widows who were also printers in eighteenth-century Charleston, considering issues of personal status, expanded private and public roles and responsibilities, and the gendered meaning of widowed freedom. King not only explores the range of personal freedoms that resulted from the move out of *feme covert* and into *feme sole* status, but also takes us inside these women's working lives. Despite tragic personal losses, she shows, these women went on to achieve a degree of family stability and enhanced status and responsibility.

Judith A. Ridner has discovered that women in frontier Pennsylvania had a practical outlook on what constituted freedom. Focusing on the Cumberland Valley, Ridner finds that the women there—whether single, married, or widowed—did not much concern themselves with abstract reasoning or political ideology in defining freedom for themselves, the heady rhetoric of the Revolutionary generation notwithstanding. Drawing on a variety of sources, including court records, legal petitions, wills, personal correspondence, and merchant account books, Ridner shows that women saw freedom instead as a tangible commodity—as "some real measure of economic autonomy."

Johanna Miller Lewis reconstructs the lives of a group of women who worked independently for their living in eighteenth-century North Carolina. Some labored as tavern keepers, and others worked as professional artisans, even monopolizing some crafts, especially spinning. Drawing imaginatively on the court records of Rowan County and the account books of area merchants, Lewis shows that such women actively participated in local society, were considered good credit risks, and enjoyed "a sense of personal freedom and self-worth that was most unusual for women in the colonial South."

8 | "What Providence Has Brought Them to Be": Widows, Work, and Print Culture in Colonial Charleston

MARTHA J. KING

In the November 21, 1743, issue of the *South-Carolina Gazette*, the recently widowed Elizabeth Timothy printed some "Verses written by a young Lady, on WOMEN born to be controul'd!" [1] Noteworthy as a rare example of poetry in the pages of her newspaper, the lines as well as their versified response reflect eighteenth-century gender differences, both of status and of perception. The young poetess viewed women as victims of a wretched fate, doomed to a life of control— "subject to Man in every State." According to the gentleman's reply, the woman's fate, while subject to father, brother, and later husband, was "free from Care, and free from Woe" because of the protection, security, and leisurely lifestyle provided by her male guardians at every stage of life.

Two women printers, Elizabeth Timothy and Ann Timothy, are the focus of this chapter. Relatives through marriage, they became widows at relatively young ages and were not immune from the tragic blows of fate. In widowhood they were free from the usual sequence of male control. At the same time, the burden of shouldering new printing responsibilities as well as single parenthood made them strangers to a life of protection, security, and leisure. Yet, in many ways the personal tragedies they bore gave them newfound freedom and opportunities for expression. The lives of Elizabeth Timothy and Ann Timothy provide a unique lens through which to view the status of women and widows in eighteenth-century Charleston.

On a mid-September day in 1731, the ship *Britannia* from London came into view of the colonial port of Philadelphia. This city of brick houses and carefully planned streets, William Penn's "greene countrie towne," was the funnel through which Europeans by the thousands passed on their way to creating new lives in America. Among the ship's passengers who took an oath of allegiance to George II on September 21, 1731, was Louis Timothée, an immigrant from Rotterdam. The French-born immigrant's family, including his four young children, accompanied their father on this trans-Atlantic passage.[2] Elizabeth, his Dutch-born wife, was not listed on the roster of newcomers, but it seems likely that she accompanied her family to the colonies. Although little is known of Elizabeth's early life, in his *Autobiography* Benjamin Franklin stated that she had achieved "a female education," which included "knowledge of accompts."[3] The Timothée family arrived in Philadelphia ready for a new start. Within three weeks of their arrival, Louis advertised for employment in the *Pennsylvania Gazette.* He hoped to establish "a publick French school" or to tutor young gentlemen and ladies in French at their homes.[4]

Certainly the decision to emigrate, to establish a new residence in a new land with the hope of earning a secure livelihood for their family, was a risk for the Timothées. Yet, it was also a chance for increased freedom and mobility, and perhaps better opportunity for their children. Years later, Elizabeth Timothy's daughter-in-law, Ann, faced similar risks and opportunities in moving to a new place. Moreover, Ann Timothy knew the exigencies of war and the struggles for American freedom in a singular way. The wife of a patriot husband, she survived in an enemy-occupied city while her husband was captured and exiled from Charleston.

Both of the women experienced a change in personal and common law status upon the death of their husbands. Neither of them avoided personal tragedy and loss. Disease and death, fires, drownings, exile, and debt touched them both. While widowhood meant shouldering the family responsibilities and running the print shop, it also opened new avenues of expression for these women printers. They shared the unique experience of being printers in a cosmopolitan southern city—of exercising editorial responsibility and liability, sometimes even in war. Unlike the woman writer in the pages of the *South-Carolina Gazette*, neither Elizabeth Timothy nor Ann Timothy, in their widowhood, experienced male control of their fates, but rather made personal decisions and choices to direct their own protection and security. That neither of them remarried may speak much about their personal desire to maintain what they had struggled to build.

Pre-Revolutionary Charleston was a receiving center for large numbers of poor Protestant Swiss, Germans, Scotch-Irish, and French Huguenots, who came to the city in response to the assembly's promise of bounties, tools, and provisions for those who would settle. Three crops grown in the low country supported Charleston's commerce: rice, indigo, and sea island cotton.[5] In the 1730s Charleston annually loaded 220 ships for Europe. The city excelled in comparison to other commercial centers; at New York in 1732 only 196 ships arrived, and at Philadelphia in 1733 only 173.[6] The coastal town bustled with activity. Each morning the city's vegetable, meat, and fish markets opened at sunrise, greeted by the ringing of market bells. Travelers reported that the most distinguished buildings in town were made of brick, and all the others were of cypress and yellow pine. Three-story single houses with balconies and piazzas lined the city's streets. City dwellers suffered from the dust and oppressive heat in dry weather and from mud in the wet season.[7]

How did Elizabeth Timothy and Ann Timothy end up in Charleston? Initially, it was the choice of their husbands to pursue a craft that led them to the city. Later, family ties, commitments, friendship networks, economic expediency, and perhaps even personal choice kept them there. For Elizabeth Timothy, it was the result of Benjamin Franklin's urging that her husband, then a journeyman for the *Pennsylvania Gazette*, take over the *South-Carolina Gazette* after its editor, Thomas Whitmarsh, died in 1733. In a six-year business agreement with Franklin dated November 26, 1733, Timothée agreed to a two-thirds share in the business. Franklin promised to supply the "necessary appurtances" of a print shop, and

Louis pledged to conduct the business and keep accurate accounts.[8] Louis arrived in South Carolina in late November 1773, but Elizabeth stayed behind in Philadelphia to settle outstanding accounts. Four months later, in March, Elizabeth and her children joined Louis in their new residence in Charleston.

In this cosmopolitan center the Timothée family settled and thrived in the early 1730s. Louis and his family became members of the city's established church, St. Philip's.[9] In April 1734, Louis anglicized his name to Lewis Timothy. He became a founder and an officer of the South Carolina Society, a social and charitable organization made up of Franco-Americans. From his printing office he participated in a subscription postal system. By 1736 the young printer had obtained for himself and his growing family land grants of six hundred acres and a town lot in Charleston.[10]

Despite this relative prosperity, tragedy struck the Timothys. By 1737 Elizabeth and Lewis had already experienced the loss of two children—one had died in Pennsylvania and one in South Carolina.[11] In 1738 a smallpox epidemic swept through Charleston. It was so devastating that Rev. George Whitefield reported that many died from neglect because there were not enough healthy people to attend the sick. In the October 12, 1738, issue of the *South-Carolina Gazette*, Louis reported a delay in publication, "myself and Son having been visited with this Fever, that reigns at present, so that neither of us hath been capable of working much at the Press."[12] Elizabeth probably helped out in the print shop in addition to nursing a sick family during this time. Two months later, in December, Lewis himself died as the result of "an unhappy accident."[13]

With young children to raise and a year left to fulfill the outstanding business contract with Franklin, the newly widowed Elizabeth had little time to wallow in her grief. She immediately assumed the business of her late husband. According to the terms drawn up with Franklin, Peter Timothy was to carry on the business in the event of his father's death and "to keep and improve ye materials of printing" until the expiration of the original partnership.[14] Because of Peter's youth (probably about fourteen years old at his father's death) and the expediency of needing a livelihood, Elizabeth assumed control of the King Street print shop. Without breaking the regular weekly publication schedule of the *South-*

Carolina Gazette, the very pregnant Elizabeth published another issue of the paper five days after her husband's burial on December 30, 1738. In this issue she told her readers, "I take this Opportunity to inform the Publick, that I shall continue the said Paper . . . and hope, by the Assistance of my Friends, to make it as entertaining and correct as may be reasonably expected." She asked all of her husband's subscribers to continue "their Favours and good offices to his poor afflicted Widow and six small Children and another hourly expected." [15]

The year following her husband's death proved a difficult one for Elizabeth as she struggled to settle Lewis's accounts, care for her family, and run the presses of the Timothy shop. Sickness took the lives of two more children. Elizabeth buried Charles on September 22, 1739, and Joseph just two weeks later.[16] In November Elizabeth ran an announcement in her paper, acting in her capacity as administratrix of her husband's estate. She asked that all those indebted to her husband pay her before the first of March 1740, "she being under an absolute Necessity of settling her said Husband's Accounts . . . in which she hath been much retarded by Sickness, as well of herself as of her Family; and as many of the Outstanding Debts are but small, she hopes no Persons will lay her under a Necessity of putting them to any charge in the Recovery thereof." [17]

With a smallpox epidemic still lingering in the memory of many Charlestonians, further tragedy befell the South Carolina city in 1740. On November 18 a terrible fire broke out at the corner of Broad and Church Streets. A northwest wind fanned the flames for nearly six hours as the fire consumed houses and stores down to Granville's Bastion, a valuable trading center of the town. The fire also spread to the west side of Church Street from Broad to Tradd. An estimated three hundred houses were reduced to ash and rubble. Parliament appropriated twenty thousand pounds sterling for the conflagration's 171 sufferers.[18] No reports exist of damage sustained directly by the Timothy shop. However, even if the printing office escaped unharmed, the fire undoubtedly took its toll on the revenues of the presses because many subscribers and customers suffered great losses.

As Charleston tried to rebuild in the 1740s in the aftermath of tragedy, so too did Elizabeth Timothy. Despite the physical strains of poor health and the emotional trauma of ongoing family losses, Elizabeth fulfilled the printing contract made years before with Franklin. The Philadelphia printer was so impressed by Elizabeth's ability that he wrote of her in his *Autobiography*. On the decease of Lewis, Franklin wrote,

> the business was continued by his widow ... [who] not only sent me as clear a state as she could find of transactions past, but continued on account with the greatest regularity and exactitude every quarter afterwards, and managed the business with such success that she not only brought up reputably a family of children but at the expiration of the term was able to purchase of me the printing house and establish her son in it.[19]

Franklin offered the life of Elizabeth Timothy as an example to young ladies and suggested that knowledge of accounts would be more useful than music or dancing in the event of widowhood and the assumption of responsibility for running a family business. In a printing family, the household was both the family domain and the production center. The needs of a printing family led to a gender-division of labor that was more flexible than in other household industries such as shoemaking. Women printers were typically engaged in composing, although it was not uncommon for them to work the presses or do whatever other task was at hand. The woman printer also served as a foster mother for the young apprentices or journeymen employed under her roof and care. All members of the household were expected to participate in production. Usually the print shop adjoined the living quarters, more closely connecting kin and craft.

On one level, to continue an enterprise after her husband died did not entail drastic change in a woman's activity, but merely an assumption of sole responsibility for what she had already been doing. On another level, being left without a spouse meant more to a woman than just the opportunity to reclaim the rights of her unmarried contemporaries. In addition to all the emotional strains, at the death of her husband a widow had to readjust her household relations depending upon such factors as her age, wealth, and family size. Her legal status, her economic position, and her social standing within the community changed drastically. Legally, the widow became a *feme sole*. She could enter into contracts, loan money, sue debtors, and dispose of property by will or deed. Economically, her spouse's death meant that the material resources of her family had been reduced, and she now faced a lower standard of living. Socially, much of the status given a married woman was derived from her husband. His death removed his own as well as his wife's position or prestige within the community. Contrary to the norms suggested by this pattern of widowed dependency, the women printers of this study took on added responsibility and often supervised or worked in partnership with their sons. These women coped, survived, and sometimes thrived in the face of loss and economic disadvantage. Such an experience can hardly qualify as dependence.[20] Circumstances rather than choice may have dictated the woman printer's decision to enter the profession, but that did not prevent her from enjoying the work or making a successful endeavor of it.

One wonders how widely known among Elizabeth's contemporaries was the work of Daniel Defoe, author of the didactic *Complete English Tradesman* (1730). Perhaps both Franklin and Lewis Timothy had recalled the author's advice. Defoe enjoined every tradesman to "let his wife into an acquaintance with his business, if she desires it, and is fit for it; and especially in case of mortality; that she may not be left helpless and friendless with her children, when her husband is gone, and when perhaps her circumstances may require it."[21] He cautioned against women who "marry the Tradesman, but scorn the trade."[22] Defoe's injunction seems to have been either consciously or unconsciously taken to heart by the male printers of this time.

Defoe further remarked on women's amazing ability to recover from misfortune. "Women," he wrote, "when once they give themselves leave to stoop to their own circumstances, and think fit to rouze up themselves to their own relief, are not so helpless and shiftless creatures as some would make them appear in the world; and we see whole families in trade frequently recover'd by their industry." "[B]ut then they are such women as can stoop to it," he added, "and can lay aside the particular pride of their first years; and who, without looking back to what they have been, can be content to look into what Providence has brought them to be."[23]

By the end of 1739 Elizabeth had been able to buy out Franklin's interest in the partnership and became the first woman in the American colonies to own and publish a newspaper. By March 14, 1743, Elizabeth had changed her publication day from Thursday to Monday. The *Gazette* maintained consistency in its format: four pages, approximately eight by thirteen inches in size, with type set in two columns (changed to three in 1745).[24] Woodcut engravings, especially those of a fugitive man, made regular appearances accompanying advertisements in Elizabeth's newspaper. Apparently Charlestonians supported the widowed printer, for there was no noticeable decline in newspaper advertising.

The exact term of Elizabeth's control of the *Gazette* before she passed it on to her son Peter is unknown. Isaiah Thomas claims she conducted the press "for a year or two."[25] She most likely relinquished her management gradually as her son grew in years and printing competence. In 1741 the Acts of the General Assembly were delivered to "Mr. Peter Timothy Printer in Charles Town." Yet only three days before, the Assembly made provisions for settling its annual printing bill with Elizabeth rather than her son. Thus it seems that although Peter may have assumed the responsibility of mechanically operating the family print shop as of 1741, his mother retained control of its overall management.[26]

Continuing in a position previously held by her husband, Elizabeth served as official printer for South Carolina. She also inherited her husband's difficulties in getting the General Assembly to pay for her work, including the publication of an edition of *Trott's Laws*. On March 16, 1741, the Committee on Petitions and Accounts advised that Elizabeth receive £191 for printing proclamations, advertisements, abstracts of laws, and the enactments of two sessions of the General Assembly up to the end of March 1738.[27] Elizabeth relied on the revenues of public printing to support her family. Between February 18, 1742, and March 13, 1746, the Commons House of Assembly authorized payments to Mrs. Timothy in an amount just over £2,406. In addition to public printing, Elizabeth ran a commercial printing business in legal blanks, handbills, broadsides, pamphlets, and stationery.

Throughout the 1740s Elizabeth maintained a good relationship with Benjamin Franklin, her husband's former partner. As recorded in his account books from 1740 to 1747, Franklin supplied the Charleston shop with printing necessities and the merchandise for retail and personal use. His shipments to Elizabeth included candles, beer, tallow, flour, and two hundred to three hundred almanacs a year. In January 1745 Franklin recorded shipping to Elizabeth one thousand copies of *Poor Richard's Almanac,* his largest single consignment to the Charleston printer.[28]

In October 1746 Elizabeth announced in her paper that she would operate a stationery and book store next to the printing office. Perhaps Elizabeth chose to run a bookstore so that she would have a means of support independent but complementary to the printing office, which she had turned over to her son Peter when he reached his legal majority. Was Elizabeth free to retain control of the print shop had she so desired? Probably she could have held control according to the common law status of widows. But most likely as she advanced in years she was glad to turn over to her son the family business that she had so proudly maintained.

Elizabeth's new daughter-in-law, Peter's bride, Ann, signed over to her a release of dower dated October 24–25, 1746.[29] By South Carolina law, before clear title to property could be obtained by a buyer, the wife of a seller had to renounce her dower or right to a portion of the property. Ann's dower signed over to Elizabeth included a parcel of land on King Street with all its gardens, orchards, fences, wells, and watercourses. The property released to Elizabeth in this agreement was adjacent to a lot already owned by Peter. Knowing that her son would have a family of his own to assist him, Elizabeth probably readily dispensed with the duties of printer herself as she resided nearby in the newfound freedom of retirement from printing office responsibilities.

In December 1746, however, she announced her decision to leave South Carolina. Elizabeth requested that all those people indebted to her late husband's estate and to herself for *Gazettes* over the last eight years make final settlement.[30] It is unclear from the surviving record whether Elizabeth was away from Charleston for all of the next decade, but by July 1756 she appears to have returned to Charleston, as evidenced by an advertisement she placed in the *Gazette* for a runaway slave named Flora.[31]

On her deathbed, Elizabeth drafted her last will and testament on April 2, 1757, and was buried two days later at St. Philip's Church.[32] No obituary appears for her in the South Carolina newspapers, including that of her son. The inventory of her estate dated July 2, 1757, shows that she did not die impoverished.[33] The value of her goods and chattels was £586.12.6. Among Elizabeth's possessions at the time of her death were a parcel of books, two French Bibles, two old desks, some china, writing paper, thirty-six ounces of silver, a marble-covered sideboard, beds, mattresses, looking glasses, pewter, a few pieces of furniture, a saw, two pots, a brass mortar and pestle, and at least six slaves, four female and two male.[34]

According to her will, Elizabeth left her accounts to her son Peter. She also placed in his care a sentimental object, the silver watch of her late husband, intended to be given to her grandson, Benjamin Franklin Timothy. Elizabeth showed great concern for the security of her widowed daughter, Mary Elizabeth Bourquin, to whom she left a small tract of land, a house on King Street, two slaves, and half her clothing and furniture. To her other married daughters, Catherine Trezevant and Louisa Richards, she left a house and three slaves.[35]

As the first woman in colonial America to own and publish a newspaper, Elizabeth Timothy played an important role in the development of pre-Revolutionary Charleston. She wielded considerable influence and possessed community status as official printer to the colony and proprietor of a bookstore and commercial printing enterprise. For almost eight years after her husband's death she continued the *South-Carolina Gazette*. Her son Peter, daughter-in-law Ann, grandson Benjamin Franklin Timothy, and great grandson Peter Timothy Marchant in turn worked the family press. Through her determination and example, Elizabeth helped to ensure that the family's printing tradition would continue for four generations.

The young Ann Donavan would unexpectedly follow in her mother-in-law's footsteps. She married Peter Timothy on December 8, 1745, in St. Philip's Church in Charleston.[36] Virtually nothing is known of Ann's early life. By working with her husband and her mother-in-law in the print shop, she quickly learned the trade and became part of the family business. For almost twelve years, she also observed how her mother-in-law, Elizabeth, went on with life as a widow and carried her grief.

Within a year after her marriage, Ann had the concerns of two generations on her shoulders. To provide for her mother-in-law, she had signed over a release of dower in October 1746. Ann and Peter also started a family of their own. In December 1746 Ann gave birth to a daughter, the first of her fourteen children. The Timothys named the baby Elizabeth Ann, probably in honor of the child's grandmother and mother. The young couple named their first son Lewis (born in 1755) after his grandfather.[37] Child-rearing became a large and time-consuming task for most of Ann's life. From the age of nineteen, when her first daughter was born, until the age of forty-four, when Benjamin Franklin Timothy was born, Ann devoted much time and energy to her role as mother. While pregnant, she often still had a child in the cradle. In addition, she had the sad lot of outliving many of her children, who died in their infancy. By the time her youngest son was born, Ann already had several grandchildren.

While his wife was busy raising children, for almost thirty-three years Peter Timothy ran the family print shop. On August 24, 1772, he wrote to Benjamin Franklin, "My natural Eyes being almost worn out, I have declined the Printing Business, and am now employed in putting my affairs in order for a settlement."[38] Peter lamented to his readers that he had often sacrificed his private interests to the public good. Ann most likely was familiar with the print shop routine and increasingly assisted her husband as his vision worsened. Peter asked Franklin to help him acquire an appointment as a naval officer (a customs, not a military post) in Charleston. In a paternalistic tone, Franklin cautioned Peter that "to leave a good Trade in hopes of an Office, is quitting a Certainty for an Uncertainty, and losing Substances for Shadow."[39] Evidently, Peter took Franklin's advice and became a printing partner in Powell, Hughes and Company as well as deputy postmaster for the southern provinces of North America. This arrangement lasted until November 1773, when Peter resumed publication of the *South-Carolina Gazette* and became printer to the Commons House of Assembly.

Amid her husband's public prosperity and recognition, Ann endured some great family losses. Most of the Timothy children did not live to adulthood. In an August 1774 letter to Franklin, Peter wrote, "My Son Benjamin Franklin has just happily got thro' the Measles, and is a fine promising Boy; but as I have lost eight Sons in Teething, my apprehensions for him will not be over till he has all his Teeth."[40] Fortunately, the youngster survived his bout with the measles. One learns this in a 1785 congratulatory note to Franklin on his return from France. Ann Timothy wrote, "I endeavour to excite in my son an emulation of what is great and noble, while I charge him never to suffer his conduct to be unworthy of the illustrious name he bears."[41]

In addition to family illnesses, the Timothys suffered other disasters. A fire swept through Charleston late in the evening of January 15, 1778, and as John Wells, Jr., a fellow Charleston printer, reported, "Timothy's Printing materials, are entirely lost."[42] Remarkably, within five months the *Gazette* was able to resume publication. On June 24, 1778, in his rejuvenated newspaper, Peter remarked that the tragedy forced him "to begin the World anew, at an advanced Period of Life."[43]

During the course of the American Revolution, Peter also became inflamed with the patriot cause. He served on the General Committee of Correspondence, on the Committee of Observation, and as clerk of the Council of Safety. During the siege of Charleston, he acted as a military observer, reporting to American authorities the British movements, troop strength, and weather changes.

When Charleston finally fell to the British in May 1780, Peter refused to take an oath of allegiance to the British Crown—a dramatic realignment of allegiances from the oath of loyalty that Peter's father had pledged in 1731. In August 1780 Lord Cornwallis ordered into exile thirty-three leading citizens of Charleston who had adopted the patriot cause during the previous months.[44] As Peter was taken aboard the ship *Sandwich*, on his way to imprisonment in St. Augustine, Ann and her children worried that they would never see him return to Charleston.

After ten months of captivity, the prisoners in St. Augustine were exchanged with the proviso that they were forbidden to return to Charleston. Many prisoners were sent to Philadelphia and arrived there in August 1781. By December the American prisoners and their families were joyously reunited. More than five hundred Carolinian exiles were in Philadelphia by the end of the year. Some members of Peter's family met him in Philadelphia, though it is unclear whether Ann made the trip or stayed behind to manage the family's affairs in Charleston. In autumn of 1782, however, Peter accompanied two of his daughters and a grandchild on a trip from Philadelphia to Santo Domingo. Peter planned to stop in Antigua, where his daughter, Frances Claudia, the widow of Benjamin Lewis

Marchant, owned some property. Along the way the ship foundered in a storm off the coast of Delaware, and all the passengers and crew perished.

When news of the shipwreck finally reached her, Ann must have been overcome with grief. No stranger to tragedy, the fifty-five-year-old widow was especially overwrought by the sudden and collective loss of a husband, two daughters, and a grandchild. Ann was probably more prepared, though, than most widows for the sudden loss of a husband. Through the exile of her husband during war, Ann already knew the pain of separation. She also recalled the example set by her mother-in-law in her own widowhood.

Prior to his exile, Peter had drafted a will while "being advanced in Years, and involved in all the Perils of a Siege, by an Enemy who do not promise to exercise all that Humanity which distinguishes a generous Foe." He left "ALL the Property I have in the World of whatever kind" to be divided and distributed among his wife, Ann, his spinster daughter, Sarah, his invalid son, Robert, and his other son, Benjamin Franklin. To his other married daughters, he left nothing, "not because less dear to me, but because the Fire in 1778, and my uniform political Conduct has not left me the Means to make that Provison I could wish for all." He invested in Ann full power and authority to execute the will and to dispose of his land as she deemed necessary "in case of my decease or not."[45] In effect, Peter had granted Ann *feme sole* privilege, not only upon his demise but also while he was imprisoned.

With few options left, Ann stoically rebuilt her shattered life. In 1782 she formed a partnership with E. Walsh to continue her late husband's business. With the help of her new partner, she resumed weekly publication of the *Gazette of the State of South-Carolina* on July 16, 1783. Shortly after commencing their partnership, Walsh became ill and retired.[46] Ann continued the paper with other assistance, and within two years, by July 1784, the paper began appearing twice a week, on Monday and Thursday. As printer of the *Gazette*, Ann changed the format of her publication and included considerable advertising. Eventually, the South Carolina coat of arms adorned the center of the masthead. In 1784 Ann moved the print shop from 100 Meeting Street to 89 Broad Street and later to the corner of Broad and King Streets. Perhaps as an outward indicator of her new commitment to move on with her life, Ann contracted with Alexander Crawford, a Charleston painter, glazier, and paper hanger, from 1786 through 1789 for several household improvements, including panes of glass and interior and exterior house painting.[47]

In addition to the newspaper, Ann printed many pamphlets and offered for sale from her print shop the usual assortment of legal blanks, handbills, and other paper products.[48] In 1783 she published the *South Carolina & Georgia Almanac for 1784*. In 1785 she published Isaac Bickerstaff's *North & South Carolina and Georgia Almanack for 1786*. As a widow herself, Ann had a special and personal interest in the publication of a small rule book published in her name in 1788 for the "Society for the relief of the widows and orphans of the clergy of the Protestant Episcopal church in the state of South Carolina."[49]

On March 3, 1783, she was appointed printer to the state "in consequence of the services rendered to it by her late husband."[50] Holding the potentially lucrative post of state printer was not without care for Ann. She repeatedly had to send the South Carolina legislature bills and reminders for payments due. On January 21, 1788, she reminded the state of its obligations to her. She

> assured this Honorable House that she advanced Money to purchase paper and pay workmen to execute the public printing Work, which could not be done otherwise; That the nonpayment of that Account has involved her in much distress for want of Cash to carry on her expensive Business, and pay debts which she owes, for the principal part whereof she is obliged to pay Interest, although allowed none from the State.[51]

Ann took her appointment as printer to the state seriously. She also did not shrink from reminding the state of its responsibility to its printer. In her January 16, 1790, petition to the South Carolina House of Representatives, Ann clearly expressed her self-identity as a public servant. She also wanted to establish her position so that male competitors would not deprive her of what she understood to be a life appointment. "Your Petitioner begs leave to remind your Honourable House of a Resolution passed in March 1785," she wrote,

> whereby she was appointed State printer in consequences of & as a reward for the services of her late husband, this she received with gratitude & assures your Honourable House that her patriotism would induce her to

serve the public for no other reward than the satisfaction she would enjoy in the reflection of her having served her country (the only recompense her predecessor received) would it be in any degree consistent with her circumstances. She wishes for no compensation for the services of her Husband—she wishes to be rewarded merely for her own, at the same time leaving it to your Honourable House to determine whether your good intentions in granting her the State Office have been answered, when she was called on in the years 1786, 1787, & 1788 to contend with men who wished to deprive her of that Office; by which means she was reduced to the necessity either of working for a very trifling consideration, or of giving up the office of State Printer, which would have been still more mortifying, whereas she had conceived on her appointment that she was to hold that office during her life. As your petitioner has still an orphan family to provide for, she humbly hopes that her situation will be taken into serious consideration & that some provision may be made in order to discharge the Debt due to her by the State.[52]

Stressing her role as family provider (even though her youngest child was by now a teenager), Ann announced her decision to stay in Charleston and not to accompany other state officials on their relocation to Columbia, the new capital. She assured the house that "any service which is in her power to render the State, by printing for the Public in Charleston, shall be most cheerfully done as far as can be accomplished by her exertions, and that she will at all times hold herself in readiness to execute your Command."[53] In many respects this document represents the epitome of Ann's self-assertion as a printer in her own right and not just as the widow of Peter. By expressing her decision not to move to Columbia, she also exercised a freedom of choice that she may not have known in her years as a married woman.

Ann continued to publish the *Gazette* without interruption until her death, at the age of sixty-five, on September 11, 1792. She left a detailed will, making specific provisions for each of her children. Of particular note is her sentimentality in bequeathing value-laden items to certain children. For example, to her daughter Elizabeth Williamson, who was "in easy and independent circumstances," Ann left no inheritance but "my large easy Chair & the Cover thereof which she worked herself as a token of the affection I have for her, and an Acknowledgment for her dutiful Behaviour and tender treatment to me through Life." To her daughter Sarah she left "my Negro Woman Sarah with her future Issue and Increase." Ann requested that her daughter make a weekly payment of "four shillings and eight pence sterling" to the slave Sarah as recompense for her "honesty and fidelity." Upon the death of Ann's daughter Sarah, Benjamin Franklin Timothy was authorized to immediately "manumit and set free from the bonds of slavery" the black woman.[54]

Ann's maternal concerns are revealed in the provision she made for her son Robert Smith Timothy "whom it hath pleased God to Afflict with grievous Infirmities." Ann left him a bed, bed linens, and bedroom furniture—all appropriate items for an invalid. Ann entreated her children "to be at all Times kind and attentive to him not only in Compassion to his Informities, but thro' Regard and respect to my Memory." To her grandsons Benjamin, Robert, and Peter Timothy Marchant, she willed "a pretty property in the West Indies which was their late Father's, and in all probability they will be better provided for than my own Children."[55]

Benjamin Franklin Timothy, whose grandmother Elizabeth had left him his grandfather's silver timepiece, now came into a more valuable but equally cherished inheritance—the printing business. Ann explained in her will, "As the printing Business has been carried on by the Father and Grandfather of my son . . . and my press is now well established and furnished I recommend to my said Son to continue this Business after my Death."[56] Obviously, Ann took pride in the family business that she had maintained for twelve years and wanted to ensure that such a legacy would continue after her passing. Through her marriage into a printing family, Ann had both learned a trade and passed it on to her own children. She not only inherited a means of livelihood from her husband and made her own distinctive mark as state printer and newspaper publisher, but also learned from her mother-in-law how to deal with the cares and woes of life and the fate of widowhood. For both Elizabeth Timothy and Ann Timothy, the fate of their husbands initially propelled them into a professional and public sphere they would not otherwise have occupied. But, as they learned to deal with what Providence had brought them to be, they exercised increased personal control and freedom as widows in colonial Charleston.

NOTES

1. *South-Carolina Gazette*, Nov. 21, 1743.

2. Louis Timothée's children—Peter, Louis, Charles, and Mary—are included on the roster of newcomers. The oath of allegiance, which included a renunciation of the Pretender, was required of all males age sixteen and above who had not obtained official permission from the English Crown to emigrate. Hennig Cohen, *The South Carolina Gazette, 1732–1775* (Columbia: University of South Carolina Press, 1953), 233. William E. Egle, ed., "Names of Foreigners Who Took the Oath of Allegiance to the Province and State of Pennsylvania, 1727–1775," *Pennsylvania Archives*, 2d ser., 17 (Harrisburg, Pa.: E. K. Meyers, 1890), 28–29, 32.

3. Edward T. James and Janet Wilson James, eds., *Notable American Women, 1607–1950: A Biographical Dictionary* (Cambridge, Mass.: Belknap Press, 1971), 3:465. The quoted material is from Benjamin Franklin, *Autobiography*, Max Farrand, ed. (Berkeley: University of California Press, 1949), 119.

4. *Pennsylvania Gazette*, Oct. 14, 1731.

5. George C. Rogers, Jr., *Charleston in the Age of the Pinckneys* (Norman: University of Oklahoma Press, 1980), 9.

6. A June 9, 1739, "Prospect of Charles-Town," published by act of Parliament, proclaimed the city "the fairest and most fruitfull Province belonging to Great Britain." Rogers, *Charleston in the Age of the Pinckneys*, 55.

7. Leila Sellers, *Charleston Business on the Eve of the American Revolution* (Chapel Hill: University of North Carolina Press, 1934), 16–17, 21.

8. "Articles of Agreement between Benjamin Franklin and Lewis Timothée, 1733," *Pennsylvania Magazine of History and Biography* 30 (January 1906):104–6.

9. Rogers, *Charleston in the Age of the Pinckneys*, 56.

10. Lewis Timothy, plat for a half-acre town lot, no. 31 in Berkley County, Sept. 8, 1735; Lewis Timothy, plat for two hundred acres of land in Berkley County, Sept. 19, 1735; Lewis Timothy, plat for four hundred acres in Berkley County, Dec. 16, 1736, South Carolina Department of Archives and History, Columbia (hereafter cited as SCA).

11. Cohen, *South Carolina Gazette*, 237.

12. *South-Carolina Gazette*, Oct. 12, 1738.

13. Ibid., Jan. 4, 1739.

14. "Articles of Agreement," 105.

15. *South-Carolina Gazette*, Jan. 4, 1739.

16. A. S. Salley, Jr., ed., *Register of St. Philip's Parish, Charles Town, South Carolina, 1720–1758* (Charleston, S.C.: Walker, Evans and Cogswell, 1904), 261.

17. *South-Carolina Gazette*, Nov. 11, 1739. For an example of a bond (dated

Oct. 5, 1738) due Lewis Timothy and later collected by his widow, see Joseph Crell to Elizabeth Timothy, mortgage of five hundred acres of land in Congaree Township, 1739–40, SCA.

18. Rogers, *Charleston in the Age of the Pinckneys*, 27–28. The November 20, 1740, issue of the *South-Carolina Gazette* included a report and description of the fire.

19. Franklin, *Autobiography*, 119.

20. Suzanne Lebsock argues for women's autonomy as a result of their return to *feme sole* status. She discovered that women of Petersburg, Virginia, from 1784 to 1860 "gained greater freedom from immediate and total dependence on particular men." See Suzanne Lebsock, *The Free Women of Petersburg: Status and Culture in a Southern Town, 1784–1860* (New York: Norton, 1984), 235.

21. Daniel Defoe, *The Complete English Tradesman in Familiar Letters*, 2 vols. (1727; reprint, New York: Augustus M. Kelley, 1969), 2:294. For more on Defoe's work, see Paul Dottin, *The Life and Strange and Surprising Adventures of Daniel Defoe* (New York: Octagon Books, 1971), 257–58; Peter Earlee, *The World of Daniel Defoe* (New York: Atheneum, 1977), 169, 234, 243.

22. Defoe, *Complete English Tradesman*, 291.

23. Ibid., 303.

24. Ira L. Baker, "Elizabeth Timothy: America's First Woman Editor," *Journalism Quarterly* 54 (1977):284.

25. Isaiah Thomas, *The History of Printing in America* (Worcester, Mass., 1810; reprint, New York: Weathervane Books, 1970), 568; A. S. Salley, Jr., "The First Presses of South Carolina," Bibliographical Society of America, *Proceedings and Papers* 2 (1907–8):29–33.

26. Cohen, *South Carolina Gazette*, 239–40.

27. J. H. Easterby, ed., *The Colonial Records of South Carolina*, 9 vols., vol. 2, *The Journal of the Commons House of Assembly, September 12, 1739–March 26, 1741* (Columbia: Historical Commission of South Carolina, 1952), 514, 531, 533.

28. George Simpson Eddy, ed., *Account Book Kept by Benjamin Franklin*, vol. 2, *Ledger "D," 1739–1747* (New York: Columbia University Press, 1929), 121.

29. Ann Timothy to Elizabeth Timothy, Renunciation of Dower, Aug. 15, 1757, SCA. By South Carolina law, before clear title to property could be obtained by a buyer, the seller's wife had to renounce her dower or right to a portion of the property. Renunciation of dower was used to assign land, buildings, slaves, and personal property, permanently to a third party. Andrea Hinding and Clarke A. Chambers, eds., *Women's History Sources: A Guide to Archives and Manuscript Collections in the United States* (New York: R. R. Bowker, 1979), 951.

30. *South-Carolina Gazette*, Dec. 15, 1746.

31. Ibid., July 8, 1756. "Runaway from the subscriber a tall strong Angola

Negro wench named Flora." In the inventory of Elizabeth's estate are listed the names of her slaves: Abram, Amsterdam, Judith, Flora, Molly, and Dina and her two children.

32. Will of Elizabeth Timothy, Charleston, S.C., Probate Court, Record of Wills, 1737–69, book 8, SCA. Elizabeth was buried on April 4, 1757, at St. Philip's. D. E. Huger Smith and A. S. Salley, *Register of St. Philip's Parish, Charles Town, or Charleston, S.C., 1754–1810* (Columbia: University of South Carolina Press, 1971), 332.

33. Arthur Hirsch concludes that Elizabeth's inventory is a "tale of solemn pathetic interest, for it contained little besides the bare necessities of life in a home." Her will seems to support quite a contrary conclusion. Elizabeth was able to bequeath to her children both property and slaves, in addition to the usual household items. Arthur Henry Hirsch, *The Huguenots of Colonial South Carolina* (Durham, N.C.: Duke University Press, 1928), 250–51.

34. Probate Inventory, vol. S, 1756–58, roll 5, 164–67, SCA.

35. Caroline T. Moore, ed., *Abstracts of the Wills of the State of South Carolina, 1740–1760* (Columbia, S.C.: R. L. Bryan, 1964), 227; Will of Elizabeth Timothy.

36. Smith and Salley, *Register of St. Philip's Parish*, 182.

37. Walter B. Edgar and N. Louise Bailey, *Biographical Directory of the South Carolina House of Representatives*, vol. 2, *The Commons House of Assembly, 1692–1775* (Columbia: University of South Carolina Press, 1977), 674–75.

38. Douglas C. McMurtrie, "The Correspondence of Peter Timothy, Printer of Charlestown, with Benjamin Franklin," *South Carolina Historical and Genealogical Magazine* (hereafter cited as *SCHGM*) 35 (1934):127.

39. Quoted by Jeffrey A. Smith in *Printers and Press Freedom: The Ideology of Early American Journalism* (New York: Oxford University Press, 1988), 145–46.

40. McMurtrie, "The Correspondence of Peter Timothy," 127.

41. Ann Timothy to Benjamin Franklin, Nov. 5, 1785, photocopy at the South Carolinia Library, University of South Carolina, Columbia.

42. John Wells, Jr., to Henry Laurens, Jan. 23, 1778, in *The Papers of Henry Laurens*, edited by David R. Chesnutt, James Taylor, and Peggy J. Clark (Columbia: University of South Carolina Press, 1990), 12:333.

43. *Gazette of the State of South-Carolina*, June 24, 1778.

44. George Smith McGowen, Jr., *The British Occupation of Charleston, 1780–82* (Columbia: University of South Carolina Press, 1972), 151. Among the first prisoners taken to St. Augustine in 1780 were Christopher Gadsden, Edward Rutledge, Josiah Smith, and David Ramsay. For more on the siege of Charleston and the exile of some of its leading citizens, see 230–31.

45. Quoted material here and above is from the will of Peter Timothy, Charleston Probate Court, book 20, Record of Wills, 1783–86, SCA. For more on *feme sole* status, see Mary Roberts Parramore, " 'For Her Sole and Separate Use':

Feme Sole Trader Status in Early South Carolina," master's thesis, University of South Carolina, 1991.

46. E. Walsh published the *Gazette of the State of South-Carolina* with Ann from July 16, 1783, until August 27, 1783. Printers' File, American Antiquarian Society, Worcester, Mass.

47. Alexander Crawford Daybook, 1786–95 (no. 34–347), South Carolina Historical Society, Charleston, 3, 6, 10, 31.

48. For an annotated list of Ann Timothy's imprints, see Christopher Gould and Richard Parker Morgan, *South Carolina Imprints, 1731–1800: A Descriptive Bibliography* (Santa Barbara, Calif.: ABC-CLIO Information Services, 1985).

49. Mabel L. Weber, comp., "South Carolina Almanacs to 1800," *SCHGM* 15 (April 1914):79. Protestant Episcopal Church in South Carolina, *Rules of the Society, for the Relief of the Widows and Orphans of the Clergy of the Protestant Episcopal Church, in the State of South Carolina; Established October 17, 1787* (Charleston, S.C.: Printed for A. Timothy, 1788).

50. Leila Sellers, *Charleston Business on the Eve of the American Revolution* (Chapel Hill: University of North Carolina Press, 1934), 82.

51. Michael E. Stevens and Christine M. Allen, eds., *Journals of the House of Representatives, 1787–1788* (Columbia: University of South Carolina Press, 1981), 186.

52. Michael E. Stevens and Christine M. Allen, eds., *Journals of the House of Representatives, 1789–1790* (Columbia: University of South Carolina Press, 1984), 372. The house accepted the recommendations of the committee that Ann be given interest on her accounts from the time they were due but was unable to remunerate her for the loss from the sale of the certificates. The house accepted the recommendations and sent them to the senate. The senate, however, did not consider the report sent from the house.

53. Stevens and Allen, *Journals of the House of Representatives, 1789–1790*, 372.

54. The quotations are from the will of Ann Timothy, Charleston Probate Court, Record of Wills, book 24, 1786–93, 703, SCA. No copy of the probate inventory has been found.

55. The quotations are from the will of Ann Timothy.

56. The quotation is from the will of Ann Timothy.

9

"To Have a Sufficient Maintenance": Women and the Economics of Freedom in Frontier Pennsylvania, 1750–1800

JUDITH A. RIDNER

When Isabella Bell came before the justices of the Cumberland County Court of Quarter Sessions in 1802 to request a license to sell beer and cider in the town of Carlisle, it was, as she explained, because her deceased husband's financial "Embarrassment" had severely impinged upon her economic autonomy both as a widow and as a mother. With her husband's property sold to pay off his debts, the family had been "Left destitute." Although Isabella had already employed "my Industry . . . to support myself and family" by running an unlicensed tippling house, she needed the approval of the court to carry on her business legally.[1]

In many respects Isabella Bell's petition typified requests for tavern licenses made in Cumberland County during the second half of the eighteenth century. The unusually detailed contents of Bell's petition, however, and the fact that she was one of only a small number of female petitioners, illustrate how women in backcountry Pennsylvania defined freedom as it applied to their own lives and experiences. For women like Bell, freedom was not about abstract notions of individual rights or theoretical conceptions of political and legal privilege. They perceived it as a tangible commodity. Circumscribed by the practical and often demanding realities of daily life and labor in the backcountry, freedom was equated with the achievement of some actual measure of the kind of economic liberty that guaranteed personal autonomy. Freedom equaled independence in women's minds. It meant being able to work within traditional gender bounds, and even within the bonds of marriage, to attain a level of economic standing or security that would ensure the continued well-being of themselves and their families.

Feminine definitions of freedom were inseparable from the circumstances and expectations that accompanied life on the early American frontier. Joining in the westward journey from longer-settled areas in and near Philadelphia or New Castle, women, like men, migrated to the backcountry of central Pennsylvania in hopeful anticipation of their families' future economic achievement. First arriving in the Cumberland Valley in the 1740s, and in greater numbers after the formation of Cumberland County in 1750, these men and women knew that the fertile and well-watered limestone soils of the valley were prime agricultural lands by eighteenth-century standards. They hoped that the valley, an ideal location for the production of a variety of grains, especially wheat, would offer them the personal and financial autonomy—or competency—that they so desired. In an era when birthright and inheritance so often determined one's fate, these aspiring men and women hoped to circumvent the predominant socioeconomic patterns of the East by achieving independence, and hence freedom, by owning land, engaging in trade, and acting as sovereign arbiters of their families' collective economic destinies.[2]

For early American women, such expectations of potential economic security on the frontier were especially appealing. Confined to the status of dependents by a legal system that denied married women any property rights apart from their husbands, women of the eighteenth century had little opportunity to achieve personal freedom or economic autonomy.[3] In the backcountry, however, where the public sphere intermingled with the private as families worked together to eke out a living and achieve the coveted status of independence, women, whether single, married, or widowed, were offered the chance to become integral and productive members of their respective family units. In contrast to their eastern counterparts, frontier women fully expected to enjoy any and all economic gains their families experienced, even if they had only limited opportunities for amassing personal wealth, owning land, or achieving a status separate from their husbands or male guardians.[4]

Life on the Pennsylvania frontier taught women to have high expectations of their own gendered role in the family. Evidence from both public and private records suggests that many, if not most, Cumberland County women recognized that they were indispensable members of the household economic unit. Indeed, the intense desire to prosper drove most backcountry families to engage in a number of diverse productive activities—from farming, to manufacturing, to retailing—placing significant and remarkably balanced demands upon all members of the family, regardless of their sex. Such developments were especially likely in Pennsylvania, where an expanding market economy in grain, a host of evolving rural industries, and a high demand for labor encouraged economic diversity. Typically, a Pennsylvania frontiersman not only farmed, but also practiced a trade. If a town dweller, he ran a retail establishment such as a store or a tavern as well. Women participated directly in broadening their families' economic interests. While they managed the domestic sector and cared for the children, a combination of necessity and aspiration also encouraged them to manufacture various household goods and assist their husbands in field, shop, or tavern. Because women were accustomed to carrying out so many key economic functions within the family unit, few backcountry women had qualms about moving outside the immediate confines of their families' homes, fields, or shops to engage in economic exchanges in the larger market economy. Single, married, and widowed women appear consistently in the account books of local merchants. Some women actually maintained their own accounts, but many others shopped regularly under their husbands' or fathers' names, not only charging merchandise to the accounts of their male guardians, but also borrowing cash from these merchant-bankers.[5] Most important, the economic authority these women enjoyed did not disappear as the frontier moved westward. In Cumberland County, public and private realms remained entwined as women maintained an economic role in both the family and the community well into the nineteenth century.[6]

Because women in the backcountry were accustomed to sizable amounts of economic responsibility, freedom had a very specific context, derived directly from the economic expectations and personal experiences that life on the frontier generated. For single women, and for widows like Isabella Bell, freedom meant having sufficient economic means and financial resources to provide an adequate and independent living for themselves and their dependents, even if it meant that they had to use the economic fruits of their own labors to achieve it. For married women, freedom was more closely allied to male notions of independence. Wives, like their husbands, were concerned about preserving the property interests of their families as a way to prevent dependence. Yet, wives linked freedom to property, not as a way to assert their manliness, but instead to ensure that they would be able to pursue their complementary feminine roles of wife, mother, domestic servant, and economic producer, free from significant economic want or worry.[7]

For many backcountry women, the American Revolution was a pivotal juncture in the establishment and maintenance of their freedom. Although this region of central Pennsylvania was distanced from the battles of the Revolution, women's lives were nonetheless dramatically affected by the war. With many of their male kin absent from home, women in Cumberland County, like women across the American colonies, were left on the home front to cope with a host of adverse conditions. Widows, in particular, often found their economic independence contested or curtailed by wartime circumstances. Yet, because economic freedom was of such basic importance to women, when they found their autonomy or the autonomy of their families challenged, they moved readily into the courts to obtain relief. The petitions local widows presented illustrate the way backcountry women defined and articulated their concepts of freedom in the public domain. Most widows sought economic relief. Few questioned their role as widowed provider. Instead, these women sought legal affirmation of their responsibilities as independent heads of households and the economic resources necessary to persist in their duties.

In 1787 Elizabeth Ross, widow of the late militia private Jonathan Ross, killed at the battle of Crooked Billet in 1778, came before the justices of the Cumberland County Orphan's Court in a last and desperate attempt to obtain some basic subsistence for herself and her family. In the wake of her husband's sudden death, she explained, she and her seven children had been left in "a Distressed Situation," made worse because several of her children "were very young and totally incapable of Supporting themselves." She went on to show that "since her husband[']s death [she] hath Laboured under real Difficulties and Distresses to procure a bare Subsistence for herself and the Children." Although Elizabeth was clearly anxious for herself and her family, she displayed pride in her work as family provider when she made it clear to the justices that, in the nine years since she had been widowed, she "hath never obtained any relief from the State." Although impoverished, Elizabeth Ross was not begging for a handout. She sought to protect her own and her family's economic independence by obtaining what she considered a just compensation from the state for her widowhood. Having "been informed that relief has been granted to many widows," Ross requested that the court "take her Situation into consideration and Extend the Provision of the act of assembly . . . for her Relief." In response to her petition, the court confirmed her status as a deserving young widow and granted her an award of 12s.6d. per month from the time of her husband's death—for a total of some sixty-seven pounds.[8]

Elizabeth Ross was not the only Cumberland County widow to assert her independence in the face of wartime adversity. Upon the death of her husband, Col. George Gibson, during one of the western expeditions against the Indians in 1791, Anne West Gibson, a member of the West family of Philadelphia merchants, struggled to preserve herself and her family while she maintained what remained of her husband's extensive landed estate in central and western Pennsylvania. Colonel Gibson, it was said, "died poor," leaving a "distressed Family." Thomas Duncan, a neighbor, friend, and advisor, observed that he did not know "in what Manner the Family are to be brought up." While he clearly respected Anne as "an industrious & managing Woman," Duncan recognized, as he acknowledged to another male friend, that in the wake of her husband's untimely death she "will have many Difficulties to encounter," not the least of which were "the Pay[men]t of his Debts" and "the Repair of the Mill."[9]

By her own testimony, the widowed Anne suffered through hard times. In a letter to another male friend and advisor in 1792, Anne outlined her situation. "Last winter my mill fell Down since which time [I] have Bought my Grain on Credit and it has taken a great quantity for a famely of 9 persons beside a large stock." Moreover, her debts continued to accumulate. Although she was "now Rebuilding the mill," she had "promis[e]d the millwrights and masons Cash when they fin[ish]," while "Every person I owe a shilling [t]o is makeing Dayly Demands." To relieve her sufferings and preserve her independence, Anne hoped to obtain a one-thousand-dollar widow's compensation from the U.S. Congress. Although she recognized fully that even with the pension she would still have to "Depen[d] [o]n my own Industry to provide for my Children," she nonetheless hoped to be able to finish rebuilding the mill that "my Dayly Bread depends on" and repay most of her family's outstanding debts.[10]

Anne Gibson faced a serious struggle against the lingering effects of wartime adversity. Yet, notably, she was willing to use her own ingenuity and labors to attain and sustain her family's autonomy. Like so many widows on the Pennsylvania frontier, Gibson was fully prepared to manage her family's farm while also taking all steps necessary to obtain relief in the public domain. When her petition before Congress was not processed promptly, for example, she pressured a politically well-connected male friend to urge those congressmen on "the side of Humanity" to make special legal provisions for "widows of the late unfortunate officers." As she saw it, a pension was a prerogative she was entitled to as an army widow: "Certainly we have as good a Right as some who have enjoyed it [a pension] long[,] for is it of more Consequence to the Publick whether a man is kill[e]d by a British or [a] savage Enemy?" On the advice of some of her late husband's Virginia friends, Anne also petitioned for compensation from the Virginia Assembly. Although "tis a long Journey for a Bad traveler," she was willing to "Exert myself for my Poor sons," Francis, George, John, and William, to make her request in person. Personal sacrifice was not an issue when the future well-being of her family was at stake. Yet Gibson's actions were nonetheless a bit paradoxical. By emphasizing the way these pension funds would literally and metaphorically "free" her from her creditors and thus ensure the future economic independence of herself and her family, Gibson, like many other backcountry widows, evidently rationalized her actions by disavowing any notion that the receipt of such funds made her a ward of the state.[11]

Most local women who petitioned for a widow's pension did so in a last-ditch effort to preserve the vestiges of their family's economic independence, but Catherine Thompson took shrewd advantage of post-war circumstances and generous pension laws to secure a compensation from the court that would guarantee her economic well-being for the rest of her life. In the early spring of 1783, Catherine, widow and "Relict" of "the honorable" William Thompson, appeared before the justices of the county court to petition for the half of her husband's military pay she was entitled to "during her Widowhood" under Pennsylvania law. Her husband, she explained, had been appointed brigadier general in the army of the united colonies in March 1776. He served faithfully until he "died in actual service," in September 1781.[12]

Catherine Thompson was not typical of Cumberland County women. Rather, at the time of her husband's death at the age of forty-five, she was one of the county's more economically and socially privileged residents. Daughter of the well-to-do Reverend George Ross of Lancaster and sister of a signer of the Declaration of Independence, in 1762, when she was twenty-three years old, Catherine Ross had married the Irish-born William Thompson. As a prominent landholder and mill owner in Cumberland County with servants and slaves to work his land, Thompson was one of many gentlemen in the backcountry who was able to provide amply for his wife, both before and after his death.[13]

Thus, the widowed Catherine had not been left to suffer as a hapless victim of wartime poverty and destitution. Survival was not at issue. Rather, her petition was meant to safeguard her status as an independent woman by guaranteeing her a financially comfortable and wholly autonomous future as a widow. The pension that the court awarded her—consisting of sizable annual payments of £281.5.0 and a hefty £421 due her in arrears—ensured that Catherine would continue to live comfortably. Indeed, in the years following she remained the proprietor of two parcels of land totaling 439 acres just outside the town of Carlisle and held at least one slave, named Jacob. Able to transport herself around the county in her stylish phaeton, Catherine made two additional court appearances, in 1784 and 1787, to renew her pension.[14] By 1790, however,

Catherine had relocated and was sending Galbreath Patterson to court on her behalf. Patterson assured the justices that even though Catherine resided in Pittsburgh, she remained William's widow and thus deserved the continuation of her pension. The court agreed, awarding £210.18.9 to Thompson in payment for three quarters. The court continued to award payments to her, on a quarterly or an annual basis, until 1794. In each court appearance, Catherine's spokesmen argued that she remained "in full life, unmarried and the Widow of the said Brigadier General." [15]

Although Catherine Thompson's pursuit of economic self-preservation was hardly exceptional among Cumberland County widows, her level of wealth and education, as well as her family's social and political connections, raised her interests to a level well above that of most women in the backcountry. As her petition for a widow's pension attests, Catherine was predominantly concerned with the conditions of her own economic freedom—in particular, the ability to continue to live in the comfortable manner to which she was accustomed. Yet, like other widows, the issue of her economic autonomy was never divorced from the larger interests of her family, and particularly of her seven children—William, George, Robert, Mary, Catherine, Juliana, and Elizabeth. Catherine sought the economic sovereignty necessary to preside as matriarch over her family. To her, as to most widows in the backcountry, her economic well-being as an individual was inseparable from the well-being of her children. [16]

The close connection between Catherine's personal interest and the collective interest of her family was most evident in her private correspondence. When her eldest son, William, an attorney in western Pennsylvania, died suddenly in 1806, Catherine wrote to his lawyer, William Orbison, being "much concerned and Surprised to hear his Affairs are so Deranged." She chided Orbison for apparently allowing others to examine her son's accounts—prompting rumors of his financial instability—but she also was most upset to hear that there was "no Possibility of Preserving the [silver] Plate or any other Effects [of the estate] for Mrs Thompson [her widowed daughter-in-law] unless She is by bond and Security to Pay for them." Indignant over the lawyer's mishandling of the case and her son's reputation, and eager to protect her personal interests and those of her family, Catherine took control of the situation. In defense of her beloved son, his widow, his children, and hence herself as his mother, she aggressively sought to protect the family's collective interest. She reminded Orbison that "Part of the Plate is mine and I may Surely with Propriety Claim it" and instructed the lawyer to "Keep it for Mrs Thompson at the Price at which it is appraised and I will be Responsible for it," adding "The Table and Bed Linnen I will also pay for." Catherine also enclosed a list of articles "which are mine which I wish you to keep for me." These articles—a carpet, a mahogany tea table, a bed, window curtains, a collection of silverware, glassware, several teapots, a coat of arms, and "his own picture" (presumably a portrait of her son)—were likely to serve not only as sentimental reminders of her son's life, but also as symbolic artifacts of a material legacy that would perpetuate the Thompsons' family history for future generations. For Catherine, the acquisition and control of these items would likely legitimate her role as family matriarch while also sustaining the long-term interests of her family.[17]

Married women's freedom, too, was affected directly and indirectly by the dislocations of war. Unlike widows, however, married women were not left as sole providers for their families. Many backcountry wives assumed temporary leadership of their households during their husbands' wartime absences, but they always remained as partners within a family unit led by a male head of household. Indeed, although evidence from inheritance patterns and personal correspondence suggests that women's authority within the family was increasing steadily during the second half of the eighteenth century, surprisingly few of the married women of Cumberland County demonstrated any overt recognition that gender relationships in the backcountry had changed in any substantial way during the Revolution. Because most wives were already accustomed to a high degree of participation in their families' fight for economic independence, women's experiences during the American Revolution did not fundamentally alter these basic expectations, but rather served to affirm them. The Revolution, and the temporarily increased authority it accorded many women, strengthened women's resolve to continue to fight for their families' collective well-being. Thus, showing few signs of becoming passive "republican mothers," the married women of Cumberland County continued to equate their self-interest with the interest of their households (albeit more intensely than in the past) and sought to safeguard their own autonomy by actively defending the economic, and specifically the property, interests of their families.[18]

As the preservation of property took on increased significance during the crisis of the Revolution, wives, like their husbands, leaped to defend their families' possessions on a moment's notice. The clash between the Mulhollan family and Robert Moore, likely provoked by war-induced economic tensions, is a good illustration. In May of 1778 Moore testified that when he went "to Distrain the Goods and Chattels" of Arthur and James Mulhollan for the rent due to their landlord, all members of the Mulhollan family—including Sarah, the wife of Neal Mulhollan—threatened him with bodily harm. Moore recounted that when he went to get the grain he had been ordered to collect, Neal Mulhollan threatened him with "a Loage [large?] Stick and Swore By God he wo[u]ld beat and Ill treat any person that wo[u]ld meddel with that Grain." Arthur and Roger Mulhollan took up farm tools and threatened Moore with bodily injury. Sarah "Swore by God She wo[u]ld Lose her Life Before any of that Grain should Go out of her house," then helped the men shove Moore out of their home and off their property, and barred the door "So that no one Could Get in again." [19]

Sarah's actions and words during the altercation are particularly significant. She clearly believed that she had an equal stake in protecting the family's resources. To Sarah, as to Neal, Arthur, and Roger Mulhollan, freedom had a precise economic context, which hinged on their ability to control their possessions collectively. After all, as tenant farmers, the Mulhollans had yet to realize the ideal state of independence that so many backcountry families coveted. The grain Moore tried to confiscate was not only the product of their combined labors, but also collateral for their future economic well-being as a family. Profits from the sale of grain, accumulated over several years or decades, offered the Mulhollans the potential to escape their dependent status. From Sarah's perspective, defending her family's possessions was not only a way to enhance her family's prospects, but also a tangible way to safeguard her own freedom as an integral part of that family unit.[20]

Other married women in the county also linked the preservation of freedom to the defense of private property. While her husband, laborer John Junks, was away in 1776, Sarah Junks purchased a cow and a calf from her neighbor, Alexander Grahams, for several pounds cash and a load of wool to be paid some months later. Backcountry wives engaged regularly in such economic exchanges, so this transaction was not unusual, but Grahams's attempt to collect his debt was. Sarah had paid him thirty shillings and two pounds of wool three months after their exchange. Nearly a year later, Grahams appeared at Junks's house to call in the remaining debt. Sarah was again alone while her husband was away serving in the militia. As she described it, Grahams confronted her, demanding the rest of the purchase price. When Sarah explained that she did not have the money because her husband had not yet received his summer wages, Grahams "pulled out his Pocket Book and opened it and counted some Money," and "came to her and put it into her hand." He then tossed more money into her lap, saying "there's your Money and y[ou]r Note and the Cow's mine Damn you." As he stormed out of her house, Sarah ran after him, flinging the money back at him. Infuriated, Grahams "Damn[e]d" her as an "old Bitch," and twice knocked her down. After the tussle, he left with the livestock. "Since that time," Sarah had "not Seen Said Cow, Heifer or Calf nor does She know Where they are." [21]

It was common practice for accounts in the county to go unsettled for a year or more, so the reason for the intensity of Grahams's attack on Sarah is something of a mystery. We do know that he was frustrated at the worsening state of the wartime economy. When Sarah told him she only awaited the receipt of her husband's militia pay to close the debt, for example, Grahams retorted that "that was always the cry to keep him out of his Money." [22] Yet, in this heated exchange between neighbors, there are hints that Sarah's gender may have heightened the severity of Grahams's attack. His physical assault and his derogatory and suggestive reference to her as an "old Bitch" may indicate not only anger, but also an attack upon her womanhood.

Although Grahams's motives remain unclear, Sarah Junks was certainly incensed by his behavior. In his assault on her property and her person, he infringed upon her economic autonomy and violated her liberty. Once Grahams fled, Junks took the dispute to court and had him brought up on charges of assault and battery. Yet, Junks was also willing to fight like a man to defend her possessions and her independence. To this backcountry woman, virtue was not yet equated with the kind of quiet, "feminine" resolution and purity that Ruth Bloch has described. Rather, virtue was manifested through a defiant, "masculine" display of courage, conviction, and physical resistance. Much like any eighteenth-century male head of household, Sarah Junks saw herself as the principal defender of her family's collective economic interest.[23]

It was no coincidence that in the era of the American Revolution issues of economic rights and the defense of private property overshadowed many women's lives. War dislocations provoked the kinds of family crises that brought many women, especially widows, into the legal domain of the courts to seek redress of their grievances. While the actions and words of these female petitioners suggest that there was some consensus on the general principles, values, or economic conditions that constituted freedom, neither before, during, nor after the Revolution did all women agree on how best to achieve these objectives. As the diversity of their requests attests, women employed a variety of methods in their petitions, inspired by their differing needs and circumstances. Aside from their obvious desire to attain or protect their freedom, these female petitioners also shared an apparent willingness to work within established institutions and traditional gender boundaries to achieve their goals. Freedom had its gendered bounds, even in the backcountry. None of these women sought overtly to challenge the socioeconomic system of which they were an integral part. Rather, in their requests for assistance or compensation, they sought only to maximize their gains from it.

For some women, the court clearly delineated the extent of those limits. Elizabeth Pattison came before the justices of the Cumberland County Orphan's Court in 1778 to present her petition for compensation from her husband's estate. Charles, she explained, had died intestate in June 1771, leaving her pregnant and with three young children to care for. "Eight weeks after the decease of said Charles she was delivered of a son whom she had Called John." Because "her lying in was Expensive to her" and because "she had maintained Cloathed and Educated her said Children ever Since" her husband's death, she asked the court to "allow her a Reasonable compensation for her Expenses" to be deducted from the shares of the estate reserved for each child. By Elizabeth's own measure, she had gone beyond the duties expected of any widowed wife and mother. As she explained to the justices, at the time of her husband's death, he had possessed two lots in the town of Carlisle and two farming plots just outside. On one of the town lots "he had Laid Logs to Raise the House another Story," but he died before this work could be completed. Elizabeth finished constructing the second story and put a new roof on it. She also completed the barn that her husband had begun to raise, and cleared and fenced one of his outlots, which was partly "grub" at the time of his death. All of these activities, she emphasized, while in the best interests of the estate, were completed at considerable personal expense to her, endangering her financial well-being. Because the rents and profits of the lots were not enough to cover the expenses these improvements had cost her, Elizabeth sought reimbursement from the estate. Her economic freedom as a widow, she clearly believed, had been encroached upon by the financial demands of her children's care and the excessive oversight her husband's estate demanded.[24]

We know little about the Elizabeth Pattison who presented her petition before the court that day in 1778, but we do know something of the Pattison family's existence in the county seat of Carlisle. Members of the Pattison family were among the town's earliest inhabitants, appearing as heads of households on the town's first tax assessment in 1753. Though a shoemaker, Charles was nonetheless a reasonably affluent man by frontier standards. As the owner of both an indentured servant and a slave, Charles's taxable property totaled some eight pounds in 1768, placing him in the top 20 percent of the town's taxpayers.[25] Because of the Pattisons reasonably comfortable financial status, we can assume not only that Elizabeth had relatively high expectations of what her life as a widow should be like, but also that she may have expected that she would continue to promote her family's economic mobility after her husband's death. The Pattisons were one of many aspiring families in the backcountry, and as Charles's actions testify, much of their attention and energy had focused on maintaining and improving their property—a practice Elizabeth carried on after his death.

Unfortunately for Elizabeth, when the court's three male auditors returned in February 1779 to report on their inquiry into her situation, they did not express unequivocal accord with her protestations of economic frustration. They adjudged that shares totaling £280 should be deducted from each child's estate for Elizabeth's "Expences and Trouble for maintaining Cloathing and Educating" each child since her husband's death. The auditors further reported, however, that "on due Examination," they found that "the Rents, Issues [and] Profits ariseing from the Lots ... Exceed the Expences which ... Elizabeth hath laid out in Repairs on the Same." Elizabeth was told she owed the estate £93.10.6.[26]

Unlike Elizabeth Pattison, some women in the county were wholly unconcerned about their authority over property or pension. Because of hardships imposed by the ravages of war, age, or illness, these women were more interested in finding a dependable male provider. Widow Isabel Neily is an example of one woman who was willing to accept some measure of dependency in exchange for a more secure economic future. The years of the American Revolution had brought enough relocation, family disruption, and economic hardship to undermine Neily's sense of personal well-being and to challenge her notions of feminine responsibility. In a petition for clemency brought before Pennsylvania's Executive Council in 1780, Neily described her wartime plight and begged state officials for indulgence in resolving her predicament. Neily, like other backcountry widows, agreed that freedom had an economic context, determined by the attainment of some basic level of financial security. Yet, in contrast to so many of her married and widowed counterparts who expressed pride in their capacities as autonomous women, Neily made no claim to being a competent widowed provider. Rather, her plea for compassion and her expressions of dependence suggested that she had a very different interpretation of how to acquire and maintain economic freedom.

Sometime before the war, the widowed Neily had "removed" herself and her two youngest children, John and Rachel, then fourteen and ten years old, respectively, from one hundred acres of "poor Land" to "better" land taken up by her oldest son, David, in the remote northwestern reaches of the county. Sometime in 1778, after several war-provoked Indian uprisings nearby, Neily and her children were "obliged to fly" from their new home on the frontier and return to their former residence. When a neighbor "Set up a Claim to Part of Their Land," a series of confrontations ensued, resulting in several fist fights. During one altercation, Neily's son beat the neighbor to death and was later convicted of manslaughter. After pleading benefit of clergy, he was "burn'd" on his left thumb with the letter "M" and jailed for six months (or until all costs of his prosecution were paid).[27]

Neily's story is a sad commentary on the Revolution's effects on many families living on the outer reaches of Pennsylvania's frontier. It also offers insight into how some women in the backcountry, particularly older women, sought to secure their freedom only within the most traditional limits of feminine existence. Portraying herself as powerless and infirm, Neily petitioned the Pennsylvania Council "to remit the Confinement of her Son that he may labour to procure Bread for his aged . . . Mother and af[f]licted Sister." While Indian raids had forced Neily and her children to flee the frontier for the refuge of their lands near Carlisle, the subsequent absence of her imprisoned son only worsened the situation. Without him to run the farm, Neily and her daughter were left helpless and destitute. Neily even implied that being women rendered them incapable of maintaining the property. In her son's absence, she noted, "the procuring of Firewood and taking Care of my two Cows and an old Mare and an Horse [had] devolved on my Daughter." In carrying out these chores, "she got Colds by which she has contracted female Disorders which your Petitioner expects will terminate in her Death," Neily added, implying that "man's work" had resulted in her daughter's "female" illnesses. According to Neily, her own and her family's future well-being was precarious at best. What "little Wheat and Rye which your Petitioner had growing . . . is almost destroyed by Creatures." Furthermore, without the labor of her son, "she has no Spring Crop in the Ground, nor a Way to procure any Person to fallow the Grains for Fall Crop." Her "temporal Circumstances" in ruin, Neily asked the Council to free her son from jail so that he could farm the family's land and earn the money necessary to preserve the economic autonomy of his aged mother and infirm sister.[28]

Neily's petition depicted female freedom in its most limited and gendered context. Women, and widows in particular, Neily believed, were entitled to an adequate financial competence. Yet, unlike most women, Neily was not only unable, but likely unwilling to labor outside the immediate confines of her home to secure that autonomy. Limited by her physical circumstances, economic freedom was a goal to be met only within precisely delineated gender boundaries. An aged widow like herself was not to be expected to engage in tasks outside the realm of her traditional domestic duties as wife and mother. She was entitled to have an able-bodied man—her son in this case—provide the basic necessities of life for her. Nor could her young daughter serve as a long-term substitute. Farm labor had, after all, brought on her mysterious "female Disorders."

Isabel Neily sought to ensure her freedom. Yet her notions of how best to achieve that posed no threat to the increasingly status-conscious men who composed the county's male elite. Neily did not assert her independence, but rather her utter dependence and subordination. Though Neily, like other widows, expected to enjoy a modest existence with her children, free from significant want or worry, she acknowledged a desperate need for a man to furnish this economic existence for her. In contrast to other backcountry petitioners, Neily asserted no spirit of self-reliance, but rather displayed a stereotypically feminine brand of helplessness. Whether as a frustrated expression of her limited physical capacities, as a representation of her genuine convictions, or as a conscious strategy to strengthen her petition's chances for approval, Neily's portrayal of herself as needy and helpless confirmed women's customary role as dependents.

Similar expectations were expressed by some younger married women as well. In May 1790 Philip DeLancey of Cumberland County placed a notice in the *Carlisle Gazette*, announcing to his neighbors that because "there has been and still subsists a misunderstanding between me and Margaret my wife," no one should issue her credit on his account.[29] DeLancey's notice seemed like a typical bed and board separation announcement until some seven months later, when in January 1791 his wife, Margaret, posted a reply in the newspaper. "I think it reasonable," she began, that "the public should know the real cause I had for leaving him; (although a quire of paper would scarce contain the many miserable abuses I have received from him by blows from his fists and kickings from his feet)." Philip, Margaret asserted, was an abusive husband. On one occasion "a blow from his fist" broke one of her ribs, and his continued mauling "cracked" her skull. He also "frequently would bid God to damn all woman[ly] flesh," referring to women as "earthly devil[s]." "Many time[s]," Margaret added, he "has swore he would murder me."

But Margaret was bothered by more than repeated beatings and cursings. She felt that her husband's cruelty severely curtailed her autonomy as a wife and mother. Philip forced her to "wrought plantation work like a man"—making her tend to the livestock and work in the fields—and "tasked her" to "assist in quarrying stone," while he "set at home by his favorite stove" and "curse[d] and imprecate[d] shocking expressions" when rain kept her from completing her chores. Occupied during the day with what she saw as men's work, Margaret was forced to perform her female domestic duties, such as spinning, "after night," leaving her tired and frustrated. In an especially memorable incident during one harvest, Philip had even hampered her ability to care for their children. Although her second child was so ill "that life was hardly expected from it," Philip made Margaret work the fields with him. As the field they were harvesting was near their house and the child was inside alone, Margaret stopped work repeatedly to tend to the child. Philip, she said, "damned" her for her actions, and "said that I loved the child better than the grain, to which I answered I did." He then "swore" her "a fool," reminding her that they "could live without the child but not without the grain."

Aside from infringing on her roles as wife and mother, Margaret also argued, Philip was not fulfilling his legal responsibilities as husband. She held that by periodically refusing to provide adequate nourishment for his wife and children, he was in effect violating his duty as the economic head of their household. "When grain was plenty in his house," she explained, Philip "would not permit any to be sent to mill to be ground." Instead, he "kept me and his children for six weeks without either bread or meal." [30] Philip, therefore, had not only forced her to transgress the bounds of her gender, he had also greatly exceeded the limits of his own.

Philip DeLancey's cruel conduct shattered Margaret's sense of well-being and undermined her sense of freedom. Although she did not deny him the legal right to make economic decisions for the family as the male head of household, she believed that his masculine authority required him to carry out certain functions within their family. His actions—and particularly his unwillingness to act as provider for his family—fractured the bond of mutual cooperation (and perhaps love) that once had held their household together and thus violated the bounds of her liberty as his wife and as mother to their children. Both as a woman and as an integral member of her family unit, Margaret felt she was entitled to the provisions of a decent livelihood. Like most backcountry women, she expected to be able to carry out her duties to home and family free from significant economic want or worry. Being beaten, half-starved, and forced to do "man's work" did not enter into her, or any other woman's, definition of freedom. In abandoning her marriage, Margaret did not challenge male authority, but only the legitimacy of her husband's conduct.

By concluding that she would leave it up to "a candid public to judge whether they [these reasons] were sufficient" cause to leave her husband, Margaret DeLancey suggested that there was some general consensus on how freedom was defined for women in the Pennsylvania backcountry.[31] Indeed, her belief was not without a basis in reality, for in all of the diverse petitions and protests presented by the many widows and wives of Cumberland County during the second half of the eighteenth century, local women implied again and again that they generally agreed upon many of the ideals, principles, or conditions that constituted freedom. To most backcountry women, freedom had a largely economic context, which was linked directly to the kind of economic autonomy that accompanied the achievement of independence. In this context freedom was equated with the ability to live a financially secure existence. Yet, freedom also had other, more gendered, overtones, even in the backcountry. Whether rich, middling, or poor, backcountry women consistently connected their personal autonomy—or freedom—to that of their family, and particularly their children. For them, the ability to live independently not only as women, but also as mothers, was essential. Though many widows and wives in Cumberland County expected to assume responsibility for their families' economic well-being, these duties, as the protests of Isabel Neily and Margaret DeLancey suggest, also had limits. During an era when talk of freedom punctuated the nation's political discourse, the women of Cumberland County clearly sought to obtain economic and personal security, their "freedom," by working within traditional gender bounds, within the bonds of marriage, and within the broader institutional framework of the backcountry to achieve their goals.

NOTES

1. Isabella Bell, Petition for a Tavern License, March 1802, Hotel and Tavern Licenses, Cumberland County Historical Society, Carlisle, Pa. (hereafter cited as CCHS). In *Republica v. Isabella Bell,* March Sessions 1802, Bell was indicted, convicted, and fined for keeping a "Tipling House." See Cumberland County Court of Quarter Sessions, docket 9, 162, Cumberland County Court House, Carlisle, Pa. (hereafter cited as CCCH).

2. The historical development of the backcountry has been steeped in a mystique of expectation and optimism. From Frederick Jackson Turner's "The Significance of the Frontier in American History," in *The Frontier in American History,* by Turner (New York: H. Holt, 1920), 1–38, to the more recent writings of such scholars as Joan E. Cashin, *A Family Venture: Men and Women on the Southern Frontier* (New York: Oxford University Press, 1991), 34–36, 101; Christopher Clark, *The Roots of Rural Capitalism: Western Massachusetts, 1780–1860* (Ithaca: Cornell University Press, 1990), 21–38; Jack Greene, "Independence, Improvement, and Authority: Toward a Framework for Understanding the Histories of the Southern Backcountry during the Era of the American Revolution," in *An Uncivil War: The Southern Backcountry during the American Revolution,* edited by Ronald Hoffman, Thad Tate, and Peter Albert (Charlottesville: University Press of Virginia, 1985), 31; Allan Kulikoff, *The Agrarian Origins of American Capitalism* (Charlottesville: University Press of Virginia, 1992), 75–77; and Alan Taylor, *Liberty Men and Great Proprietors: The Revolutionary Settlement on the Maine Frontier, 1760–1820* (Chapel Hill: University of North Carolina Press, 1990), 1–10, historians have suggested that settlers moved to the frontier because they hoped to better themselves in some noticeable way—they hoped to achieve independence. Scholars most often define *independence* in an economic sense, explaining how, by moving from the status of dependent tenant farmers in the East to that of independent freeholders—or "yeoman farmers"—in the West, westward-migrating settlers thereby came to control fully the agricultural means of production. For the early history of Cumberland County, see George P. Donehoo, *A History of the Cumberland Valley in Pennsylvania,* 2 vols. (Harrisburg: Susquehanna History Association, 1930), 1:259; Milton E. Flower and Lenore E. Flower, *This Is Carlisle: A History of a Pennsylvania Town* (Harrisburg, Pa.: J. Horace McFarland Co., 1944), 2–30; Frederic A. Godcharles, *Chronicles of Central Pennsylvania,* 4 vols. (New York: Lewis Historical Publishing Co., 1944), 2:94–95; *History of Cumberland and Adams Counties, Pennsylvania* (Chicago: Warner, Beers, 1886), 4–37, 66–70, 208–62.

3. For the legal status of early American women, see Mary Beth Norton, *Liberty's Daughters: The Revolutionary Experience of American Women, 1750–1800* (Boston: Little, Brown, 1980), chap. 2; Marylynn Salmon, *Women and the Law of Property in Early America* (Chapel Hill: University of North Carolina Press, 1986), chaps. 1 and 7.

4. Joan M. Jensen, *Loosening the Bonds: Mid-Atlantic Farm Women, 1750–1850* (New Haven, Conn.: Yale University Press, 1986), 43, 79; Mary M. Schweitzer, *Custom and Contract: Household, Government, and the Economy in Colonial Pennsylvania* (New York: Columbia University Press, 1987), 21–35; Carole Shammas, "Early American Women and Control over Capital," in *Women in the Age of the American Revolution*, edited by Ronald Hoffman and Peter Albert (Charlottesville: University Press of Virginia, 1989), 134–54. Shammas speculates that early American women had a rather ambivalent relationship to capitalism. I would suggest that on the early American frontier this relationship was more direct. See also Julie Roy Jeffrey, *Frontier Women: The Trans-Mississippi West, 1840–1880* (New York: Hill and Wang, 1979), chap. 3.

5. The diversity of Pennsylvania's rural economy has been well documented by several scholars. See Paul G. E. Clemens and Lucy Simler, "Rural Labor and the Farm Household in Chester County, Pennsylvania, 1750–1800," in *Work and Labor in Early America*, edited by Stephen Innes (Chapel Hill: University of North Carolina Press, 1988), 110–12; James T. Lemon, *The Best Poor Man's Country: A Geographical Study of Early Southeastern Pennsylvania* (Baltimore: Johns Hopkins University Press, 1972), 118–40; Schweitzer, *Custom and Contract*, 67–80. For women's role in that diversification, see Jensen, *Loosening the Bonds*, 79; Mary P. Ryan, *Cradle of the Middle Class: The Family in Oneida County, New York, 1790–1865* (New York: Cambridge University Press, 1981), 27; Billy G. Smith, *The "Lower Sort": Philadelphia's Laboring People, 1750–1800* (Ithaca: Cornell University Press, 1990), 185. For women's role as backcountry shoppers, see Elizabeth A. Perkins, "The Consumer Frontier: Household Consumption in Early Kentucky," *Journal of American History* 78, no. 2 (1991):486–510. Women's participation as consumers in Cumberland County strongly supports Perkins's argument and challenges Daniel B. Thorp's picture of backcountry retail life in "Doing Business in the Backcountry: Retail Trade in Colonial Rowan County, North Carolina," *William and Mary Quarterly*, 3d ser., 48, no. 3 (1991):387–408. For specific evidence of women's shopping (and borrowing money) in Cumberland County, see the Samuel Postlethwaite Ledger, 1760–78; Anonymous Account Book 2, Ledger, Carlisle, 1769–70; and Anonymous Account Book 3, Daybook, Carlisle, 1790–92—all found in the James Hamilton Papers, Historical Society of Pennsylvania, Philadelphia, Pa. (hereafter cited as HSP).

6. Several scholars have suggested that in the earliest stages of frontier settlement and development gender bounds were transgressed temporarily and patriarchy undermined for a time. See, for example, Susan C. Boyle, "Did She Generally Decide? Women in Ste. Genevieve, 1750–1805," *William and Mary Quarterly*, 3d ser., 44, no. 4 (1987):785–87; Lois Green Carr and Lorena S. Walsh, "The Planter's Wife: The Experience of White Women in Seventeenth-Century Maryland," *William and Mary Quarterly*, 3d ser., 34, no. 4 (1977):542–71; Ryan, *Cradle of the Middle Class*, 20–22. In contrast, I have found that some of these patterns—

especially in the economic sphere—persisted well past Cumberland County's beginnings as a frontier settlement. Indeed, as Linda K. Kerber suggests in "Separate Spheres, Female Worlds, Woman's Place: The Rhetoric of Women's History," *Journal of American History* 75, no. 1 (1988):9–39, public and private spheres may not have been as separate and distinct as many historians have thought. Kerber's views are well supported by Lisa Wilson, *Life after Death: Widows in Pennsylvania, 1750–1850* (Philadelphia: Temple University Press, 1992).

7. Clark, *Roots of Rural Capitalism*, 21–38; Greene, "Independence, Improvement, and Authority," 31; Taylor, *Liberty Men and Great Proprietors*, 1–10. The notion that female conceptions of freedom were closely connected to male interests in property is supported in part by Jeffrey, *Frontier Women*, chap. 3; and Wilson, *Life after Death*, 5–6. In contrast, Cashin, *A Family Venture*, 108–12, argues that the quest for independence drove an often irreparable psychological wedge between many husbands and wives.

8. Petition of Elizabeth Ross, Feb. 21, 1787, Cumberland County Orphan's Court, docket 3, 18, CCCH.

9. Thomas Duncan to William Irvine, Feb. 1792, 10:127, Brigadier General William Irvine Papers (hereafter cited as Irvine Papers), HSP. For information about Anne West Gibson and her husband, George, see William H. Egle, *Some Pennsylvania Women during the War of the Revolution* (Harrisburg, Pa.: Harrisburg Publishing Co., 1898), 70–72.

10. Anne Gibson to William Irvine, June 14, 1792, 11:15, Irvine Papers, HSP.

11. Anne Gibson to William Irvine, Oct. 28, 1792, 11:35, Irvine Papers, HSP.

12. Petition of Catherine Thompson, Mar. 1, 1783, William Thompson Papers, CCHS. For the presentation of her petition in court, see Cumberland County Orphan's Court, docket 2, April 23, 1783, 323, CCCH. Although Catherine claimed that William "died in actual service," he had actually died some years after his return from a lengthy imprisonment by the British in Canada. Thompson had been captured in the summer of 1776, following an unsuccessful American attempt to capture the British post at Three Rivers on the St. Lawrence River. Though he was not officially exchanged until October 25, 1780, he had been placed on parole and returned to Pennsylvania by 1778. For information on William Thompson, see *The Dictionary of American Biography*, 2d ed., s.v. William Thompson. Catherine was evidently responding to the supplement of the law entitled "An Act to settle and Adjust the Accounts of the Troops of this State, in the Service of the United States, and for other purposes therein mentioned," passed October 1, 1781. See James T. Mitchell and Henry Flanders, eds., *The Statutes at Large of Pennsylvania from 1682 to 1801*, 32 vols. (Harrisburg: C. M. Busch, State Printer of Pennsylvania, 1896–1919), 10:372. Section 4 states that "the widows and children of the officers of the said regiments, ... who have fallen in battle or died in captivity, shall be and are hereby entitled to receive the half pay of such officers from and since the time of their death."

13. For information about Catherine and William Thompson, see Egle, *Some Pennsylvania Women*, 189–91.

14. "Negro Jacob" was the slave named in Catherine Thompson's will of 1808, in which she stated: "It is my will and desire that Negro Jacob shall at my decease become free" — presumably as a reward for a long period of service. See will of Catherine Thompson, Lycoming County, Pennsylvania, Mar. 8, 1808, William Thompson Papers, CCHS. For information about Catherine Thompson's material status, see Cumberland County Tax Rates, Middleton Township, 1787, CCHS.

15. Cumberland County Orphan's Court, docket 3, Sept. 13, 1792, 108, CCCH. For Catherine Thompson's many appearances in court after 1783, see Orphan's Court, docket 2, April 23, 1784, 240; docket 3, Sept. 28, 1787, 34; April 27, 1790, 73; July 18, 1791, 92; Feb. 16, 1792, 101; Sept. 13, 1792, 108; April 6, 1793, 111; Aug. 6, 1793, 117; Sept. 10, 1793, 118; Feb. 11, 1794, 131; May 14, 1794, 141. Catherine was one of a small number of women in the county who bequeathed large amounts of property to their heirs. With a 287–acre tract called "Liberty," a ninety-eight-acre tract referred to as "Sugar Bottoms," and another three hundred acres known as "Chatsworth" in Westmoreland County, Thompson remained an exceptionally well-situated woman even at her death. See will of Catherine Thompson, Mar. 8, 1808, William Thompson Papers, CCHS. For examples of other women in the county who deeded real estate to their heirs, see will of Margaret Cummins, Cumberland County Wills, book D, Aug. 14, 1779, 97–100, CCCH; will of Margaret Douglass, Wills, book G, Sept. 3, 1804, 39–40, CCCH; will of Mary Sanderson, Wills, book G, Oct. 9, 1805, 59–60, CCCH; will of Catharine Russ, Wills, book G, Aug. 24, 1806, 182, CCCH; will of Hannah Collier, Wills, book G, Oct. 25, 1804, 256–57, CCCH; will of Ellenor Pollock, Wills, book H, Aug. 29, 1808, 32, CCCH.

16. In this respect Thompson was much like Lisa Wilson's Chester County widows. See Wilson, *Life after Death*, 1–9.

17. Catherine Thompson to William Orbison, Jan. 24, 1806, William Thompson Papers, CCHS. In another letter William Orbison (very likely a relative of Catherine's son-in-law, James Orbison) replied rather defensively to Catherine's charges. Although he largely defended his handling of her son's business affairs, he conceded her claim to the household goods, remarking "your claim to the plate . . . shall be duly attended to." See William Orbison to Catherine Thompson, Feb. 14, 1806, in the William Thompson Papers, CCHS. There is evidence to suggest that the intensity of Catherine's response to Orbison was likely a reflection of the fact that William was the only one of her sons who had not proven to be a disappointment. In a letter Maria (Mary) Thompson Reed wrote to her brother William Thompson in 1804, she warned her brother to watch his "Delicate Constitution," because "Our Dear Mother . . . how much must she be affected should any thing Befal you: So Unhappy has she been in all her Sons but

you . . . may not her Gray hairs yet go Down in Sorrow to the Grave." See Maria Thompson Reed to William Thompson, May 5, 1804, William Thompson Papers, CCHS.

18. My interpretation contrasts somewhat with the arguments presented by Linda K. Kerber in *Women of the Republic: Intellect and Ideology in Revolutionary America* (Chapel Hill: University of North Carolina Press, 1980), 11–12, 199–200, 269–88; and Norton, *Liberty's Daughters,* 228–99. For the development of my argument, I am indebted in part to the work of Joan Hoff-Wilson, "The Illusion of Change: Women and the American Revolution," in *The American Revolution: Explorations in the History of American Radicalism,* edited by Alfred F. Young (DeKalb: Northern Illinois University Press, 1976), 383–446. For more general information about the changes taking place in Cumberland County marriages during the second half of the eighteenth century, see Judith A. Ridner, " 'A Handsomely Improved Place': Economic, Social, and Gender-Role Development in a Backcountry Town, Carlisle, Pennsylvania, 1750–1810," (Ph.D. diss., College of William and Mary, 1994), esp. chap. 6.

19. Testimony of Robert Moore before John Agnew, May 19, 1778, John Agnew Papers, CCHS.

20. Even after being indicted, convicted, and fined on charges of assault and battery on Moore, the Mulhollans remained convinced of the righteousness of their actions and protested their innocence to the court. See *Pennsylvania v. Henry Mulhollan, Roger Mulhollan, Arthur Mulhollan, Sarah Mulhollan, and Neal Mulhollan,* July Sessions 1778, Court of Quarter Sessions, docket 6, 49–50, CCCH.

21. Testimony of Sarah Junks before John Agnew, Mar. 13, 1777, John Agnew Papers, CCHS.

22. Testimony of Sarah Junks before John Agnew, Mar. 13, 1777, John Agnew Papers, CCHS.

23. Testimony of Sarah Junks before John Agnew, Mar. 13, 1777, John Agnew Papers, CCHS. See also *Pennsylvania v. Alexander Grahams,* April Sessions 1778, Court of Quarter Sessions, docket 6, 29, CCCH. Although it is not clear how the case was finally resolved, Grahams was indicted for assault and battery, and Sarah Junks was called to testify before the next session of the court. For the evolution of the multifaceted meanings of *virtue* during the late eighteenth century, see Ruth Bloch, "The Gendered Meanings of Virtue in Revolutionary America," *Signs* 13, no. 1 (1987):37–58. For examples of the length of time it often took to settle accounts in Cumberland County, see the Samuel Postlethwaite Ledger, 1760–78; and Anonymous Account Book 2, Ledger, Carlisle, 1769–70, in the James Hamilton Papers, HSP.

24. Petition of Elizabeth Pattison, Nov. 18, 1778, Orphan's Court, docket 2, 232, CCCH.

25. For information about the Pattisons, see Cumberland County Deeds, book 2A, 300–302, CCCH. See also entries for John and Charles Patteson, Tax Rates,

Carlisle, 1753, 1764, 1768, CCHS; and Merri Lou Schaumann, "A History and Genealogy of Carlisle, Cumberland County, Pennsylvania, 1751–1835" (Dover, Pennsylvania, photocopy, 1987), 216.

26. Report of Robert Miller, John Pollock, and Samuel Laird, Feb. 18, 1779, Orphan's Court, docket 2, 251, CCCH. For Elizabeth the court's ruling must have generated mixed emotions. Although she came away with a net gain of some £180, she suffered a decline in her financial status in the decade or more that she remained in Carlisle, falling into the seventh decile of wealth holders by 1779 and remaining there in 1787. It is not clear whether her loss of status was due to her widowhood or to the economic effects of the American Revolution. Despite any hardships she may have suffered, Elizabeth raised her two eldest sons, Charles and George, to be prosperous local artisans. See Tax Rates, Carlisle, 1779, 1782, CCHS. For information about Charles Pattison, carpenter, and George Pattison, Esq., saddler, see Tax Rates, Carlisle, 1787–1800, CCHS.

27. Petition of Isabel Neily to the Supreme Executive Council of Pennsylvania, Aug. 25, 1780, Records of Pennsylvania's Revolutionary Government, Clemency Files, 28–30, available on microfilm at the David Library of the American Revolution, Washington Crossing, Pa. The "poor land" Neily refers to was likely the land blacksmith James Thompson granted to Andrew Steel and Robert Morrison in April 1774—John Neily's heirs are mentioned as occupants at this time. See Cumberland County Deeds, book D, 206–7, CCCH. Neily and her family likely relocated to 306 acres in Armagh Township at the east end of the Kishoquillas Valley. See Deeds, book E, 82–84, CCCH. After Neily's husband, John, died intestate, she came before the justices of the county Orphan's Court to report her account of the administration of the estate, listing herself and six children as the beneficiaries of her husband's small estate—amounting to only twenty pounds. See Orphan's Court, docket 2, May 18, 1773, 177.

28. Petition of Isabel Neily to the Supreme Executive Council of Pennsylvania, Aug. 25, 1780, Records of Pennsylvania's Revolutionary Government, Clemency Files, 28–30, microfilm, David Library of the American Revolution, Washington Crossing, Pa.

29. *Carlisle Gazette*, May 12, 1790. For a comprehensive analysis of such bed and board separation notices, see Merril D. Smith, *Breaking the Bonds: Marital Discord in Pennsylvania, 1730–1830* (New York: New York University Press, 1991), 139–55.

30. *Carlisle Gazette*, Jan. 6, 1791.

31. *Carlisle Gazette*, Jan. 6, 1791.

10 Women and Economic Freedom in the North Carolina Backcountry

JOHANNA MILLER LEWIS

When the first settlers rambled down the Great Wagon Road into the backcountry of North Carolina in the mid-eighteenth century, they were far removed from the staple crop, plantation economy and culture for which the colonial South was famous. The backcountry was that area of the South located "in back" or west of the first coastal settlements in the region; it ran toward (and later into) the Appalachian mountains. More than distance separated the coastal South from the backcountry. Because of the different geography, the two areas were, in fact, almost complete opposites.

Although settlement of the southern colonies gradually progressed inland as the coast became full, this tide of settlement never really reached the backcountry in North Carolina.[1] For as settlers moved west, the hills, the lack of navigable rivers, and the different (albeit fertile) soil type made the area unsuitable for staple crop agriculture.[2] Without the plantation system, the strong economic ties of the southern coastal cities to England, and the higher standard of living, which resulted from a trans-Atlantic economy, the backcountry did not attract the same type of people, or the same number of people, who settled the eastern areas of the South.

In fact, as early accounts document, the first handful of people who wandered into the backcountry were either unsuccessful former inhabitants of coastal areas or too poor even to have attempted living on the coast.[3] When William Byrd II, a member of the Virginia gentry, visited the North Carolina backcountry in 1728 to help survey the dividing line between that colony and Virginia, he was appalled to find "the wretchedest Scene of Poverty I had ever met with in this happy Part of the World."[4] Yet, in the midst of his bleak portrayal of these early backcountry settlers, Byrd acknowledged one bright spot: "the Distemper of Laziness seizes the Men oftener much then the Women. These last Spin, weave and knit, all with their own Hands, while their Husbands, depending on the Bounty of the Climate, are Sloathfull in everything but getting of Children."[5] For female settlers the frontier conditions in the backcountry provided a challenge absent from the civilized plantations and towns of the coastal South, and some women found opportunity in that challenge. One historian observed that "the frontiersman's remoteness from the waterways and highways and his lack of a marketable staple crop prevented his trading much with the outside world and made it necessary for him and his wife to provide almost everything consumed in their household." Such a life, however, created "superior women ... strong, daring, and self-reliant, as well as skillful and industrious."[6]

Those few early stragglers who meandered into the backcountry from the east never made up a substantial portion of the frontier population. By contrast, the later settlers to the backcountry, male and female alike, sensed the challenge of the wilderness and moved to the region in ever-increasing numbers, not out of desperation, as the first settlers had, but out of hope for the future. In much the same way that geography discouraged staple crop planters from an east-west migration into the backcountry, it encouraged settlers migrating west from southeastern Pennsylvania to head south when they ran into mountain ranges that literally funneled them down the Shenandoah Valley of Virginia and into what became Rowan County, North Carolina, by 1753.

Who were these people who came to the backcountry of North Carolina, and why did they come? Because of the port of Philadelphia, southeastern Pennsylvania served as a major source of immigrants from Scotland, Ireland, Germany, and England. Advancing land prices and the rapid diminution of unoccupied land in the hinterlands of Philadelphia led to the opening up of new areas and the rapid spread of Middle Colony settlement patterns into the backcountry. Between 1730 and 1760, as southeastern Pennsylvania exploded in terms of population growth, rate of occupation, and the organization of new counties, towns, and trade, many new people moved west and then south into Maryland, Virginia, and North Carolina.[7]

The first wave of settlers reached Anson County in the North Carolina backcountry in the late 1740s. Since they were not recent immigrants to the New World (they had already lived in Pennsylvania, New Jersey, Maryland, or Virginia), many of the settlers already knew each other, traveled together, and decided to live as neighbors in the backcountry. Consequently, the earliest backcountry settlements maintained the ethnic flavor of the groups who founded them: English, Scotch-Irish, and German.[8] By 1752 enough people lived in northern Anson County to petition the colonial legislature to create a new county with a more conveniently located courthouse.[9] Named after Governor Matthew Rowan and covering the entire northwest quadrant of the colony, Rowan County became the largest county in North Carolina at its formation in 1753.[10]

If a foreign visitor to the thirteen colonies stumbled into Rowan County in the 1750s or 1760s, he might very well have thought he was in southeastern Pennsylvania. The gently rolling landscape dotted with small to midsize farms; a county seat at the crossroads of two main thoroughfares, featuring a courthouse and jail, taverns, and stores; and a diverse population of European extraction, speaking various dialects of English as well as German—all could mislead the visitor. In essence, Rowan County was Pennsylvania "hearth culture" transplanted to the South.[11]

At first glance the only opportunity this landscape seemed to offer women was one for hard work, especially in the earliest years of settlement. As in Pennsylvania, the wives and daughters of the male landowners were responsible for all of the household or domestic chores, while husbands and fathers worked the land, improved it with houses, barns, and fences, and maybe practiced a trade in the "off hours." In the early years of the county, before Salisbury, the county seat, developed into the economic center of the county, complete with artisans, specialty shops, and general merchandise stores, the workload for women and men was daunting. The description of frontiersmen and their wives having to make everything they consumed was not far from the truth. Not only did the settlers have to carry out their everyday responsibilities, including cooking, gardening, butchering, sewing, milking, and so on, but they also had to repair anything that broke and improvise necessary tools and equipment, because replacement items and specialty goods were difficult if not impossible to procure.

Though the "subsistence frontier" most certainly existed during the first years of settlement, economic specialization and commercialism was not far behind. For instance, even though permanent agriculture stood at the forefront of Rowan's economy, other activities soon supplemented commercial farming. When Rowan became a county, people lined up at court for licenses to provide basic goods and services to the newest arrivals and visitors. Taverns offered overnight accommodations, meals, and intoxicating spirits to weary travelers, and ferries allowed them more expeditious ways to cross the backcountry's many streams and rivers.

Further economic specialization in the county depended on the growth of both the population and agriculture. Additional farms and higher crop yields paved the way for commercial agriculture. The profit received could be spent purchasing the products of local artisans or goods at the general store. Rowan County's increasing number of artisans and trades reflected the growth and development of the economy, from just twenty-two artisans in eight trades in 1753, to 126 artisans in twenty-two trades by 1759, and finally to 328 artisans in thirty-four trades in 1770.[12]

Men were not the only participants in Rowan County's fledgling economy. Women actively worked for the growth and development of the region, too. For example, at least 26 of the 328 artisans working in the county in 1770 were female.[13] Plying a trade for wages was a path followed out of necessity, and by only a few women in the backcountry. Most of the adult female residents were housewives. Unfortunately, the participation of women as housewives in the economy of early America has been vastly underrated, if not ignored, by the assumption that domestic or household production, which mainly fell into the female domain, could not become commercial. Such assumptions ignore the realities of everyday life in early America—that women produced goods at home for consumption, exchange, and sale.[14] Trading between neighbors, of eggs for butter, milk for yardage, and the like, made up the "underground" economy of early America—a series of vital yet anonymous trade networks between the women of a community that kept their families clothed and fed. Unlike other informal local trade networks in early America, which usually disappeared upon the development of an external market and more formal trade networks,[15] the underground economy of women never totally ceased to exist.

Rowan County had such an underground economy. Only faint traces of it remain, however, because women rarely recorded such informal economic transactions. Traces appear when male household members traded surplus "domestic products" for merchandise from the local store. Robert Brevard, to cite one example, once traded Salisbury merchant William Steele one pair of stockings for sundries, a silk handkerchief, some fabric, and a pair of garters.[16]

As important as the underground economy was to the daily life of most Rowan County inhabitants, the informal nature of the transactions did not provide the women who made them with much economic power. If anything, it allowed those women a small measure of control over how they spent their time. By contrast, the married, widowed, and single women such as Mary Carter Boone, Elizabeth Steele, and Isabella Moore, who worked at a trade, not only were able to make and in many cases control their own incomes, but the ability to do so seems also to have afforded them a sense of personal freedom and self-worth that was most unusual for women in the colonial South. For unmarried working women, who were not bound by the laws of *feme covert*, managing one's own income and property provided a precious (and unavoidable) sense of autonomy, which may in turn have subjected them to the moral, and sometimes violent, reactions of society. Widowed women, on the other hand, were allowed to control their income and property and seemed to enjoy the respect of society in return for the years they had spent as wives and mothers.

The court of pleas and quarter sessions records of Rowan County clearly demonstrate that women worked as professional artisans in the North Carolina backcountry.[17] Employed mainly in the textile arts, such as weaving and sewing, women artisans even held a monopoly on the craft of spinning. For these women, gaining control over their personal financial destiny was so important that they took advantage of the gendered division of labor to advance their economic status. Choosing an occupation that fell within the nebulous bounds of *housewifery*, the domestic responsibilities performed by the female sex,[18] certainly made it easier for these women to get work. Working within the accepted female sphere also allowed these women (the married artisans, especially) to schedule and accomplish their work at home while still carrying out their regular household duties.

As we will see, the married, widowed, and single female artisans of Rowan County faced special challenges as a result of the economic roles they played. For married women the challenges were organizational and legal. How could they find the time to work for an income while fulfilling the expected roles of wife, mother, and housewife? How could they circumvent the legal tradition of *feme covert*, which prevented married women from owning and controlling their own personal property and income? Widows faced the challenge of time: was the financial security of remarriage worth risking the economic autonomy that accompanied their advancing age and declining productivity? For single women (who did not need to worry about the property laws) the challenge came from society. Whether these women chose to remain single in order to retain control over their economic affairs, or were forced to work and remain in control of their finances because they were single, being a single working woman in frontier society was an unusual status that had profound, sometimes even violent, consequences.

In Rowan County some married women, such as Mary Carter Boone, daughter of one of the richest men in the county, wife of a local artisan, and sister-in-law of the intrepid frontiersman Daniel Boone, worked as professional spinsters. They spun fibers into thread to make money, not to be self-sufficient. Far from being a group of unmarried women past their prime, they held a monopoly on the craft of spinning in Rowan County. Considering that it took the output of seven spinsters to supply a full-time weaver with adequate amounts of thread and yarn, and that there were forty-six weavers working in Rowan County in 1770, these women were obviously an integral cog in the wheel of backcountry textile production. And yet, for the notable role they played in the local economy, these women seem strangely absent from the county's official records. When one does appear, it is usually when she signs a deed with her husband or settles his estate.

Most adult women were married, but they are missing from the public records of Rowan County because those official records deal mainly with property transactions. *Feme covert* status meant that no married woman had the legal ability to act independently with regard to property.[19] When a woman married, all of her property became her husband's. However, women's names frequently appeared with their husbands' on land titles, especially if the land had originally belonged to the wife, a small detail the court was duty-bound to acknowledge. If the justices of the peace had reason to believe that the husband's desire to sell the wife's land was not in the best economic interest of the woman or her heirs, they could question the wife in private about the transaction before allowing it. In Rowan County the justices questioned some women, including Mary Thorton, Susanna Verril, and Jenet Kerr. Nor were they afraid to act on their suspicions in protecting married women from scoundrel husbands. In 1767, for example, the Rowan Court actually prohibited Henry France from selling 157 acres of his wife's land.[20]

Over the years, historians have surmised that *feme covert* status prevented working married women from controlling their own incomes. To support this view, historians have noted that merchants would not grant store credit to married women because the women could not be held accountable (sued) for their debts, but their husbands could be.[21] Yet, the private records of some of the county's merchants tell a very different story. The account books of three Rowan County merchants, in particular, reveal much about the buying habits of backcountry residents, as well as how they paid for their purchases. Account books and some other records still exist for William Steele's store and tavern in Salisbury in the 1760s, for Alexander and John Lowrance's combination tavern and store on Beaverdam Creek, ten miles west of Salisbury from the 1750s to the 1790s, and for John Nisbet's store northwest of Salisbury near Ft. Dobbs in the 1770s. These private records hold valuable information about the economic status of women in Rowan County because all three merchants conducted business with women. In fact, thirty-six women appear in Steele's book, seven in Lowrance's, and four in Nisbet's.[22]

The most revealing information comes from William Steele's store. Steele, a tavern keeper and merchant, followed meticulous accounting procedures, and the fact that most of his customers paid for their purchases in cash reflects his careful consideration of the individuals to whom he would extend credit. He consistently listed his accounts under the name of the person ultimately responsible for them. If Steele denied someone credit, the only way he or she could purchase on credit was to use someone else's account—someone Steele already had judged would be good for the debt. If one individual drew off another person's account, it was always listed as such, and not as a separate account. Accordingly, on September 14, 1760, "Catherin" Smith paid Steele cash for some fabric and notions, a knife, and "sundrys per yr husband, sundrys another time." Steele not only granted credit to this married woman, but he also allowed her husband, who did not have an account, to draw on her credit. Smith may not have been the only married woman in Steele's book, either. The title "Mrs" appears before the last names of Gamble, Woods, Duffel, Miller, Forsyth, and Chambers. These women could have been widows, but two other women, Donaldson and Rarion, had the descriptor "widow" before their names.[23]

William Steele may have had a special understanding of the needs and desires of working married women to maintain their own economic autonomy, because of his own wife, Elizabeth. A thirty-year-old property-owning widow when he married her in 1764, Elizabeth was the only female tavern owner and operator in Rowan County to hold a tavern license. Elizabeth learned how important her economic autonomy was during her first marriage, when her husband's business partnership almost bankrupted them. Despite the fact that her tavern keeping (and spinning and weaving skills) helped keep them solvent, by virtue of her sex and marital status Elizabeth was a pawn in the legal tangle. Since married women did not legally exist, Elizabeth could not actively participate in the court proceedings to recoup debts owed them and to protect the few assets they had, even though the outcome would decide her and her children's fate.[24] She would never forget the sense of frustration caused by her legal invisibility.

At her husband's death two years later, Elizabeth realized that she had the legal status that had eluded her when she was married, and she became determined to make the most of it. She purchased a tavern in her own name, settled her husband's estate, and frequently went to court to sue her delinquent patrons for the debts they owed her.[25] While Elizabeth and William may have combined their respective tavern operations after their marriage in 1764 (they were neighbors), Elizabeth's property remained solely in her name, and she resumed responsibility for operating the tavern at William's death in 1773. At her own death in 1790, Elizabeth was one of the wealthiest women in Rowan County.[26]

Account books provide a glimpse of married women's economic activity, but most of the women encountered in the private and public records of Rowan County were single. They usually appear in the account books without descriptors before their name, although John Nisbet carefully noted that one of his customers, "Miss Marey Gayley," was a stocking knitter.[27] Many of these single women, who had to work to support themselves, were artisans, while others worked as tavern keepers and farmers.[28] Needing control over their finances, they were allowed to own property as well. For most single women, working for a living was a brief stage in their lives before marriage. In New England and Pennsylvania, for example, the teenage daughters of local families frequently worked for neighbors and received wages for spinning, weaving, and doing household chores.[29] Given Rowan County's similarity to southeastern Pennsylvania, the same type of work situations no doubt occurred, and the Rowan County Orphans Court clearly placed female orphans with local families to learn domestic skills.[30]

However, for at least some women in Rowan County, working for a living clearly was not a brief stage before marriage—it was a career. Exactly how this happened remains somewhat of a mystery, but one possible explanation may be that the single and widowed professional women in Rowan County achieved real economic independence and became reluctant (or unable) to abandon control of their hard-earned incomes to husbands. In a rural society such as Rowan County, which was organized around family-run household economies (in which single women had no permanent role), this became a difficult situation.[31] Back-country society failed to sympathize with, or even to comprehend, the need of these women to promote their independence as wage earners in their own right. Working widows had an easier time in society than women who never married, because they had fulfilled the gender roles of wife and mother that society expected. In addition, most widows remarried rather than trying to make it on their own, but there were exceptions.[32] One advantage that widows had over both married and single female artisans was the ability to take an apprentice, providing them with a supply of labor. Single women could not take an apprentice at all, and married women could obtain apprentices only through their husbands.

Left with at least two underage sons at home following the death of her husband, Michael, in 1776, Anna Baker chose to create her own financial security by expanding her spinning and weaving operation with at least one apprentice, Nansey Jolley. Six years later, with one son grown and gone from home, Baker was doing well enough to be one of a handful of women on the Surry County tax list. And when the census taker surveyed in 1790, Anna Baker headed a household that included two males over age sixteen, six males under sixteen, and two other females.[33] Further east, in Randolph County, Rachel Dennis followed a similar course. As a widow in 1786, Dennis took on two-year-old Elizabeth Alexander as her apprentice and adopted daughter to learn the "art and mystery" of a spinster. Four years later the census taker recorded her household as having three males over sixteen, and three females.[34]

Twice widowed and still running her tavern in August 1781, Elizabeth Steele took Allen Campbell, orphan of Collin Campbell, as an apprentice to learn the trade of weaver.[35] With five slaves in her household, Elizabeth certainly did not need young Campbell to build up her spinning and weaving operation. However, the Revolution had taken male artisans away, and the Orphan's Court's naming of Elizabeth in the indenture (the only case of a male apprentice being sent to work with a female master) acknowledges her stature as a businesswoman and artisan in the community.

Thirty-five when her husband, Thomas, died in 1781, Sarah Butner did not remarry, but chose rather to support herself and her three underage children with her weaving and tailoring skills. She was obviously talented and successful at her trade, for when she applied to the Moravian Church to live in the town of Salem, she was accepted despite the church's strict rules regarding the regulation of trades. At the time, the Aufseher Collegium (the church board charged with overseeing economic matters) instructed Butner to limit her skills to weaving. Eleven years later, Sarah had far surpassed her original instructions and was so deluged with tailoring work that she turned to the Collegium to obtain additional help. The members were not impressed with her success, especially since her profits had cut into those of the church-sponsored tailor shop, from which the church received a percentage. After deciding that Butner's livelihood was not dependent on the extra money her business would clear with an added employee, the Collegium refused her request.[36]

Widows who chose not to remarry for personal or financial reasons had experienced the close physical relationships of marriage. Some single women may have eschewed the legal restrictions marriage imposed on their economic autonomy, but they were not necessarily willing to forsake the intimacy marriage afforded. The Rowan County records are littered with references to their illegal cohabitation and illegitimate or "base born" children. Three spinsters and their partners, Sarah Stamon and William Watson, Sarah Barrs and Joseph Thomas, and Sarah Pincer and Francis Metcalf, appeared before the Rowan Criminal Court in April 1768 because "diverse times" they "did criminally copulate and cohabit and live together in the constant habitual practice of Fornication against the decency and good order of Society an evil example to all others."[37]

Women paid a high price for having sex without matrimony. In 1764 Elizabeth Steele forfeited her coveted economic status as a widow for marriage when she found herself pregnant by William Steele.[38] If, on the other hand, a child resulted from such a union and the couple did not marry, the Orphan's Court would take the child from its mother for placement in a "decent" home. Such maneuvers served two purposes: to raise the child in a wholesome environment in the early years, and to train the child in a skill in later years, to become self-supporting. Spinster Isabella Moore's son, James Craig, was sent to live with John Johnson for the first ten years of his life, then bound out to William Ireland for the next eleven years to learn the "art of Cordwainer."[39] Whether the orphans were in great demand as labor, or the court was merely eager to place them in a "moral" atmosphere, on one occasion in 1769 the court acted too quickly in taking base-born Sarah Shaver away from her mother, Margaret, and placing her with Mr. James Potts. Two years later, Margaret and her husband, John Joist Shaver, appeared in court to reclaim Sarah after proving they were legally married.[40]

Sadly, some bastardy cases took a double toll on the women who could least afford it: female indentured servants. Servants and apprentices were not allowed to marry, as they were usually bastard or orphaned teenagers who had been placed with a master until they reached the age of majority, eighteen for a woman and twenty-one for a man.[41] If a woman serving a term of indenture became pregnant, not only did she lose her child to the legal system, but her term was extended by one year as a punishment. Christiana Bibby served an extra year with tailor Thomas Allison after she gave birth, and Ann Waltsir served two additional years "for unlawfull Getting Two Base Born Children within the time of her Servitude." Such a system had the potential to hold women prisoner almost indefinitely if they became pregnant by their masters, willingly or unwillingly. Women like Charlotte Dearmont, who bounced from one master to the next, her term extended under each of them because of pregnancy, were either terrible victims of the system or terrible burdens on their various masters.[42]

Having one's children taken away was only one unpleasant reality encountered by the working women of Rowan County. The social stigma these women faced as a result of working and being single was so great that it exploded into violence at times. The criminal records of both the Rowan County Court of Pleas and Quarter Sessions and the Salisbury District Superior Court contain references to female artisans being abused by men. Warrants sworn out by Mary and Agnes Osborough accused hatter William Williams of assaulting the two sisters in separate incidents in 1762. Butcher and entrepreneur John Lewis Beard purportedly "beat wounded and evilly treated" Agnes earlier the same year. Sometimes the attacks were more serious, as when William Nettle was accused of raping spinster Catherine Evington.[43] Although the trial records and verdicts are not extant, these female accusers felt enough anger and ill will toward these men that they wanted to publicly damage their names and reputations at the very least, and perhaps see them go to jail.

Working women were not the only victims of crime. Professional women surface in the court records both as plaintiffs and as defendants. The frequency with which working women, especially single women, appeared in court raises the question of whether they were special targets for harassment for their unusual lifestyle. Isabella Moore is a good example. Moore appeared in county court three times and in district superior court two times. One of the few female property owners in the county, Moore seems to have had a difficult time staying out of trouble — or did she?

In 1763 Moore was a successful artisan who purchased lot number four in the east square of Salisbury from Andrew Bailie. The following year she experienced a reversal of fortune when she found herself pregnant and embroiled in a slander case with a local hatter, Robert Johnston, which may have forced her to sell her land to pay a lawyer.[44] Over the course of the next four years Moore suffered some great hardships. Her baby was taken away from her and placed with a guardian. She lost the slander case to Johnston and found herself in jail when she could not afford the fifty-pound fine. To get out of jail she had to declare herself destitute and petition for relief on the basis "that she is not worth forty shillings sterling money in any worldly substance working tools and wearing apparel excepted." Once out of jail, she was attacked by James Townsley, the local tinsmith.[45] She ended up in county court two more times for charges of petit larceny and theft. Convicted of the latter charge, Moore was sentenced "to receive 30 lashes on her bare back at the public whipping post at 3 o'clock this afternoon."[46]

Amazingly, four months later, in August 1768, Moore's signature appears on a deed for a minor, Jane (Jean) Bailie, to purchase some land in the west square of Salisbury.[47] What sounds like an incredible story of beating the odds and overcoming a personal history of adversity may actually have been the manipulations of a shrewd businesswoman. A closer look at the timing of Moore's land sale and repurchase suggests that she sold her property to avoid losing it in the slander suit Robert Johnston brought against her (preferring to stay in jail rather than pay the fine) and then repurchased a comparable lot through the minor when her legal problems had ended.

In the backcountry of North Carolina, women gained freedom by working. And the greater the freedom, the higher the price women paid. For the female participants in the underground economy of Rowan County, extra work doing one domestic chore, such as setting hens, meant freedom from another task, such as making soap. Small freedom, small price. For women who chose to pursue a trade or a profession, the aptitude to make and control an income produced a sense of financial freedom and increased self-esteem. Greater freedom, but at a greater price. For married women who worked, the price to pay was *feme covert*, the restrictive property laws that only a handful of women were able to surmount. For widows the price was foregoing the financial security of remarriage. For single working women with complete economic freedom, the price varied. Economic freedom frequently came at the cost of various personal freedoms. For those women who wanted permanent economic freedom, marriage was not an option. For those women who attempted to live a fulfilling life without marriage, other freedoms were at risk, including the ability to keep one's personal life private or to raise one's child. For those women who merely worked to support themselves, economic freedom may have come at the cost of personal safety. Nonetheless, for many women of Rowan County, the achievement of economic autonomy was so precious that, if necessary, they endured legal irritation—and even physical violence—to maintain their freedom.

NOTES

1. In other southern colonies some east-to-west migration did occur. For instance, the Virginia Southside was settled by emigrants from the Tidewater region who emulated the slave-based, agricultural economy and accompanying tobacco culture and extended it into that area. See Richard R. Beeman, *The Evolution of the Southern Backcountry: A Case Study of Lunenburg County, Virginia, 1746–1832* (Philadelphia: University of Pennsylvania Press, 1984).

2. The geographical description of North Carolina is drawn from Harry R. Merrens, *Colonial North Carolina in the Eighteenth Century: A Study in Historical Geography* (Chapel Hill: University of North Carolina Press, 1964), 37–41, 46–67.

3. A. Roger Ekirch, *"Poor Carolina": Politics and Society in Colonial North Carolina, 1729–1775* (Chapel Hill: University of North Carolina Press, 1981), 31.

4. William G. Boyd, ed., *William Byrd's Histories of the Dividing Line betwixt Virginia and North Carolina* (New York: Dover, 1967), 304.

5. Boyd, *Byrd's Histories of the Dividing Line,* 66.

6. Julia Cherry Spruill, *Women's Life and Work in the Southern Colonies* (1938; reprint, New York: Norton, 1972), 81, 83.

7. Jack P. Greene, *Pursuits of Happiness: The Social Development of Early Modern British Colonies and the Formation of American Culture* (Chapel Hill: University of North Carolina Press, 1988), 125, 127; James T. Lemon, *The Best Poor Man's Country: A Geographical Study of Early Southeastern Pennsylvania* (Baltimore: Johns Hopkins University Press, 1972), 222.

8. Merrens, *Colonial North Carolina,* 8, 12; Robert Ramsey, *Carolina Cradle: Settlement of the Northwest Carolina Frontier, 1747–1762* (Chapel Hill: University of North Carolina Press, 1964), 10–22.

9. David L. Corbitt, *The Formation of North Carolina Counties, 1663–1943* (Raleigh, N.C.: State Department of Archives and History, 1950), 8.

10. Stephen B. Weeks, ed., *The Colonial Records of North Carolina* (Raleigh, N.C.: Printers to the State, 1886–1900), 23:390.

11. Lemon, *Best Poor Man's Country,* 2–7, 114–16, 222.

12. Johanna Miller Lewis, *Artisans in the North Carolina Backcountry* (Lexington: University Press of Kentucky, 1995), 55, 74.

13. For more information see Johanna Miller Lewis, "Women Artisans in Backcountry North Carolina, 1753–1790," *North Carolina Historical Review* 68 (July 1991):214–36.

14. Allan Kulikoff, "The Transition to Capitalism in Rural America," *William and Mary Quarterly,* 3d ser., 46 (January 1989):133, 137–38.

15. James A. Henretta, "Families and Farms: Mentalité in Pre-Industrial America," *William and Mary Quarterly,* 3d ser., 35 (January 1978):15.

16. William Steele's Cash Account, John Steele papers, vol. 2, Southern Historical Collection, University of North Carolina at Chapel Hill.

17. Lewis, *Artisans,* 94–112.

18. For additional information on the definition or interpretation of housewifery in the region, see Lewis, *Artisans,* 96–97.

19. Marylynn Salmon, *Women and the Law of Property in Early America* (Chapel Hill: University of North Carolina Press, 1986), xv.

20. Jo White Linn, *Abstracts of the Minutes of the Court of Pleas and Quarter Sessions, Rowan County, N.C. 1753–1762* (Salisbury, N.C.: Mrs. Stahle Linn, 1977), 83, 86, 72.

21. Daniel B. Thorp, "Doing Business in the Backcountry: Retail Trade in Colonial Rowan County, North Carolina," *William and Mary Quarterly,* 3d ser., 48 (July 1991):398.

22. General Merchandise Store Ledger, Nisbet Collection, Southern Historical Collection; Account Book, 1784–96, Rowan County, John Dickey Papers, Manuscript Collection, Perkins Library, Duke University, Durham, N.C.; Account Book, Alexander and John Lowrance Papers, 1749–96, Manuscript Collection, Perkins Library; William Steele Account Books, John Steele Papers, Southern Historical Collection; Thorp, "Doing Business," 398.

23. William Steele Account Book, John Steele Papers, Southern Historical Collection. Incidentally, none of the other women's accounts mention men.

24. On July 23, 1757, Robert Gillespie (Elizabeth's husband) sued Peter Arrand and Jacob Frank for debt and recovered close to fifty-five pounds. Eighteen months later, Gillespie dodged some further debts against his failed partnership by swearing in court that his net worth was less than forty shillings sterling. See Linn, *Rowan Court Abstracts, 1753–1762*, 77, 101.

25. Linn, *Rowan Court Abstracts, 1753–1762*, 112, 114; Rowan County Deeds, North Carolina Division of Archives and History, Raleigh (cited hereafter as DAH), 4:241, 5:308, 309; John Steele Papers and Anonymous Lawyer's Account Book, Macay-McNeely Papers, Southern Historical Collection.

26. Linn, *Rowan Court Abstracts, 1753–1762*, 114, 153; Jo White Linn, *Rowan County, North Carolina Deed Abstracts, 1753–1762: Books 1–4* (Salisbury, N.C.: Mrs. Stahle Linn, 1972), 4:241; Jo White Linn, *Abstracts of the Court of Pleas and Quarter Sessions, Rowan County, N. C. 1763–1774* (Salisbury, N.C.: Mrs. Stahle Linn, 1979), 158; Archibald Henderson, Biography of Elizabeth Maxwell Steele, Henderson Family Papers, Steele Series, Southern Historical Collection, typescript.

27. General Merchandise Store Ledger, Nisbet Collection, Southern Historical Collection, 80.

28. Linn, *Rowan Court Abstracts, 1753–1762*, 15, 70, 153.

29. Laurel Thatcher Ulrich, *A Midwife's Tale: The Life of Martha Ballard, Based on Her Diary, 1785–1812* (New York: Knopf, 1991), 77–81; Joan M. Jensen, *Loosening the Bonds: Mid-Atlantic Farm Women, 1750–1850* (New Haven, Conn.: Yale University Press, 1986), 38; Paul Clemens and Lucy Simler, "Rural Labor and the Farm Household, Chester County, Pennsylvania, 1750–1820," in *Work and Labor in Early America*, edited by Stephen Innes (Chapel Hill: University of North Carolina Press for the Institute of Early American History and Culture, 1988), 131.

30. See Lynne Howard Fraser, "Nobody's Children: The Treatment of Illegitimate Children in Three North Carolina Counties, 1760–1790," (Master's thesis, College of William and Mary, 1987); Kathi R. Jones, " 'That Also These Children May Become Useful People': Apprenticeships in Rowan County, North Carolina from 1753 to 1795," (Master's thesis, College of William and Mary, 1984).

31. In *Loosening the Bonds*, 207, Jensen notes the organization of rural areas around the family and that frequently single, working women relocated to cities.

32. Either the social pressure or the financial need for most widows to remarry

was so great that Rowan Court of Pleas and Quarter Minutes show numerous women, such as Jane Beby, who remarried before a first husband's estate was settled. Linn, *Rowan Court Abstracts, 1753–1762*, 155. Suzanne Lebsock found that the better a widow's financial status was, the less likely she was to remarry. See Suzanne Lebsock, *The Free Women of Petersburg: Status and Culture in a Southern Town, 1784–1860* (New York: Norton, 1984), 26–27, 36.

33. Surry County split from Rowan in 1771. Jo White Linn, *Surry County, N.C., Will Abstracts*, vols. 1–3, 1771–1827 (Salisbury, N.C.: Mrs. Stahle Linn, Jr., 1974), 1:84; Surry County Court Minutes, February 11, 1782, and Surry County Tax List, 1782, DAH; *Heads of Families at the First Census of the United States Taken in the Year 1790: North Carolina* (Washington: Government Printing Office, 1908; reprint, Baltimore: Genealogical Publishing Co., 1966), 123 (page references to the reprint edition).

34. Randolph County Apprentice Bonds, DAH; *Heads of Families at the First Census*, 123.

35. Rowan County Court of Pleas and Quarter Minutes, Aug. 9, 1781, DAH.

36. Jo White Linn, *Abstracts of Wills and Estates of Rowan County, N.C., 1753–1805, and Tax Lists of 1759 and 1778* (Salisbury, N.C.: Mrs. Stahle Linn, Jr., 1980), 21; *Aufseher Collegium Protocol*, April 11, 1786, Oct. 10, 1797, translated by Erika Huber, Archives of Moravian Church, Southern Province, Winston-Salem, N.C.

37. Rowan County Criminal Action Papers, file C.R.085.326.1, DAH.

38. Although the exact sequence of events is unclear because of a lack of extant sources, Elizabeth probably married William Steele shortly after confirming her pregnancy in early 1764. As late as April 1765 Elizabeth is referred to by her first husband's surname, "Gillespy," in a deed selling Steele sixteen lots in the east square of Salisbury, adjacent to Elizabeth's property. Rowan Deeds, 6:160, 161, DAH; Linn, *Rowan Court Abstracts, 1763–1774*, 591. Nineteenth-century histories of Rowan County give 1763 as the year Elizabeth and William were married, but no primary sources substantiate the date.

39. Linn, *Rowan Court Abstracts, 1763–1774*, 45; Rowan County Court of Pleas and Quarter Minutes, Feb. 8, 1775, DAH.

40. Linn, *Rowan Court Abstracts, 1763–1774*, 89, 129.

41. Weeks, *Colonial Records*, 23:577–83.

42. Linn, *Rowan Court Abstracts, 1753–1762*, 88, 93. Rowan County Court of Pleas and Quarter Sessions, Jan. 17, 1769; May 6, 1772; May 5, 1774.

43. The warrant actually charged that Nettles "an assault did make and then and there did violate, lie with, and carnally know" Evington. Rowan County Criminal Action Papers, C.R.085.326.1, DAH; Salisbury District Superior Court Criminal Action Papers, D.C.S.R. 207.326.1, DAH.

44. Linn, *Rowan Deed Abstracts*, 5:450, 451, 537; Linn, *Rowan Court Abstracts, 1763–1774*, 24, 28; Anonymous Rowan County Lawyer's Account Book, Macay-McNeely Papers, Southern Historical Collection.

45. Linn, *Rowan Court Abstracts, 1763–1774,* 45; Salisbury District Superior Court Reference Docket, 1767–69, D.S.C.R. 207.322.2, DAH; Salisbury District Superior Court Miscellaneous Records 1754–1807, D.S.C.R. 207.928.1, DAH; Rowan County Civil Action Papers, C.R.085.325.1, DAH.

46. Salisbury District State (Crown) Docket Superior Court, 1762–1779, D.S.C.R. 207.321.2, DAH; Rowan County Criminal Court Papers, C.R.085.326.1, DAH; Linn, *Rowan Court Abstracts, 1763–1774,* 79.

47. Linn, *Rowan Deed Abstracts,* 7:92, 93; Linn, *Rowan Court Abstracts, 1763–1774,* 92.

IV Marriage and the Family

Throughout history, women have been most defined, and in some ways most limited, by their experience as wives and mothers. The chapters in this section explore that experience for early American women from very different directions. Merril D. Smith introduces us to eighteenth-century Pennsylvania women who found unexpected freedom when their husbands died or deserted them. Abandoned women often appeared in court records as they attempted to handle the myriad legal complications of suddenly being left to fend for themselves. Drawing on such information, Smith contrasts the experiences of deserted women with those of widows. The abandoned faced special problems. Friends and family helped, but desertion did not legally end a marriage; it left even absentee husbands in control of family estates and wives "in precarious, if not desperate situations." Widows enjoyed more respect than abandoned women, but legal battles over inheritances significantly restricted their freedom. Both groups of women faced emotional upheaval, unaccustomed dependence upon others, and—in extreme cases—the breakup of their families as hungry children were placed in other households to work for their keep. Such daunting realities notwithstanding, Smith concludes, these women "frequently managed to support themselves and their families, and even to prosper."

Seventeenth-century Puritan writers often used marriage as a metaphor for government. Many, including John Milton, emphasized the importance of the wife's submission and obedience to her husband, just as subjects must be subordinate to their leaders. Yet, as Elizabeth Dale shows, there were many understandings of women's rights and responsibilities within marriage. By examining how William Gouge, John Winthrop, Elizabeth Poole, and others used marriage as a metaphor for government in political theory disputes, Dale reveals the complexity and diversity of seventeenth-century English views of marriage. As she notes, considering that complexity and diversity should remind us to further consider, rather than merely to assume we know, what the actual experience of marriage was for women in early America.

Were widows poor and powerless in colonial America, as some scholars have insisted, or did they often have considerable control and authority, as others have maintained? Focusing on the lives of widows during the 1633–1750 years, Vivian Bruce Conger addresses this question. Through a careful analysis of the wills left by these women across more than a century, she offers some surprising revelations. Proportionately more women than men left wills, for example, and—contrary to previous scholarly assumptions—substantial numbers of women left real property behind. Their pointed bequests to daughters and granddaughters reveal a quiet but persistent challenge to prevailing gender roles. In the end, Conger shows, notwithstanding a pervasive ideological vision of women as inferior players in colonial society, in practice widows—and not only the very wealthy ones—"possessed a surprising amount of social and economic freedom."

11

"Whers Gone to She Knows Not": Desertion and Widowhood in Early Pennsylvania

MERRIL D. SMITH

On 19 February 1793 the Guardians of the Poor in Philadelphia noted in their Daily Occurrence Docket the death of Nancy Beety's one-month-old baby girl. When the mother and infant had been admitted two weeks earlier, Beety stated that "her Husband is a labouring man that left her two months ago & whers gone to she knows not." Unable to work because of the recent birth of her child, poor, probably cold, hungry, and unsure of her marital status, Beety had sought shelter in the almshouse.[1] Twenty-seven years earlier, Margaret Hill Morris had also delivered a baby girl in the absence of her husband. Morris, however, was not a deserted wife; she was a widow. She had a defined legal and social status, although death had changed her situation drastically and permanently. Differing from Nancy Beety, she knew what had happened to her husband; he was gone forever. Having this knowledge, she and her family could grieve, comforted by their Quaker faith. Like Beety, Morris was concerned about her financial condition, but rather than being a burden, her daughter, Gulielma, was the "dear last Pledge of Happiest Love."[2]

Despite the obvious class differences and the passage of time, these women had much in common. Both found themselves without husbands and forced to cope in some fashion. All deserted and widowed women faced this situation. Unlike single women or those who chose to leave or divorce their husbands, they did not select independence. Like many others, Beety and Morris found themselves in a position that they neither anticipated nor desired. For those who depended wholly or partly on the financial support of a husband, his sudden absence could cause considerable pecuniary suffering, as well as emotional distress, especially if there were no family members to help bear the burden. Morris, however, through family connections and her own common sense, managed to live comfortably into old age.[3]

Yet, there were also many differences between women who had been abandoned by their husbands and those whose spouses had died. Although both groups of women had to cope emotionally with the loss of their mates, deserted wives differed from widows both legally and socially. By law a married woman was under coverture; her property, wages, and inheritance belonged to her husband. This system did not change substantially until the 1830s and 1840s.[4] Desertion itself did not lawfully end a marriage. Thus, women like Nancy Beety found themselves in a predicament: legally, their husbands retained control over family finances and property. But if they held control, they also had responsibilities. Therefore, Pennsylvania statutes, passed in the 1770s, required husbands to support their wives as long as they were lawfully wed, so that the wives would not become burdens on their communities. Unfortunately, this meant very little if the husbands could not be found, owned no property that could be sold, or simply refused to provide for their wives and families.[5] Family and friends provided for deserted women and widows when they could. Those without resources or family members who would care for them had to resort to charity. Yet, in order to gain relief, poor and deserted wives sometimes found that they had to prove their worthiness, as well as their need. The Philadelphia Almshouse, for example, generally required that prospective inmates come with a recommendation from a reputable citizen. Once admitted, they were to behave respectably and show the proper deference to authority.[6] In 1796 Sally Brown, "a free black woman," was admitted to the Philadelphia

Almshouse. The entry recorded Mayor Hilary Baker's remarks, noting that she was "a lewd disorderly Woman," whose husband had left her because of her intimacies with other men in his absence. She had become "disordered" due to her relationships. "It is therefore proper in my Opinion," Baker reported, "that when she is cured, she ought to make compensation to the Managers by Servitude."[7] In contrast, Catharine Cannon, deserted and pregnant, came "well Recommend'd" to the Philadelphia Almshouse by a shoemaker in the city. Unfortunately, she died ten days later, the result of smallpox and the ordeal of childbirth.[8]

The "worthy poor" came in a wide variety. Some women even demonstrated their worthiness by admitting their sins, leaving the almshouse as "Magdalens," after proving to the Magdalen Society that they could be reformed. Commonly, the story these women told was of being seduced, then deserted, and finally left without any means of support or family or friends to help them. The Magdalen Society was a private charitable organization designed to rescue women "fallen from a condition of innocence and virtue." One Magdalen, Rachel Brooks, was deserted by her husband in Maryland. A year later she came to Philadelphia, "where being much exposed to temptation, was Seduced & led astray," becoming diseased and being forced to enter the almshouse. In 1808 the Magdalen Society placed her with "An orderly pious family, about 25 Miles distant from the City, where it is believed she will be likely to do well."[9]

Because entering the almshouse was such a demeaning experience—inmates were stripped of their meager belongings and forced to endure a prisonlike atmosphere—the majority of people ventured there only when desperate.[10] For deserted women, this meant when they were about to give birth, were sick, or could not work because of their young children. Between 1796 and 1815, 354 women who had been deserted by their husbands entered the Philadelphia Almshouse. Of these, 202 (57.1 percent) were pregnant or had children with them. As might be expected for that group, most of the abandoned wives in the almshouse (258 or 73 percent) were also under forty. Of them, 189 were under thirty years old. Nearly a third of the women, including those who were pregnant or had children, were also ill; one in ten of those had venereal disease. The majority of the women were native born white. Thirty-four were listed as black; eighty were Irish, and seven were German.[11]

Margaret Hunter, Isabella Johnson, and Ann Wiges are typical examples. On 27 October 1801 Margaret Hunter was admitted, pregnant. Her
husband, Thomas, had enlisted "in the land service" six months before,
but she did not know his regiment or company. She had not heard from
him since he left her, but, according to the docket, "she dont appear to
be more than two or three weeks distant from her down lying and having
no resource come here." Enlisting or shipping off were common ways
men left their spouses. Isabella Johnson's husband, Robert, went to New
York and "enter'd on board the United States frigate call'd the New
York." He also deserted her when she was pregnant.[12] Ann Wiges' unhappy marital situation led her to the poorhouse more than once. When
she entered in December 1802, she was twenty-seven years old with
three young children. Her husband, Samuel, was a blacksmith, but the
overseers noted that "he drinks hard, and neglects providing for his
family, by which, they suffer, and she being sick with fever and ague, was
obliged to come here." Four years later Ann returned after her husband
had deserted her. She was sick again and had two new children, one a
four-week-old infant.[13]

Institutional settings were unpleasant at best, inhuman at worst.
Women who had other choices went elsewhere. Recognizing that there
were limited childbirth services for poor pregnant women without husbands, the Philadelphia Lying-In Charity, for attending indigent females
at their own houses, was established in 1832. In the preamble to the first
annual report, the managers noted that at the Pennsylvania Hospital,
where there were only limited facilities for poor married women, children
could not be admitted with their mothers when they came to give birth,
"and to provide for their welfare during her absence, if at all practicable,
may require an expense beyond her means." If the mother went to the
almshouse instead, her children were taken from her. The report also
noted that "there will always exist no small number whose reluctance to
lying-in, in a public institution is so great, that rather than consent, they
will undergo the greatest suffering and inconvenience at home."[14] Until
the twentieth century, most women did not deliver their babies in hospitals, but poor women could not always afford even a doctor or a midwife
to assist in the birth. The authors of the report were well aware of the
numbers of babies who were stillborn and believed that the association

could help prevent infant deaths. Nevertheless, they also noted that "great care will be taken to discriminate between the deserving and the undeserving." [15]

It was not only those without resources who suffered. Even women who owned some property sometimes encountered problems when deserted by their husbands. Mary Taylor's husband, William, was a silversmith in Philadelphia. Mary was forced to leave him suddenly in 1777 because of his frequent rages and abuse. She fled to her mother's house in Burlington, New Jersey, with their young child. William refused to support them, then left Mary and went to sea after he "sold all of the Household Goods and Effects (which belonged partly to her Mother and partly to herself before her intermarriage with the said William Taylor)." Fortunately, Mary owned property inherited from her father. This inheritance consisted of a plantation and land in the township of Moyamensing that had been leased to Joseph Johnson five years before at a yearly rate of £150. Johnson, however, refused to pay the rent. Mary petitioned for assistance, and the court ordered him to remit all sums in arrears and to "pay rent for [the] plantation as it becomes due." [16] Although British forces were occupying Philadelphia while Mary was in Burlington, no mention of the war was made in this case. Daily life continued, it seems, despite war and politics.

Other women discovered that their husbands had fled with their money. Catherine Rumler, for example, had held a bond of four hundred dollars against James Shively before she married her husband, Mathew. "Just before he absconded," Mathew hired a lawyer to sue and collect the sum. When Catherine went to the Directors of the Poor in Chester County to gain some support in 1837, they tried to collect the money from the sheriff who was holding it. [17]

Ownership of property clearly did not guarantee that a deserted wife would prosper, especially if her husband returned. Johanna Delany entered the Philadelphia Almshouse in 1797, although she apparently owned two or three houses. She refused to sign these properties over to her mariner husband, with whom she had not cohabited for years and who had lately returned from sea. He probably returned only to make some money from her properties. When she refused to give them to him, he beat her. Johanna was also ill with venereal disease. The disease and perhaps her husband's ill treatment must have made it impossible for her to support herself.[18]

Some women, who may not have had any money or property in their own names, tried to make their errant husbands support them through court-decreed separate maintenances. In 1790 Elizabeth Ireland, for example, complained that her husband, Andrew, had deserted her "without good Cause and refuses to contribute towards her support." The court ordered Andrew to pay "one dollar & a Half every week" for her support "to be paid on every Wednesday in the Forenoon from this Day." Andrew refused to pay and was ordered to jail until he complied. William Garwood, a shipwright from Southwark, then sent in thirty pounds on the condition that Andrew would comply with the order.[19] The affairs of the Irelands underscore the fact that desertion, unlike the death of a spouse, was not always permanent. In June 1796 Elizabeth Ireland once again came before the court and declared "her free and voluntary Consent and Agreement to cohabit and dwell with her said Husband again." They asked that Garwood be discharged from the surety, and the court agreed.[20]

The Poor Law required that grown children support their parents when necessary.[21] In the case of Isabella Adair, it was the estate of her deceased son that had to maintain her. Isabella's husband, James, had deserted her, leaving the county of Chester to provide for her. James and Isabella's son, Nathaniel, died intestate. He had never married and had no children. In November 1836 the court ruled that his real estate be sold to pay his debts and that the balance go to support Isabella.[22]

Wanting a more permanent solution than a separate maintenance, some deserted Pennsylvania women chose to divorce their husbands. Under the Pennsylvania Divorce Act of 1785, desertion for more than four years was grounds for divorce. In 1815 the period of desertion was changed to two years. Divorce ended the *feme covert* status of the wife. A divorced woman could conduct business as a single woman or a widow did. She could also remarry. Yet relatively few women attempted to divorce during this time, and fewer still actually succeeded. For most, divorce was probably a last resort. For one thing, the process involved time and money. First, the court had to be petitioned, then subpoenas had to be issued, the witnesses had to give depositions, and finally the justices had to make their decision. There were also expenses involved, including lawyer fees and court costs. In addition, before a new 1804 law permitted women or men to sue for divorce in their county courts, divorces were tried before the Supreme Court of Pennsylvania, in Philadelphia. This meant some people had to travel a considerable distance, find lodgings or impose on friends, and take time from work and family. Finally, unless it was explicitly requested in a divorce from bed and board (more like a legal separation), alimony was not granted.[23]

Although desertion was probably easier to prove than other grounds for divorce, such as adultery or cruelty, there was no guarantee that a divorce would be granted. Plaintiffs had to demonstrate that they were "worthy" and that there was no collusion between the spouses. The court listened to the testimony of witnesses to determine if the so-called deserted wife really simply did not want to live with her husband. Had she been fulfilling her duties as a wife? Had her husband really abandoned her? Was he willing to now live with her? Women who had been deserted tended to emphasize that they had been left destitute. Between 1785 and 1815, fifty-four women applied to the Supreme Court of Pennsylvania for divorce on desertion grounds. Of these, thirty-four were granted divorces. In rural Chester County, twenty-three women filed on desertion only grounds between 1804 and 1840. Sixteen divorces were granted.[24]

The story of the notorious Ann Carson provides an example of a woman who did not understand the technicalities of divorce; she was a deserted wife and ultimately a widow, too. Ann's parents convinced her to marry Capt. John Carson shortly before her sixteenth birthday. The marriage was not a happy one. When Carson abandoned her, leaving her without money, Ann decided to open a china shop. While her husband was away, she supported her three young sons and her parents with the profits made there. Believing her husband to be dead, Ann, who apparently never lacked male admirers, was kidnapped by Lt. Richard Smith, who forced her to marry him. Despite this unconventional beginning, the two were happy during their brief marriage. Then Carson returned home, and Smith killed him in a fight.[25]

In her memoirs, Ann wrote that at one time she did inquire about a divorce. She knew that the law required that her husband be absent without supporting her for at least two years. According to Ann, the lawyer she consulted told her that if her husband was alive, she would have heard from him, so why should she bother with the trouble of trying to obtain a divorce? After her marriage to Smith, Ann demonstrated an imperfect knowledge of the law and of her first husband, believing that "he would never claim a woman he had voluntarily abandoned for such a length of time; and moreover I believed he could not claim me as his wife." [26]

Carson's memoirs may not tell the whole truth, but Judge Rush's charge to the jury on 28 May 1816 does define the legal position of wives, deserted or not. Although it was clear that John Carson had deserted his wife for a period of over two years, Rush noted, it was also clear that he was her legal husband at the time he was murdered. As her husband, "he had a right to settle his differences with his wife, and to receive her again into his arms." [27]

"It being universally understood and known," the judge continued,

> that the property of the wife, is the property of the husband, and that he alone had the control over it, the consequence is, that John Carson had an undoubted right to take possession of the house and goods which belonged to his wife, on his return in January last, to this city and to his family. It follows that Richard Smith, the prisoner, was an intruder, and had acquired possession of the wife, of the house, and of the goods and chattels of John Carson. [28]

According to the law, everything that Ann had acquired by her own efforts belonged to a man who had abandoned her years before. As a deserted wife, she had supported her family, scorning help from male admirers and their offers of marriage. It appears that she had a good sense for business, and she relished the freedom she had. Yet, if Carson had lived, all she owned would have been his. Moreover, if her marriage to Carson had been declared invalid, her belongings still would not have belonged to her; they would have been the property of her second husband, Richard Smith.

But that was not to be, either, for Smith was convicted and executed. Ann was declared innocent as an accomplice to murder, although she spent much of the rest of her life in and out of prison. In fact, she died there, guilty of passing counterfeit bills in order to earn her living. Her experiences had left her a penniless widow, after being a deserted wife, and she had no one to turn to for help. Because of her scandalous behavior, even her family abandoned her, and her reputation kept her from respectable Philadelphia society.[29]

Ann Carson probably lived better as a deserted wife than she did as a widow. She managed to keep her family clothed and fed by her efforts in her china shop, until Captain Carson returned home. As a widow, however, she had problems supporting herself, but that was because all her possessions were sold by her family to pay for her court costs and the support of her children while she was imprisoned.

The death of one's husband ended coverture. Yet, as the cases of Ann Carson and others show, this did not make a widow's status necessarily less precarious. For example, Caroline Shock's husband, Samuel, died after deserting her. She later attempted to gain control of his estate from the Directors of the Poor of Chester County, who had seized it to support her. Six years later, in 1846, Caroline tried to get the sum of money she had been allotted increased, since she was seventy years old and had broken her right arm.[30]

Sometimes a widow's inheritance caused friction in a subsequent marriage. Elizabeth Clandennin had inherited a sizable estate from her husband, William Woodward. When she married John Clandennin in February 1779, her real and personal property became his. By December 1780 Elizabeth had already left John because he physically abused her. She went to court to demand a weekly allowance, which the court granted. The couple reconciled for a brief period, but Elizabeth moved out of the house again in August 1785 and filed for divorce with alimony in April 1786. The court granted the divorce from bed and board, but court papers note an attachment for contempt against John for nonpayment of support. Money was one issue that caused strife in this marriage. Elizabeth no longer had any control over it, and John did not want to give up anything he had gained from his marriage to the former Widow Woodward. Indeed, John was literally ready to fight for the money, and Elizabeth received her divorce because of his "cruel and barbarous treatment."[31]

Most widows during this time did not remarry.[32] Ann Carson, for example, did not want to "resign her liberty," and Margaret Morris, who was given a house in Burlington by her brother, Henry Hill, in 1770, chose to sell medicines in a small store she opened in 1780. Perhaps there were too many strings attached to her brother's generosity. She kept the shop a secret from him. Nevertheless, during her store's brief existence, she achieved some independence as well as extra income.[33]

Whether a widow remarried or not, she still had to settle the estate of her late husband in order to provide for herself and her family. Pennsylvania law required that creditors be paid before the widow received her share. As Lisa Wilson has demonstrated, however, Pennsylvania law was not always as harsh as it appears. Many widows ignored or found ways around the law, as did deserted wives, and they managed to support themselves and their families. In other cases an inheritance might not provide enough, or the husband may not have left anything at all. In that case the widow had to work to support herself, depend on her family or friends, or obtain relief from the poorhouse, either as an inmate or as a recipient of outrelief.[34]

Both widows and deserted wives worked. Some women maintained the businesses or farms they and their husbands had operated. After Jacob Bristol's death, for example, his widow, Sarah, continued to run the bakery they had opened. Others, including Margaret Morris and Ann Carson, opened stores after their husbands died or abandoned them. After her shop closed, it is likely that Morris earned additional income by performing medical treatment or giving medical advice. Although she could not have obtained formal medical training, Morris had gained some knowledge from her physician father, Dr. Richard Hill. Other women taught school or kept boardinghouses or taverns.[35]

Sewing was probably the most common way that women earned money. Books and articles on child rearing and education, from the late eighteenth century and into the nineteenth, advised mothers and teachers to teach their daughters needlework because it was a respectable and useful way to keep occupied, and it was a way that a woman could earn her living, if she had to. These essays do not discuss the long hours spent bent over in poorly lighted rooms, nor do they mention the meager remuneration received for such labor.[36]

In contrast, Mathew Carey reported in his *Essay on the Public Charities of Philadelphia* that seamstresses earned on the average one dollar per week, while their lodgings cost about half a dollar. Furthermore, they were often unemployed during slow seasons. Carey explained that women who did needlework at home had five choices: "to beg—to depend on the overseers of the poor, a species of begging—to steal—to starve—or to sell themselves to pollution—to misery and disease here, and perhaps to misery hereafter." [37]

A year later, in a public letter, Carey asked Mary Queen, the matron of the Provident Society, how many women employed by the society in the winter of 1828–29 were widows. "I should think," she replied, "that at least six hundred of them were widows. At least two thirds of them said they had children to support. The recompense they received averaged about fifty cents per week, while they took out work." [38] The matron also noted that few of the women lived in the city. Carey added that for those coming from Kensington, there was a two-mile walk each way. It took about three days to make four shirts. When completed, the women returned the shirts to the society and received fresh materials. However, if the new supplies were not available, they had to make an extra trip at a later date. [39]

Ann Taylor, in rural Chester County, also took in sewing to support her family when living apart from her drunken, abusive husband. Taylor's case demonstrates in addition the importance of community bonds, even in the 1830s. In her divorce petition, Taylor noted that she "was thrown upon the charity of her neighbors to save herself and two small and helpless children from starvation." Her witnesses in the divorce proceedings corroborated her account. Thomas Woodward, a farmer, reported that neighbors "had occasionally to assist her with the means of living," and Lewis W. Williams noted that she often received flour from his father's mill. [40]

Widows fortunate enough to inherit farms from their husbands also required help from sons, tenants, and maybe outside laborers as well, in order to maintain the farms and their families. Lisa Wilson's study of Chester County widows indicates that before the 1830s, practical Chester County farmers generally left their widows part of the house, supplies, and farm produce. The widow would live in the house with her young children as well as an older son or a tenant who could help to run the farm. In this way the farm widow had shelter, a business, laborers, and a product to sell or consume. [41] This could mean crowded living conditions.

The widow Esther Lewis's household consisted of family members, including mentally handicapped relatives, tenants, hired laborers, and boarders. By the 1840s Lewis had made plans to build a new house.[42] In addition to her farm, which she was actively involved in running, Lewis discovered iron ore on her property and soon had a mine that brought additional income to support her dependents. However, the farm remained her primary concern.[43]

Besides working outside of the home, widows and deserted women, whether in the city or on the farm, had to care for their children. Those unable to do so, and who were without the help of relatives, were forced to send their children to the almshouse. The deserted wife of Marcus Rickars, a Philadelphia blacksmith, brought her fourteen-month-old son to the almshouse. The overseers declared that the "poor infant" seemed to be "half starved." The mother informed them that "Mr. Crook Stevenson, will provide places, for her other two Children; he sent this one here."[44] We can assume that the other two children were old enough to work for Stevenson. Children, some as young as three, who were brought to the almshouse were indentured, sometimes over the protests of their parents. This was true both in Philadelphia and in rural areas outside the city. For poor widows and deserted wives struggling to support themselves, any child who could work did so.[45]

On the other hand, at least one adult woman and her widowed mother entered the Philadelphia Almshouse together. Margaret Cooper's mother, Ann Atley, probably lived with or depended upon her daughter. When Margaret's husband, Gilbert, deserted her, she found that she could not support them because she was "sick with Rheumatism." Margaret and Ann had been born in Bermuda and perhaps had no friends or other kin in Philadelphia.[46]

Both law and custom demanded that grown children care for parents, if necessary. Grown children would provide financial support as well as affection to their parents, especially widowed mothers.[47] Moreover, mothers communicated this sense of mutual obligation to their own children. For instance, Gulielma M. Smith wrote to her mother, Margaret Hill Morris, in reference to her own young daughter, that she hoped that she was "sensible of the obligation she is under to thee, [and I] am in hopes she may with me be favoured to have an opportunity of repaying thee, tho it will be but in a small measure for thy care and trouble of us."[48] Although women without husbands sometimes had difficulties raising children alone, children also brought comfort. Margaret Hill Morris wrote, "For now I see that in losing [their] dear Father, I lost not quite all, for it seems as if it would please Heaven to raise up Comforters to me in the children of my beloved Husband."[49]

Each widow had to cope with her grief in her own way. Morris found solace in her religious beliefs, as well as in her children. Others relieved their tears and anxiety by keeping busy with all the things they now had to do. But a widowed woman's position was at least clear, the estate could at least be settled, and the family could grieve. By the nineteenth century, widows even dressed in a distinctive fashion that indicated their status and set them apart from other women.[50] Even Ann Carson noted this in distinguishing her state of separation from that of a widow. "No weeds of widowhood covered a light heart, or demanded the sympathy and commiseration of the world; yet I was a widow in every sense of the world, except in public estimation."[51]

Because a widow's situation was clear—she had been legally married, but her husband was dead—she might be considered more respectable than a deserted wife. After all, people might wonder what the wife did to drive her husband away. Unmarried mothers sometimes pretended that they had been deserted or widowed, but creating a dead husband certainly made things less complicated for a woman seeking a new past. Several times the minister of Gloria Dei Church in Philadelphia recorded that he had refused to marry a couple because he was not sure that the woman was really a widow. For example, in August 1806 he reported: "A man about 30 came with a widow, as she said. He was a little in liquor. A Man who came for evidence was more so. On being refused the woman was very angry."[52] The Philadelphia Almshouse also treated with suspicion the stories of several inmates. In February 1798 they noted that Catherine Leaman was "a pregnant Woman [who] says she is married." Her husband supposedly was a mariner whose ship was lost at sea, but she provided no details. Catherine also said she could produce a marriage certificate but did not have it with her. The entry concluded that "from her appearances her whole story is very dubious or Equivocal."[53]

Some deserted wives may have mourned the loss of husbands, and some may have hoped for reconciliations. Widowhood, however, was permanent. Those wives who had loved their husbands truly mourned them. Grief was expressed in different ways. In a public tribute to her husband, Elizabeth Haddon Estaugh wrote, "My loss is as far beyond my Expressing as is his Worth." Margaret Hill Morris noted privately, "I believe I shall always suspect that sorrow to be the deepest wch is most silent; loud complaints vent themselves & are soon over." In the nineteenth century Deborah Norris Logan wrote, "My heart is sore, and wounded, and widowed," after her husband, George, died.[54]

Both widows and deserted wives faced emotional upheaval as well as a change in status. This did not change throughout the period of time studied here. Quaker beliefs emphasizing family bonds and a strong sense of religious community may have helped some Pennsylvania women to withstand this difficult transition period. What did change in Pennsylvania were some of the laws regarding divorce, married women's property, and the poor. This enabled *some* women to gain financial support when left without husbands. Moving into the nineteenth century, a re-form spirit brought an increase in public charities designed to take care of widows, deserted women, and their children.[55] In the most desperate situations, these women might have to go to the almshouse or split up their families, sending children to live with various relatives, or placing them in the households of others to work. In general, women who were poor before being widowed or deserted remained so. For both widows and deserted women, the support of family members—both emotional and financial—made a crucial difference in how they maintained them-selves and their families. Having some assets, especially in their own names, gave women some financial and legal advantages. A deserted wife, however, could lose everything if her husband returned.

No doubt many grieving widows would have given up everything to have their beloved husbands return. Independence was not necessarily a blessing. Nevertheless, in a period when marriage was considered to be the ideal condition for adults, and the partnership of husband and wife was sometimes necessary for economic survival, these women who lost their mates frequently managed to support themselves and their families, and even to prosper.

NOTES

The author gratefully acknowledges assistance from a Gest Fellowship at the Quaker Collection, Haverford College, and an Andrew W. Mellon Fellowship at the Library Company of Philadelphia. She wishes to thank the staffs of both institutions.

1. Daily Occurrence Docket, 19 Feb. 1793, Guardians of the Poor, Philadelphia City Archives, Philadelphia (hereafter cited as PCA).

2. Margaret Hill Morris, 18 Aug. 1766, ms. 955, box 6B, folder 2, Edward Wanton Smith Collection, Quaker Collection, Haverford College Library, Haverford, Pa. (hereafter cited as QC).

3. See "Biographical Sketch of Margaret (Hill) Morris," in *Margaret Morris, Her Journal with Biographical Sketch and Notes*, John W. Jackson (Philadelphia: George S. McManus, 1949).

4. Coverture came from the English common law. "An Act Relating to Orphans' Courts," passed in 1832, *Laws of the General Assembly of the State of Pennsylvania* (Harrisburg, Pa., 1832), 190–213, sec. 48, forced husbands to post security before receiving a wife's inheritance, to make sure that at least after the husband's death, she would receive the money. For more on this see Merril D. Smith, *Breaking the Bonds: Marital Discord in Pennsylvania, 1730–1830* (New York: New York University Press, 1991), 159–62. For more on common law, see Marylynn Salmon, "Equality or Submission? Feme Covert Status in Early Pennsylvania," in *Women of America*, edited by Carol Ruth Berkin and Mary Beth Norton (Boston: Houghton Mifflin, 1979), 92–113, esp. 99–101.

5. See "An Act for the Relief of the Poor," *The Statutes at Large of Pennsylvania from 1682 to 1801* (Harrisburg, Pa., 1896), 7:93–94. Husbands could be imprisoned for nonsupport, but again this assumes they had some assets.

6. John K. Alexander, *Render Them Submissive: Responses to Poverty in Philadelphia, 1760–1800* (Amherst: University of Massachusetts Press, 1980), 23. He also notes that the more industrious inmates were given extras, whereas those seen as lazy or disreputable were punished, 119–20.

7. Daily Occurrence Docket, 30 Nov. 1796, PCA.

8. Ibid., 1 May 1792, 11 May 1792.

9. Magdalen Society Minutes, 1800–1810, vol. 1, June 7, 1808, 110–11, Historical Society of Pennsylvania, Philadelphia (hereafter cited as HSP).

10. Alexander, *Render Them Submissive*, 95.

11. These numbers are based only on inmates whose marital status was stated in the Daily Occurrence Dockets *and* who had been admitted because their husbands had deserted them. Dockets from October 1790 to February 1792 and August to December 1799 were missing. Billy G. Smith finds that of the residents of the almshouse in 1800–1801, 6 percent were deserted or abused wives, and

almost one-third of the women admitted had venereal disease or were pregnant. See his *The 'Lower Sort': Philadelphia's Laboring People, 1750–1800* (Ithaca: Cornell University Press, 1990), 168–69. My thanks to Douglas G. Smith for the statistical help.

12. Daily Occurrence Docket, 27 Oct. 1801, 3 Nov. 1800, PCA.

13. Ibid., 9 Dec. 1802, 10 April 1806.

14. Preamble, "First Annual Report of the Managers of the Philadelphia Lying-In Charity, for Attending Indigent Females at Their Own Houses," Library Company of Philadelphia, Philadelphia 1833 (hereafter cited as LCP).

15. Catherine M. Scholten, *Childbearing in American Society: 1650–1850* (New York: New York University Press, 1985), 104–5. Scholten links the move to hospital births after World War I with the rising use of anesthesia, which could be used only in hospitals. Preamble, "First Annual Report, Philadelphia Lying-In Charity."

16. Quarter Sessions Docket, Dec. 1779, PCA.

17. *Directors of the Poor v. Mathew Rumler,* 17 Aug. 1837, Quarter Sessions Records Related to the Directors of the Poor, Warrants to Directors, 1826–39, Chester County Archives, West Chester, Pennsylvania (hereafter cited as CCA).

18. Daily Occurrence Docket, 16 Mar. 1797, PCA.

19. Quarter Sessions Docket, Mar. 1790, PCA.

20. Ibid., June 1796.

21. See "An Act for the Relief of the Poor," *Statutes at Large,* 7:93–94.

22. Quarter Sessions Docket, Nov. 1836; Quarter Sessions Records Related to the Directors of the Poor, Nov. 1836, CCA.

23. See "An Act concerning Divorce and Alimony," *Statutes at Large,* 12:94; "A Supplement to the Act entitled 'An Act concerning Divorces and Alimony,'" *Laws of the Commonwealth of Pennsylvania* (Philadelphia, 1810), 4:182; "Act of 13th March, 1815" and "Act of 26th February 1817," in *Digest of the Laws of Pennsylvania, 1700–1846,* edited by George M. Straub (Philadelphia: Thomas Davis, 1847), 314–18.

24. I am primarily concerned in this essay with women who did not divorce. For more on divorce in Pennsylvania, see Smith, *Breaking the Bonds,* esp. chap. 1 on divorce and chap. 5 on desertion.

25. Mrs. M. Clark, ed., *Memoirs of the Celebrated and Beautiful Mrs. Ann Carson, Daughter of an Officer of the U.S. Navy, and Wife of Another,* 2d ed. (Philadelphia, 1838), 40, 76–77, 136–46, 152–65.

26. Ibid., 116, 146.

27. *The Trial of Richard Smith and Ann Carson, alias Ann Smith, as Accessary, for the Murder of Captain John Carson* (Philadelphia, 1816), 70.

28. Ibid.

29. Clark, *Memoirs of Ann Carson,* vol. 2.

30. Quarter Sessions Records Related to the Directors of the Poor, 3 Aug. 1840, CCA.

31. "The Petition of Elizabeth Clendinnin, Wife of John Clendinnin of Philadelphia County, Inn holder," Philadelphia Quarter Sessions Docket, Dec. 1780, PCA; *Elizabeth Clandennin vs. John Clandennin*, 1786, Petition of Elizabeth Clandennin, Divorce Papers, 1785–1815, Division of Archives and Manuscripts, Records of the Supreme Court, Eastern District, Pennsylvania Historical and Museum Commission, Harrisburg, Pa. Also see Smith, *Breaking the Bonds*, 160–61.

32. Lisa Wilson, *Life after Death: Widows in Pennsylvania, 1750–1850* (Philadelphia: Temple University Press, 1992), 2.

33. Clark, *Memoirs of Ann Carson*, 171; Jackson, "Biographical Sketch," 27; Margaret Hill Morris, "Memorandum for my Children," 7 June 1770, ms. 955, box 6B, additions, folder 2, Edward Wanton Smith Collection, QC.

34. Wilson, *Life after Death*, chap. 2.

35. Smith, *The 'Lower Sort,'* 36–37. Jackson, "Biographical Sketch," 27–28.

36. For one example, see *Thoughts on Domestic Education the Result of Experience by a Mother* (Boston: Carter and Herndee, 1829), 59.

37. Mathew Carey, *Essay on the Public Charities of Philadelphia*, 4th ed. (1829), vii. Carey was concerned about what happened to the children of these women, who he said were often sent out to beg, and thus to begin lives of crime.

38. Mathew Carey, Letter to Samuel Breck, "Sir, Apprehensive that in my past communications on the subject of the inadequacy of the wages of various species of female labour," 28 April 1830, LCP.

39. Ibid.

40. *Taylor vs. Taylor*, 1832, Petition of Ann Taylor, Depositions of Thomas Woodward and Lewis W. Williams, Common Pleas Papers, CCA.

41. Wilson, *Life after Death*, chap. 4, esp. 110–11.

42. Joan M. Jensen, *Loosening the Bonds: Mid-Atlantic Farm Women, 1750–1850* (New Haven, Conn.: Yale University Press, 1986), 132–33.

43. Ibid., chap. 8. Jensen describes Esther Lewis's life in great detail in this chapter.

44. Daily Occurrence Docket, 3 July 1802, PCA.

45. Billy Smith notes that "indentured children accounted for 25 percent of the blacks who lived in white households in 1790." See Smith, *The 'Lower Sort,'* 196, also 166–67. For rural indentures see Jensen, *Loosening the Bonds*, 72–73.

46. Daily Occurrence Docket, 13 Jan. 1804, PCA.

47. For an account of Deborah Norris Logan's reliance on her grown sons, see Terri L. Premo, *Winter Friends: Women Growing Old in the New Republic, 1785–1835* (Urbana: University of Illinois Press, 1990), 32–33.

48. Changes in the relations between parents and children are beyond the scope of this chapter. For one view, see Jay Fliegelman, *Prodigals and Pilgrims: The*

American Revolution against Patriarchal Authority, 1750–1800 (Cambridge: Cambridge University Press, 1982). See also "An Act for the Relief of the Poor," *Statutes at Large*, 7:93–94; Gulielma M. Smith to Margaret Hill Morris, undated letter, box 10, folder 2, Gulielma M. Howland Collection, QC.

49. Margaret Hill Morris to Sister, 12 Mar. 1769, box 7, folder 1, Gulielma M. Howland Collection, QC.

50. Wilson, *Life after Death*, 11–12.

51. Clark, *Memoirs of Ann Carson*, 93.

52. "Remarkable Occurrences," Aug. 1806, Marriage Records of Gloria Dei Church, HSP.

53. Daily Occurrence Docket, 20 Feb. 1798, PCA. Leaman returned to the almshouse in June 1800, pregnant again, reportedly the wife of a Swedish mariner.

54. Elizabeth Estaugh, "Elizabeth Estaugh's Testimony to the Memory of her beloved Husband John Estaugh, deceased," in *A Call to the Unfaithful Professors of Truth*, by John Estaugh (Philadelphia, 1744); Margaret Hill Morris, "Memo," additions, folder 2, Edward Wanton Smith Collection, ms. 955, box 6B, QC.

55. For example, The Philadelphia Indigent Widows and Single Women's Society, The Female Association of Philadelphia for the Relief of Women and Children in Reduced Circumstances, and The Philadelphia Infant School Society. On the Philadelphia Almshouse, see Priscilla Ferguson Clement, *Welfare and the Poor in the Nineteenth Century, Philadelphia, 1800–1854* (Rutherford, N.J.: Fairleigh Dickinson, 1985); Jensen, *Loosening the Bonds*, discusses changes in how the poor were cared for in the Brandywine Valley, 57–76.

12

The Marriage Metaphor in Seventeenth-Century Massachusetts

ELIZABETH DALE

In 1638 Anne Hutchinson stood trial in Massachusetts, first before a civil court and then before her church congregation. Toward the end of her church trial, one of the ministers accused her of stepping out of her place. As that minister, Hugh Peters, put it, Hutchinson preferred rather "to be a husband than a wife, . . . a preacher than a hearer, and a magistrate than a subject."[1] With that comment Peters defined his view of Hutchinson's offense and one view of the place of women in Massachusetts. Women, in his equation, should be passive, silent, and subordinate. Men, in contrast, ruled their families and acted as political and religious leaders. In this view Hutchinson, who had spoken publicly, had acted outside her proper role and should be punished.

Peters's comments not only explain his view of Hutchinson's conduct; they also indicate how marriage was used as a metaphor in the seventeenth century. Marriage as a metaphor reminded people that women should be subordinate and demonstrated how limited the lives and freedoms of women were. The idea of women captured in the marriage metaphor also shapes our understanding of women's lives in seventeenth-century Massachusetts.[2] Yet, perhaps we make a mistake when we rely on that metaphor without examining it carefully.

There are hints, for example, that not everyone shared Hugh Peters's feelings about what Hutchinson did. Even during her trials some people defended her comments and her right to make them. Some of those people went into exile with Hutchinson when she was banished. Others supported the decision to banish Hutchinson but still argued that she should not be punished for speaking publicly. For members of this second group, it was what Hutchinson said that justified her punishment, not the fact that she had spoken in public.[3]

Other uses of the marriage metaphor confirm that there were various views of women and their place in early Massachusetts. In this chapter I consider several different examples of how the marriage metaphor was used. Representing individuals in both England and New England, these examples demonstrate that people understood marriage in a variety of ways and that they employed the marriage metaphor for different purposes.

The marriage metaphor was popular in the seventeenth century, and it has been considered by numerous historians of the period.[4] Most studies that discuss the marriage metaphor in the seventeenth-century Anglo-American world read it as depicting the hierarchical view of marriage suggested by Hugh Peters at Hutchinson's trial and set out in Milton's famous description in *Paradise Lost* of the relation between Adam and Eve—"He for God only, she for God in him."[5] These studies infer from such descriptions that women were uniformly subordinated.

And certainly, many seventeenth-century texts provided a very hierarchical view of marriage. In his conduct manual, *Of Domesticall Duties*, the English Puritan William Gouge elaborated one such view. There, Gouge began his discussion of the obligations of all household members by explaining the way the household was arranged in parallel hierarchies: the husband was superior to a wife, just as parents were superior to children and masters to servants. Gouge then described that hierarchical structure using several other parallels, most famously by comparing the family to the state, asserting that "a family is a little Church, and a little commonwealth." [6]

This parallel had several implications for Gouge's view of the status of women. Most obviously, it meant that married women were the equivalent to citizens in a state, a group Gouge pointed out were subject to higher authority. At other points in his work, Gouge made the depth of that subordination clear. For Gouge, the superiority of the husband over the wife was amply demonstrated by the titles given to husbands in scripture—lord, master, guide, head, and "Image and glory of God." [7] These terms confirmed what other scriptural commands demonstrated, that God gave superiority and authority to the husband over the wife and "said to women, He shall rule over thee." [8]

Gouge reinforced the hierarchy inherent in his description of a marriage by comparing it to another popular model—the body. As Gouge noted, "heathens" often understood hierarchy in terms of a body, where a ruler was counted as the head and the ruled took the place of other parts of the body. Gouge argued that his example made precisely the same point, and he frequently used the body to describe a marriage and, by implication, the state. [9]

Significantly, Gouge used the body as a metaphor for a marriage the way political theorists used the body as a metaphor for a state run by a king—the king was both the head of the state and the state itself; the king and the body politic were one. [10] So too, in Gouge's understanding, a husband was the head of a marriage and the head of his wife, while she was the body of the marriage and the body of her husband. In Gouge's view, the body that a marriage created was essentially male and was the husband. [11]

Because of this hierarchy, because a husband was "to [a wife] as Christ [was] to the Church," a wife had to submit herself to her husband. [12] This additional parallel, comparing the husband to Christ and the wife to the church, had yet another implication. Given the extent to which Christ was superior to the church, a husband was clearly superior to any woman he took as a wife. This meant, Gouge argued, that it was inconceivable that a husband would naturally love his wife. Rather, he had to learn to do so, as Christ loved the church even though it was unworthy and imperfect. And that meant that he had to change her, for just as Christ made the church lovable, the husband had to make his wife lovable even though she was unworthy of his love. And that meant he had to instruct her and correct her, though he could not do so physically.[13]

All this suggests yet another aspect of Gouge's view of marriage and women. He noted that although wives were inferior to their husbands, they were all too often unwilling to accept their inferior status. Given their natural lack of inclination to do so, they had to be trained to accept their subordination for their own good. But they also had to be trained to be subordinate so that other inferiors (particularly children and servants) could learn from their example.[14]

The hierarchical marriage was thus a model, actual and metaphorical, for other relations, religious and political. It was a natural model to the extent that it was a training and testing ground for men, "whereby trial may be made of such as are fit for any place of authority, or of subjection in Church or Commonwealth." Here, it was "a school wherein the first principle and grounds of government and subjection are learned: whereby men are fitted to greater matters in Church or Commonwealth."[15]

But Gouge was not simply concerned with marriage as a school to train men who might one day lead church or state. He was also interested in using marriage as a metaphor to describe the condition of others, who would not be leaders in the state. In the state, although some became leaders and so retained some of the authority that Gouge attributed to husbands, others had to assume the position of subordinates given to wives. Likewise, in the context of religious communities, all members of the congregation were subordinate, as wives were, to the ministers, who were in the position of husbands.[16] In this respect wives were models not only for children and servants; they became models for citizens.

This use of marriage as a metaphor to describe a hierarchical state had one further implication. Within a marriage, Gouge noted, "though a husband in regard to evil qualities may carry the image of the devil, yet in regard to his place and office [in the family], he beareth the image of Christ." A husband's evil nature, though regrettable, was not a ground for divorce.[17] Gouge appeared, in these passages, to contradict his earlier claim that husbands could never correct a woman physically, suggesting that husbands had complete authority over their wives to the point of doing them physical harm. But actually, his message was more ambiguous. Wives had to remain subordinate to husbands who resembled devils, but Gouge did not believe it was natural for husbands to act that way. Those who did beat their wives were, in Gouge's view, actually possessed by the devil.[18] Thus, Gouge did not approve of husbands doing harm to their wives, but he made no provision for wives who were subject to that sort of abuse.

The same ambivalence appeared implicitly in his brief discussions of state and of church. Good leaders did not harm or oppress their subordinates, but Gouge did not discuss what those subordinates should do when their leaders were bad. By implication, they had to do what wives did. The leader or minister might be evil and do harm, but the people, like wives married to an evil husband, had no authority to remove themselves from the harm.

Although Gouge presented a very complete version of the hierarchical model of marriage, his was not the only one. Others used similar metaphors, though they did not emphasize the same aspects or draw precisely the same conclusions that Gouge did. Elizabeth Poole, a sectarian prophet in England during the civil war, relied on the marriage metaphor when she argued in a 1649 pamphlet that Parliament could not execute Charles I.[19] Like Gouge, her basic premise was that a king had the same relationship to his people (including Parliament) as a husband had to his wife.

Just as Gouge had, Poole explained the marriage metaphor by means of parallels. One was a comparison straight out of Gouge: she also argued that the relations between king and people and husband and wife could be explained by reference to a third image—the body. For Poole, as for Gouge, the king and the husband were the head, the people and the wife, the body.[20]

There were several implications to Poole's use of this comparison. Most obviously, by equating marriage and a body, Poole suggested that marriage was hierarchical. She also implied that it was a natural and inevitable hierarchy. Her emphasis on the natural aspect of this hierarchy had implications of its own. Because bodies could not exist without heads, her comparison suggested that people could not exist without rulers and that wives could not exist without husbands. Her argument that Parliament could not behead Charles I made this implicit point explicit.

To this extent Poole's view of marriage as a hierarchical relationship resembled that of Gouge. Yet in other respects her view was more extreme. The sense in which her view of the nature of marriage was more hierarchical is first suggested by the way she collapsed husbands and fathers. Although Gouge had compared fathers to parents and wives to children in drawing his parallels, at other times he explicitly distinguished the husband and father categories, noting that fathers could physically correct their children, but husbands could not physically correct their wives.[21] Poole did not make that distinction, but rather referred to the king as both husband and father. It was no accident that she collapsed those categories, since she suggested that husbands could physically correct, and potentially even physically harm, their wives.[22] In this respect the husband in Poole's understanding of marriage had a type of power that he did not have in Gouge's description.

There was, then, both a practical and a theoretical difference between the images of hierarchical marriage provided by Gouge and Poole. On the practical level, Poole understood that a husband's authority over his wife included physical control, whereas Gouge denied that such authority should exist. And this meant that at a theoretical level, they described different phenomena—Gouge described a hierarchical marriage, where husbands had considerable, but limited, authority; Poole described a patriarchal one, where husbands' power was seemingly unrestricted.

Poole's description of a patriarchal marriage had implications for the other part of her parallel: just as a wife could not rid herself of her husband, no matter how evil or abusive a king might be, his people had to submit to him. In Poole's view of the relation between husband and wife, a wife could only try to restrain her husband; she could never do more.[23] So, too, the people could not resist or kill their king, regardless of his failings or the harm he did.

When Poole employed the body as a third term that explained the parallels between the relations of king and people and those of husband and wife, she reinforced the extent to which the hierarchical model depended on nature. Insofar as it rested on that appeal to nature, Poole's model assumed some mutuality because neither part could survive without the other. But while kings and husbands needed people and wives in order to fulfill their roles, in Poole's eyes that need created mutuality but not equality.[24] For the potential for abuse by kings and husbands that Poole's image both granted and accepted made it clear that in her view neither force nor power flowed both ways in the relationships.

Whereas Elizabeth Poole used a patriarchal model to emphasize the extent of the hierarchy she described and the extent to which submission was required in relations between king and people and husband and wife, John Winthrop focused on another aspect of the metaphor and drew other lessons from it.[25] Arguing in 1637 that the Massachusetts government could choose to bar some people from entering its community, Winthrop claimed that exclusion was permissible by analogy to the family. Just as a family "was a little commonwealth," the converse was true as well, and a commonwealth was like a family. Because a family did not open its doors to anyone, but could choose to entertain only those it pleased, a commonwealth could also admit some and not others.[26]

Here, Winthrop's analysis began with language identical to that used by Gouge; but in contrast to Gouge, Winthrop focused not on marriage as a relation between husband and wife, but on the family. This shift in focus had several implications. Initially, it meant that Winthrop emphasized the integrity of the family unit more than the hierarchical aspect of the family run by the father and husband. He reinforced this aspect of his analysis by comparing the colony to a corporation and a church, both of them—in New England at least—institutions with power to exclude.[27]

Though that comparison played down the hierarchical element, hierarchy was still present in Winthrop's discussion. In a subsequent text elaborating his reasons for supporting the act excluding strangers, Winthrop specifically noted that the magistrates could legitimately outlaw otherwise lawful dissent. As Winthrop put it, arguing otherwise would mean that "a wife, a child, [or] a servant may do anything that is lawful, though the husband, father, or master, deny their consent." The result "will be anarchy." Winthrop later repeated his earlier argument that a family could exclude, but he argued that such power rested in the master of the family, who could bar anyone from the family home and from its chambers, even a chamber given over to the exclusive use of one member of the family.[28] These elaborations made clear that in Winthrop's view wives and children were subordinated to husbands and fathers just as citizens were subordinated to those who ruled.

Winthrop's image of family and society was hierarchical, although not in quite the same manner as the images offered by Gouge or Poole. His focus on the family rather than on marriage to some extent suggested Poole's patriarchal model, since both equated fathers and husbands. But Winthrop did not go as far as Poole. His rulers, like Gouge's husbands, were not supposed to harm. They were supposed to protect their people, just as husbands and fathers protected their wives and children.

Because Winthrop's model did not give as much power to husbands, fathers, or rulers, it was not as patriarchal as Poole's. It is probably more accurate to say it was a paternalistic model instead. But his paternalism did not lack bite. As Winthrop's treatment of Anne Hutchinson and his other writings made clear, paternalism as he understood it subordinated women just as much as Gouge's hierarchical model of marriage.[29] In those writings Winthrop described women as perpetual children, who should not be permitted to think or appear to challenge the authority of their husbands or leaders. Here, his view of women differed from that offered by Gouge. Where Gouge was concerned with the number of women who refused to accept their subordinate status, and urged correction and instruction to end that response, Winthrop believed that only unnatural women challenged their position.[30] Likewise, his other works established what his writings in support of the act against strangers suggested: he believed people should accept the decisions of their leaders, who were more qualified to understand situations and make decisions.[31]

Responding to Winthrop's argument that a commonwealth, like a family, could exclude, Henry Vane, a previous governor of Massachusetts and later one of the people executed for complicity in the death of Charles I, mocked Winthrop's use of the analogy. Vane objected that the comparison gave too limited a picture of the freedom of individuals within the state.[32] Thus, while he rejected the analogy, Vane did not reject the assumptions upon which it was based. To refute Winthrop's argument, Vane played off the notion of the hierarchical family. A colony, he maintained, could not exclude people by analogy to the exclusive nature of a family; as observation indicated, a colony was not as hierarchical as a family. Where a family was ordered so that the husband and father had complete control over all the family property and could dispose of it as he wished, no government could dispose of its people's property in the same way.

Further, Vane declared that in the particular case of Massachusetts, the analogy was inapt for two reasons. First, some in that colony might not be citizens, so the Massachusetts government had political authority over some who were not fully part of it. Government thus lacked the complete integrity of a family. Second, the colony was under the authority of the king and therefore was not as independent as a family might be. There was too "great [a] disparity" between the family and the state for the one to provide an accurate image of the other.[33]

By rejecting the equation of family and state, Vane rejected the hierarchical model of the state offered, in different ways, by Gouge, Poole, and Winthrop. But his quarrel was with the use of the metaphor as applied to the state, not with the hierarchical image of a marriage upon which it rested. Indeed, Vane's comments suggested that he rejected the metaphor because he shared the general view that marriage was a hierarchy subordinating wives. He wanted to avoid that sort of hierarchy in describing the state.

Richard Mather, in his *Apologie of the Churches of New England*, drafted in 1639 and published in 1643, presented a significantly different picture of marriage. Mather, a minister in Dorchester, Massachusetts, wrote the *Apologie* to explain the nature of the church covenant in New England. In the course of doing so, he discussed a variety of other sorts of covenants, including the marriage covenant, in depth. The result is a text that asserted that marriage was a proper metaphor for the state but denied that marriage should be chiefly understood as hierarchical.

Mather began by noting that there were several types of covenants in Scripture. Sometimes, covenants were no more than "firm appointment[s] or promise[s] of God, when man does not promise unto God anything back again." Other times, the "covenant [was] taken more strictly and properly for an agreement which God does make with men, when he promises some blessing unto man, and binds them to perform some duty back again to him."[34] But Mather went on to observe that there were other types of covenants, such as covenants within cities or other political organizations. These covenants shared particular qualities, chief among them being that they could not oblige some "to take upon them authority or power over free men without their free consent, and voluntary and mutual covenant or engagement."[35] In Mather's view, even the covenant between God and God's people had to reflect this voluntariness. Indeed, as Mather saw it, any voluntary covenant had to reflect these requirements of liberty, freedom, and equality. This was also true of the marriage covenant, which Mather explicitly described as voluntary. In fact, Mather used marriage as the model of a voluntary covenant that explained all others of that sort.[36]

To define the voluntary covenant, Mather distinguished it from relations based on nature or conquest. Doing so, he separated his view of marriage from that offered by the hierarchical model. Where that model, especially as it was set out by Poole, emphasized the extent to which the relation between husband and wife was itself modeled on that between parents and children, Mather declared that these were relations of different types. The relation between parent and child was the classic example, in Mather's view, of a natural relation. There, the parties could not choose to enter into the relation, and this lack of choice dictated the nature of the relationship throughout the course of its existence.[37]

In Mather's schema, the relation between a parent and a child bore a close resemblance to a relation based on conquest. These relations, resulting from war or some other undertaking, were also involuntary, at least from the perspective of one of the parties.[38] In this sort of relation, the complete absence of choice on the part of the conquered party was the defining element of the relation and continued to define it throughout its existence.

The result was that in both involuntary and natural relations, a second defining criterion was the imbalance of power between the parties. Parents had authority over their children, and conquerors had power over those they conquered, but neither children nor conquered peoples had reciprocal power. The first great difference between a voluntary covenant and one of these two types of relations was that both parties to a voluntary covenant had freely consented to enter that covenant. This requirement of free consent was mandated by "moral equity," and Mather specifically found it in marriage, political, and religious covenants.[39]

Voluntary covenants also had, as part of their essential nature, reciprocity.[40] Thus, just as a king and his people undertook mutual responsibilities when they created a political covenant, so too a husband and wife undertook mutual responsibilities when they married. This said, there were limits to the agency that Mather's description of a marriage allowed women. He did, in one place, argue that a woman entering into marriage "gave herself unto her husband," implying that marriage subordinated women to men. Yet, shortly thereafter, he argued that when the marriage covenant brought a man and woman together, it gave "them mutual power over each other as husband and wife." A few pages later he refused to describe marriage as a relation in which wives were naturally subordinated to their husbands. Instead, he argued that marriage was created by a woman's voluntary undertaking, to marry a particular man and assume the duties of a wife.[41]

A further sense of Mather's view of marriage can be derived by comparing it to the church covenant. There, the covenant had several aspects. Two are particularly notable here. From one perspective it was a covenant between a minister and a particular congregation. In this sense it was a hierarchical relationship, since Mather (a minister himself) hardly intended to deny that the minister led the congregation. Yet, even here the relation was reciprocal. Ministers had no inherent, or natural, power. They derived their power from the fact that a particular congregation called them. Their power came from, and was thus controlled by, the congregation. That power was limited further by the fact that they were the servants of the congregation. The congregation did not exist for their benefit; they existed for the congregation's.[42]

But there was another perspective on the church covenant. It was also a covenant between the members of the congregation. Here, the relationship between the parties was completely reciprocal. The members of the congregation had obligations to each other and existed as a congregation in order to fulfill them. Indeed, they gathered into a church in order to undertake those obligations, and the evidence of a covenanted church was that the members of the congregation undertook them to each other.[43]

In Mather's view, the political covenant had similar dimensions. In a civic covenant, as Mather described it, the people called their leaders and the leaders undertook the obligations of protection and leadership involved in that calling. Though the leaders held power, that power was derived from the covenant and was not an expression of some inherent authority.[44]

Mather's understanding of political and church covenants defined his understanding of marriage. As was the case in the political and religious covenants, the marriage covenant had more than one aspect. One was religious. This aspect had two consequences for a marriage. First, it meant that the covenant, although between the husband and the wife, was actually a covenant with a third party—God. As a result the hierarchy that the covenant reflected did not set husband over wife. Rather, it set God over both. This led to the second aspect of the marriage covenant. Just as a failure of the rulers in the state, or of the ministry in a church, could lead God to punish the covenanting parties, so too a failure of the parties to the marriage to live up to their obligations to each other could lead God to punish them.[45]

In all of these cases, the significance of the covenant was not simply that it obligated all the parties to each other. More significant were two other aspects. First, the covenant created a new entity, and that entity made new people of the parties to the covenant: just as the civic covenant created a state, the religious covenant created a church, and the marriage covenant created a marriage.

And there were new roles for the parties within these new relationships. A citizen of the state was different from a stranger, a member of a covenanted church was different from a believer who was not part of the church, and a woman or a man within a marriage was different from one outside it.[46] This led to the other, more important aspect of the covenants. Each covenant created a new liberty for the parties within it, a liberty that resulted from the reciprocal duties of the covenantors. In Mather's construction, liberty was manifested by acting in a manner consistent with the authority one attains from behaving as Scripture commanded. That liberty gave each woman the power to "make herself a wife by her own voluntary covenant."[47] It also included the capacity to determine that the other party had failed to follow those commands, and to leave the covenant when that occurred, even in a marriage.[48]

Mather's notion that a marriage was a voluntary covenant meant that he understood it to include a greater freedom for both wives and husbands than Peters, Gouge, Poole, Winthrop, or Vane did. But while his view was the most expansive, it was not unique in being different from the idea of marriage offered by Peters. The several people whose writings are considered in this chapter all understood marriage differently and brought a variety of meanings to the marriage metaphor and to their understanding of the lives of women.

Those different views were significant, particularly because Gouge, Winthrop, Vane, and Mather were all seventeenth-century Puritans. It suggests that there was not a single view of women and that our understanding of how women lived during that time must take those different perspectives into account.[49] Women's freedom was undeniably limited in seventeenth-century Massachusetts, yet the range of meanings people brought to the marriage metaphor suggests that we should be careful to examine, rather than to assume, how women actually lived in early America.

NOTES

1. Comments of Hugh Peters before the Boston Church. "Report of the Trial of Mrs. Anne Hutchinson before the Church in Boston," in *The Antinomian Controversy, 1636–1638: A Documentary History*, edited by David D. Hall, 2d ed. (Durham, N.C.: Duke University Press, 1990), 382–83.

2. See, for example, Jane Neill Kamensky, "Governing the Tongue: Speech and Society in Early New England" (Ph.D. diss., Yale University, 1994), 185; John Demos, *A Little Commonwealth: Family Life in Plymouth Colony* (New York: Oxford University Press, 1970), chap. 5; Edmund S. Morgan, *The Puritan Family: Religion and Domestic Relations in Seventeenth-Century New England* (New York: Harper and Row, 1966), 162–68.

3. See the comments of John Cogshall and William Colburn during the civil trial of Anne Hutchinson in November 1637. "Examination of Mrs. Anne Hutchinson at the Court at Newtown," in Hall, *The Antinomian Controversy*, 311, 331, 332–33, 344, 345, 347, 348. For other comments supporting Hutchinson during the church trial, see "Report of the Trial," 356, 386. For an example from the second group, see "Examination of Mrs. Anne Hutchinson," 316–17 (comments of Simon Bradstreet). For an extended discussion of this, see Elizabeth Dale, "Debating—and Creating—Authority: A Legal History of the Trial of Anne Hutchinson" (Ph.D. diss., University of Chicago, 1995), esp. chap. 4.

4. Susan Dwyer Amussen, *An Ordered Society: Gender and Class in Early Modern England* (New York: Basil Blackwell, 1988), 55–66.

5. John Milton, *Paradise Lost* (London, 1667), book 4, line 299; Demos, *A Little Commonwealth*, 82.

6. See William Gouge, *Of Domesticall Duties, Eight Treatises in the Works of William Gouge in Two Volumes*, 2d ed. (London, 1627), vol. 1 (misnumbered in the printing), 10a, relying on Ephesians 5 and 6, and 10b. (Because this text is printed in double-column pages, page citations indicate the column by *a* or *b*.)

7. Gouge, *Domesticall Duties*, 158b.

8. Ibid., 158b (citing Gen. 3:16), and 159b-160a.

9. Ibid., 17a-b, 44a, 159a-160a.

10. See Ernst H. Kantorowicz, *The King's Two Bodies: A Study in Medieval Political Theology* (Princeton, N.J.: Princeton University Press, 1957); and Stephen L. Collins, *From Divine Cosmos to Sovereign State: An Intellectual History of Consciousness and the Idea of Order in Renaissance England* (New York: Oxford University Press, 1989), chap. 1.

11. Gouge, *Domesticall Duties*, 44a, 158b-159a, 159a-b.

12. Ibid., 17a.

13. Ibid., 44b, 224b, 225a-b, 226a.

14. Ibid., 12a, 13b, 14b, 14b-15a.

15. Ibid., 10a-b.

16. Ibid., 3a-b, 8b.

17. Ibid., esp. "Treatise 2," 14b-15a.

18. Ibid., 249b.

19. Elizabeth Poole, *An Alarum of War, Given to the Army and to Their High Court of Justice (so called) revealed by the will of God in a vision to E. Poole* (London, 1648), 7–9. For another discussion of this passage, see Amussen, *An Ordered Society*, 62.

20. Poole, *An Alarum*, 7–9.

21. Gouge, *Domesticall Duties*, 224b.

22. Poole, *An Alarum*, 7.

23. Kathleen M. Brown, "Brave New Worlds: Women's and Gender History," *William and Mary Quarterly*, 3d ser., 50 (April 1993):311, 324.

24. Cf. Gouge, *Domesticall Duties*, 159b.

25. John Winthrop, "A Defense of an Order of Court Made in the Year 1637," in *Hutchinson Papers*, reprinted in *The Publications of the Prince Society*, vol. 2 (Albany, N.Y.: Joel Munsel, 1865), 79, 81.

26. Ibid., 81.

27. Ibid., 80.

28. See John Winthrop, "A Reply to an Answer," in *Hutchinson Papers*, reprinted in *The Publications of the Prince Society*, vol. 2 (Albany, NY: Joel Munsel, 1865), 99, 106, 104.

29. John Winthrop, *Journal, or A History of New England*, James Kendall Hosmer, ed., 2 vols. (New York: Scribner's, 1908), 1:282–83, 285–86, 2:93.

30. Ibid., 1:285–86.

31. Ibid., 2:237–39, 339–40.

32. See Henry Vane, "A Brief Answer to a Certain Declaration," in *Hutchinson Papers*, reprinted in *The Publications of the Prince Society*, vol. 2 (Albany, N.Y.: Joel Munsel, 1865), 84, 89–90, 90.

33. Ibid., 90.

34. See Richard Mather, *An Apologie of the Churches of New England* (London, 1643), 2.

35. Ibid., 9.

36. Ibid., 7, 9, 11–12, 15, 21–23.

37. Ibid., 22.

38. Ibid., 22.

39. Ibid., 9, 22–23, 24.

40. Ibid., 7–8, 15.

41. Ibid., 15, 24.

42. Ibid., 23.

43. Ibid., 15, 23.

44. Ibid., 23.

45. Ibid., 7, 12, 16, 24.

46. Ibid., 7.

47. Ibid., 24 (rejecting a more limited reading of Eph. 5:22). Cf. Gouge, *Domesticall Duties.*

48. Mather, *Apologie*, 22, 24.

49. For a more general discussion of this point, see Janice Knight, *Orthodoxies in Massachusetts: Re-reading Puritanism* (Cambridge: Harvard University Press, 1994).

13

"If Widow, Both Housewife and Husband May Be": Widows' Testamentary Freedom in Colonial Massachusetts and Maryland

VIVIAN BRUCE CONGER

On January 25, 1709, a Boston merchant named Thomas Banister wrote his will, which included a lengthy rationale for his bequest to his wife, Sarah. He explained that it "draws tears from mine Eyes" to leave her nothing more than she was legally allowed by dower law (one-third of his real property for her lifetime and one-third of his personal estate forever). Except token bequests of money to his married daughter, a grandson, and others, he divided his entire estate among his three sons. He maintained that his widow wanted no more and that her thirds would be "ample provision" for her. Then he revealed what perhaps was his real reason for not providing his widow with more than her thirds: "Altho, if you and I were to live together to the longest Age of man I should not fear your wronging our Children, unless by your overkindness & Tenderness toward them, Yet it often falls out otherwise upon Second mariages as Experience daily shews." In a codicil attached six months later he said he was "informed" that he had not provided for Sarah as he "intended and expected" he had. To remedy the oversight, he left Sarah an additional one thousand pounds out of his personal estate. Thomas Banister need not have worried that Sarah would wrong their children. Two years later she died a widow and followed the inheritance pattern established by her husband. Except for money and clothing given to her daughter and money to her grandson, she divided her entire estate among her three sons.[1] In both cases the testators seemed to assume that their married daughter would be cared for as Thomas had cared for Sarah.

Nearly twenty years later, on October 1, 1728, Sarah Wheeler, also of Boston, wrote a will in which she too explained her various bequests to her children and grandchildren. She noted that although she had divided her entire estate among her son, Samuel, two married daughters, and her unmarried daughter, Sarah Wheeler, she was giving Sarah an additional £90 for her to "procure Houshold Goods" in case Sarah the elder died before her daughter married, "because She has not had so much Advantage as some of my Children have had to get for herself."[2] Sarah Wheeler wanted her unmarried daughter to buy the requisite goods to marry well—or perhaps to support herself if she did not marry. In devising her estate to both sons and daughters, Sarah Wheeler implicitly expressed a fear that her two married daughters might need her economic support, and she explicitly argued that her unmarried daughter needed even more help than the others because she had not had the opportunity to better her economic situation on her own.

The differences in the bequests provided by Thomas Banister, Sarah Banister, and Sarah Wheeler represent different approaches to widows' will making in colonial Massachusetts and Maryland between 1639 and 1750 that will be explored in this chapter. Widows who controlled family wealth had some power to contribute to the families' prosperity before their own deaths, and they had some power to contribute to their children's prosperity through their own wills. Widows' estates might have been small, or at least smaller than their husbands', but as female heads of households, they played an important role in the distribution of wealth and power in colonial communities, as members of those communities recognized.

The way early American widows devised their estates reflects a complex account of how they responded to gender roles promulgated in advice literature (sermons and conduct books), family obligations, gen-

dered notions of property, and changing economic and demographic circumstances. Through their bequests of realty, household goods, slaves,
and intangible goods, and the conditions they attached to them, widows
sometimes conformed to, but often deviated from, male-determined public norms. In doing so they openly exerted their legal and personal wills,
exercised a great deal of autonomy and discretion, and provided for their
daughters in ways that male testators did not.

Historians are only beginning to examine women's wills. Their slow-
ness to do so is due partly to an implicit assumption that those wills add
nothing to our understanding about the family because they simply
reflected male bequeathing patterns. Their findings suggest that the
assumption is not valid. Studies by Susan Amussen, Vivian Brodsky,
Joan Jensen, and Suzanne Lebsock, for example, show that widows in
sixteenth- and seventeenth-century England and late eighteenth- and
early nineteenth-century America had the freedom or flexibility to bequeath more widely among cousins, nieces, nephews, and nonkin than
men did. These historians claim that widows could do this for two
reasons: men, who bore the primary responsibility for establishing their
children's economic futures, had previously provided for their children in
their wills, and thus widows were free from parental responsibility and
could bequeath more widely; and widows simply had fewer unmarried
children and more grandchildren and near kin to bequeath to than men
had. Such widows bequeathed according to their heirs' needs rather than
according to guidance offered in books and from pulpits.[3] The arguments
presented in these studies imply that widows' responsibilities to their
immediate families were less compelling and perhaps less important than
those of men.

In colonial America, between 70 and 80 percent of all Massachusetts
and Maryland widows' bequests of real property, household goods, slaves,
and intangibles went to their children and grandchildren, belying widows'
so-called freedom from parental responsibility.[4] Focusing on widows'
bequests to near kin and nonkin, therefore, ignores their significant
contribution to the family economy. A cursory examination of the general
characteristics of the testators reveals another important point: a large
proportion of widows had dependent children under their care and responsibility. Widows in Massachusetts named grandchildren as legatees

approximately one-third more often than male testators did, and widows in Maryland did so twice as often as did male testators. Because male testators appear to have been younger than widow testators, they may have been under more pressure to ensure the economic survival of their sons, often at the expense of bequests to daughters. Concomitantly, widows may have had the freedom to be more equitable in dividing their estates. Regardless, a third of the widows in Massachusetts and over half the widows in Maryland named dependent children as heirs, suggesting that they shared their husbands' sense of responsibility to the next generation.

The English settlers of the American colonies brought with them particular beliefs about household and community structures. Both husbands and wives, according to one popular English author, had "certain things in the house that only do pertain to the authority of the husbands . . . [and] there are other things in which the husband giveth over his right unto the woman."[5] The specific tasks they performed enabled the household to survive as an interdependent unit. Thomas Tusser, author of one of England's most popular books on "husbandry" and housewifery from the sixteenth through the nineteenth centuries, captured the essence of this relationship when he wrote, "Take weapon away, of what force is a man? Take housewife from husband, and what is he then?"[6] These lines suggest that both husbands and wives fulfilled important but different responsibilities within the household—until death disrupted the complementary relationship. Tusser then described how a widow's (and for that matter, a widower's) life changed upon the death of a spouse: "If widow, both housewife and husband may be, what cause hath a widower less than she?"[7] The complementary roles of husband and wife devolved upon the widow, as she was expected to assume both. Widows, then, acquired new responsibilities to the household and to the community.

Colonial ministers and advice-book authors expected and taught widows to assume rights and responsibilities within an intricate web of communal standards of gender and status. Upon the death of their husbands, wives became not only widows, but heads of households. Sermons and conduct books advised widows to "supply the place of both parents" and to add "to the tenderness of a mother, . . . the care and conduct of a father."[8] They explicitly pointed out that a widow became a "father as well as mother to the orphans with whom she is left entrusted."[9] Widows' newly assumed responsibilities as both mother and father of the household entailed the duty to safeguard their children's fortunes. An ideological disjunction arose, however, between their responsibilities and how ministers and authors expected widows to carry them out, because most colonial writings assumed that parenthood signified that the masculine head of the household would and should oversee his children's financial future.

Although conduct-book authors cautioned widows against using their sons' estates to help them find second husbands, they cared little about the price a daughter paid for her mother's remarriage because they assumed that land and its resources rightfully belonged to men. For example, *The Whole Duty of Man*, a book widely read in the colonies, instructed the wealthy parent to "distribute [his estate] to his children, remembering that since he was the instrument of bringing them into the world, he is, according to his ability, to provide for their comfortable living in it."[10] Although books and sermons admonished both parents to nourish their children's physical and spiritual well-being, they directed the father to bequeath *his* wealth to *his* children. It was no accident that this advice, ostensibly given to both mothers and fathers, targeted the father alone.[11]

Given this bias toward male parental responsibilities and male control over various forms of property, it is almost impossible to learn why some widows left wills and others did not. Testators, especially those in Maryland, rarely explained their actions. The few who did, however, are revealing. Some widows left explanations, like that of Joanna Newman of Dorchester, Massachusetts, who claimed that "the frame and Constitution" of her husband's will required her to "Sett my house in order."[12] Similarly, widows such as Elizabeth Hearsey of Hingham left wills because their husbands' wills instructed them to bequeath to their children the goods the husbands had bequeathed (usually for the widow's lifetime only) to their wives.[13] Many colonists, especially in Massachusetts, linked this material responsibility to a spiritual responsibility. For example, widows claimed that—according to Scripture—it was their responsibility to "sett [their] house in order." In addition, widows asserted—again according to Scripture—that if they did not provide for their children through their wills, they at best neglected Christian teachings and at worst behaved like pagans or heretics.[14]

At the funeral of the widow Mary Rock, Cotton Mather told his audience that "Pious Parents have their Piety often Rewarded in the Prosperity of their Children. They get their Estates Honestly; they wear well; their Children Inherit the Earth which they leave unto them." To make sure his listeners understood his message, he added that "The Parents devise Libral Things; the Children reap the Harvest of that Liberality. The Alms dispensed by the Parents, are a Seed sown in the Earth for the Children."[15]

Playing on widows' sense of piety and understanding of Scripture, Mather specifically used Mary Rock as an exemplar for widows in the community. Through her, he tried to demonstrate that their children's prosperity rewarded widows who dutifully carried out their role as temporary guardians of their children's fortunes by generously dividing their estates among their children. In linking piety and will making, he showed that, as heads of households, widows had an economic and social stake in their community, in the survival of their offspring, and in the structure of the family. Living up to their responsibilities as heads of households entailed dividing their estates among their heirs and legatees. It also symbolized the ambiguity in gender roles that urged widows to act as both mother and father to their children.

Mary Baker's will, in which she declared that she had by her "Industry and care Acquired some Estate of my own ... and not only well nigh cleared my said husbands Estate From Debts, but much advanced the same," suggests perhaps the most significant reason widows left wills. Like Baker, Ann Pollard of Boston proudly declared that "the Estate left by my said Husband is Considerably Advanced and bettered by the Disbursements, I have made thereon, in buildings, and otherwise since his Decease." She then elaborated on her self-reliance, claiming that she paid for these disbursements "out of my own proper gettings by my Labour and Industry over and above what I have acquired in Plate and other things." Other widows noted that they had, through their own "hard and difficult" endeavors, "gotten and Acquired" since their husbands' deaths a (sometimes considerable) separate estate (including land and household goods they purchased) to bequeath.[16]

Widows left wills because they understood their economic responsibilities as heads of households, because they had worked hard to increase the estates left to them by their husbands, and because they wanted to control the distribution of those estates. The motivations of these widows provide new insight into the way widows viewed their individual and familial responsibilities and call into question the prevalence of the interdependent but gender-segregated responsibilities of the patriarchal household. Widows themselves did not draw clear distinctions between the categories of male-female, father-mother, or husband-wife. In their role as heads of households in a male-dominated society, they took the skills they had learned as deputy husbands and applied them to their role as fathers. They did not question their responsibility to work hard to increase their own estate and to secure the economic future of those upon whom they chose to bestow their estates.

Men in both colonies controlled more wealth than did widows. Across time, the mean value of widows' estates equalled 54 percent of men's estates in Massachusetts and 82 percent of men's estates in Maryland. To say that men possessed larger estates than widows, however, does not negate the fact that some widows controlled substantial wealth in colonial America. The contest over Hannah Sharpe's estate illustrates that widows in Massachusetts or Maryland constituted neither a widespread "widowarchy" nor a large group of economically dependent and powerless women.[17] In questioning the appraisal and final settlement of Sharpe's estate, a relative claimed that the administrator of the estate (Hannah Sharpe's son-in-law, Benjamin Gallop) presented a fraudulent account because it was "very Improbable that a Woman of Mrs. Sharpe['s] frugality & Carrecter who always lived in very good Credit & Reputation, her house well furnished till she removed to Mr. Gallops, should die & leave among all hir household stuff not a plate, dish or anything Else of pewter."[18] The widow Sharpe was poor enough (and perhaps sick enough) to move into her married daughter's household, but she was not so poor, according to one incredulous relative, as to lack valuable pewter goods among her final possessions. Many widows possessed real and personal estates to bequeath, and they bequeathed them in detail to their daughters and sons.

Both a widower's and a widow's death represented the final dissolution of the parental nuclear family and presented the last opportunity for providing for the family's long-term financial well-being.[19] Yet, widows in Massachusetts and Maryland bequeathed their property to children differently from the way men did. In general, between 1630 and 1750, men increasingly favored sons over daughters, whereas widows increasingly granted daughters a larger portion of their estates. The difference between male and widow bequeathing practices reflects their understanding of advice literature as well as their conception of an efficient and effective distribution of their families' wealth. More specifically, bequests widows made of their real property, slaves, household goods, and intangibles reveal not only how gendered identities influenced the way colonial American widows devised their estates, but also how widows used each category of goods to reconstruct those identities in various and complicated ways. Let us examine those patterns in detail.

REAL PROPERTY

Land and housing, real property, are traditionally considered the most valuable and probably the most seemingly masculine property in early America. In the aggregate, widows in Massachusetts and Maryland, a third of whom bequeathed real property, named sons as recipients of that property more than twice as often as they did daughters. Although fewer widows in Maryland than in Massachusetts had real property to bequeath, over time widows increased their bequests of realty to daughters, while they decreased such bequests to sons. Between 1690 and 1719 Massachusetts widows bequeathed real property to sons more than twice as often as they did to daughters, and Maryland widows did so three times more often. Between 1720 and 1750 both Massachusetts and Maryland widows narrowed those gaps by bequeathing realty slightly less than twice as often to sons as to daughters. Over the entire time, men in both colonies favored sons over daughters by nearly a four-to-one ratio.

Although the improving situation of widows' daughters (and the concomitant declining position of sons) was not drastic, it represents widows' changing beliefs about the kind of property their daughters rightfully deserved; and in comparison to male bequests, it is significant. The pattern becomes more striking when we realize that the percentage of widows who bequeathed real property (and thus had property to bequeath) declined over the same period of time by 10 percent.[20] At a time when widows' access to land decreased and the proportion of male testators who bequeathed land increased, widows expanded their daughters' access to land.

Urban and rural widows bequeathed realty slightly differently. Overall, urban widows favored sons approximately twice as often as they did daughters, but specific patterns reveal a steadily improving outlook for daughters of widowed testators. Urban men named sons as recipients of land nearly five times more often than they did daughters. Rural testators of both sexes, on the other hand, favored sons over daughters as recipients of real property. The tendency to keep land in the hands of men remained strong, particularly among male testators, in rural areas where land was the most crucial to the economic viability of succeeding generations. Although rural widows did not overtly overturn this assumption as consistently as urban widows did, many ignored it by granting their daughters a slowly increasing access to land, thereby implicitly calling the assumption into question.

Bequeathing patterns of specific types of real property also illustrated changing gender roles and expectations. Mothers in both colonies understood the importance of houses for their daughters, if only as a way to insure they would have a place to live after their mothers' deaths. Seven out of ten Massachusetts widows and four out of ten Maryland widows bequeathed houses to their daughters. That fewer Maryland widows than Massachusetts widows did so suggests that Maryland widows may have been dependent on sons who had been bequeathed the dwelling house by their fathers, but it also suggests that widows more highly valued bequests of other types of real property, especially given the predominance of agriculture in that area. Bequests of land clarify the point.

In Massachusetts, if widows possessed only land, they were nearly five times more likely to give such land to sons than they were to daughters, while men who possessed only land gave it to their sons seven times more often than to their daughters. By contrast, when the bequest of realty included a house, widows favored sons only two and a half times more often than they did daughters, whereas men favored sons more than five times over daughters. In Maryland, on the other hand, land played a much more important role in the bequests of both mothers and fathers. Nearly seven out of ten widows gave daughters land alone (about four times the rate at which they gave them a dwelling house alone), but only four out of ten male testators bequeathed land alone to daughters. These bequeathing patterns reveal the long-standing relationship between land and economic survival in the Chesapeake. A house alone, or even a house with a small plot of land, would not provide economic security in a colony that relied heavily on growing and selling tobacco and other cash crops. Land could be worked or it could be rented out. By bequeathing land alone to daughters so often, like widows in Massachusetts who understood the importance of houses for economic well-being in more urban New England, widows in Maryland ensured their daughters' economic security. Neither group of widows wanted their daughters to be dependent on their brothers, husbands, or sons for subsistence.

SLAVES

Because only twelve widows and five male testators without spouses bequeathed slaves in Massachusetts, our discussion of slave bequests will focus on Maryland. Twenty percent more widows than men bequeathed slaves, and widows clearly and steadily bequeathed slaves more often to daughters and less often to sons as time went on. Between 1690 and 1719 widows bequeathed slaves nearly twice as often to sons as to daughters, while male testators, by a nearly six-to-one ratio, favored sons over daughters as recipients of their slaves. But by the 1720–50 period widows bequeathed slaves nearly evenly to children of both sexes, and male testators bequeathed all of their slaves to their sons. The situation for daughters of male testators grew worse over time, rather than better.

These bequeathing patterns reflect not only gender role expectations of male testators, but widows' rejection of those expected gender roles. Widows bequeathed slaves to daughters twice as often as male testators did, while male testators bequeathed slaves to sons twice as often as widows did. Widows apparently believed in securing the future of their daughters through bequests of slaves more than men did. Widows' concern for their daughters grew over time as the means to work the land became more valuable and as the pressure to look after their children increased. As Maryland widows bequeathed land increasingly often to their daughters, they also more frequently bequeathed to their daughters the slaves with which to work that land.

Widows in Maryland appeared to believe that it was their responsibility to secure the economic future of their daughters, even at the expense of their sons. Such goals represent a significant reshaping of gender roles since the men at best took a different view of how those economic futures would be secured and at worst neglected the needs of their daughters. Both women and men likely assumed that daughters would marry and their husbands would care for them, but widows seemed more reluctant than men to leave their daughters' lives in the hands of fate. Slaves remained critical to carrying on the efficient operation of Chesapeake households, and widows increasingly turned their attention to ensuring that their daughters would have the means to participate in those operations. Maryland widows contested the notion that slaves, as a concomitant to real property, belonged only to men.

HOUSEHOLD GOODS

In examining the receiving and giving of bequests such as household goods and intangibles (traditionally feminine categories), the realm of established gender roles becomes even more complex, especially considering the well-defined gender roles presented in the contemporary prescriptive literature. Nearly 60 percent of widows in Massachusetts and over 65 percent of widows in Maryland bequeathed household goods. Not surprisingly, widows bequeathed household goods at approximately twice the rate of men in both colonies. What is surprising is the testators' distribution of these goods among children.

Across time Massachusetts widows consistently favored daughters over sons, and by 1720 they did so at a two-to-one ratio. Male testators demonstrate a strikingly different pattern. Until 1720, much like widows, they favored daughters over sons as recipients of household goods, but after 1720 they overwhelmingly favored sons over daughters. The same pattern holds for testators in Maryland. Although Maryland widows favored daughters over sons as recipients of household goods not quite two-to-one for the entire period, widows narrowed the gap between them as time went on. Male testators, conversely, always favored their sons as recipients of their household goods. Like bequests of slaves, these figures call into question the well-worn tenet that men bequeathed real property to their sons and made up for this imbalance by bequeathing more household goods to their daughters. Men appeared to be ensuring that their sons would have all the necessary tools at hand to establish an independent household. By their actions, and in contrast to male testators, widows declared that women needed and should have the family's household goods.

These findings suggest that widows used bequests of household goods, much more than did male testators, to provide their daughters a means of economic support. As male testators after 1720 shifted their bequests of household goods from daughters to sons, widows shifted their bequests of the same from granddaughters to daughters. Although household goods may not have provided daughters with substantial wealth in the first half of the eighteenth century, such bequests did provide them with the means to establish and maintain a viable household. Recall the widow Sarah Wheeler who desired that her unmarried daughter receive ninety pounds more than her brother and two married sisters so that she could buy the household goods so necessary for establishing a new conjugal unit.

INTANGIBLES

Intangibles—bequests such as money, debts due from others, and cancellation of debts due to the testator—played a significant role in all testators' lives. In Massachusetts, widows' bequests of intangibles to their daughters, composing roughly one-third of all such bequests, remained steady over time. Their bequests of intangibles to sons gradually but steadily increased. Bequeathing their intangibles evenly to daughters and sons before 1690, widows thereafter named sons over daughters by a slight margin. These figures suggest that widows saw intangibles as neither inherently male nor female property. In revealing contrast, men in Massachusetts clearly envisioned cash and debts as rightfully female property. Here is probably where they made up for not bequeathing daughters as much real property as they did sons.

Intangible goods appear much more gendered in the Chesapeake than they were in New England, at least in the early years of settlement. In Maryland, widows initially seemed to view intangibles as female property when they bequeathed such goods to daughters four times more often than to sons. By contrast, male testators initially named sons as recipients of intangibles five times more often than they named daughters. However, this pattern shifted dramatically. After 1720 widows favored sons over daughters by a slight margin, while male testators favored daughters over sons by a slight margin. For whatever reason, both female and male testators in Maryland came to see intangibles as generally gender neutral. This gave daughters relatively equal access with their brothers to their parents' cash and outstanding debts due, thus providing them with liquid assets that they could readily use as a means of economic security.

Comparing urban and rural bequests of intangibles reveals additional ways in which widows undermined the gendered economic order. Urban male testators, like male testators in both colonies, clearly saw intangibles as female property. In urban areas, where market-dominated relationships made intangibles more important to the economic life of the family and its individual members, widows bequeathed relatively evenly to daughters and sons across all periods. They wanted to ensure that both their daughters and their sons would have the same likelihood of surviving in the city.

Rural testators differed from urban testators. They were not much concerned with bequeathing intangibles. Just over 50 percent of rural male and female testators left intangibles. In an interesting twist, rural widows always favored sons over daughters as recipients of their cash and debts, while rural male testators favored daughters twice as often as sons as recipients of intangibles. For the most part, men envisioned intangibles as female property. The difference between widowers and widows here suggests that widows viewed intangibles as more than a token or "lesser" bequest and adhered to an ideology that implied that such goods, like slaves, needed to be attached to the plantation, which they still tended to believe belonged more rightfully to sons than to daughters.

Examining the types of intangibles testators bequeathed, and to whom, allows a more in-depth exploration of gender-role expectations and of the rejection of those roles. Because widows in Maryland bequeathed only cash, this discussion will focus primarily on Massachusetts. The overwhelming majority (75 percent) of Massachusetts widows bequeathed cash only, and they bequeathed it nearly equally to sons and daughters. When they did bequeath debts due from others, they similarly did so nearly equally to daughters and sons. Gender bias in widows' bequests appeared only in two categories: cancelation of debts to the testator and profits from the land. Widows were slightly more likely to bequeath to their sons (or sons by law) the cancelation of a debt due, probably because sons were more likely to borrow from mothers than were daughters, and because it was an easy way to fulfill their obligations to their sons without taking away from others. Widows gave profits from land approximately four times as often to daughters as to sons. This was probably an additional way widows compensated for the fact that they and their husbands favored sons over daughters as recipients of land. If the sons were going to take possession of the land itself, the daughters at least could share in the profits from that land.

Male testators in Massachusetts bequeathed only cash more often than did widows, and like widows they bequeathed it nearly equally to sons and daughters. Unlike widows, they bequeathed debts due from others three times more often to sons than to daughters, while they bequeathed profits from the land to daughters nearly three times more often than to sons. Given the prescription that widows should not "meddle" in the "resort of men & gathering of people," because to do so would call their honesty and chastity into question,[21] it could be that male testators believed it would be much easier for their sons than their daughters to recover those outstanding debts. Concomitantly, they might have believed the easiest way to get intangibles into their daughters' hands would be by leaving them profits from the estate.

Given the urban nature of Massachusetts, it is not surprising that widows there participated in the debt network to a greater extent than did widows in Maryland. Approximately one-half of Massachusetts widows had debts due from others listed in their inventories, whereas only a third of Maryland widows did. In addition, widows in both Maryland and Massachusetts were more likely than male testators to have debts due from others and debts due to others listed in their inventories, which suggests that widows were more likely than men to rely on an active debt network for economic survival.

Although it is impossible to determine whether there was a direct correlation between changing male and female bequeathing patterns, it is significant that as men shifted their bequests of intangibles from sons to daughters, widows shifted their bequests of intangibles from daughters to sons. A large proportion of testators of both sexes bequeathed intangibles, but by 1720 widows (and particularly urban widows) more than men viewed intangible goods as being equally important to daughters and sons. Unlike male testators and rural testators of either sex, widows probably felt little pressure to ensure that their daughters inherited the bulk of their cash or debts due from others simply because widows made sure that their daughters inherited other equally valuable, perhaps even more valuable, items from their estate. In an intriguing reverse of the male pattern, widows may even have felt pressure to bequeath their sons more intangibles than they did daughters because widows worked so hard to give their daughters a large portion of realty, household goods, and slaves.

• • •

Massachusetts widows appeared to be more willing than Maryland widows to push and redefine gender boundaries, and widows used different strategies for accomplishing that goal according to which goods they were bequeathing. Yet, in both colonies there was a clear shift between 1690 and 1750 from widows overwhelmingly favoring sons to bequeathing more equitably to sons and daughters. How can these shifts be explained?

Several interrelated factors led to widows' changing bequeathing patterns. The scarcity of productive land and constricted economic conditions in the late seventeenth and early eighteenth centuries determined, in part, how testators divided their estates. During this period of economic stagnation, inheritance became even more crucial in determining children's economic success than it normally was. Fathers responded to the situation by generally bequeathing all of their land to their sons and a small amount of personal goods, such as livestock and slaves, to their daughters.[22] Beginning in 1690, married daughters found it less likely that they would find a second husband, and unmarried daughters found it less certain that they would marry at all; this pattern had intensified by 1720. More evenly balanced sex ratios (if not a surplus of women because of declining mortality rates and the large number of young men migrating west in search of land or employment) and increasing rates of permanent widowhood meant that inheritance of more than personal goods became as important for daughters as for sons.[23]

Colonial widows in both Massachusetts and Maryland learned to deal with these changing social and economic conditions. Giving either real or personal goods to daughters did not provide them with independence or power because once the daughters married, their husbands managed or absolutely possessed those bequests.[24] Still, widows clearly envisioned that their bequests would provide their daughters with some economic security and thus some degree of independence and power.

Individual wills indicate that widows wanted the estates that they bequeathed to their daughters to remain under their daughters' control. In the seventeenth century most widows would not have given such bequests directly to their daughters; instead they would have given the estates indirectly to their daughters through their daughters' husbands. Even then it is possible to discern widows' growing concern for their daughters. Elizabeth Minor's bequest to her daughter Elizabeth Barnes is a good example. Minor noted that she was giving Barnes the money Minor's son-in-law owed her for some land, and "he not paying it, to her sol use I give that Land to her and her heires."[25] Taking an unusual step for the time, Elizabeth Hardy of Salem gave her daughter real and personal property with the provision that it "was to be at her proper disposing without having any Relation to her Husbands Leave in it." Such bequests became more frequent after 1700. Although Elizabeth Walker of Boston technically bequeathed all of her moveable estate to a good friend, it was for the sole use and benefit of her daughter. She specified that her son-in-law could not have use or interest in it. Likewise, Martha Clark stipulated that her daughter's estate remain in the hands of three male overseers and "the Profits arising there from shall be paid for her sole & separate use exclusive of her Husband." Susanna Condy's will stipulated that her son pay such money "into her [Elizabeth Russell's] own proper Hands, and not into the Hands of her said Husband

Thomas Russell . . . for her sole & separate Use and her said Husband to have no medling with the same."[26] Such cases indicate that widows increasingly favored giving their daughters some social and economic power within the family and the community.

In addition, specific bequests of real and personal property suggest that although widows may not have seen their bequests solely as instruments of independence and power, they believed they could help their daughters achieve a better life in two ways. First, at a time when marriage—or at least an economically sound marriage—was less certain than it had been in the past, they could provide their unmarried daughters with estates that enabled them to marry well and start out with more economic security than their fathers had provided, or than their husbands could. It may have been that seventeenth-century daughters, especially those in Maryland, needed only "cattle, bedding, linens, and cooking pots"[27] to marry a landowner, but that was not the case by the mid-eighteenth century. In the crude, consumer-oriented language of the "marriage market," these daughters became more valuable commodities. Secondly, widows could provide their married daughters with assets that could see them through their own widowhood, an event that became increasingly likely after 1720.

Widows might also have discussed with their husbands how each parent would assume testamentary responsibility over the family and each simply carried out his or her part of that joint decision. However, that appears generally not to be the case. Thomas Banister's fears about his wife's remarriage and how that would harm the economic well-being of his children (and his resulting unwillingness to bequeath his wife more than her thirds) suggests that many male testators felt solely responsible for establishing their children's economic future and did so by focusing on their sons as directed by prescriptive literature and their understanding of the patrilineal system. More important, I based my analysis on a comparison between widows and widowers, not all male testators. If male testators believed it was important that both their sons and daughters be given an equal or nearly equal opportunity to share in the family's economic resources and thus be able to establish economically viable households in the community, then there would not have been such sharp differences between widowers' and widows' bequests. Widowers would have understood that it was their responsibility to settle their estates more evenly on both sons and daughters.[28]

Moreover, widows' bequests were atypically gendered in two ways. First, widows redefined accepted notions of property as appropriately male or female by giving what was envisioned as male property to their daughters. Second, although mothers usually did not correct the inequity between sons and daughters, they played a major part in redefining what it meant to be mother and father. They did not believe in establishing only their sons on a solid economic footing—as cultural ideology suggested fathers should. They expanded their duties to include ensuring their daughters' economic well-being.

One historian has argued that widows' bequests of land and slaves to daughters suddenly increased in the late eighteenth century because of the American Revolution with its ideology of equality and liberty.[29] But the shift really began around 1690. It did so because widows in early eighteenth-century Massachusetts and Maryland, in essentially similar ways, responded to changing economic resources and reinterpreted the ideology of inheritance and gender proclaimed by authors and clergy alike. They demonstrated their ability to live up to their ambiguous gender role as both mother and father through bequests of realty, household goods, slaves, and intangibles. Widows defined their world in neither patriarchal nor egalitarian terms, for either position would have been anachronistic. As widows they were not supposed to exert inordinate economic and social power, but in their role as fathers they had the responsibility to ensure that their children would be able to establish independent households. Eighteenth-century widows helped redefine and reshape the economic structure of the colonial family according to the often ambiguous gender roles open to them. In doing so they provided their daughters with greater financial security than they might otherwise have had.

NOTES

I wish to thank Will Scott, my colleague and friend at Kenyon College, for the time and effort he put into reading this chapter. His comments were invaluable in helping me make it better and more clearly argued.

1. Suffolk County Probate Records, Suffolk County Courthouse, Boston, Mass., 16:606–8, 17:284–86 (hereafter cited as SCPR).

2. SCPR, 29:227–30, 287, 31:95–96.

3. Susan Dwyer Amussen, *An Ordered Society: Gender and Class in Early Modern England* (Oxford: Basil Blackwell, 1988), 91–93; Susan Dwyer Amussen, "Governors and Governed: Class and Gender Relations in English Villages, 1590–1725," (Ph.D. diss., Brown University, 1982), 176–82; Vivian Brodsky, "Widows in Late Elizabethan London: Remarriage, Economic Opportunity, and Family Orientations," in *The World We Have Gained: Histories of Population and Social Structure*, edited by Lloyd Bonfield, Richard M. Smith, and Keith Wrightson (Oxford: Basil Blackwell, 1986), 52; Joan M. Jensen, *Loosening the Bonds: Mid-Atlantic Farm Women, 1750–1850* (New Haven, Conn.: Yale University Press, 1986), 25–26; Suzanne Lebsock, *The Free Women of Petersburg: Status and Culture in a Southern Town, 1784–1860* (New York: Norton, 1984), chap. 5, "Women Alone: Property and Personalism," esp. 77–79, 136–38; Jean Butenhoff Lee, " 'Land and Labor': Parental Bequest Practices in Charles County, Maryland, 1732–1783," in *Colonial Chesapeake Society*, edited by Lois Green Carr, Philip D. Morgan, and Jean B. Russo (Chapel Hill: University of North Carolina Press, 1988), 325; Gloria L. Main, "Widows in Rural Massachusetts on the Eve of the American Revolution," in *Women in the Age of the American Revolution*, edited by Ronald Hoffman and Peter J. Albert (Charlottesville: University Press of Virginia, 1989), 89.

4. The larger study from which this material is drawn included South Carolina, but I chose to ignore South Carolina widows in this chapter. For computer analysis, I coded information from wills ($N = 1,599$) probated between 1633 and 1750 of all widows and an equal number of men in Charles, Prince George's, and Kent Counties in Maryland, as well as Suffolk, Essex, and Hampshire counties in Massachusetts. Next I created a subset of wills ($N = 811$) in which the testator had at least one son and one daughter in order to examine whether testators preferred daughters to sons (or vice versa) as heirs. Finally, to more accurately analyze the difference between male and widow testators, I created a subset ($N = 320$) of the "children" data set in which the male testators were widowers. The widowers data set was used in analyzing the information for this chapter. In assessing change over time, I grouped the information into three broad periods— 1633 to 1689 (the early period), 1690 to 1719 (the middle period), and 1720 to 1750 (the late period). All of the data have been analyzed using Stata, version 3.1, Stata Corporation, College Station, Texas. See Vivian Bruce Conger, " 'Being Weak of Body but Firm of Mind and Memory': Widowhood in Colonial America, 1630–1750" (Ph.D. diss., Cornell University, 1994).

5. Juan Luis Vives, *The Office and Duty of an Husband*, 1529, Thomas Paynell, trans. (London, [1555?]), as quoted in Joan Larsen Klein, *Daughters, Wives, and Widows: Writings by Men about Women and Marriage in England, 1500–1640* (Urbana: University of Illinois Press, 1992), 32.

6. Thomas Tusser, *The Points of Housewifery, United to the Comfort of Husbandry* (London, 1580, collated with editions of 1573 and 1577), in Klein, *Daughters, Wives and Widows*, 211.

7. Tusser, *The Points of Housewifery*, 211.

8. [Richard Allestree], *The Ladies Calling in Two Parts, By the Author of the Whole Duty of Man, the Causes of the Decay of Christian Piety, and the Gentlemans Calling* (Oxford, 1673), 70; John Dunton, *Letters Written From New-England . . . In Which are Described His Voyages by Sea, His Travels on Land, and the Characters of His Friends and Acquaintances* (Boston: Published for the Prince Society, 1867), 108.

9. Cotton Mather, *Ornaments for the Daughters of Zion or the Character and Happiness of a Vertuous Woman: In a Discourse which Directs the Female-Sex how to Express, the Fear of God, in every Age and State of their Life; and obtain both Temporal and Eternal Blessedness* (Boston, 1692), 100–101.

10. *The Whole Duty of Man, laid down in a Plain and Familiar Way for the Use of All, but especially the Meanest Reader . . . Necessary for All Families* (London, 1701), 288.

11. See, for example, Cotton Mather, *Nepenthes Evangelicum . . . A Sermon Occasion'd by the Death of a Religious Matron, Mrs. Mary Rock* (Boston, 1713), 42; Thomas Prince, *Be Followers of Them, who . . . inherit the Promises* (Boston, 1755), 22; Thomas Fuller, *The Holy State* (Cambridge, 1642), 15–20; *The Laws Respecting Women*, with a foreword by Shirley Raissi Bysiewicz (London: J. Johnson, 1777; reprint, Dobbs Ferry, N.Y.: Oceana Publications, 1974), 399 (page reference is to the reprint edition).

12. Will of Joanna Newman, SCPR, 6:341 (1680).

13. Will of Elizabeth Hearsey, SCPR, 7:161–63 (1705). See also the wills of Elizabeth Mercer, SCPR, 20:383–85 (1718), and Elizabeth Rozer, Maryland Wills, Maryland State Archives, Baltimore, Md., 20:674–75 (1733). For a historian who argues that widows left wills because they were fulfilling their husbands' wishes, see Lisa Wilson Waciega, "Widowhood and Womanhood in Early America: The Experience of Women in Philadelphia and Chester Counties, 1750–1850" (Ph.D. diss., Temple University, 1986), 233.

14. In fact, the "frame and Constitution" of Joanna Newman's husband's will did require her to do so. See SCPR, 6:341. According to 2 Kings 20:1, the Lord commanded Hezekiah to "set thine house in order; for thou shalt die." Many colonial sermons addressed to "old and young, male & female" proclaimed the virtue of doing as Hezekiah was commanded. See, for example, sermons 132, 133, 134, and 136 in Parsons Family Papers, box 1, folder 2, American Antiquarian Society, Worcester, Mass. The exhortation to provide for one's own family comes from 1 Tim. 5:8. One widow writing to her children implied that this phrase referred to the spiritual and religious well-being of children and not to "the temporal things of this world." See Dorothy Leigh, *The Mother's Blessing: or, The Godly Counsel of a Gentlewoman not long since deceased, left behind her for her children*

... *Proverbs 1:18.* "*My son, heare the instruction of thy father, and forsake not the law of thy mother*" (London, 1616), in Klein, *Daughters, Wives, and Widows,* 292.

15. Cotton Mather, *Nepenthes Evangelicum,* 43; Cotton Mather, *Ecclesia Monilia ... [The Funeral Sermon] of Mrs. Elizabeth Cotton, and Certain Instruments and Memorials of Piety, Written by that Valuable & Honourable Gentlewoman* (Boston, 1726), 29–30. David Hall makes a similar argument about the connection between the material and spiritual dimensions in his exploration of the rhetoric of inheritance found in prescriptions about infant baptism in seventeenth-century Massachusetts. See David D. Hall, "From 'Religion and Society' to 'Practice': Reflections on Religion in Early New England" (paper presented at Possible Pasts: Critical Encounters in Early America, the annual meeting of the Institute of Early American History and Culture, Philadelphia, June 5, 1994).

16. Will of Mary Baker, SCPR, 18:120–21 (1713); will of Ann Pollard, SCPR, 24:328–31 (1726). See also the wills of Elizabeth Bowdoin, SCPR, 21:801–3 (1720); Joanna Bulkley, SCPR, 19:296–98 (1717); Johanna Carthew, SCPR, 18:291–93 (1714); Sarah Dolbear, SCPR, 37:377–80 (1745); Susanna Newell, SCPR, 21:751–52 (1720); Sarah Oliver, SCPR, 21:184–85 (1718); Sarah Pemberton, SCPR, 16:594–95 (1709); Sarah Vincent, SCPR, 26:183–86 (1728); Mary Wilson, SCPR, new ser. 5:302–3 (1700); Ruth Allin, Hampshire County Wills, Hampshire County Courthouse, Northampton, Mass. 7:41–42, 131–32 (1746). Although Maryland widows included no such comments in their wills, it is likely that they shared the same sense of accomplishment and empowerment. I compared the wealth the husband bequeathed the widow to the wealth she died possessed of to see if Maryland widows improved the value of their estates as Massachusetts widows claimed they did. I have information available for eight couples (14 percent of the data set). Assuming the husbands bequeathed their wives only their legal third of their estates, then all eight widows added to the value of the estates. In fact, most of them doubled and several of them tripled the value of their thirds. Assuming the husbands bequeathed their wives their entire estate, only two of the eight widows improved their estates. Yet, those estates that declined in value did so by an average of only 34 percent (the range was 7 percent to 59 percent). The number of those who actually improved their estates probably falls in between the two assumptions. See Maryland Inventories, Maryland State Archives, Baltimore, Md., 4:11–21, 5:50–51, 6:155–59, 8:407, 10:31–44, 288–89, 15:163–64, 17:578–81, 22:518–20, 24:192–93, 27:191–93, 42.C:124–26; Maryland Accounts, Maryland State Archives, Baltimore, Md., 1:129–31, 6:81, 7:137–38, 324–26, 16:229, 19:513–19, 21:432–42, 22:45–47, 39.C:134; Maryland Inventories and Accounts, Maryland State Archives, Baltimore, Md., 15:318–23, 19:127–31, 36.C:290–92, 298–99, 37.A:4–6, 112–13, 130–31, 37.B:181, 37.C:222–26, 39.C:82.

17. Edmund S. Morgan, *American Slavery, American Freedom: The Ordeal of Colonial Virginia* (New York: Norton, 1975), 164–65. For a discussion of wealthy

widows, see Kim Lacy Rogers, "Relicts of the New World: Conditions of Widowhood in Seventeenth-Century New England," in *Woman's Being, Woman's Place: Female Identity and Vocation in American History*, edited by Mary Kelley (Boston: G. K. Hall, 1979), 27, 33–34, 40, 49–50; Lois Green Carr and Lorena S. Walsh, "The Planter's Wife: The Experience of White Women in Seventeenth-Century Maryland," *William and Mary Quarterly*, 3d ser., 34, no. 4 (1977): 555–57, 560. For an example of those who focus on the poverty and powerlessness of widows, see Carole Shammas, "Early American Women and Control over Capital," in Hoffman and Albert, *Women in the Age of the American Revolution*, 137, 143, 147, 150.

18. SCPR, new ser. 9:522–23.

19. David Sabean, "Aspects of Kinship Behavior and Prosperity in Rural Western Europe before 1800," in *Family and Inheritance*, edited by Jack Goody, Joan Thirsk, and E. P. Thompson (Cambridge: Cambridge University Press, 1976), 103; E. P. Thompson, "The Grid of Inheritance: A Comment," in Goody, Thirsk, and Thompson, *Family and Inheritance*, 337.

20. Between 1639 and 1750, the percentage of widows bequeathing real property declined from 37.8 percent to 27.9 percent.

21. Juan Luis Vives, *A Very Fruitfull and Pleasant Booke Called The Instruction of a Christian Woman* (Richard Hyrde, 1540), 395–96.

22. Allan Kulikoff termed this "domestic patriarchy." See Allan Kulikoff, *Tobacco and Slaves: The Development of Southern Cultures in the Chesapeake, 1680–1800* (Chapel Hill: University of North Carolina Press, 1986), 7, 51–52, 85; Philip Greven, Jr., *Four Generations: Population, Land, and Family in Colonial Andover, Massachusetts* (Ithaca, N.Y.: Cornell University Press, 1970); Russell Menard, *Economy and Society in Early Colonial Maryland* (New York: Garland Publishers, 1985), 320. See also Jack P. Greene, *Pursuits of Happiness: The Social Development of Early Modern British Colonies and the Formation of American Culture* (Chapel Hill: University of North Carolina Press, 1988), 95.

23. The proportion of remarrying women in all colonies decreased by half, from 11 percent in the seventeenth century to 5.5 percent in the eighteenth. The ratio of men to women in eighteenth-century Essex County fell to 84 women per 100 men. Even in Maryland, a colony well known for its extraordinarily imbalanced sex ratios, the ratio of men to women fell from a high of four to one in the 1650s to three to two in 1704, and finally to eleven to nine in 1712. Douglas Lamar Jones, *Village and Seaport: Migration and Society in Eighteenth-Century Massachusetts* (Hanover: University Press of New England, 1981), 79, 96–98; Carr and Walsh, "The Planter's Wife," 552, 567; Lois Green Carr, Russell R. Menard, and Lorena S. Walsh, *Robert Cole's World: Agriculture and Society in Early Maryland* (Chapel Hill: University of North Carolina Press, 1991), 158; Susan Grigg, "Toward a Theory of Remarriage: A Case Study of Newburyport at the Beginning of the Nineteenth Century," *Journal of Interdisciplinary History* 8, no. 2 (Autumn 1977):196; Kulikoff, *Tobacco and Slaves*, 48, 52; Lois Green Carr, "Inheritance in

the Colonial Chesapeake," in Hoffman and Albert, *Women in the Age of the American Revolution*, 171.

24. Mary Beth Norton, "Reflections on Women in the Age of the American Revolution," in Hoffman and Albert, *Women in the Age of the American Revolution*, 486–87.

25. SCPR, 9:110–11.

26. Will of Elizabeth Hardy, in *The Probate Records of Essex County, Massachusetts*, 3 vols. (Salem, Mass.: Essex Institute, 1917–20), 1:200–201 (1654); will of Elizabeth Walker, SCPR, 18:250–52 (1714); will of Martha Clark, SCPR, 33:514–17 (1738); and will of Susanna Condy, SCPR, 40:258–62 (1747).

27. Carr, Menard, and Walsh, *Robert Cole's World*, 149.

28. I analyzed the same pattern for all male testators with both daughters and sons, and the differences between the two groups were quite revealing. Very generally, in the group with no wives (relative to the group with wives), the positions of daughters improved absolutely and relatively to sons. Male testators with no wives tended to be more generous to their daughters, and so the widowers' data set is the "best case scenario" for daughters, which makes the contrasts between male testators and widows even more startling.

29. Lee, "Land and Labor," 341.

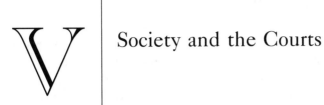

Society and the Courts

Among the most important sources for studying women in early America are the records kept by officials to preserve their dealings with those who came before them. The chapters in this section extensively employ such sources to explore the lives and experiences of early American women in diverse circumstances and places. Ruth Herndon has found several hundred transient women who appeared before town officials to face expulsion in early Rhode Island. Her findings challenge long-held assumptions about the "warning out" process in early New England and offer fascinating insights into the lives of women in early America.

Drawing on an unusually complete base of county and church records, Julie Richter reconstructs the lives and social relationships of free women, both African American and white, who lived in Charles Parish, Virginia, across more than a century. The world of these women, she shows, extended beyond their dwellings and the surrounding acreage. Women from all social levels played active roles in their neighborhoods and parishes and made extensive use of the legal system to protect their families as well as their individual interests and personal freedom.

Women in colonial America lived under a host of restrictions in their personal and economic lives, had few legal rights, were allowed only limited access to the judicial system, and appeared relatively infrequently in court records. Yet, Deborah Rosen shows that colonial women managed with few formal rights and relatively little access to the courts because they enjoyed an alternative path to justice. Drawing on a wide range of court records and legal documents from eighteenth-century New York, Rosen demonstrates that women commonly sought informal and discretionary justice outside of the formal judicial system. Far more than men, they avoided litigation and chose informal avenues of redress, including petitions to governors, assemblies, and chancery courts. Their social, economic, and legal status, as well as the high costs of litigation, tended to keep women out of the courts; and in any event playing the meek and conciliatory role thought appropriate for women worked better in asking for help than battling in court would have. In pursuing informal justice, women were often successful. That success declined, however, as the eighteenth century came to a close, increasingly restricting women's access even to informal justice. That loss of freedom helped lay important foundations for the rights-based move toward varieties of female emancipation in the nineteenth century.

14

Women of "No Particular Home": Town Leaders and Female Transients in Rhode Island, 1750–1800

RUTH WALLIS HERNDON

In 1754 a newcomer to the town stood before the councilmen of Exeter, Rhode Island, and told the story of her travels. Born in "old England," Mary Roose had immigrated to Massachusetts in 1743. After living one year in Boston and several more in Braintree, she "moved a long Toward Newport" and then migrated to Westerly, on the Connecticut border. From there she moved north to Exeter, where the town fathers, having judged Mary as a person "not haveing a good Cerrector," refused to let her reside in their community; they ordered that she "forthwith Depart this town." [1]

Nearly fifty years later, in 1800, a newcomer to Providence told that town council a similar story. Described by the clerk as "mulatto," Nancy Brown had been born free in Colchester, Connecticut, but she left that state when she was fifteen and had not gone back. After living in Boston for a few years—long enough to earn the nickname "Boston Nance"—she came to Providence, but she did not find a warm welcome. The councilmen, acting on information that she "conducts herself in a very disorderly manner and is an unfit person to be at large," sent her to

Bridewell, the recently built house of correction for troublers of the peace. Two days later the councilmen ordered constable William Givens to take her from Bridewell and "conduct her without the Limits of this Town."[2] The clerk recording Nancy Brown's story noted that this eighteen-year-old woman had "no particular home," and she found none in Providence.

These two stories illustrate the dilemma faced by many unpropertied women in the latter half of the eighteenth century in southeastern New England. Open borders between towns and colonies invited them to move wherever their personal circumstances enabled them to go, and that freedom of movement seemed to promise that they could shape their own lives by sampling opportunities and finding a congenial place to live and work. But the promise often proved hollow. People without property were indeed free to move from one place to another, but they were not free to settle where they chose. Town leaders were dedicated to curtailing efforts by transients (especially women) to settle in their communities, fearful that these people would swell the town's relief lists and disturb the peace of the community. Every town council wanted to "control the absence" of transients by sending them elsewhere ("warning them out").[3]

Transient in the eighteenth century conveyed meanings very different from those it has today. Then, the word referred neither to travelers nor to homeless vagrants. Instead, it specifically identified a person who had been living in a town but had not become a legal inhabitant of that town. Inhabitants had rights and privileges; transients, however, remained in residence only by the permission of town leaders. Colony law stated clearly how a person qualified as a legal inhabitant of a town (birth, servitude, or—for white adult males—the purchase of real estate), and those who did not qualify continued as transients no matter how long they lived within the town.[4] But the legal meaning of the term was not the whole story, for negative interactions between transient people and settled inhabitants added the connotation of "undesirable" to the word. For many propertied people of the late 1700s, *transient* signified noise, dirt, rudeness, illiteracy, and disorder. To be a transient person was not only to be denied the legal privileges that inhabitants enjoyed; it was also to be regarded as a potentially troublesome person who represented the opposite of everything those respectable inhabitants valued.

This chapter explores transience from two points of view: that of town leaders and that of transient people, particularly women unrepresented by men. I discuss who these women were, what they did that leaders found so problematic, and how they tried to manipulate the system of warning out to their own advantage. Woven through the discussion is the issue of race: how the racial identity of transients became of such great concern to town leaders that by 1800 a Nancy Brown was more likely to be warned out than a Mary Roose.

To reveal the experience of these transient people, I draw on a base of more than 1,800 warnout orders and close to 800 transient examinations— official interviews conducted by councilmen to determine where transient people legally "belonged." All of these documents were recorded by the clerks of fourteen Rhode Island towns over a period of fifty years.[5] Each order and each examination was directed technically at one individual, but that individual's family also suffered the judgment of the council. Transient documents focused on heads of households, but the transient world in reality included hundreds of wives and children whose points of view are missing from the official records. Fortunately, half of the warnout orders and half of the examinations were directed at women unrepresented by men, and these documents allow us to study how many women experienced transience. It is a selective sample, to be sure—single women, women cohabiting with men, wives separated from their husbands, divorced women, and widows. Wives in the company of their husbands did not have the opportunity to speak for themselves, nor did the many children who were sent packing with their mothers and fathers because of a warnout order. Even so, the voices of women that come through the warnout orders and the transient examinations provide an unusual opportunity to learn what it was like to be transient and female in the eighteenth century.

The stories of Mary Roose and Nancy Brown bracket an era that produced a flood of transient people and, in response, a burst of activity on the part of local government officials, who tried to identify and control them. The unsettledness expressed in the women's tales and the rejection expressed in the town councils' judgments were familiar stories to the leaders of southeastern New England communities in the latter part of the 1700s. The extensive town welfare system that supported indigent inhabitants with "the necessities of life" from cradle to grave had a dark side that showed up in official attempts to interview, warn away, and physically remove all transient people who seemed "likely to become chargeable" or who caused disturbances in the town. Town leaders relied heavily on welfare and warning out in the second half of the eighteenth century as a series of upheavals fragmented the lives of numerous inhabitants. The Seven Years' War, the Revolutionary War, and postwar depression in the 1780s imposed severe economic hardships on the region. The influx of European immigrants and the migration of ex-slaves freed during the Revolution and by later gradual emancipation led to increases in the number of displaced New Englanders. Transients became a familiar presence in southeastern New England as people followed the army and hunted for work.[6]

The juxtaposition of the stories of Mary Roose, a white English woman, and Nancy Brown, a woman of color, illustrates the increasingly racial focus of the warning out system as the century wore on. Over the entire fifty-year period, about 14 percent of the people warned out were identified as nonwhite, but this statistic masks the dramatic change that took place. For the first thirty-five years of the era, clerks noted only haphazardly when a transient was not white; but as emancipations produced a growing population of free people of color, the record-keepers showed more diligence.[7] In the 1750s only 5 percent of those warned out were designated as people of color; but by the 1790s this figure averaged 22 percent and was climbing rapidly. Part of the increase is due to greater precision in record keeping, and part is due to a greater representation of people of color in the transient population. Both point to the growing presence of race in town council deliberations. When "Boston Nance" came before the Providence councilmen in 1800, people of color constituted half of all transients warned out of Rhode Island that year—an astonishing statistic in light of the facts that "Negroes" represented only 6.3 percent of the population of Rhode Island in 1790 and that the figure had decreased to 5.3 percent ten years later.[8]

Women—Native American, European, and African—accounted for

half of the transient people examined by councils. From the town fathers' point of view, these daughters, sisters, mothers, and wives were not in their proper place, disconnected as they were from the settled, patriarchal households on which white New England was officially built. They spoke for themselves before the councilmen and they were named on the warnout orders. Although this concentration of women detached from male heads forms a skewed sample of the female population at large, it is not a surprising phenomenon, given the legal foundation of the warning out process. This humiliation could be visited only on unpropertied people—people who had not purchased a *freehold* in the community. Since women could never achieve *freeman* status, with its attendant political rights, they could not become inhabitants by their own action. Women's settlement status always came through men. By virtue of birth, they claimed their fathers' place of residence; by virtue of labor, they claimed their masters' residence; by virtue of marriage, they claimed their husbands' residence. But fathers, masters, and husbands might prove to be frail reeds; the female examinants in this study include women married to hapless or ill men who offered no protection from poverty, women abandoned by fathers and husbands in places far from home, and women released by masters to provide for themselves. Separated from their home communities, these women became transients; separated from their husbands, fathers, and masters, they could never become inhabitants anywhere else.

The widespread uprooting and resettling in southeastern New England meant that every town had within its borders numerous people not born and raised there. Poor newcomers without freeholds were watched with particular care, since they would be dependent on others for their jobs and livelihood, and that dependence might, in a time of crisis, slide over into poor relief. But even people who had lived within a town for decades might still be transients in the eye of the law, and so subject to warning out, once incapacitated by old age or illness. Sixty-nine-year-old widow Abigail Carr, for example, had lived in Providence for thirty years when the council ordered her out to her "legal settlement" in Newport, the place where she had married her husband some four decades earlier.[9]

From the town fathers' point of view, warning out served as a weapon against economic disorder, for it allowed officials to limit the number of people receiving public assistance from the town—of special import during the 1780s, when poor costs spiraled upward during the postwar depression. Councilmen frequently used the phrase "likely to become chargeable" when they explained their reasons for warning out an individual or a family. This indicated some condition that would cause these people to need support: illness, injury, an absent husband or father, or a large number of children dependent on a feeble breadwinner.

"Likely to become chargeable" had particular resonance for women. The impending birth of a "bastard" child brought more female examinants before councils than any other cause. In this context mothers, not fathers, bore the burden of illegitimacy, for it was the mothers who suffered removal on the eve of childbirth to a place that might or might not be "home." In a typical case, Exeter councilmen warned out Abigail Cleveland, "a Singal woman," in 1780 because "She is with Child and Near the Time of her Delevery and Likely to be Chargeable." From the council's perspective, this hurried removal made sound financial sense. Every council wanted to avoid both the immediate costs of caring for a recovering mother and her newborn and also the long-term costs of raising a fatherless child born within their jurisdiction. As soon as the councilmen became aware of the impending birth of a "bastard," they acted to prevent such liability. Mary Johnston was ordered to appear before the Cumberland councilmen in 1769 because they had "Great suspicion that She will very Soon Become Chargeable," but it was too late; their intended removal of Mary "was prevented by her Lying in." The East Greenwich councilmen never had a chance: there, in 1800 Susan James came into town, "Taryed one Night and one Day and on the Second Night was Delivered of one other Child." The costs associated with Susan's month-long recovery and "Necessary Cloathing" for herself and her older child added substantially to the town's poor relief bill. This was the sort of expense councilmen hoped to avoid by removing women in the last stages of pregnancy.[10]

Warning out served also as a weapon against social disorder, for it allowed councilmen to monitor and intimidate noninhabitants who might disturb the peace of their community. The process of bringing people before the town council for questioning was invested with drama and was designed to impress transients with the power of the authorities. The town sergeant, citation in hand, conducted the examinant away from friends and family to the place of meeting in the good house of a respectable inhabitant. The councilmen and clerk, in their meeting-day clothes, sat behind their table, with their official papers and records. These five or six authorities volleyed questions at the individual before them. When the interview was complete, the clerk read aloud his transcription of the conversation and handed the pen to the examinant for a signature or a mark that would transform this paper into a legal document that might be used in a court dispute. Relatively few examinants were literate, and even those who could sign their names usually did so in an awkward, untrained hand.[11] Unable to read what they signed, most examinants (particularly women of color, among whom literacy was most rare) were dependent on the integrity of the council and clerk to make a faithful record of their spoken words. Signing thus emphasized the power and authority of the highly literate town fathers in contrast to the uneducated transients.

Having gathered information and intimidated the examinant, the councilmen then discussed among themselves the problem this person represented. Was it a problem of indigence brought on by adverse circumstances? Or was it a problem of behavior that disturbed the quiet, ordered lives of propertied people? The Glocester town councilmen decided the latter in 1752, when they warned out Mary Worsley, a newcomer "from some remote parts" who was annoying people with her "unRuley tongue and no Good Behavouer"; they agreed with the judgment of the overseer of the poor, who felt "it is not prudent or Safe for the Town to Let her tarry long in it." And in 1784 the Hopkinton councilmen chose to rid the town of Mercy Lawton, Amy Prince, and "other asosiates," whom they judged to be "harbourers of Evil practises & of a bad fame & Reputation."[12] In neither of these cases was there any hint that the women were a financial liability to the town; their offenses were against the peace of the community.

Councilmen viewed warning out, for reasons of both economic and social control, as a way of fulfilling their responsibilities as town fathers. Paternalism dictated that councilmen take seriously their responsibilities to all suffering people within their communities—even transients. To some extent, the reputation of town leaders depended on their treatment of such unfortunate souls. The Attleboro authorities were appalled when the Providence town council sent to them Anna Fuller and her two children "in the most destitute and disagreable Circumstances," filthy from head to foot and without sufficient clothing. The Attleboro men were not surprised to see dirt, lice, and tattered rags on transient poor people; but they were greatly dismayed that town leaders had not alleviated the wretched condition of these "most abandoned and worst of Characters" before they removed them.[13] The Providence town councilmen had failed to care for people who could not or would not care for themselves, and their failure was both noted and censured by their peers.

Unfortunately for town leaders, not everyone wanted to be cared for. Often transient women and men resisted having their circumstances reordered by town officials, who used the law, public money, and their particular sense of what was fitting to design "suitable" lives for the less fortunate. Transient people were interested in the freedom to settle where they chose, and this freedom local leaders frequently denied them. Women and men who hoped to build a life in a particular place without official interference instead found themselves in conflict with authorities.

Town fathers devoted a good deal of time to solving problems these transients posed for the town—at least, to certain settled inhabitants of the town. Councilmen were not all seeing and all knowing; they responded to information brought to them by overseers of the poor and others. Some of the unofficial informants were well-meaning people who hoped to improve the material condition of those in need. Others were sharp-eyed and sharp-eared neighbors annoyed at the presence of these unsettled residents. Transients came before authorities because someone lodged a complaint against them. Although councils undoubtedly dismissed many complaints as frivolous, enough resulted in council action that transients quickly learned the hazards of irritating neighbors.[14]

In some ways transients looked no different from their legally settled neighbors. The women examined by councils were younger (averaging twenty-eight years old) than the men (averaging forty years old). Both female and male examinants tended to have dependent children: two or three was the norm. And these family units were not usually vagrant or homeless in the twentieth-century meaning of those terms, though a small fraction of such footloose people counted in the transient population. Instead, most examinants showed a certain determination to settle; they had lived in the towns an average of five years before being examined. In many if not most cases, then, warning out displaced persons who had a great deal to lose by removal: jobs, neighbors, connections, a sense of place. Even family cohesion was at risk, since officials might decide that siblings "belonged" to different towns or that an unmarried, cohabiting man and woman should return to their separate home communities.

In other ways transients looked very different from their settled neighbors. Only a third of the examinants lived within patriarchal families. Men without wives and children accounted for 10 to 20 percent of the examinants; and women without husbands, fathers, or masters accounted for 50 percent. These women supported themselves by their own labor and did not depend on men to provide for them. Although a handful mention a craft or a trade, most women performed domestic service in the homes of better-off residents. Further, these women formed alternative nonpatriarchal living arrangements for support and comfort. A number of female examinants built their households around mothers and daughters. Patience Havens, for example, headed a household that included three underage children, two adult (married) daughters, and a son-in-law.[15] Sometimes mothers banded together, as did Mrs. Tower, Mrs. Meachins, and Mrs. Manning, three women whose husbands were at sea and who had formed their own household with their eleven children.[16] Women living by their own labor in nonpatriarchal households doubtless worried town fathers and "respectable" inhabitants and gave them additional incentive to monitor transient women.

Also unlike their settled neighbors, transient people had a certain familiarity with moving. Over half of the examinants had lived in at least one other community before coming to the town where they were examined. They understood the work of packing up possessions, traveling to a new town, finding a place to live, and finding a job. This last was often the primary motivation for a family to move. Providence, with its booming economy and promise of jobs, held a particular attraction for transient people: three-quarters of the examinations on which this study rests were recorded by Providence clerks. And word of opportunities in Providence obviously spread throughout the region, since well over half of Providence examinants came from towns that were at least twenty miles away but not more than sixty miles away—a band of land that cut through all of southeastern New England. Transients in other Rhode Island towns came mostly from nearby communities, often just across the border in Connecticut or Massachusetts. All told, about one-half of the transients examined in Rhode Island originated outside Rhode Island, suggesting that political boundaries presented less of a barrier than might be expected.

In Providence one noticeable difference between transient people and their settled neighbors was a matter of color, for a free black community emerged there toward the end of the eighteenth century.[17] Few of these people of color were legal inhabitants. Instead, nonwhites from throughout the region migrated purposely to this port town, which had weathered the Revolution intact (in contrast to Newport) and which promised work for laborers in its thriving mercantile economy. Its black community also gave nonwhite transients a place to mingle and hide away from white authority. Clearly, Providence was viewed as a place where Native Americans and African Americans could live and work largely unmolested. Women were particularly likely to come there: nearly 90 percent of all nonwhite female examinants show up in Providence records. And these were not women who edged across a nearby border: two-thirds of the nonwhite female examinants in Providence originated in moderately distant towns scattered throughout the region.

These women were purposeful settlers. Black and Native American female examinants had lived in the towns where they were examined an average of seven years—two years more than the average for all examinants. Some of them had spent a lifetime in a community. Phillis Yamma had lived in Providence twenty years and Deborah Church twenty-five years.[18] At the time of warning out, most nonwhite women had been in the town long enough to build a social network and become an integral part of the community. Several women of color even operated boarding houses for other transients. Margaret Fairchild, for example, rented "the old Gaol House" in Providence during the Revolutionary War and took in as tenants both black and white women. Similarly, Jenny Rose supported herself and her two children while her husband was at sea by "go[ing] out to day's work," "tak[ing] in washing," and taking in boarders, including Isaac Rodman and James Taylor, two black sailors.[19]

There is no obvious explanation for the long residence of these women. It may be that they were better able than others to support themselves adequately over the long haul and to conduct themselves with sufficient quietness to avoid council attention. It may also be that town fathers were more willing to tolerate their presence in the town because their labor was so valuable to influential inhabitants. In several instances people of substance objected to the removal of nonwhite women, suggesting that the departure of a valuable servant constituted a significant loss to a household. In 1794 one Providence tavern keeper went so far as to take direct action. When the council ordered that Sarah Mason, "a mulatto Girl," be removed to Westerly, Esek Aldrich hid Sarah and refused to surrender her to the constable. There is no indication of what Sarah thought about this drama—whether she welcomed or resented Esek's interference; but in any case it was in vain. Sarah was removed eventually, and the council scolded and fined Esek for his "unwarrantable and high handed procedure," but the point was made that he saw this removal as an injury.[20]

It is not surprising that nonwhite women were valued for their work; their narratives often tell of bound labor. Whereas about one-quarter of all examinants reported servitude or slavery in their past, the figure doubles for nonwhite women: well over half of them named a former master. This is probably a low figure, for examinants had reason to deny legal bondage and thus avoid being returned to a master; some of those who claimed to be "born free" probably were not. A few women claimed to have been emancipated but could not produce the evidence. Abigail Carr, for example, said "she gave her said Master Thirty Pounds for her Freedom, which she had in Writing, but cannot at present find it." Others reported being freed in a casual way, denied the proof of a manumission paper. In 1782, for example, Margaret Fairchild Bowler reported that her master "Verbally gave her her Freedom without any Instrument in Writing about Five Years ago."[21] Warning out carried the possibility of return to bondage for some women of color.

Whether Indian, white, or black, a typical female examinant emerges from the records. She was a poor, young, and illiterate mother familiar with hard work. She displayed determination and endurance sufficient to uproot herself from her home community, move to a new place, and build a new social network. She had the strength and will to support herself and her family for five or more years before a crisis of ill health, pregnancy, or conflict with neighbors brought her to the attention of the town council. Female examinants were not, on the whole, helpless and submissive. The temporary circumstances that made them vulnerable to the council's attention did not strip them of their ability to negotiate their fate.

A close look at the transient interviews reveals a number of ingenious ways women countered official attempts to displace them. These strategies highlight the distance between town leaders and most female examinants. These women did not share the privileges, education, wealth, comforts, and status of those in positions of authority; they did not have powerful husbands or fathers to protect them. Yet these women had a power of their own. They lived by their own labor; they knew how to survive outside the circle of "suitable lives" that officials would draw for them; and they understood the paternalism of their antagonists, never hesitating to use it to their own advantage. Throughout the warning out process, the ostensibly powerless found ways to frustrate the powerful.

Some women avoided the entire process by refusing to come before the council; they hid out or left town until the crisis had passed, the latest "complaint" or "information" against them forgotten or dismissed. In 1750 the Middletown councilmen sent the town sergeant to summon "the Stranger" at Mr. Upham's house. He discovered "She was gone Before he Came there." In 1780, when Drusilla Jillson refused to appear when summoned, the Cumberland councilmen ordered the town sergeant to search diligently for this transient who "Secreets her Self in the Said Town." [22] A few women made their resistance even more obvious. In 1773 the Middletown sergeant came to council without bringing Frances Doggett; he reported that when he went to collect her, "She Went up Stairs and Some time after I Inquired after her but She would not be Seen But Locked her Self up in a Room." In 1786 Sarah Brown told another Middletown sergeant that she "would not appear unless he had Brought her by force." [23]

But women could not always outrun or outfox the town sergeant, so strategies for the council meeting were in order. Here, female examinants' skills of persuasion were put to the test; their ability to tell their own stories could help determine their fate. Councilmen had wide discretion in their own "courtroom," and penitents who showed the right attitude might find sympathy. The unfortunate Jerusha Townsend did not "render a sattisfactory and intelligible account of herself" to the Providence councilmen, who ordered her removed "immediately" from the town.[24] But other women were more skillful at stressing the pathetic elements in their situations. They told of husbands who were casualties of war, victims of Indian attacks, lost at sea, and even one killed by a falling tree. Others reported being abandoned by husbands, left to raise young children by themselves. Several women described the nightmare of discovering that they were married to bigamists and their children were illegitimate. One Providence town clerk was sufficiently moved by a transient woman's distress to write an unusual note in the margin of the page when he entered her testimony into the official record: "Examination of the unhappy Miss Phebe Newcomb." He appended a Latin quotation from Virgil's *Aeneid*, obviously comparing Phebe to Dido, whose grief over her lover's abandonment ended in suicide.[25] That one of the town fathers could be so impressed by a transient woman's narrative underscores how the drama of the situation could serve the goals of the examinant as well as those of the authorities.

Such presentations did not normally dissuade councilmen from issuing a warnout, but they did frequently result in the examinant gaining an extension of time before leaving—two weeks, two months, and even longer, depending on the circumstances presented. Some relieved souls took this to be a complete pardon and continued to live and work in the very towns where councilmen had examined them. And they had reason to act that way, since councils were sloppy about following up on their own deadlines if they did not perceive the examinant to be an outright threat to the community. In many cases the councilmen contented themselves with having intimidated and subdued people during the council meeting, and they often overlooked the business of sending out the town sergeant with a warrant for removal on the day appointed.

In a few cases town fathers were so impressed by a woman's circumstances that they completely changed their minds about removal. Polly Fitch showed such "great averseness to be[ing] Removed" that the councilmen decided to write the Sherburne selectmen to see if they would support Polly if she remained in Providence. Likewise, Elizabeth Stonehouse, an elderly widow who had been living in Providence since she was forty, moved the clerk to note that she "is now advanced in Life [and] is poor and Indigent and in Need of Assistance." Instead of removing her, the councilmen wrote their counterparts in Newport, asking them "to contribute to her Relief without her being Sent to that City." Five years later, Elizabeth was still being supported in Providence, living with and sharing relief funds with another elderly widow.[26] Clearly, a well-staged appeal to the paternal feelings of town leaders could be highly effective.

The color and status of the pentitent mattered in such an appeal. White women of "respectable" families were better positioned to identify with the town fathers and had a particular advantage when presenting their stories. The clerk gave Elizabeth Stonehouse the title of "Mrs.," for she was a white woman whose father had "owned a valuable Estate" in Newport; likewise "Miss" Phebe Newcomb's father was "a Freeholder and a Man of Estate" in Windham, Connecticut. These two women found sympathy at the council table, in some measure perhaps because they told their stories well; but it is also likely that the councilmen were swayed by the wealth and influence of these women's relatives and saw an opportunity to earn the good will of powerful men. Women of color had no such connections, and they did not receive the same courtesies or consideration.

Some women, perhaps understanding their handicaps before the councilmen, ignored the possibilities of appealing to paternalism and chose instead to express their disdain for the conventions and procedures of the authorities. Women were never recorded as being openly contentious before the town council, but they did use more subtle words and actions. When the South Kingstown councilmen asked Mary Fowler, an "Indian Woman," if she were married, she responded that she had been living with a man "for about thirty Years and had Ten children by him . . . but never was Married to him in the Manner white People are married in these parts." [27] Patience Butler, questioned by the council because her husband was too ill to attend the meeting, "utterly Refused" to put her name or mark on the clerk's written version of her interview, forcing the councilmen to make a special trip to see her husband and get his testimony.[28] Judah Wanton, a black woman confined to labor in the workhouse, also refused to sign because "She never did Sign any Writing." [29]

Although these assertive women did not win any privileges from the town councilmen, they did demonstrate that the values of the authorities were not universally embraced.

Strategies of resistance did not always end with removal. Some women simply returned later. The town records actually document the return of thirty-five such women (9 percent), but this is almost certainly only a fraction of the real figure: many women would have avoided being caught by the authorities a second time, and in other cases the council found it convenient to ignore a returning transient who was not causing a problem. The women who were cornered a second and third time seemed quite hardened to the entire business of warning out—even to a stiff fine or public whipping, the statutory punishment for repeat offenders.[30] Sarah Gardner returned to Providence repeatedly in defiance of official order. Even the threat of whipping did not deter her—or the four adult daughters who accompanied her. The council considered the five women to be "of bad Character and Reputation" and clearly wanted them elsewhere, but the Gardners' determination to live in Providence was even stronger, perhaps because it was the only place where they could survive together as a household.[31] Sarah Mathewson showed she had a sophisticated grasp of the system when, after returning illegally to Providence, she "concealed herself from the Officer until she got into her present Pregnant State when . . . it became improper to inflict the Punishment prescribed by Law." [32]

The two examinations of Phillis Merritt Wanton illustrate particularly well the problems female examinants faced and the strategies they used. Her narratives also highlight the specific concerns of women of color, for Phillis was identified first as "a Negro Woman" and later as "a black woman." In her first narrative in 1784, she said that she was born a slave to Robert Sanderson in Attleboro, Massachusetts, but raised in the house of John Merritt of Providence—the man whose name the clerk assigned to her. After John Merritt's death, she was sold to a Boston leather breeches maker, John Field, who eventually announced that he was leaving the country and "told her she might go and Get her own Living." Phillis returned to Providence, where she supported herself by "go[ing] out to washing" and lived mainly with one Mrs. Goodwin, "whose House she made her Home." [33] When the councilmen ignored Phillis's subtle plea to stay in her adopted "Home" and warned her out to Boston, Phillis hid from the sergeant to avoid removal.[34]

Phillis subsequently melted out of the council's vision and memory, and when she came before a different group of Providence councilmen sixteen years later, she had changed her name and her story. Now Phillis Wanton, she told of marrying Jack Wanton, an African-born slave freed in 1791, and of bearing three children—two bound out as servants elsewhere and one four-year-old with her. Her husband was absent; he was back in Newport, his place of settlement, because he was "at Times insane." When asked to explain her own settlement, Phillis again told of slavery under William Sanderson (in Attleboro), John Merritt (in Providence), and John Field (in Boston), but she added a new master: "Mr. Peck" of Boston, to whom John Field had sold her. It was this Mr. Peck who told her "to seek and provide for herself," an informal emancipation that she dated suggestively "about the Time of the Blockade of [Boston] by the British." Phillis further tweaked the conscience of the councilmen by claiming that when she first came back to Providence after being set free in Boston, she "lived in the family of Moses Brown," the prominent and wealthy abolitionist. But the unpersuaded councilmen ordered Phillis and her daughter removed to Newport, where her husband lived.[35]

Phillis had employed several of the strategies transient women used to good effect. She laced her examination with tidbits of information designed to elicit sympathy from the councilmen, she hid from the town sergeant to avoid removal, and she changed her story to supply information that might strengthen her case on her second hearing. Phillis also embodied the particular problems faced by women of color. Illiterate, she signed her examination with an "x." She had known slavery, and her status as a free woman was not clear. And she drew the attention of the council twice because she was so obviously not within a patriarchal household—she was, after all, a black person without a master and a woman without a husband.

Phillis's two examinations mark out a time of change in official perceptions of transients. When she was first examined in 1784, gradual emancipation was newly born, but by the time of her second examination in 1800, a growing population of free blacks had made its presence felt in Providence. Throughout the 1790s, councils around Rhode Island (and especially in Providence) examined and warned out growing numbers of nonwhite people—and noted their color in the official record. Women of color became particularly visible to councilmen and prone to examination, since they represented a double affront to patriarchy as women without male heads and servants without masters. For the white town fathers of Providence, who examined twice as many women of color as white women in 1800, the Phillis Wantons and Nancy Browns had come to embody female transience.

NOTES

I wish to thank Joanne Melish and Ann Plane for their extensive support and help with this essay.

1. Town council meeting of 12 Feb. 1754, Exeter Town Council Records, 1:157. Town council and town meeting records cited in this chapter are located in the town clerk's office of each respective town.

2. Town council meetings of 29 Apr. and 1 May 1800, Providence Town Council Records, 7:452–55.

3. I wish to thank Joanne Melish for the creation of this phrase.

4. *Acts and Laws of the English Colony of Rhode-Island and Providence Plantations in New-England, in America* (Newport, R.I.: Samuel Hall, 1767), 228–32; *The Public Laws of the State of Rhode Island and Providence Plantations* (Providence: Carter and Wilkinson, 1798), 352–58. The law also stipulated that a resident could become an inhabitant by living for one entire year in a town without being warned out. Town councils usually prevented this from happening by keeping such people "under warning" by means of a yearly citation. While this fell short of an official warnout order, it kept long-term "transient" residents from ever claiming the town as their legal settlement.

5. The records contain far more warnout orders than examinations for two reasons. First, an examination was not necessary when transient people complied with colony or state regulations by asking the council's permission to live in the town and voluntarily providing information about their legal settlement. Second, not every town included examinations in the official record books. Instead, the clerks documented the fact that an examination was made and noted the particulars of the subsequent warnout order, but the actual examination was filed away with the clerk's papers for possible later reference. The vast majority of these loose documents have disappeared over time. The recorded examinations reflect particular styles among the record keepers. Some clerks presented examinations in a question-answer format that suggests a verbatim transcription of the conver-

sation. Usually, however, the clerk condensed and paraphrased the questions and answers and thus injected his own voice into the record. The difficulty of distinguishing the voice of the clerk from that of the examinant cautions us to read these documents with care. The examinant may have withheld or falsified information; and the clerk selected what information would go into the record and in what form. Thus, these examinations are far from being an unmediated source; but they do give us the substance of conversations between the councilmen and transient persons, and they allow us to hear people who would otherwise be voiceless.

6. Ruth Wallis Herndon, "Governing the Affairs of the Town: Continuity and Change in Rhode Island, 1750–1800" (Ph.D. diss., American University, 1992), 295–301, esp. figs. 17 and 18.

7. Even when the clerks did identify people of color, they routinely blurred racial distinctions. It was commonplace for a clerk to refer to the same person as "mulatto" in one place and "mustee" in another or to use the terms "Indian" and "Negro" to describe the same person within one document. In addition, clerks showed preferences for certain designations, one favoring "mulatto" and another favoring "black," for example. Because of such quirks and inconsistencies, it is difficult to distinguish Native American from African American transients in the records or to make an accurate count of the people of color warned out during the era. Despite this handicap, it is possible to identify certain trends. Up through 1775, transients designated "Indian" or "mustee" constituted well over half of all those identified as people of color. From 1776 through 1800, however, less than one-tenth of the nonwhite transients were so described. The Revolution apparently served as some sort of watershed in official perceptions of racial identity. Town leaders may have determined that intermarriage between indigenous and African peoples obscured the racial heritage of Native Americans, and some Rhode Island towns began to claim, as New Shoreham did in 1780, that "the native Indians [are] extinct in the Town." Town meeting of 22 Apr. 1780, New Shoreham Town Meeting Records, 5:8. But more significantly, after the Revolution began, the number of indigenous people among the transient population was eclipsed by the far greater number of African people freed as a result of wartime military service, voluntary manumissions inspired by Revolutionary fervor, and gradual emancipation legislation and court decisions.

8. U.S. Bureau of the Census, *Negro Population 1790–1915* (Washington, D.C.: Government Printing Office, 1918), 51.

9. Town council meeting of 2 July 1787, Providence Town Council Records, 6:10. Abigail claimed to have been living in Providence thirty-seven years, but her husband, in his examination thirty years before, had stated that he and Abigail had been in Providence just two months. Town council meeting of 31 Dec. 1757, Providence Town Council Records, 4:168. It is possible that Jack Carr lopped seven years off their residence, but more likely that Abigail inflated her figure

three decades later in an attempt to impress the council with her sense of belonging in the community.

10. Town council meeting of 7 Feb. 1780, Exeter Town Council Records, 4:71; town council meetings of 3 Feb. and 10 Apr. 1769, Cumberland Town Council Records, 2:109–10, 114; town council meetings of 1 and 24 Feb. and 29 Mar. 1800, *East Greenwich Town Council Records*, 4:331–35. The problem of pregnant unmarried women inflating town welfare costs reached epidemic proportions in some communities. In 1784, when the Exeter town councilmen learned "there is a Number of Very poor people Come into the Town of Exeter Belonging to other Towns Some of Which are Now prignent and Likely to Be Chargable to This Town," they issued a blanket order that all of these offenders "Immediately Depart out of this Town" or expect to be removed by the town sergeant. Town council meeting of 14 Oct. 1784, Exeter Town Council Records, 4:134.

11. Since the official town record books usually contained a clerk's *copy* of the original examination, the examinant's "signature" is often in the clerk's hand. In some seventy cases, however, the official record books contain the examinant's original signature or mark.

12. Town council meeting of 26 Jan. 1752, Glocester Town Council Records, vol. 1; town council meeting of 15 Mar. 1784, Hopkinton Town Council Records, 2:131.

13. Letter from overseers of the poor of Attleboro to the Providence town council, 13 Dec. 1796, Providence Town Papers, Rhode Island Historical Society, Providence, R.I., 26:74.

14. When the flood of transients into communities became particularly heavy in the decade after the Revolutionary War, town councils strengthened this "neighborhood alert" system by passing regulations designed to enforce long-standing colony laws that required all residents to report any newcomers staying with them, thus tightening the net around transients who might hide out in a community with sympathetic friends or relatives. *Acts and Laws of Rhode Island*, 228–29. In 1790, for example, the Hopkinton council ordered the clerk to post "Notifications" that all inhabitants who took in transient people "without giving proper Notice" could expect to be "dealt with according to Law"—that is, fined. Town council meeting of 4 Jan. 1790, Hopkinton Town Council Records, 2:311.

15. Town council meetings of 23 Oct. 1793 (see also examination of Pompey Brown) and 31 Aug. 1797 (see also examinations of Deborah Green and Nancy Hazard), Providence Town Council Records, 6:299–300, 7:167–68.

16. Town council meeting of 31 Dec. 1757, Providence Town Council Records, 4:167.

17. For a thorough discussion of the changing attitudes toward race that accompanied emancipation, see Joanne Pope Melish, "Disowning Slavery: Emancipation in New England, 1780–1840" (Ph.D. diss., Brown University, 1996). I am particularly grateful to Melish for sharing with me her ideas on race, poverty, and

transience in post-Revolutionary New England. Her insights into the power relationships between Black and White revealed in the warnout orders and transient examinations have richly informed my own thinking and helped me build a better context for understanding transience.

18. Town council meetings of 8 Nov. 1796 and 13 Aug. 1787, Providence Town Council Records, 7:118, 6:16.

19. Town council meetings of 24 July 1782, 21 Oct. 1799, and 28 Oct. 1800, Providence Town Council Records, 5:215, 7:407, 586.

20. Town council meetings of 7 July and 8 Aug. 1794, Providence Town Council Records, 6:349–50; Providence Town Papers, 20:80.

21. Town council meetings of 2 July 1787 and 24 July 1782, Providence Town Council Records, 6:10, 5:215.

22. Town council meetings of 15 and 27 Oct. 1750, Middletown Town Council Records, 1:233–34; town council meetings of 29 Aug. and 9 Sept. 1780, Cumberland Town Council Records, 3:37–38.

23. Town council meetings of 2 and 4 June 1773, 19 June 1786, and 20 Aug. 1787, Middletown Town Council Records, 2:57, 157–58, 171.

24. Town council meeting of 6 June 1796, Providence Town Council Records, 7:97.

25. Town council meeting of 16 Mar. 1780, Providence Town Council Records, 5:164.

26. Town council meetings of 15 May 1788 and 5 Sept. 1785, Providence Town Council Records, 6:50–51, 5:239; relief orders on the town treasury, Providence Town Papers, 12:44, 59, 13:106.

27. Town council meeting of 14 May 1796, South Kingstown Town Council Records, 6:230.

28. Town council meeting of 22 Apr. 1793, Providence Town Council Records, 6:259–60.

29. Town Council meeting of 20 Mar. 1780, Providence Town Council Records, 5:169; Providence Town Papers, 5:39.

30. Rhode Island law allowed councils to collect a fine of not more than forty shillings or inflict a whipping of no more than thirty-nine stripes on a person who had returned after being removed. *Acts and Laws of Rhode-Island*, 231–32. Councils usually ordered fewer stripes for women than for men.

31. Town council meetings of 5 Mar. 1770, 17 Feb. 1772, 20 Mar. and 4 Apr. 1780, and 1 Oct. 1787, Providence Town Council Records, 4:299, 322, 5:168–69, 172, 6:23; Providence Town Papers, 10:148.

32. Letter to Rehoboth Overseers of the Poor, town council meeting of 18 May 1778, Providence Town Council Records, 5:113–15.

33. Town council meeting of 3 Feb. 1784, Providence Town Council Records, 5:256.

34. Town council meeting of 6 Feb. 1784, Providence Town Council Records, 5:527; warrant for removal of Phillis Merrit, Providence Town Papers, 13:11; Henry Bowen's account against the town, Providence Town Papers, 13:103.

35. Town council meetings of 3 and 4 Oct. 1800, Providence Town Council Records, 7:549, 551.

15 The Free Women of Charles Parish, York County, Virginia, 1630–1740

JULIE RICHTER

In December of 1727 Ann Robinson, the widow of Anthony Robinson, traveled to Virginia's York County Court. She told the justices of the peace "that her said dece[ase]d Husband hath made a Will in prejudice to the Rights that she hath by the law of Virginia to his Estate and praying that so much of the said Will as Concerns her Interest may be declared void according to the Act of Assembly in that Case made and provided."[1] Robinson was one of Charles Parish's wealthiest residents, and his widow wanted more than a slave girl, a feather bed and furniture, and a horse and saddle. The magistrates granted her petition.

Ann Robinson was only one of the seventeenth- and eighteenth-century female residents of Charles Parish who made use of her legal rights. The appearances of women in the York County Court indicate that females from all levels of the parish's social order played a public role in their community and knew how to use the county court system to protect their freedom, interests, and families. York's court records also reveal that members of both sexes called upon married and unmarried women to provide evidence in civil court cases, to witness documents, and to administer estates. The appearances of Charles Parish women in the York County court records can be divided into four categories: women, social crimes, and the parish community; labor and economic activities; women and the public use of household authority; and relationships between husbands and wives.[2]

It is necessary to have some background information on Charles Parish before turning to the court records. Charles Parish, established in 1634, was in southeastern York County, approximately twenty-one miles southeast of present-day Williamsburg. At just under fifty-nine square miles, it was the smallest of the three parishes in colonial York County. The mortality rate in the parish was high, and there was a constant turnover in the population from the immigration of new settlers and the emigration of individuals who hoped to gain possession of property that was more fertile than the land in much of Charles.[3]

The men, women, and children who stayed in the parish formed friendship and family ties with one another. Marriage, child rearing, and peaceful relationships among neighbors helped to give the Charles Parish community a sense of security. In addition, local officials used their authority to foster social stability and to take action against individuals who violated standards of moral behavior. Charles's leaders depended on females to serve as petitioners and witnesses because their actions helped to maintain the parish's social order. They also knew that it was easier for women than it was for men to investigate some incidents, such as childbirth.

Women played an important part, for example, in an inquiry into the circumstances surrounding an infant's death in 1658. Early in April of that year, Christopher Calthorpe learned that a child had died soon after its birth. The mother, Margaret Barker, was an indentured servant of his neighbor, Ralph Hunt. Calthorpe investigated the matter in his role as a justice of the peace. He asked another neighbor, John Ensworth, a parish constable, to send women to talk to Barker about the death of her infant. On 6 April 1658 Elizabeth Dunn, Elizabeth Taylor, and Mary Sables told Calthorpe that Eleanor Hunt had lifted the dead infant out of a cradle and showed it to them. The female deponents also stated that Barker was in a weak condition and that they did not speak to her.

The initial report did not satisfy Calthorpe, and he had Ensworth send

Elizabeth Dunn and Elizabeth Taylor back to Hunt's house the following day. Elizabeth Rooksby, Elizabeth Johnson, Margaret Booth, and Elizabeth Ensworth joined Elizabeth Dunn and Elizabeth Taylor on the second trip. The six women reported that they spoke to Barker, who at first denied that any harm had been done to her or to her child. However, when the women examined Barker's body, they found that her loins were black and blue. The servant said that her mistress had beaten her on the day that she gave birth. She speculated that the beating had harmed her child. Barker also told the women that Ralph Hunt had never hit her.

Information in the second set of depositions gave Calthorpe sufficient evidence to charge Eleanor Hunt with infanticide. On 24 June 1658 the justices reviewed the evidence. It is likely that the magistrates paid special attention to the statement that Barker gave Calthorpe seventeen days after she talked to the six women. She told him that she had fainted while she was doing some washing. When she regained consciousness, she was in labor. Eleanor Hunt delivered the baby because there was not enough time to send for a midwife. Barker said that her mistress had hit her on her back on the Friday before her child was born and had struck her about three weeks before the delivery. In spite of the evidence that Hunt had beaten Barker, it was not enough to convict her of infanticide. York's magistrates ordered Ralph Hunt to enter into a bond of five thousand pounds of tobacco to guarantee his wife's good behavior, especially toward Barker.[4]

The servant woman's deposition helped Hunt more than the others' statements. Barker changed her testimony when she told Calthorpe that she fell on the day she gave birth to the child. She also neglected to inform him that the beatings she received from her mistress had left her black and blue. Why did the indentured woman alter her testimony? Perhaps Eleanor Hunt was in the room while Barker talked to Calthorpe. She may have persuaded or forced Barker to change her story about her infant's death during the seventeen days between the questioning by the deponents and Calthorpe's visit. Barker was in a dependent position without any family support in Charles Parish. She probably was afraid of what her future would be in the Hunt household if the justices decided to send Hunt to Jamestown for a murder trial and she was found guilty.

Also, it was undoubtedly easier for Barker to tell other women about the events in the household and the birth and death of her child than it was for her to tell Calthorpe, one of the parish's most prominent residents.

Charles's churchwardens did not charge Barker with fornication or with bearing an illegitimate child, both sins and crimes that she had committed.[5] Nor did they ask her to name the father, though the evidence suggests that it was Ralph Hunt. Perhaps he quietly paid Barker's fine before the churchwardens presented her. It is possible that church officials dropped the case to protect the reputation of Hunt, a parish constable, and other local leaders who did not accuse him of adultery. It is likely that they wanted to put this incident and the disruption that it had caused to rest.

Church officials presented other individuals who did not live up to behavioral standards and who committed crimes that threatened the parish's social stability. In 1659 the churchwardens charged Elizabeth Knight and Nicholas Taylor with fornication. The testimony of a nineteen-year-old woman provided evidence to help convict Taylor. Mary Hazelgrove stated that Taylor lived near her landlord, Charles Dunn, and was quite familiar with Dunn's servant, Elizabeth Knight. Taylor remained in the house "untill the family was abedd & sometimes staying all night where upon this depon[en]t se[e]ing their great familiarity did acquaint Mrs Dunne with it." The young woman did not approve of the behavior that she witnessed and informed her landlady about what happened in her house during her absence. Though not a servant, Hazelgrove was in a dependent position in the Dunn household, and it is possible that she was afraid that Taylor would attempt to gain "great familiarity" with her as well. The justices of the peace fined Taylor two hundred pounds of tobacco and court costs. Knight died, possibly in childbirth, before the magistrates decided the case.[6]

The birth of an illegitimate child often became a financial burden on Charles's residents because the parish supported the infant if the father could not be identified. The cost of illegitimate children was a concern to Anthony Franklin, one of the parish's churchwardens, who charged a servant named Rebecca Noble and Thomas Hayrick with adultery and fornication in June of 1661. Franklin intended to use Hayrick and Noble as an example for the rest of Charles's residents because he believed that the couple had committed fornication and then tried to conceal their crime.

In August of 1661 Hayrick told the justices that he and Rebecca Noble had never had intercourse. In addition, he said that she was known to have kept company with a slave belonging to Colonel Matthews and that she almost married a slave owned by Colonel Read. The justices of the peace dropped the charges against Hayrick. Noble's reputation as "a woman of a very evill life & conversacon" counted against her. The officials sentenced Noble to receive ten lashes on her bare back. In addition, the constable was to make sure that "the next Lords day she do penance in the said poquoson p[ar]ish Church by standing in a white sheet & asking open forgiveness on hir knees of God almighty for hir said offence before the whole Congregation and also that shee forthwith aske forgiveness of the Court." [7]

The prosecution of adultery also provides evidence of the value that parish and county officials placed upon marriage. In 1692/93 an indentured man named Cornelius Cornute turned to the county court in order to protect his wife, Ann, against his former master. Cornute told the justices of the peace that Stephen Pond "kept & detained his wife from him & made it his frequent custom to lye w/her openly boasting thereof to s[ai]d Cornute & others together w/diverse other rude behaviors & unjust actions." Four depositions, including statements from Cornute's female neighbors, Elizabeth Harding and Sarah Keys, helped to persuade the justices to rule in his favor. [8]

The status of Cornute and his spouse make this case and the decision of the justices revealing. Cornelius and Ann Cornute were husband and wife before he began a four-year indenture with Stephen Pond in December 1691. A short time later, Pond assigned Cornute's indenture to a man named John Gardiner. Cornute was still a servant when he charged his former master with sleeping with his wife. Since Ann Cornute was probably indentured to Pond during the time that he boasted that he slept with her, the only thing that separated her from other servant women who were forced to lie with their masters was that she had a husband. Her marriage proved to be the critical factor in the case. The fact that the justices allowed Cornute to appear in court and that the members of the jury ruled in his favor indicates that a marriage bond was more important to the preservation of the social order than was a master's power over a servant.

Charles's planters did not always succeed in their attempts to regulate the sexual behavior of their female servants. They wanted to control indentured women because pregnancy affected their productivity and threatened to reduce the authority that masters had over their laborers. Seventeen of the twenty-two women presented for either fornication or bearing an illegitimate child between 1630 and 1720 were servants. In addition, the fact that only one of this group married the father of her child probably helped to associate immoral behavior with poverty in the minds of Charles's leaders. Katherine Pond also married after bearing children out of wedlock. She was the mother of three free black children—Mary, William, and Matthew Cattilla—by 1672, when she married Stephen Pond. Katherine Pond had a unique position in Charles. She acted as the link between the free black and the white members of her family and parish. Pond apprenticed her son William so that he would learn a skill and have a record of his status as a free person. Matthew Cattilla served as a witness for his white half-brother, John Pond, in 1695. In December of 1699 Mary Cattilla and Katherine Pond gave depositions in support of the nuncupative will that they had persuaded their neighbor, a white woman named Jane Merry, to make because "itt would be a great Satisfaccon to her selfe & ease her friends of a great deal of trouble." [9]

Eleven women bore illegitimate children between 1720 and 1740. Ten were young and unmarried. The other, Elizabeth Patrick, was a widow. They came from all levels of the social scale, from Sarah Woodfield, who asked her brother-in-law, Justinian Love, to pay her fine because she could not afford to do so, to Eleanor Hayward, who had the money to pay her own. The marriage prospects for women who gave birth out of wedlock all but disappeared after 1700 because of the greater number of females in the Chesapeake and the increased importance that prospective husbands placed on women's reputations. In an October 1729 defamation case, the plaintiff, an unmarried woman, argued that "no greater misfortune can befall a young Woman whose well being depends upon her having a good Husband than to be reputed a Whore." Sarah Woodfield and Eleanor Hayward did not have to worry about the impact that a rumor would have on their reputations. Their illegitimate children were proof of their illicit behavior.[10]

York's officials accepted unions between free blacks, and the children born of them, as legal. They also recognized the marriage between John Combs, a white man, and Sarah Whiting, a free woman of color. The same was not true for unmarried free black women like Judith Cattilla, a free black granddaughter of Katherine Pond. When she appeared in court in 1729 to answer the charge of bearing an illegitimate child, the father was neither present nor named. This suggests that he was a slave. Judith Cattilla was only one of the members of her family to face this charge in the eighteenth century. With the number of potential partners limited by the fact that free blacks accounted for only 2 to 4 percent of Charles's population, some free black women probably found slave partners or became involved with white men who did not acknowledge the relationships in public. Their illegitimate children could have been the result of relationships that parish leaders did not recognize, especially if the union was with a slave man.[11]

Women who were guilty of adultery or fornication, or who gave birth to illegitimate children, breached standards of moral behavior. Local leaders punished them in order to maintain the parish's social order. Charles's officials also regulated women whose actions disrupted economic pursuits and neighborly relations. In 1705 John Cox, an ordinary keeper, accused Thomas and Sarah Sclater of illegally selling liquor. Four years later, the grand jury summoned the husband and wife to answer the same charge. The Sclaters probably sold food and drink for less than the price set by law, undercutting Cox's business. That the grand jury included Sarah Sclater's name in both presentments suggests that she helped her husband operate the ordinary. It is also possible that Sarah was the guilty party but had to be sued in her husband's name. Thomas Sclater did not keep an ordinary after Sarah's death in December of 1709, another indication that she played a large role in the business.[12]

Neighborly relations became strained when an individual blocked a small path or a road in the parish. Charles's residents depended on the roads to attend church on Sundays, to do business, and to visit friends. In 1716 the grand jury presented Mary Taylor for preventing travelers from using the road that passed through her land. Taylor charged the surveyor of the highways, Robert Kerby, with trespassing upon her land because she did not want the road to run through her cornfield and reduce the size of her harvest. Two of her four witnesses, Sarah Burkhead and Elizabeth Cockerill, were women who lived a short distance away from her plantation. Taylor called on women from the lower end of the social scale to appear as witnesses, suggesting the existence of gender-based networks that transcended social layers.[13]

Women helped Charles's political leaders enforce statutes and punish those individuals, male and female, who violated behavioral standards and harmed neighborly relations by committing social crimes. Women's labor also helped to maintain a sense of stability in Charles. Many of the daily tasks that women did in their homes and around their plantations did not come under the purview of the York County court. However, several petitions and depositions contain details about the situation of indentured servants and about the labor that independent women performed. The parish's women, whether bound laborers, single women, wives, or widows, did what was necessary to protect and support themselves. Charles's females, like its males, had varying degrees of success in their economic endeavors, depending upon their standing in the parish community and their abilities.

Several bonded laborers turned to the court for protection from masters who violated the terms of their indentures. In 1665 the justices awarded Judith Walker her freedom dues (clothes and a barrel of corn), which Edmund Chisman had refused to give her. Ann Gray successfully petitioned against her former master in 1715/16. Simon Stacy continued to treat Gray as a servant even though she had completed her servitude. The court decision enabled her to move freely in the parish. In March 1682/83, Mary Adney complained that John Wright, Charles's minister, treated her cruelly. Testimony from several witnesses helped the justices to find Wright guilty of treating his servant in "a most grosse, inhumane & barbarous manner, to the great scandall & infamy of this Country." He entered into a bond to guarantee his good behavior toward Adney and all the rest of his servants.[14]

Rebecca Groom supported herself by working for hire. In 1714 she received a payment of £3.11.10 for the wages owed to her by the estate of Henry Hayward. It is probable that Hayward had hired Groom to help his second wife, Elizabeth, care for their six children and the five minor children from his first marriage. Groom, a trusted member of the household, was one of the witnesses to Hayward's last testament. The will that Groom wrote a month before she died in June of 1745 reveals that she maintained a close relationship with the Hayward family, possibly by helping to raise Hayward's grandchildren. She named Hayward's daughter, Elizabeth, as her executor, asked Francis Hayward to witness her will, and left her personal possessions to Elizabeth Hayward and four of Henry Hayward's granddaughters. The inventory of Groom's estate indicates that she had been able to save £18 and to acquire items including a bed, earthenware dishes, and eating utensils. She stored her clothing in a chest of drawers and possibly kept her Bible and prayer book on top of the chest.[15]

Hired workers were not the only women to work for pay. Unmarried women, wives, and widows undertook a variety of activities in order to add to the incomes of their families and to assist their neighbors. These tasks included endeavors associated with the female sex and undertakings usually identified with their male counterparts. In November 1679 John Phipps's executor paid Thomas Wray a small sum because his wife had nursed Phipps's infant son, Thomas, after the death of his mother nine months earlier. In June of 1697 Francis Callowhill noted that he had paid a midwife one hundred pounds of tobacco to deliver a daughter born to his servant woman, Mary Hughson, in February of the same year.[16]

Charles's women also managed plantations and businesses. Jane Cox took over the operation of the family's plantation after the death of her husband, Thomas. She decided to rent out to Thomas Hazelton the property that her husband had patented and to lease a tract from John Hayward. It is likely that Cox, as the first owner of the land, had not cleared enough ground to grow the tobacco, corn, and wheat that his family needed. His widow thought it would be easier to tend her own crops on land that was already cleared, such as the Hayward parcel. As it turned out, her decision was not wise. Jane Cox could not make ends meet as a tenant, so she asked Hazelton to leave her property. Hazelton agreed but later changed his mind, so Jane Cox sued him for damages amounting to five thousand pounds of tobacco. After losing the case, she turned to an attorney, Hugh Owen, who obtained an injunction against Hazelton. However, York's magistrates decided that the proceedings were illegal and dismissed her suit. The widow Cox and Hazelton may have shared the seventy-nine-acre plantation until the end of his lease; there is no evidence that either of them rented a different tract of land. Jane Cox retained the plantation, and her son Thomas tended fields on his father's property after he reached his majority in 1711.[17]

Elizabeth Hayward, daughter of Henry Hayward and his second wife, Elizabeth, became the owner of a plantation when she purchased two hundred acres of land in March 1721/22. Hayward remained a single woman throughout her life, and because of her status she was able to serve as the executor of her mother's will in 1731 and of the last testament written by her stepbrother, Edward Tabb, ten years later. In addition, her mother placed her in charge of "all my crop of Corne wheat & what hogs are now put up to fatten as alsoe what other provision is in or aboute my house for the fomoly' use." The fact that Elizabeth Tabb and her stepson chose Elizabeth Hayward, not her brother Francis Hayward, a justice of the peace, to probate their estates is an indication of her abilities. Hayward kept control of her plantation until her death in 1772. Appraisers valued her estate at £940, evidence of her skill as a plantation manager. Three nieces and a nephew fought for possession of their deceased aunt's land. Perhaps the fact that her nieces represented themselves in the chancery suit would have pleased this woman who had lived an independent life.[18]

Three of Charles's female residents involved themselves in endeavors that required them to enter into economic agreements with other parish residents. First, Lydia Harwood and her brother-in-law, Thomas Chisman, ran Chisman's mill in 1678, the year after the death of her first husband, Edmund Chisman, and the year of her marriage to Thomas Harwood. Jane Cully was a teacher. As the 1721 settlement of her estate indicated, several prominent residents of Charles owed her small sums of money "for Schooling" their children. Finally, Mary Ward followed in her husband Plany Ward's footsteps as an ordinary keeper when she petitioned for her first license in May 1734, three months after her husband's death. Ward operated the ordinary and collected almost £348 of the £440 that individuals owed to her husband's estate during the seven months following his death. In 1734/35, Ward purchased ten acres of land and became the owner of the ground on which the ordinary stood, something that her husband had not been able to do. It is likely that Ward continued to work as an ordinary proprietor until she sold her tract of land to her neighbor, Edward Tabb, in January 1744/45.[19]

The parish's working women came from up and down the social scale: indentured servants, widows of middling planters, and even the daughter of one of Charles's most prominent residents. Jane Cox did not have the managerial abilities or the productive land that Elizabeth Hayward did. Mary Ward proved herself as able an ordinary keeper as her husband had been. Rebecca Groom probably fared better than did the majority of women who worked in someone else's household. The fact that many of Charles's females were able to provide for themselves and their families meant that they did not need assistance from the vestrymen, thereby reducing the tax burden on their neighbors.

Charles's women also took public actions in order to provide support for their children, grandchildren, and godchildren. There were several ways in which the females could make sure that they and members of their families had access to land to plant, to laborers to help tend fields, and to personal possessions that might make life a bit more comfortable. The options available to the women were related to their marital status and legal identity.

Married women knew that by law their husbands were to leave them a third of their estates. If a legacy did not equal her legal portion, a widow could petition the court in order to gain her due. In 1692 Margaret Booth successfully did just that. She was the widow of William Booth, a justice of the peace and the owner of 340 acres of land. In spite of the fact that Booth left a large portion of his estate to his grandchildren, his legacy to his widow, though less than a third, would have been large enough to support her during her widowhood. The widow Booth insisted on her dower portion because it was her right, not because she needed the real and personal property.[20]

Not all of the parish's widows were as fortunate as Margaret Booth. Small planters were not always able to leave estates large enough to support their wives and children. As a result the widows of poor men turned to the court and to their neighbors for help in making ends meet.

In February 1673/74, the justices decided to allow Susanna Crandall "to gather in & dispose of what debts she shall find belonging to her husbands estate for her owne & childrens sustenances." Three years later, Mary Floyd appeared before York's magistrates because the death of her husband, Thomas, left her "in a very poore & lowe condicon with a sucking child at her breast." They "ordered that she have three Barrells of Indyan Corne if there be soe much, her bedd & provisions for the maintenance of her selfe and Infant." [21]

Martha Provo had a difficult life after the death of her husband, James. He was not among the successful members of the parish. In June of 1692 Provo asked to be discharged from the payment of public and county levies because he was "very aged & poore haveing sustained losses & charge of children to maintain." Provo died in December of 1693, and it is likely that he left Martha a very small estate with which to support herself and their two surviving children, Ann, who died in November of 1697, and Mark. By 1698 Martha was forced to bind out her son to John Miller.[22]

The widow Provo also worked as a servant, an unusual circumstance for a woman who had been married and widowed. In July 1701 Richard Dixon and Henry Hayward, the churchwardens of Charles Parish, complained that Thomas Nichols refused "to entertain his servant woman Martha Pervoo widd of James Pervoo but in her poor & weak condition haveing illegally imposed the s[ai]d servant upon Charles P[ari]sh afores[ai]d & denying to receive her again but that she may become a charge to the s[ai]d P[ari]sh." We do not know if Martha remained in the service of Nichols, but she was clearly among the poor of Charles Parish—a widow in ill health and unable to support herself. Parish officials may have provided support for Martha until her death in June of 1703.[23]

Several women who inherited real estate and personal possessions from their husbands took steps to make sure their children would gain possession of their legacies when they reached adulthood. Margery Jolly Griggs Hay and her third husband, William Hay, entered into a marriage agreement in 1655. Margery wanted to insure that her two young children from her second marriage received good care from their stepfather and that he did not waste their inheritances or the five hundred acres of land that she had purchased in 1653. Hay promised "to bring up the s[ai]d children in good Education and Learning and to finde and allowe them sufficient meate drinck & app[ar]ell washing & lodgeing and all other necessaries ... w[i]thout any Charge to the Childrens Estate." Hay's wealth enabled him to cover the expenses of rearing Margery and John Griggs. The majority of Charles's stepfathers and guardians charged the costs of maintenance to the orphans' estates. Hay raised his stepchildren after his wife died, looked after their cattle, tended their fields, and remembered them in his 1669 will.[24]

Hannah Bennett Turner Tompkins Arnold used a deed of gift to make sure that her children would gain possession of her real and personal property. The only surviving child of Samuel and Joan Bennett, Hannah inherited her father's 450–acre tract in the 1630s and made it her home for the rest of her life. Her first husband, Abraham Turner, worked to secure the title to her land after her stepfather, Thomas Chapman, attempted to claim part of the tract for her mother. It was important that Turner retain possession of the whole plantation; he had no land of his own. Turner reached an agreement with Chapman in June of 1646, but he died by the following January.[25]

The widow Turner settled her husband's estate with the help of Humphrey Tompkins, the man who became her second husband. Tompkins served as an estate appraiser, guardian, and surveyor of highways. He probably received the charge to maintain roads in the parish because of the status he acquired by marrying a woman who had 450 acres of land. Tompkins wanted his wife, not one of his neighbors, to settle his estate after his death. In November of 1673 Edmund Watts and Walter Chapman testified that Tompkins had stated "that what Estate hee was possest of hee had it with his wife & I have noe intent to give any thing from her my Children being all her owne & therefore I give all that I have to my wife & let her dispose of it as she pleaseth amongst her children & I make my wife sole Exec[ut]r[i]x."[26]

Hannah decided to "dispose of some part of my estate to the natural use of" her five surviving children, Samuel, William, Humphrey, John, and Ann, in a deed of gift in April of 1674. She was forty-four years old when she decided to give a portion of her real and personal property to her children. The widow Tompkins had buried two husbands and six children in addition to seeing many of her friends and neighbors die in their late thirties and early forties. If she married again, she might not outlive a third husband and be able to bequeath her real and personal property to her sons and daughter. Hannah thus used a deed of gift as a will to provide for her five children and to insure that a stepfather would "not in any Waies hinder any of my children." [27]

Hannah's third husband, William Arnold, was one of the witnesses to the deed of gift to her children. It is likely that Hannah had known Arnold since the 1660s and wed for a third time for companionship. Like Tompkins, Arnold did not possess property in his own name and received his appointment as surveyor of the highways after his marriage to Hannah. When Arnold died in February 1683, he left a gold ring to his stepson Samuel, a silver cup to his stepson William, and the rest of his estate to his wife. Arnold made no mention of the plantation in his will, a sign that he and Hannah probably had entered an agreement about the property before their marriage. Hannah Arnold lived on the land she had inherited from her father until her death in June 1693 at the age of sixty-three. Her descendants retained possession of the family plantation throughout the eighteenth century.[28]

Women who remained widows used wills to transfer real and personal property to their children, family members, friends, and neighbors. Some of Charles's women wrote wills because their husbands had died intestate or had not made specific bequests in their last testaments. In 1687 Elizabeth MacIntosh was the sole legatee and executor of her husband, Enos MacIntosh. The widow MacIntosh carefully divided his real and personal estate among their six surviving children in her 1692 will. One of Elizabeth MacIntosh's neighbors, Amy Moore, wrote her last testament in June of 1700, a month after she had petitioned for a commission of administration on the estate of her deceased husband, John Moore. Her decision to leave a written record of legacies for her seven children and to appoint her cousin, Peter Starkey, as the guardian of her underage sons and daughters turned out to be an important one. She died in December 1700.[29]

Women lucky enough to live long lives bequeathed remembrances to their heirs in addition to cattle and laborers. In 1722/23, twice-widowed Ann Chapman Callowhill willed livestock, jewelry, clothing, money to buy mourning rings, and slaves to her sons and daughters, their children, and her godchildren. Twelve years later, Elizabeth Nutting's will contained a detailed list of personal possessions that she had collected over the course of her life and was passing on to her children, grandchildren, and great-grandchildren. Elizabeth Nutting turned to her daughter, Katherine Armistead, to execute her estate. Armistead had gained experience in probating estates when she served as the executor for her first husband, William Sheldon, in 1727, and for her sister, Elizabeth Doswell, in 1728. She inventoried her mother's possessions and served as the executrix even though she was a married woman. Robert Armistead appeared as a coplaintiff with his wife in order to collect the debts owed to his mother-in-law's estate.[30]

Women's gender role gave them the duty and responsibility of caring for their children. Charles's women had public ways of providing for their own support and that of their sons and daughters. The women knew that they could petition the local magistrates for assistance if their husbands did not leave them a large enough estate, as Mary Floyd and Susanna Crandall did. Charles's women relied upon three legal measures to transfer real and personal property to their sons and daughters, grandchildren, godchildren, and children of friends. First, single women who were about to marry or widows who planned to remarry used deeds of gift to convey their possessions. Second, a small number of women, including Margery Jolly Griggs Hay, entered into marriage agreements with their new husbands to make sure that their children received their legacies from their fathers. Third, unmarried women and widows relied upon wills to transfer real and personal property to their legatees. The public actions that women took to provide support for their families and godchildren were especially important in Charles Parish because of its high mortality rate. Women who appeared before the court demonstrated that they, like their husbands, knew they needed to make provisions to insure the welfare of their children against a stepparent or a guardian who might try to take advantage of their stepchildren or wards.

Charles's couples also looked out for the well-being of their spouses when they were in happy marriages. Details about the relationships between some of Charles's married men and women are a part of the court proceedings. Some of the parish's husbands trusted their wives to represent them in court; other couples did not have happy relationships.

These men and women had to resolve their difficulties because divorce was not an option. A troubled marriage was disruptive to their family and to their community. Estranged spouses found various solutions to their marital problems, including apparent reconciliations, decisions that wives could work to support themselves apart from husbands, and formal separation agreements.

The power of attorney that a husband granted to his wife was a public indication of the trust that the couple shared. It conveyed the authority to make decisions that affected the family's prosperity and landholding. When Christopher Calthorpe left Charles Parish for Carolina in early 1661/62, he appointed his wife, Ann, not one of his friends, as his attorney. In spite of his confidence in her abilities, Ann Calthorpe may have felt that it would be difficult for her to settle her husband's estate in Charles Parish and in England and look after their four young children, all under the age of fifteen, after his death. In April of 1662 she appointed her husband's friend, Armiger Wade, as her attorney to administer his estate.[31]

Men in the lower portion of the social order also turned to their wives for assistance. In November 1679 Joseph Disarme "gave his wife full power to plead and implead in a case [against] Mr Joseph Davis merchant or his attor[nie]s & likewise ag[ains]t Edward Johnson & Lewis Roberts." Elizabeth Disarme was experienced in the courtroom. She had settled the estates of her first two husbands and had overseen the property of her son, John Murray. The fact that Disarme gave his wife the authority to represent him in three cases suggests that he planned on being away from home for an extended period of time.[32]

The Reverend James Sclater turned to his wife, Mary, as his attorney on two occasions, in 1693/94 and in 1703, even though a male relative lived in the parish. James Sclater gave his wife wide-ranging powers to exercise on his behalf, an indication of the trust he had in her and of the length of time that he intended to be away from Charles. In January 1693/94 the minister authorized his wife to act in his name to collect debts, to represent him in court in civil cases, and to serve as his attorney. He appointed his wife and sons, James and John, to execute his last will and testament. Mary and James Sclater received probate of the minister's estate in August 1724. The widow Sclater presented the inventory of her husband's possessions to the justices of the peace by herself in September of the same year, an indication that she handled the administration of her deceased husband's will on her own.[33]

The trust between the Calthorpes, the Disarmes, and the Sclaters did not characterize all of the marriages that joined Charles's men and women. Some females received harsh treatment from their husbands, and others did not get along with their spouses. Although a married female did not have a separate legal identity in colonial Virginia, a *feme covert* could turn to the local magistrates for assistance if her husband treated her cruelly. In January 1691/92 Mary Savory petitioned the members of York's bench for relief from her husband, Henry, because "her life as well as her bodily health is dayly indangered by him." She requested "certaine necessaries out of their estate" and received "her bed, a pott, a frying pan & some spoones, 2 trayes, a gridiron & 2 chests & that he pay all costs of suite." If the two lived apart, it was probably only for a short time. Their two daughters, Lydia and Mary, were born in 1698 and 1702.[34]

When the marriage of Nicholas and Mary Martin became troubled in 1693, he warned "all maner of persons whatsoever from haveing any dealings in the least w/my wife Mary Martin any farther than her owne labour goes for if they doe they shall not receive any satisfaction from y[ou]r loveing friend & neighbor." It is interesting that Martin was willing to let his wife support herself with money she earned; he obviously believed her capable of living on her own. The justices granted Martin's wish that she be permitted to keep the money she earned instead of turning it over to him.[35]

Ann Eaton was more fortunate than Mary Martin. She had dower rights to property owned by her first husband, David Lewis, to fall back on when she requested a separation from her second husband, John Eaton. Ann told the justices of the peace "that her husband John Eaton will not suffer her to live peaceably or quietyly with him nor allow her a separate maintenance." The court decided that she should receive support from her husband and gave her "the rent of her plantacion in Cha. Parish to be yearly paid her by her s[ai]d husband." The Eatons did not repair their relationship, and he did not leave his wife anything in his

1717 will. Ann petitioned the local magistrates for her dower in his property and received one-third of the value of her husband's land.[36]

In March 1726/27 Ann Chisman Irwin petitioned for a separation from Jones Irwin after less than two years of marriage. She also wanted an agreement that would be sufficient to support her and her four minor children from her first marriage. The separation agreement contained hints about their problems. Jones Irwin said he would give his wife the rent from two plantations, pork, beef, tallow, corn, wool, wheat, cider, and milk each year, adding that she must not incur more debt than her tobacco crop would cover. He agreed to help when he could, but if he could not, Ann was not to "disturb with ill language but be Content with my Answer." She was to put locks on the doors and to keep them locked when she was not home. Ann would have a horse and a servant to take her to church on Sunday mornings. Ann Irwin stayed in Charles Parish and lived in the half of the dwelling house she received when she and her husband separated. Jones Irwin moved to Yorktown and had four children by his mistress, Elizabeth Morris. After he died in October of 1751, Ann successfully petitioned the York and Warwick county courts for her dower in his estate. Ann Irwin lived in Charles until her death in 1754.[37]

Some of Charles's women had close relationships with their husbands, whereas others had unhappy marriages. Mary Slater was an able representative for her husband, the parish's minister. Ann Eaton and Ann Irwin assured themselves of support from their estranged husbands. Mary Martin proved that she was capable of supporting herself apart from her husband as if she were a single woman. Neither the local officials nor the parish's inhabitants questioned the propriety of women thus living apart from their husbands. Separated spouses posed less of a threat to Charles's social order than did couples who could not live under the same roof without fighting or threatening each other with physical abuse.

The appearances of women before members of the county court indicate that Charles's females played a public role in their community and knew how to use the York County court to protect their interests and those of their families. In addition, they helped to maintain social stability and to uphold behavioral standards in their community. The females presented for social crimes did not themselves provide positive examples of moral behavior, but justices of the peace used their actions to publicly define right and wrong for the rest of the parish's residents. Whether women appeared before the justices of the peace voluntarily or involuntarily, their actions helped to define standards of appropriate and moral behavior. Women who petitioned for their share of a husband's estate and to provide for their children, as well as those who granted deeds of gift and wrote wills, used their authority as wives and mothers in a public manner. Several of Charles's women showed that they were able to support their children and keep their families off the list of residents who needed financial assistance from the parish.

Gender roles restricted legal activities of married women, but they could turn to local officials for help if they received cruel treatment from their husbands. Indentured servants also had the right to petition the members of York's bench if their masters did not treat them according to the terms of their indentures. Demographic characteristics of Charles also shaped the experiences of the women who lived in the parish. During the period under study, females made up a minority of the community's population. Because of the small number of women in Charles, the female residents formed friendship ties that extended miles from their homes and, at times, outside their social positions. The relationships that men formed with each other tended to be based more closely on residential location and economic standing. Like the parish's men, the women were aware of the need to provide for their children's welfare because they knew that they probably would not see their sons and daughters reach adulthood.

The justices of the peace and Charles's local-level officials depended on women to participate in public life because their actions helped to keep families together and to maintain social order in the parish community. On occasion the local magistrates allowed the parish's married females to exceed their legal authority. Lydia Harwood helped to operate a mill and Katherine Armistead administered estates while each was a *feme covert*. The members of the county bench probably permitted Charles's females to expand the range of their public actions as a way to add some stability to the community. These activities did not threaten gender roles in Charles because the parish's women did not habitually step outside of the part that colonial Virginia society gave them to play in their community.

NOTES

1. All biographical information in this chapter is from the York County Project Master Biographical File, Department of Historical Research, Colonial Williamsburg Foundation, Williamsburg, Virginia. See also Julie Richter, "A Community and Its Neighborhoods: Charles Parish, York County, Virginia, 1630–1740," (Ph.D. diss., College of William and Mary, 1992). Quotations are taken from six series of York County Court records, all at York County Courthouse, Yorktown, Va.: Deeds and Bonds (hereafter cited as DAB); Deeds, Orders, and Wills (hereafter cited as DOW); Judgments and Orders (hereafter cited as JO); Orders and Wills (hereafter cited as OW); Orders, Wills, and Inventories (hereafter cited as OWI); and Wills and Inventories (hereafter cited as WI). OW 16:495 (18 Dec. 1727).

2. I use the term *public use of household authority* to refer to the public actions women took to provide for the support of their children and godchildren.

3. Women accounted for 30 to 40 percent of the parish's population between 1630 and 1740. Females who were born in Charles and reached the age of twenty could expect to celebrate their forty-fourth birthday. Pregnancy and childbirth probably reduced the life expectancies of the parish's women during their childbearing years. However, when they reached middle age, the number of years they could expect to live increased. In fact, women of forty-five and fifty years of age could anticipate enjoying more years than Charles Parish men of the same ages could, and close to the same life span at ages fifty-five and sixty.

4. DOW 3:28, 29 (6 Apr. and 7 Apr. 1658); DOW 3:21 (24 Apr. 1658); DOW 3:27, 29 (24 June 1658).

5. Fornication and bastardy were sins as well as crimes until the late 1650s. The judges were concerned with sin because Virginia had no ecclesiastical court. By the early 1660s, Virginia's officials viewed bastardy as an offense that could be costly to parishes. Local magistrates tried to identify the father so that he, and not the parish, would support the child. Kathleen M. Brown, *Good Wives and Nasty Wenches: Gender, Race, and Power in Colonial Virginia* (Chapel Hill: University of North Carolina Press for the Institute of Early American History and Culture, 1996), chap. 6; William H. Seiler, "The Anglican Parish in Virginia," in *Seventeenth-Century America: Essays in Colonial History*, edited by James Morton Smith (Chapel Hill: University of North Carolina Press for the Institute of Early American History and Culture, 1959), 119–42.

6. DOW 3:66, 68 (24 Oct. 1659).

7. DOW 3:125, 129 (26 Aug. 1661); Brown, *Good Wives and Nasty Wenches*, chap. 6. Until 1692 Charles Parish was named New Poquoson Parish.

8. DOW 9:202 (13 Feb. 1692/93).

9. Brown, *Good Wives and Nasty Wenches*, chap. 6. Only Ann Callowhill named the father. See DOW 7:214 (24 Sept. 1686) and Charles Parish Birth Register, Library of Virginia, Richmond, Va. Pond, DOW 7:61 (24 Mar. 1684/85); DOW 10:141 (13 Apr. 1695); DOW 11:269–70 (dated 14 Oct. and recorded 14 Dec. 1699). Katherine Pond probably lived in Elizabeth City County when she gave birth to Mary, William, and Matthew. Perhaps the justices of the peace in that county presented her for bearing illegitimate mulatto children.

10. Patrick and Hayward, OWI 18:155 (18 Nov. 1734). Woodfield, OW 17:29 (16 Feb. 1729/30). *Mutlow v. Ballard*, Oct. 1729, quoted in "Carted Whores and White Shrouded Apologies: Slander in the County Courts of Seventeenth-Century Virginia," by Clara Ann Bowler, *Virginia Magazine of History and Biography* 85 (1977):426.

11. Combs, DOW 12:344 (24 July 1705). Cattilla, OW 17:12 (15 Dec. 1729). Women made up just over 50 percent of the free black population in Charles before 1740.

12. DOW 12:353 (24 Sept. 1705); DOW 13:187 (25 Jan. 1708/9); Charles Parish Death Register, Library of Virginia, Richmond, Va.

13. DOW 14:471 (16 Jan. 1715/16); DOW 14:511 (22 May 1716); OW 15:31 (17 Sept. 1716).

14. Walker, DOW 4:9 (24 Apr. 1665). Gray, DOW 14:420 (20 June 1715); DOW 14:475 (20 Feb. 1715/16). Adney, DOW 6:493–94 (24 Apr. 1683).

15. DOW 14:146–48 (dated 4 Nov. 1711 and recorded 17 Mar. 1711/12); DOW 14:371–73 (recorded 15 Nov. 1714); WI 20:3 (dated 15 May and recorded 16 Dec. 1745); WI 20:7 (dated and recorded 18 Nov. 1745).

16. Phipps, DOW 6:151 (18 Nov. 1679). Callowhill, DOW 10:423–24 (24 June 1697).

17. DOW 9:281 (dated 26 Feb. 1692/93 and recorded 24 Nov. 1693); DOW 10:74 (27 Nov. 1694); DOW 10:89, 105 (24 Jan. 1694/95); DOW 10:109 (25 Feb. 1694/95); DOW 10:122 (25 Mar. 1695); DOW 14:337 (21 June 1714).

18. DAB 3:383–84 (dated 17 Mar. and recorded 19 Mar. 1721/22); OW 17:249–50 (dated 23 Nov. and recorded 20 Dec. 1731); WI 19:49 (dated 5 Jan. 1735 and recorded 20 July 1741); WI 20:3 (dated 15 May and recorded 16 Dec. 1745); WI 20:7 (dated and recorded 18 Nov. 1745); WI 22:172–73 (recorded 17 May 1773); JO 3:316 (19 July 1773).

19. Harwood, DOW 6:38 (24 Apr. 1678). Cully, OW 16:129 (19 Mar. 1721/22). Ward, OWI 18:106–7 (recorded 18 Mar. 1733/34); OWI 18:112 (20 May 1734); DAB 4:340–41 (dated 16 Jan. and recorded 20 Jan. 1734/35); DAB 5:111–12 (dated 19 Jan. and recorded 21 Jan. 1744/45). That Mary Ward collected the majority of the debts owed by individuals to her deceased husband suggests that

Plany Ward had kept running accounts for his neighbors and regular customers. When the debtors paid their accounts to the tavern keeper's widow, they reciprocated the neighborliness that he had extended to them.

20. William Waller Hening, ed., *The Statutes at Large; Being a Collection of All the Laws of Virginia, From the First Session of the Legislature, in 1619*, 13 vols. (Richmond, New York, and Philadelphia, 1819–23; reprint, Charlottesville: University of Virginia Press for the Jamestown Foundation of the Commonwealth of Virginia, 1969), 2:212, 303; 3:371–74; 5:447 (page references are to the reprint edition). DOW 9:140 (24 June 1692).

21. Crandall, DOW 5:62 (24 Feb. 1673/74). Floyd, DOW 6:22 (10 Dec. 1677/78 [*sic*]).

22. DOW 9:142 (24 June 1692); DOW 11:80–81 (24 Aug. 1698); DOW 11:153 (24 Apr. 1699).

23. DOW 11:479 (24 July 1701) and Charles Parish Death Register.

24. DOW 1:168–69 (2[5] Sept. 1655); DOW 4:229 (dated 13 Jan. and recorded 10 Mar. 1668/69).

25. DOW 2:133–34 (16 June 1646); DOW 2:418 (dated c. Nov. 1646 and recorded 26 Sept. 1648).

26. DOW 2:412 (26 Sept. 1648); DOW 3:167 (24 June 1662); DOW 3:175 (24 Oct. 1662); DOW 5:58 (dated 8 Nov. and recorded 24 Nov. 1673).

27. DOW 5:65–66 (dated 14 Apr. 1674 and recorded [24 May 1674]). See note 3.

28. DOW 5:91 (26 Nov. 1674); DOW 6:494 (dated 30 Jan. 1682/83 and recorded 24 Apr. 1683).

29. That MacIntosh's three sons, Daniel, Enos, and Samuel, were minors when he wrote his will in 1687 may have played a part in his decision to name his wife as his executor. There is evidence that he trusted Elizabeth's judgment. When MacIntosh granted a deed of gift to his three daughters in 1671, he also gave "my s[ai]d wife Elizabeth in case of mortality of my s[ai]d children as afores[ai]d full power to dispose of them [cattle] as she shall thinke fitt" (MacIntosh, DOW 4:380 [11 Jan. 1671/72]). DOW 7:322 (dated 6 Feb. 1686/87 and recorded 4 May 1687); DOW 10:217–19 (dated 26 Nov. 1692 and recorded 24 Sept. 1695). Moore, DOW 11:332 (24 May 1700); Charles Parish Death Register; DOW 11:424 (dated 10 June 1700 and recorded 24 Feb. 1700/1701).

30. Callowhill, OW 16:186–87 (recorded 18 Feb. 1722/23). Nutting, OW 16:456–57 (dated 7 Apr. and recorded 15 May 1727); OW 16:506 (dated 24 Sept. 1727 and recorded 15 Jan. 1727/28); OWI 18:230–31 (dated 13 Sept. 1733 and recorded 15 Sept. 1735); OWI 18:250 (dated and recorded 15 Dec. 1735).

31. DOW 3:164 (dated 23 Apr. and recorded 24 Apr. 1662).

32. DOW 4:196 (24 June 1668); DOW 6:76 (24 Feb. 1678/79); DOW 6:157 ([18 Nov. 1679]).

33. DOW 10:119 (dated 10 Jan. 1693/94 and recorded 25 Mar. 1695); DOW

12:164 (dated 27 July and recorded 24 Dec. 1703); OW 16:298–99 (dated 16 Jan. 1722/23, codicil dated 29 Nov. 1721, and recorded 17 Aug. 1724); DOW 16:304 (recorded 21 Sept. 1724).

34. DOW 9:91 (25 Jan. 1691/92) and Charles Parish Birth Register.

35. DOW 9:262 (25 Sept. 1693).

36. The quotation is from DOW 13:108 (24 Jan. 1707/8); OW 15:174–76 (dated 7 Dec. and recorded 16 Dec. 1717); OW 15:180–81 (20 Jan. 1717/18); OW 15:198 (17 Feb. 1717/18).

37. The quotation is from OW 16:446 (20 Mar. 1726/27); JO 2:88 (17 Aug. 1752); Warwick County Minute Book, Library of Virginia, Richmond, Va., 1748 to 1762, 212 (1 Mar. 1753).

16 | Mitigating Inequality: Women and Justice in Colonial New York

DEBORAH A. ROSEN

Women's freedom was restricted in early America in many ways. Typically, women were subjected to a variety of personal, economic, and legal limitations. As a general rule, without her husband's participation a married woman in early America could not write a will, sue or be sued, spend money she had earned, or sell property she had brought to the marriage. When their husbands died, women still did not gain control over all the property. They ordinarily received a life tenancy, but not full ownership rights, in only one-third of the real property. Because married women also could not sign contracts individually in their own names, they were unable to establish private legal obligations. Consequently, they could not create private rights to mitigate the restrictiveness of their limited legal rights.[1]

In the nineteenth century women would try to obtain legislation removing those limitations and would attempt to find a place for themselves in the rights-oriented legal system of that period. Before the nineteenth century, however, women actually had less need to fight for access to the formal legal system and for the rights that would make such access meaningful because an alternative path to justice was available to them. That alternative was not rights-based, but rested on official discretion. Women sometimes took their disputes to court, but they also pursued informal and discretionary justice more often than men did. This alternative did not actually grant women rights or entitlements, but under certain circumstances it helped mitigate the negative aspects of their limited personal freedom.

In colonial New York only a small number of women went to court to obtain redress for grievances or resolution of disputes, and the proportion of litigants who were women declined during the eighteenth century. At no level of jurisdiction did women constitute more than 10 percent of litigants, and typically the figure was much lower. Furthermore, only about half of female plaintiffs and defendants were single, nonexecutor litigants.[2]

Rather than seeking formal justice in court, women often sought informal remedies for their grievances and for resolution of their disputes. Outside of official government channels, a woman might be able to turn to her church for resolution of a dispute if she was having a problem with a fellow church member. Newspapers from the period regularly published notices by women requesting payment of debts or demanding an end to offensive behavior. For example, in 1735 Gertruid Winkler, the widow of Herman Winkler, published an advertisement giving notice "to all Persons indebted to the Estate of the said Mr. Winkler, to pay their several and respective Debts as soon as possible and prevent further Trouble and Charge," and in 1750 Cathrine Williams, a New York widow, tried to stop slanderous statements against her, and to limit the damage to her reputation caused by such statements, by publishing a notice in the *New-York Weekly Journal*. She wrote, "I . . . have long lain under the Aspersion of several slanderous Tongues, and that to my great Detriment, having thereby lost both my credit, my Livlihood, and good Name, . . . they have even gone so far as to call me a wicked Woman, and a Thief, which is not so." She proceeded to assert her good character: "for I have lived in this City many Years, always under the Character of a good House-wife, an Honest, and Industrious Wife, Frugal and Cleanly, and my Honour untainted." At the end of the notice, she demanded (though from whom is not clear) a sum of £12,000—£5,000 for the loss of her livelihood, £6,000 for the loss of her character, and £1,000 for fear of being killed.

Newspapers also occasionally included articles describing incidents in which women resorted to physical violence to "resolve" disputes. For example, a 1743 newspaper account described the injuries inflicted by the landlady of a tavern on a patron with whom she had been quarreling. "Last Night a Sailor being at a Publick House, drinking a Pot of Syder, happened to have some difference with his Landlady," according to the account, "upon which she took up a Chopping Knife, and gave him 6 or 7 cutts in the Head, [and] bruised him otherwise so that he lies in a very poor Condition."[3] Obviously, this was not a uniquely or typically female approach to conflict. Men, too, sometimes used physical efforts to "resolve" disputes.

A more unusual example of women using self-help measures was described in the *New-York Weekly Journal* in 1735. "Last week at a Vendue held there [in Chester County, Pennsylvania], a Man being unreasonably abusive to his Wife upon some trifling Occasion, the Woman form'd themselves into a Court, and ordered him to be apprehended by their Officers and brought to Tryal: Being found guilty," the *Journal* continued, "he was condemn'd to be duck'd 3 Times in a neighbouring Pond, and to huve one half cut off, of his Hair and Beard (which it seems he wore at full length) and the Sentence was accordingly executed, to the great Diversion of the Spectators."[4]

It is a commonplace that even when disputes do not become lawsuits, or when lawsuits are resolved out of court, the way the court would have resolved the case affects the outcome of the private dispute resolution. That is, even when the law does not directly decide a case, it often provides the determinative bargaining chips. The women's mock trial in 1735, though, goes even further in mimicking the actual court process in order to provide a justificatory framework for punishing a man who overstepped proper bounds of public behavior toward his wife. The last clause in the article, "to the great Diversion of the Spectators," indicates that the women were able to accomplish what they wanted without appearing to be too aggressive. The men in the crowd watching the women's mock trial could have felt attacked or criticized as a group, or they could have felt that the women had inappropriately taken on male functions of justice. That they did not so react means the women must have kept their proceedings light and humorous enough that the men were able to laugh at their friend's plight rather than feel uncomfortable about the whole incident. The mock trial was an empowering assertion of women's interests. Such assertiveness was, it appears, rare. Women were not expected to be too quick to demand rights or to impose remedies themselves.

Somewhere between law court justice and self-help there was another option in colonial New York: discretionary official justice. Appealing to the governor for his protection was the most common, and most informal, kind of discretionary official justice. The governor was not limited to purely legal solutions but was free to offer more flexible, discretionary remedies. Another possibility was applying to the Chancery Court for help. Chancery (or equity) Court justice was somewhat more formal than petitionary gubernatorial justice, but its discretionary nature and the variety of remedies at its disposal made it distinctly less formal than standard law court justice. Indeed, equity courts were originally established to mitigate the inflexibility and harshness of rigid common law justice, and in colonial New York they were seen as providing remedies not available in the law courts. In 1704, for example, Mary Lawrence expressly noted that she was petitioning the governor because she could not obtain redress for her grievance in the courts of law and the governor had suspended the court of chancery. She asked him to withdraw the suspension of the Chancery Court so that she could obtain the relief she sought.[5]

The governor and the Chancery Court, as well as the justices of the peace and the assembly, were in a position to rescue women who were trapped in difficult, even desperate, legal and economic situations, so women regularly appealed to them for help. Men and women both petitioned on occasion for official executive authority required under the law. They sought, for example, permission to buy land from the Indians or to serve as administrator of someone's estate. Furthermore, groups of men frequently petitioned the governor for broad political change. Although men felt comfortable appealing to the governor on matters of official policy, it was not common for individual men to petition authorities for protection or relief in personal or property matters. There were exceptions, of course. Some men petitioned for help—freedom from debt imprisonment, remission of fines or fees, and the like. But as a general rule, men who had personal legal grievances went to court for remedies. Women, in contrast, often found it necessary to make petitionary appeals to the governor for protection and help in personal or property matters.

Women's causes of petition fell into five categories. They petitioned for protection against interference with property, for special permission to take otherwise prohibited legal acts, for permission to beg, for financial support, and for protection against their husbands and masters. One of the most common forms of petition in the first category, protection against interference with property, was a widow's appeal to the governor for help in obtaining possession of her deceased husband's estate. In 1706 Susannah Walgrave obtained the governor's order to the sheriff of Westchester County to allow her to take possession of the property of her husband, George, who had committed suicide. Two years earlier, in a successful petition to collect his debts, Walgrave had explained that George's death had left her and her children "in a most miserable and forlorne condition without anything to support or subsist them." She made explicit the most convincing reason for helping her and other widows like her: with access to the debts and other property, she said, she would be able to provide necessities for herself and her children for the coming winter and would therefore be able to avoid becoming "a burthen to the Citty."[6]

Women often also petitioned for protection against interference with their administration of their deceased husbands' estates. In 1693 Audry Wandell petitioned for relief from vexatious lawsuits brought against her by a "pretended heir" of land her husband had willed her. Six years later she was still having problems. In 1699 she complained to the governor that the clerk and one of the justices of the Supreme Court had countenanced continued trespasses and forcible entries into her property by Richard Alsop.[7] Women whose husbands had been charged with disloyalty or convicted of treason found themselves in a particularly awkward and vulnerable position with regard to their husbands' property.[8]

Even in situations in which men would turn to the law courts, women often petitioned the governor for help. For example, whereas most men would bring an ejectment action in court to assert title to land occupied by another, a replevin, detinue, or trover and conversion action to regain or obtain possession of personal property wrongfully held by another, or an assumpsit action to obtain payment for services rendered, the records reveal numerous circumstances in which women instead petitioned the governor for help. For example, in 1699 Lydia Rose requested the governor's help in collecting payment for nursing and maintaining Jacob Smith, the son of Jacob Smith and Mary Griggs, both deceased. She pointed out in the petition that she was a "poor widow" with "nothing to depend on but the payment of this debt for her future maintainance." The governor ordered the executors of Mary Griggs's will, John Buckley and William Bickley, to appear before the council to answer Rose's petition. Evidently her claims were eventually allowed, though she continued to have trouble actually collecting the money. Eleven years later Rose petitioned the governor to order the attorney Jacob Regnier to pay her money collected on her behalf from William Bickley.[9]

We cannot always take literally people's claims to poverty—petitions, like pleadings, tended to have a common rhetoric. But the reality of colonial life was that most widows were left in poverty and unable to support themselves; that widows regularly tried to achieve their goals by portraying themselves as helpless is a reflection of that societal reality. Examples of widowed women petitioning instead of bringing a trespass, or trespass and ejectment, action include Elizabeth Joriss, who in 1690 petitioned the governor to recover for her land wrongfully withheld from her by Robert Burgess; Elizabeth Bancker, who in 1691 appealed to the governor to end the interference by Thomas Clarke in her attempt to build on a lot in New York City; and Hester Glen, who in 1693 petitioned the governor to confirm her right to land being claimed by Richard Owen. Examples of women petitioning instead of bringing a replevin action include Dorothy Worsoncroft, who petitioned the governor in 1691 to order Peter Chock to give her certain papers belonging to her; Bathshua Wessells, who complained to the governor in 1695 that her brother John Pells detained her cattle; and Rebeccah Randall, who petitioned the governor in 1699 to order the collector Ducie Hungerford to restore certain goods of hers taken by him.[10]

Women petitioned the governor or the assembly for permission to engage in legal transactions that otherwise would be forbidden to them, particularly if they were married. Although the law limited married women's rights to control property, for example, occasionally the Chancery Court could, in the interests of fairness, recognize legal acts by women. Such recognition did not always reflect a concern for the economic well-being and independence of women, nor did it necessarily even benefit women. Sometimes women's "rights" were recognized only retrospectively, after the woman no longer controlled the property in question. In one case the Chancery Court recognized the right of a woman to mortgage inherited property, but the ruling was made only after her death in conjunction with a property dispute that emerged between her son and the man to whom she had mortgaged property during her lifetime.[11]

Arbiters of discretionary justice typically gave a living woman permission to take a specific economic action only when she had no source of male support and would otherwise have to turn to the state. Such petitions came from single and widowed women and from married women whose husbands were away. Most commonly, such a petition requested a special legislative act to enable a widow who held only a life estate in land to sell a portion of it. Mary Bradt, Sarah Crego, and Isabella Davis were three such petitioners. Typically, if the woman otherwise would fall into difficult economic circumstances, the legislature granted her petition.[12]

Women sometimes were so desperate that they requested permission to beg. Although married women occasionally submitted such petitions, widowed women were more likely to need to beg for support. In 1720, for example, Mary Barnet, a widow living on Staten Island with her four small children, lost her house and property to fire. Supported by certificates—signed not only by the justices of Richmond County but also by ministers of the English, French, and Dutch Churches—stating that she was a proper object for charity, she requested a license "to ask and receive the voluntary charity or benevolence of well disposed people throughout the whole province" so that she could buy food and other necessaries for herself and her children. An example of a married woman who petitioned the governor for permission to beg is Elizabeth Collins, whose husband was off at sea in 1711, leaving her and her children without sufficient resources to maintain themselves. She had to petition the governor for permission to beg for the support of her family.[13]

Women also petitioned for orders of financial support, particularly if they were single and pregnant. An accusation that a woman had borne a bastard child could ruin her reputation in the community. The actual birth of a child outside of wedlock brought not only social disgrace but also economic strain. It was difficult to raise a child without the help of someone who had economic rights (a man). Given the legal and economic limitations on women in colonial New York, only the rare woman was in any position to support herself or her family independently. Poor women whose male partners also had no financial resources sometimes ended up defending themselves in criminal court after they had dealt with the problem on their own in the most brutal fashion: infanticide.[14]

Most pregnant single women, however, came before government officials voluntarily, to force the fathers of their children to support them. In most cases their petitions were successful. We cannot determine how many single women had to take this course because not all such cases were recorded in the minute books. Among surviving rural Dutchess County documents, however, are recognizances or orders related to bastardy in approximately forty-five cases between 1752 and 1770, so bastardy was hardly an unusual situation.[15] Typically, the justice of the peace ordered the father to make weekly payments of two or three shillings toward the support of the child. As a general rule, the justices of the peace and the courts supported single mothers' claims. Authorities were eager to make sure that the burden of maintaining illegitimate children fell on fathers rather than on the community, and they were unwilling to give women more freedom and opportunities to support themselves and their children.

Requests by married women for support were less common but not unknown. For example, just before the Revolution, in 1771, Elizabeth Pugsley brought a bill to the Chancery Court requesting that the chancellor and masters order her husband, Israel, to pay maintenance for herself and their children. When they married in 1763, she said, she brought about five hundred pounds to his estate. They had six children together. She claimed that she had lived with him in an "affectionate and reputable

Manner until he took to Drinking to excess, attempted to Strangle her and after other Violences and ill Treatment," he finally "drove [her] out of Doors with two of her Children then with her forbidding them upon Pain of Death ever to return." She asked that Israel be forced to support her and the children. Israel answered that Elizabeth had left the house voluntarily and without any just provocation from him. He said his income was scarcely sufficient to maintain himself and that his assets were little more than sufficient to pay his debts. After hearing all the evidence, the court nevertheless decreed that Israel Pugsley pay twenty pounds a year—not directly to Elizabeth Pugsley, but to Lewis Morris, a friend of the family who would hold the money for Elizabeth's use and support. It was common in early America for money to be held and managed for women by male trustees.[16]

Women were often in the position of petitioning the governor for protection against their societal superiors, those on whom they were directly dependent for support, particularly their husbands and their masters. In 1699 Ann Everendon of Brooklyn filed two petitions for relief against her husband, Robert, who had ill-treated her and wasted her estate and was now about to abandon her. In 1710 Elizabeth Sydenham petitioned the governor for protection against abuse by her husband, George. Five years later she petitioned the governor for a separate maintenance from her husband.[17]

A number of women who were unhappy in their marriages resorted to the simplest kind of self-help: they left their husbands. Many such acts are known to us only when the husband placed a notice in the newspaper announcing the wife's desertion and disavowing any debts she might incur. Other women elected to pursue official procedures, though their options for doing so under English law were extremely limited. In the brief period during which the Dutch regained control of New York, from July 1673 to October 1674, several English women were able to invoke Dutch law and petition for divorce from their husbands.[18] Women even petitioned to prevent marriages. For example, in 1712 the widow Magtelt Niessepat asked the governor to protect her daughter Elizabeth, who was of unsound mind. She explained that John Dene and some friends had deceitfully obtained a marriage license for him and Elizabeth without Magtelt Niessepat's permission. She requested a proclamation forbidding any minister or justice of the peace to marry Elizabeth Niessepat to John Dene.[19]

Enslaved women had even more need than free women to seek protection from the governor. Abused slaves could not assume with confidence that the law would protect them or punish their masters. Slaves in general, and female slaves in particular, thus sought means to obtain freedom from slavery altogether. Three examples were an African woman named Mando, an African woman named Mary Drew, and a Native American woman, Sarah Robinson. Mando petitioned the governor for her freedom and the freedom of her daughter Hagar in 1701. She claimed her freedom based on a stipulation made by her former master that her current master refused to carry out. Mary Drew petitioned for freedom from her master, Michael Harding, on account of neglect. Sarah Robinson petitioned for her freedom in 1711. She said she was born of free parents but had been taken from New York and sold as a slave in the Island of Madeira. After the English consul arranged for her passage back to New York, Robinson, who feared being enslaved anew by her former employers, petitioned the governor to declare her a free woman.[20]

The problem of abuse of female servants is evidenced by a newspaper advertisement of 1734 that presents the terms on which women in financial straits would offer themselves as servants: "Here are many Women in this Town that these hard Times intend to go to Service, but as it is proper the World should know our Terms, we think it reasonable we should not be beat by our Mistrisses Husband, they being too strong, and perhaps may do tender Women Mischief." On those terms, the women were willing to work as servants.[21] Unfortunately, many servant women did become the victims of abuse at the hands of their masters. Those servants—or their mothers—sometimes brought petitions requesting that their obligation of service be terminated because of abuse. Examples from colonial New York include an eleven-year-old apprentice who was being harshly disciplined by her master, another young girl whose master was sexually abusing her, a female servant whose master tried to claim longer service than originally agreed upon, and a newly arrived Scottish woman whom the ship captain had tried to sell as a servant.[22]

Women's legal behavior was clearly determined by external conditions. The fact that women were less likely than men to go to court and more likely to petition the governor can reasonably be attributed to their different social, economic, and legal position. Men's claims fitted more clearly into established legal categories and rights provided by law, so they were more likely to find redress in court for their problems. As a practical matter women had to be more conciliatory and had to seek alternative paths to justice because the legal system did not adequately protect them. Furthermore, in the social environment of early New York, it was considered more appropriate for women to seek redress not as litigants invoking rights but as petitioners asking for male protection. One can easily understand why women in the colonial period would be more likely to get what they wanted if they took an approach that was consistent with their assigned roles and with their presumed characteristics as women, and if that approach was not threatening to the basic social order (because it implicitly acknowledged the established gender hierarchy).[23]

As one writer in a New York newspaper observed in 1734, women should stay out of public affairs. "Policks is what does not become them," he wrote, "the Governing Kingdoms and Ruling Provinces are Things too difficult and knotty for the fair Sex." The problem was not only that women were incapable of understanding political matters, but also that dealing with such issues would make them less feminine: "It will render them grave and serious, and take off those agreeable Smiles that should always accompany them." Women should stick to their domestic duties, he concluded, rather than "Discommoding their pretty Faces with Passion and Resentment." The next month a poem, submitted by an anonymous man and entitled "Advice to a Lady," expressed similar sentiments. Women should not strain themselves trying to understand complex matters: "Nor make to dangerous Wit a vain Pretence: / But wisely rest content with common Sense," he wrote, "For Wit, like Wine, intoxicates the Brain, / Too strong for feeble Women to sustain." Nor should they abandon their feminine qualities of modesty ("Seek to be good, but aim not to be great"), passivity ("A Woman's noblest station is Retreat; / Her fairest Virtues fly from public Sight"), and eagerness to please others ("Bless'd is the Maid, and worthy to be bless'd / . . . [who] asks no Power but that of pleasing most").[24] Clearly the courtroom, like the legislative meeting hall, was considered primarily a male, not a female, place.

Women's options for pursuing justice in the courts were further limited by the high cost of litigation. In a typical lawsuit resolved by jury trial in the New York Supreme Court in the 1750s, the plaintiff would have to pay a total of some fifteen pounds for more than fifty feeable services, and even if the lawsuit were resolved or terminated before trial, the plaintiff's legal and court fees normally ranged from four pounds to seven pounds.[25] If the plaintiff won the case, all or part of her costs might be paid by the defendant, but if she lost the case, she usually had to pay the defendant's costs on top of her own. Some paupers received the benefit of free legal services, though this was not common. The fact that people lived in colonial New York who were too poor to purchase adequate food, clothing, and firewood suggests that there was a considerable population that had difficulty gaining access to the courtroom. Many of those people were women. Newspaper advertisements, for example, asked for charitable contributions to "Poor House Keepers, Widdows, and other necessitous People as may stand most in Need of Relief." [26]

Women's economic opportunities were limited. They usually had no independent wage income, and if single or widowed, they lived on fixed assets inherited from others. Some women did have the resources to use courtroom procedures. The average assessment of female taxpayers in New York City in 1734 was not, after all, significantly different from the overall average assessment. But though the wealth of women who had enough property to be taxed did not differ much from that of property-owning men, many women were too poor to be taxed at all. Of the 450 tenants mentioned on that city tax list, 66 were widows or other single women, and of the 62 people mentioned on the list whose assessment was zero pounds, 35 were widows or other single women. (The only woman listed with a man was Mary Colex, who was listed with an unnamed "Free Negro." Otherwise, only the male head of household's name appeared on the tax lists.)[27] The arrest in 1753 of twenty-two "Ladies of Pleasure" from "several Houses of Ill Repute" may further suggest some women's desperate financial plight.[28] Women were more likely than men to be poor, so the impact of class fell more heavily on women.

Finding themselves unprotected by the law, limited by societal expectations that women be passive and subordinate, and lacking financial resources, early American women found little support or help in formal justice. They were able to compensate to some extent by regularly turning to less formal, and less rule-determined, methods of obtaining official justice rather than going to court.

Manuscript records do not always reveal the outcome of either petitions or lawsuits, particularly for cases resolved out of court, so it is difficult to compare the success rates of formal and informal mechanisms. It does appear, however, that petitions most often were successful, and therefore women were probably more likely to attain their goals through informal petitions than through formal means. The apparently high success rate of petitions did not, however, make them more desirable than lawsuits. Nor did it mean that one could necessarily obtain through petitions everything that others could obtain through litigation or that informal justice was good for women. In particular, unlike litigation, the petition process itself required and reinforced deference and subservience on the part of the petitioner. Thus, informal official justice was far from the equivalent of formal litigation and only partially mitigated colonial women's lack of freedom.

Increasingly during the colonial period, the opportunities for obtaining informal justice declined. As the legal system became more formalized in the eighteenth century to suit the needs of commercial people, who required more rationality and predictability in the law, it appears that the number of petitions to the governors declined. Since other documents relating to the governors' business in the late colonial period are extant, it seems unlikely that the decline in the number of petitions is attributable to a higher rate of survival of earlier than of later petitions. A more likely explanation is that, because discretionary justice was not good for business, redress through petitions was increasingly being discouraged and justice through the law courts was being promoted as the only fair and proper official form of dispute resolution.[29] Excluding women from justice was neither a purpose nor a reason for the decline of informal law; nevertheless, that decline had a significant impact on women. Having taken fuller advantage than men did of the opportunities for discretionary justice early in the colonial period, women were affected more significantly when such opportunities diminished in the last decades before independence.

At the same time as the newly rationalized system left women little room for discretionary justice, they were being increasingly marginalized from formal justice. Women's decreased participation in the formal legal system was largely a result of New Yorkers' increased reliance on formal contracts as the colonial economy expanded beyond the local community. Since married women could not make enforceable contracts on their own, the contractualization of relationships guaranteed for them a peripheral role in the growing market economy of the eighteenth century and consequently a reduced presence in the courtroom.[30] Thus, expanded commercialization of New York society was largely responsible both for the decline of informal justice and for women's increasing marginalization from formal justice.

In the twentieth century women have made significant progress through reliance on arguments based on rights. In fact, Sally Engle Merry's work has shown that in recent years women's relative power-lessness in personal relationships and reluctance to resort to violence has made them more likely than men to take their personal problems to court, at least to a mediation-oriented local court.[31] But in the increasingly individualistic eighteenth century, the "individual" who held rights was a man, and women were more likely to find resolution of personal problems outside of the formal courtroom. Indeed, the legal changes of the eighteenth century, which were designed to help people resolve their commercial disputes more quickly and predictably, made the courts even less hospitable to close interpersonal disputes than they had previously been. As the legal system increasingly narrowed into a more rigid rights-based conception of law in the colonial period, and as it came to focus on the interests of people engaged in long-distance and more capital-intensive economic relationships, women were increasingly marginalized from formal official justice, even as the opportunities to obtain informal justice were being closed off.

Although the changes in legal practice of the mid-eighteenth century may have been good for the economy and for the legal system, and they may have benefited men (or some men, anyway), they were not good for women. In early America the social, economic, and legal environment of women was clearly different from that of men. That different environment shaped the way in which women resolved conflicts and legal problems and, particularly, ensured that their approach was not the same as men's. In the early colonial period there was room for both men's and women's approaches to justice. Most notably, there were opportunities to obtain informal justice through petitions to the governor, the Chancery Court, and the legislature. By the end of the colonial period, although women still suffered the same constraints that formerly had led them to pursue discretionary justice, such justice was no longer so readily available. No longer were women able to find official channels for mitigating their lack of formal equality. The path to justice had narrowed considerably, and its accessibility to women had become substantially more restricted.

NOTES

1. On the legal rights of women in colonial New York, see Marylynn Salmon, *Women and the Law of Property in Early America* (Chapel Hill: University of North Carolina Press, 1986); Linda Briggs Biemer, *Women and Property in Colonial New York: The Transition from Dutch to English Law, 1643–1727* (Ann Arbor: University of Michigan Press, 1983); Joan R. Gundersen and Gwen Victor Gampel, "Married Women's Legal Status in Eighteenth-Century New York and Virginia," *William and Mary Quarterly*, 3d ser., 39 (1982): 114–34. Note that formal legal restraints did not always function as total restraints in practice—antenuptial agreements, separate estates, and agency arrangements provided loopholes for a few women.

2. New York City Mayor's Court Minutes, Hall of Records, New York, N.Y.; Dutchess County Court of Common Pleas Minutes, Dutchess County Clerk's Office, Poughkeepsie, N.Y.; Orange County Court of Common Pleas Minutes, Orange County Clerk's Office, Goshen, N.Y.; Westchester County Court of Common Pleas Minutes, Westchester County Records Center and Archives, Elmsford, N.Y.; Justice of the Peace Roswell Hopkins Records (1764–65), New York State Archives, Albany, N.Y., handwritten transcription, 1895; Supreme Court of Judicature Minutes, Hall of Records, New York, N.Y.

3. *New-York Weekly Journal*, Sept. 8, 1735 (Winkler), Nov. 26, 1750 (Williams), Nov. 21, 1743.

4. *New-York Weekly Journal*, May 5, 1735.

5. New York Colonial Manuscripts, New York State Archives, Albany, N.Y. (hereafter cited as NY Col Ms) 49:18.

6. NY Col Ms 43:28, 50:41 (the source of the quotations), 51:182. For similar examples, see NY Col Ms 39:99, 48:158, 166, 168, 169, 49:18, 51:71, 53:15.

7. NY Col Ms 39:114, 43:28 (Wandall). For similar examples, see NY Col Ms 42:108, 46:143, 47:114, 48:55, 33:39.

8. See, for example, NY Col Ms 42:18, 73, 74, 37:87, 45:99.

9. NY Col Ms 42:138, 53:158.

10. NY Col Ms 36:142 (Joriss), 37:243 (Bancker), 39:108 (Glen), 37:57 (Worsoncroft), 40:81 and 84 (Wessells), 43:61 (Randall). For help in protecting their property, women also appealed to the Chancery Court.

11. Chancery Court Minutes, Hall of Records, New York, N.Y., 1711–19, 53–55.

12. NY Col Ms 59:86 (Mary Bradt), 60:7 (Sarah Crego), 62:181 (Isabella Davis).

13. NY Col Ms 63:13, 16 (Barnet), 54:171 (Collins).

14. See, for example, the cases of Anna Maria Cochin and Angle Hendricks. NY Col Ms 61:146; Albany County Court of General Sessions Minutes, 1717–23, Feb. 4, 1719, and June 3, 1719 (Cochin); NY Col Ms 22:63–75 (Hendricks).

15. Dutchess County Ancient Documents, Dutchess County Clerk's Office, Poughkeepsie, N.Y. The adult (over age sixteen) population of Dutchess County was about 6,300 in 1756 and about 10,500 in 1771. Edmund B. O'Callaghan, ed., *The Documentary History of the State of New York* (Albany: Weeds, Parsons and Co., 1849–51), 1:473, 474.

16. Chancery Court Minutes, 1770–76, 28, 40, 48, 51, 60, 63, 66 (the source of the quotations).

17. NY Col Ms 43:83, 84 (Everendon), 54:46 and 60:18 (Sydenham). Interestingly, in 1701 Allite Doornes, Elizabeth Sydenham's widowed mother, had also petitioned for relief from ill treatment by her daughter and son-in-law. NY Col Ms 44:139.

18. Examples include Catherine Lane, Elizabeth Loper, and Abigail Darling. NY Col Ms 23:234 and 330 (Lane), 32:82 (Loper), 23:269 and 29:130 (Darling).

19. NY Col Ms 58:72.

20. NY Col Ms 44:147, 47:18, 19 (Mando), 43:26 (Drew), 56:96 (Robinson).

21. *New-York Weekly Journal*, Jan. 28, 1734.

22. New York City Court of General Quarter Sessions Minutes, Hall of Records, New York, N.Y. (Margaret Anderson); NY Col Ms 33:28 (the daughter of Elie Coppin); NY Col Ms 31:148 (Alice Fisher); NY Col Ms 32:56 (Elizabeth Stratton).

23. Carol Karlsen points out that in colonial New England, women who were assertive or who questioned the authority of (i.e., failed to defer to) ministers, magistrates, masters, or husbands could be branded witches. Carol F. Karlsen, *The Devil in the Shape of a Woman: Witchcraft in Colonial New England* (New York: Norton, 1987). See especially chap. 4.

24. *New-York Weekly Journal*, Aug. 19, and Sept. 30, 1734.

25. Estimates of costs of litigation are based on William Smith, "A Scheme for

Drawing out Bills of Costs in the Supream Court of New York Digested into Tables," William Smith Papers, vol. 9, New York Public Library, Rare Books and Manuscripts Room, New York, N.Y.; from William Livingston, "The Lawyers Fees for the Supreme Court" and "A Regulation for the Taxation of Costs in the Supreame Court" in Livingston's "Lawyer's Book of Precedents," New York State Archives, Albany, N.Y., 412–14, 448–59; and from William Livingston's "Cost Book," New York Public Library.

26. See especially *New-York Weekly Journal*, Jan. 19, 1741; see also the *Journal* for Jan. 5 and 12 and for Feb. 16, 1741. The frequency of statutes providing for poor relief further indicates the existence of serious poverty in colonial New York before 1760.

27. New York City Tax Lists, New York State Archives, Albany, N.Y. (available on microfilm).

28. *New York Mercury*, July 23, 1753. The twenty-two were committed to the workhouse, and five of them received fifteen lashes "before a vast Number of Spectators" with orders to leave town within forty-eight hours.

29. Informal unofficial justice did not, of course, die out completely. Various unofficial means of dispute resolution continued or developed anew, such as resolution in the churches or in occupational or ethnic organizations. In 1768 even merchants formed their own organization, the Chamber of Commerce, and some specialized commercial problems were resolved there, among themselves, rather than in the courts.

30. Cornelia Hughes Dayton has found a similar decline in formal litigation by women in eighteenth-century Connecticut. She attributes that decline primarily to the inability of women to gain access to credit because of their low literacy rates, limited economic resources, and scarcity of intercolonial contacts, and to the increased emphasis on the public sphere as an exclusively male domain. Dayton, "Women before the Bar: Gender, Law, and Society in Connecticut" (Ph.D. diss., Princeton University, 1986), 86–87.

31. Sally Engle Merry, *Getting Justice and Getting Even: Legal Consciousness among Working-Class Americans* (Chicago: University of Chicago Press, 1990).

Selected Bibliography

This selected bibliography does not by any means contain every source cited in the foregoing chapters. It is designed only to provide a reference to works of general interest related to women in early America. For more detailed source materials, the reader should consult the endnotes accompanying each chapter.

Abbott, Edith. *Women in Industry: A Study in American Economic History.* New York: D. Appleton, 1910.

Amussen, Susan Dwyer. "Gender, Family, and the Social Order." In *Order and Disorder in Early Modern England,* edited by Anthony Fletcher and John Stevenson. Cambridge: Cambridge University Press, 1985.

———. *An Ordered Society: Gender and Class in Early Modern England.* Oxford: Basil Blackwell, 1988.

Anderson, Bonnie S., and Judith P. Zinsser. *A History of Their Own: Women in Europe from Prehistory to the Present.* Vol. 1. New York: Harper and Row, 1988.

Anderson, Karen. *Chain Her by One Foot: The Subjugation of Women in Seventeenth-Century New France.* London: Routledge, 1991.

Applewhite, Harriet B., and Darline G. Levy, eds. *Women and Politics in the Age of the Democratic Revolution.* Ann Arbor: University of Michigan Press, 1990.

Axtell, James, ed. *The Indian Peoples of Eastern America: A Documentary History of the Sexes.* New York: Oxford University Press, 1981.

Baine, Rodney M. "Myths of Mary Musgrove." *Georgia Historical Quarterly* 76 (1992):428–35.

Baker, Ira L. "Elizabeth Timothy: America's First Woman Editor." *Journalism Quarterly* 54 (1977):280–85.

Baker, Paula. "The Domestication of Politics: Women and American Political Society, 1780–1920." *American Historical Review* 84 (1984):620–47.

Baron, Ava. "Women and the Making of the American Working Class: A Study of the Proletarianization of Printers." *Review of Radical Political Economics* 14 (1982):23–42.

———, ed. *Work Engendered.* Ithaca: Cornell University Press, 1991.

Bay, Edna G., ed. *Women and Work in Africa.* Boulder, Colo.: Westview Press, 1982.

Beard, Mary Ritter. *Women as A Force in History.* New York: Macmillan, 1946.

Beauchamp, William. "Iroquois Women." *Journal of American Folklore* 13 (April–June 1900):81–91.

Becker, Marshall J. "Hannah Freeman: An Eighteenth-Century Lenape Living and Working among Colonial Farmers." *Pennsylvania Magazine of History and Biography* 114 (April 1990):249–69.

Beckles, Hilary. *National Rebels: A Social History of Enslaved Black Women in Barbados, 1627–1838.* New Brunswick, N.J.: Rutgers University Press, 1989.

Benson, Mary Sumner. *Women in Eighteenth-Century America: A Study of Opinion and Social Usage.* New York: Columbia University Press, 1935.

Berkin, Carol Ruth, and Clara M. Lovett, eds. *Women, War, and Revolution.* New York: Holmes and Meier, 1980.

Berkin, Carol Ruth, and Mary Beth Norton, eds. *Women of America: A History.* Boston: Houghton Mifflin, 1979.

Biddle, Gertrude B. *Notable Women of Pennsylvania.* Philadelphia: University of Pennsylvania Press, 1942.

Biemer, Linda. *Women and Property in Colonial New York: The Transition from Dutch to English Law, 1643–1727.* Ann Arbor: University of Michigan Press, 1983.

Billings, Warren M. "The Cases of Fernando and Elizabeth Key: A Note on the Status of Blacks in Seventeenth-Century Virginia." *William and Mary Quarterly,* 3d ser., 30, no. 4 (1973):467–74.

Blewett, Mary H. *Men, Women, and Work: Class, Gender, and Protest in the New England Shoe Industry, 1780–1910.* Urbana: University of Illinois Press, 1988.

Bloch, Ruth. "The Gendered Meanings of Virtue in Revolutionary America." *Signs* 13, no. 1 (1987):37–58.

Bodle, Wayne. "Jane Bartram's 'Application': Her Struggle for Survival, Stability, and Self-Determination in Revolutionary Pennsylvania." *Pennsylvania Magazine of History and Biography* 115 (April 1991):185–220.

Bolding, Elise. *The Underside of History: A View of Women through Time.* Boulder, Colo.: Westview Press, 1976.

Bowler, Clara Ann. "Carted Whores and White Shrouded Apologies: Slander in the County Courts of Seventeenth-Century Virginia." *Virginia Magazine of History and Biography* 85 (1977):411–26.

Boydston, Jeanne. *Home and Work: Housework, Wages, and the Ideology of Labor in the Early Republic.* New York: Oxford University Press, 1990.

Boyle, Susan C. "Did She Generally Decide? Women in Ste. Genevieve, 1750–1805." *William and Mary Quarterly,* 3d ser., 44, no. 4 (1987):775–89.

Braund, Kathryn E. Holland. "Guardians of Tradition and Handmaidens to Change: Women's Roles in Creek Economic and Social Life during the Eighteenth Century." *American Indian Quarterly* 14 (1990):239–58.

Brewer, Priscilla J. "Tho of the Weaker Sex: A Reassessment of Gender Equality among the Shakers." *Signs* 17 (1992):609–35.

Brink, Jean R., Allison P. Coudert, and Maryanne C. Horowitz, eds. *The Politics of Gender in Early Modern Europe.* Kirksville, Mo.: Sixteenth Century Journal, 1989.

Brodsky, Vivian. "Widows in Late Elizabethan London: Remarriage, Economic Opportunity, and Family Orientations." In *The World We Have Gained: Histories of Population and Social Structure*, edited by Lloyd Bonfield, Richard M. Smith, and Keith Wrightson. Oxford: Basil Blackwell, 1986.

Brown, Elisabeth Potts, and Susan Mosher Stuard, eds. *Witness for Change: Quaker Women over Three Centuries*. New Brunswick, N.J.: Rutgers University Press, 1989.

Brown, Jennifer S. H. *Strangers in Blood: Fur Trade Country Families in Indian Country*. Vancouver: University of British Columbia Press, 1980.

Brown, Judith K. "Economic Organization and the Position of Women among the Iroquois." *Ethnohistory* 17 (1970):151–67.

Brown, Kathleen M. "Brave New Worlds: Women's and Gender History." *William and Mary Quarterly*, 3d ser., 50 (1993):311–28.

———. *Good Wives and Nasty Wenches: Gender, Race, and Power in Colonial Virginia*. Chapel Hill: University of North Carolina Press for the Institute of Early American History and Culture, 1996.

Brownlee, W. Elliot, and Mary M. Brownlee. *Women in the American Economy: A Documentary History, 1675 to 1929*. New Haven, Conn.: Yale University Press, 1976.

Buel, Joy Day, and Richard Buel, Jr. *The Way of Duty: A Woman and Her Family in Revolutionary America*. New York: Norton, 1984.

Burnard, Trevor. "Inheritance and Independence: Women's Status in Early Colonial Jamaica." *William and Mary Quarterly*, 3d ser., 48 (1991):93–114.

Bush, Barbara. *Slave Women in Caribbean Society, 1650–1838*. Bloomington: Indiana University Press, 1990.

Bynum, Caroline Walker, ed. *Religion and Gender: Essays on the Complexity of Symbols*. Boston: Beacon Press, 1987.

Calhoun, Arthur W. *A Social History of the American Family from Colonial Times to the Present*. Vol. 1. New York: Barnes and Noble, 1945.

Carr, Lois Green, and Lorena S. Walsh. "The Planter's Wife: The Experience of White Women in Seventeenth-Century Maryland." *William and Mary Quarterly*, 3d ser., 34, no. 4 (1977):542–71.

Cashin, Joan E. *A Family Venture: Men and Women on the Southern Frontier*. New York: Oxford University Press, 1991.

Chafe, William H. *Women and Equality: Changing Patterns in American Culture*. New York: Oxford University Press, 1977.

Chambers-Schiller, Lee Virginia. *Liberty, a Better Husband: Single Women in America: The Generations of 1780–1840*. New Haven, Conn.: Yale University Press, 1984.

Choquette, Leslie. " 'Ces Amazones du Grand Dieu': Women and Mission in Seventeenth-Century Canada." *French Historical Studies* 17 (1992):627–55.

Cleary, Patricia A. " 'She Merchants' of Colonial America: Women and Commerce on the Eve of the Revolution." Ph.D. diss., Northwestern University, 1989.

Clover, Carol. "Regardless of Sex: Men, Women, and Power in Early Northern Europe." *Representations* 44 (Fall 1993):1–28.

Cohen, Sheldon S. "The Broken Bond: Divorce in Providence County, 1749–1809." *Rhode Island History* 44 (1985):67–79.

Cometti, Elizabeth. "Women in the American Revolution." *New England Quarterly* 20 (1947):329–46.

Conger, Vivian Bruce. " 'Being Weak of Body but Firm of Mind and Memory': Widowhood in Colonial America, 1630–1750." Ph.D. diss., Cornell University, 1994.

Coontz, Stephanie. *The Social Origins of Private Life: A History of American Families, 1600–1900.* London: Verso, 1988.

Coontz, Stephanie, and Peta Henderson, eds. *Women's Work, Men's Property: The Origins of Gender and Class.* London: Verso, 1986.

Cott, Nancy F. "Divorce and the Changing Status of Women in Eighteenth-Century Massachusetts." *William and Mary Quarterly*, 3d ser., 33 (1976): 586–614.

———. "Eighteenth-Century Family and Social Life Revealed in Massachusetts Divorce Records." *Journal of Social History* 10 (1976):20–43.

———. *The Bonds of Womanhood: Women's Sphere in New England, 1780–1835.* New Haven, Conn.: Yale University Press, 1977.

Cott, Nancy F., and Elizabeth Pleck, eds. *A Heritage of Her Own: Toward a New Social History of American Women.* New York: Simon and Schuster, 1979.

Coulter, E. Merton. "Mary Musgrove, 'Queen of the Creeks': A Chapter of Early Georgia Troubles." *Georgia Historical Quarterly* 11 (1927):1–30.

Covert, Catherine L. "Journalism History and Women's Experience: A Problem in Conceptual Change." *Journalism History* 8 (Spring 1981):2–6.

Cowell, Pattie. "Womankind Call Reason to Their Aid: Susannah Wright's Verse Epistle on the Status of Women in Eighteenth-Century America." *Signs* 6 (1981):795–800.

Cowell, Pattie, ed. *Women Poets in Pre-Revolutionary America, 1650–1775: An Anthology.* Troy, N.Y.: Whitson, 1981.

Crane, Elaine Forman. "The World of Elizabeth Drinker." *Pennsylvania Magazine of History and Biography* 107 (January 1983):3–28.

———. "Dependence in an Era of Independence: The Role of Women in a Republican Society." In *The American Revolution: Its Character and Limits*, edited by Jack P. Greene. New York: New York University Press, 1987.

———. "The Socioeconomics of a Female Majority in Eighteenth-Century Bermuda." *Signs* 15 (Winter 1990):231–58.

———. *The Diary of Elizabeth Drinker.* 3 vols. Boston: Northeastern University Press, 1991.

Crawford, Patricia. *Women and Religion in England, 1500–1720.* New York: Routledge, 1993.

Dayton, Cornelia Hughes. "Women before the Bar: Gender, Law, and Society in Connecticut." Ph.D. diss., Princeton University, 1986.

De Barr, Mirjam. " 'Let Your Women Keep Silence in the Churches': How Women in the Dutch Reformed Church Evaded Paul's Admonition, 1650–1700." In *Studies in Church History*. Vol. 27. *Women in the Church*, edited by W. T. Shiels and Diana Wood. Oxford: Basil Blackwell, 1990.

Degler, Carl N. *At Odds: Women and the Family in America from the Revolution to the Present*. New York: Oxford University Press, 1980.

DeMarce, Virginia Easley. " 'Verry Slitly Mixt': Tri-Racial Isolate Families of the Upper South—A Genealogical Study." *National Genealogical Society Quarterly* 80 (March 1992): 19–36.

Demeter, Richard L. *Primer, Presses, and Composing Sticks: Women Printers of the Colonial Period*. Hicksville, N.Y.: Exposition Press, 1979.

Demos, John. *A Little Commonwealth: Family Life in Plymouth Colony*. New York: Oxford University Press, 1970.

———. *The Unredeemed Captive: A Family Story from Early America*. New York: Knopf, 1994.

Deutrich, Mabel E., and Virginia C. Purdy, eds. *Clio Was a Woman: Studies in the History of American Women*. Washington, D.C.: Howard University Press, 1980.

Devens, Carol. *Countering Colonization: Native American Women and Great Lakes Missions, 1630–1900*. Berkeley: University of California Press, 1992.

Dexter, Elisabeth Anthony. *Colonial Women of Affairs: Women in Business and the Professions in America before 1776*. Boston: Houghton Mifflin, 1931.

———. *Career Women of America, 1776–1840*. Francestown, N.H.: Marshall Jones, 1950.

Dillman, Caroline Matheny, ed. *Southern Women*. New York: Hemisphere, 1988.

Ditz, Toby L. *Property and Kinship: Inheritance in Early Connecticut, 1750–1820*. Princeton: Princeton University Press, 1986.

Douglas, Ann. *The Feminization of American Culture*. New York: Knopf, 1977.

Dube, Leela, Eleanor Leacock, and Shirley Ardener, eds. *Visibility and Power: Essays on Women in Society and Development*. Delhi: Oxford University Press, 1986.

DuBois, Ellen Carol, and Vicki L. Ruiz, eds. *Unequal Sisters: A Multicultural Reader in U.S. Women's History*. New York: Routledge, 1990.

Earle, Alice Morse. *Colonial Dames and Good Wives*. Boston: Houghton, 1895; classics edition, New York: Frederick Ungar, 1962.

———. *Home Life in Colonial Days*. New York: Macmillan, 1898.

Egle, William H. *Some Pennsylvania Women during the War of the Revolution*. Harrisburg, Pa.: Harrisburg Publishing Co., 1898.

Ellet, Elizabeth F. *The Women of the American Revolution*. 2 vols. New York: Baker and Scribner, 1849; reprint, Philadelphia: G. W. Jacobs, 1900.

Ember, Carol. "An Evaluation of Alternative Theories of Matrilocal versus Patrilocal Residence." *Behavior Science Research* 9, no. 2 (1974):135–49.

Evans, Elizabeth. *Weathering the Storm: Women of the American Revolution.* New York: Scribner's, 1975.

Evans, Nesta. "Inheritance, Women, Religion, and Education in Early Modern Society as Revealed by Wills." In *Probate Records and the Local Community,* edited by Philip Reden. Gloucester, Eng.: Alan Sutton, 1985.

Fineman, Martha Albertson, and Nancy Sweet Thomadsen, eds. *At the Boundaries of Law: Feminism and Legal Theory.* New York: Routledge, Chapman and Hall, 1991.

Finley, Lucinda M. "Breaking Women's Silence in Law: The Dilemma of the Gendered Nature of Legal Reasoning." *Notre Dame Law Review* 64 (1989): 886–910.

Fliegelman, Jay. *Prodigals and Pilgrims: The American Revolution against Patriarchal Authority, 1750–1800.* Cambridge: Cambridge University Press, 1982.

Ford, Margaret Lane. "A Widow's Work: Ann Franklin of Newport, Rhode Island." *Printing History* 12 (1990):15–26.

Fraser, Lynne Howard. "Nobody's Children: The Treatment of Illegitimate Children in Three North Carolina Counties, 1760–1790." Master's thesis, College of William and Mary, 1987.

Fraser, Walter J., Jr., R. Frank Saunders, Jr., and Jon L. Wakelyn, eds. *The Web of Southern Social Relations: Women, Family, and Education.* Athens: University of Georgia Press, 1985.

Frost, J. William. *The Quaker Family in Colonial America.* New York: St. Martin's, 1973.

Garcia, Hazel. "Of Punctilios among the Fair Sex: Colonial American Magazines, 1741–1776." *Journalism History* 3 (Summer 1976):48–63.

Goldin, Claudia. "The Economic Status of Women in the Early Republic: Quantitative Evidence." *Journal of Interdisciplinary History* 16 (1986):375–404.

Goody, Jack, Joan Thirsk, and E. P. Thompson, eds. *Family and Inheritance.* Cambridge: Cambridge University Press, 1976.

Gough, Deborah Mathias. "A Further Look at Widows in Early Southeastern Pennsylvania." *William and Mary Quarterly,* 3d ser., 44 (1987):829–39.

Greaves, Richard L., ed. *Triumph over Silence: Women in Protestant History.* New York: Greenwood Press, 1985.

Green, Gretchen L. "Molly Brant, Catharine Brant, and Their Daughters: A Study in Colonial Acculturation." *Ontario History* 81, no. 3 (1989):235–50.

Green, Rayna. "The Pocahontas Perplex: The Image of Indian Women in American Culture." *Massachusetts Review* 13 (1975):698–714.

———. "Native American Women: A Review Essay." *Signs* 6 (1980):248–67.

Greven, Philip, Jr. *Four Generations: Population, Land, and Family in Colonial Andover, Massachusetts.* Ithaca, N.Y.: Cornell University Press, 1970.

———. *The Protestant Temperament: Patterns of Child-Rearing, Religious Experience, and the Self in Early America.* Chicago: University of Chicago Press, 1977.

Griffiths, Naomi Elizabeth Saunders. *Penelope's Web: Some Perceptions of Women in European and Canadian Society.* Toronto: Oxford University Press, 1976.

Gundersen, Joan R. "The Double Bonds of Race and Sex: Black and White Women in a Colonial Virginia Parish." *Journal of Southern History* 52 (1986): 351–72.

Gundersen, Joan R., and Gwen Victor Gampel. "Married Women's Legal Status in Eighteenth-Century New York and Virginia." *William and Mary Quarterly,* 3d ser., 39 (1982):114–34.

Hafkin, Nancy J., and Edna G. Bay, eds. *Women in Africa: Studies in Social and Economic Change.* Stanford, Calif.: Stanford University Press, 1976.

Hamill, Frances. "Some Unconventional Women before 1800: Printers, Booksellers, and Collectors." *Bibliographical Society of America Papers* 49 (1955):300–314.

Harris, Barbara J. *Beyond Her Sphere: Women and the Professions in American History.* Westport, Conn.: Greenwood Press, 1978.

Harris, Barbara J., and JoAnn McNamara, eds. *Women and the Structure of Society: Selected Research from the Fifth Berkshire Conference on the History of Women.* Durham, N.C.: Duke University Press, 1984.

Hawks, Joanne V., and Sheila L. Skemp, eds. *Sex, Race, and the Role of Women in the South.* Jackson: University Press of Mississippi, 1983.

Henderson, Roger C. "Demographic Patterns and Family Structure in Eighteenth-Century Lancaster County, Pennsylvania." *Pennsylvania Magazine of History and Biography* 114 (July 1990):349–83.

Hendricks, Margo, and Patricia Parker, eds. *Women, "Race," and Writing in the Early Modern Period.* London: Routledge, 1994.

Henretta, James A. "Families and Farms: Mentalité in Pre-Industrial America." *William and Mary Quarterly,* 3d ser., 35 (1978):3–32.

Hewitt, J.N.B. "Status of Women in Iroquois Polity Before 1784." *Annual Report of the Board of Regents of the Smithsonian Institution for 1932.* Washington, D.C.

Hinding, Andrea, and Clarke A. Chambers, eds. *Women's History Sources: A Guide to Archives and Manuscript Collections in the United States.* New York: R. R. Bowker, 1979.

Hobby, Elaine. *Virtue of Necessity: English Women's Writing 1646–1688.* London: Virago Press, 1988.

Hoff-Wilson, Joan. "The Illusion of Change: Women and the American Revolution." In *The American Revolution: Explorations in the History of American Radicalism,* edited by Alfred F. Young. DeKalb: Northern Illinois University Press, 1976.

Hoffer, Peter C., and N.E.H. Hull. *Murdering Mothers: Infanticide in England and New England, 1558–1803.* New York: New York University Press, 1981.

Hoffman, Ronald, and Peter J. Albert, eds. *Women in the Age of the American Revolution.* Charlottesville: University Press of Virginia, 1989.

Howard, George E. *A History of Matrimonial Institutions.* Chicago: University of Chicago Press, 1904.

Hudak, Leona M. *Early American Women Printers and Publishers 1639–1820.* Metuchen, N.J.: Scarecrow Press, 1978.

Hull, N.E.H. *Female Felons: Women and Serious Crime in Colonial Massachusetts.* Urbana: University of Illinois Press, 1987.

Hutchinson, Sophie Drinker. *Hannah Penn and the Proprietorship of Pennsylvania.* Philadelphia: National Society of the Colonial Dames of America in the Commonwealth of Pennsylvania, 1958.

Hymowitz, Carol, and Michele Weissman. *A History of Women in America.* New York: Bantam Books, 1978.

Ingle, H. Larry. "A Quaker Woman on Women's Roles: Mary Penington to Friends, 1678." *Signs* 16 (Spring 1991):587–96.

James, Edward T., and Janet Wilson James, eds. *Notable American Women, 1607–1950: A Biographical Dictionary.* 3 vols. Cambridge, Mass.: Belknap Press, 1971.

James, Janet Wilson. *Changing Ideas about Women in the United States, 1776–1825.* New York: Garland, 1981.

———, ed. *Women in American Religion.* Philadelphia: University of Pennsylvania Press, 1980.

Jensen, Joan M. *Loosening the Bonds: Mid-Atlantic Farm Women, 1750–1850.* New Haven, Conn.: Yale University Press, 1986.

Juster, Susan M. " 'In a Different Voice': Male and Female Narratives of Religious Conversion in Post-Revolutionary America." *American Quarterly* 41, no. 1 (March 1989):34–62.

———. "Sinners and Saints: The Evangelical Construction of Gender and Authority in New England, 1740–1830." Ph.D. diss., University of Michigan, 1990.

Karlsen, Carol F. *The Devil in the Shape of a Woman: Witchcraft in Colonial New England.* New York: Norton, 1987.

Katz, Ester, and Anita Rapone, eds. *Women's Experience in America: An Historical Anthology.* New Brunswick, N.J.: Transaction Books, 1980.

Katz, Maude White. "She Who Would Be Free—Resistance." *Freedomways* (Winter 1962):60–70.

Kelley, Mary, ed. *Woman's Being, Woman's Place: Female Identity and Vocation in American History.* Boston: G. K. Hall, 1979.

Kerber, Linda K. *Women of the Republic: Intellect and Ideology in Revolutionary America.* Chapel Hill: University of North Carolina Press, 1980.

———. "Separate Spheres, Female Worlds, Woman's Place: The Rhetoric of Women's History." *Journal of American History* 75 (June 1988):9–39.

Kerber, Linda K., Nancy F. Cott, Robert Gross, Lynn Hunt, Carroll Smith-

Rosenberg, and Christine M. Stansell. "Beyond Roles, Beyond Spheres: Thinking about Gender in the Early Republic." *William and Mary Quarterly,* 3d ser., 46 (1989):565–86.

Kessler-Harris, Alice. *Women Have Always Worked: A Historical Overview.* Old Westbury, N.Y.: Feminist Press, 1981.

―――. *Out to Work: A History of Wage-Earning Women in the United States.* New York: Oxford University Press, 1982.

Keysar, Alexander. "Widowhood in Eighteenth-Century Massachusetts: A Problem in the History of the Family." *Perspectives in American History* 8 (1974): 83–119.

Kidwell, Clara Sue. "Indian Women as Cultural Mediators." *Ethnohistory* 39 (1992):87–107.

Kirwen, Michael C. *African Widows.* Maryknoll, N.Y.: Orbis Books, 1979.

Klein, Joan Larsen. *Daughters, Wives, and Widows: Writings by Men about Women and Marriage in England, 1500–1640.* Urbana: University of Illinois Press, 1992.

Kleinberg, S. Jay, ed. *Retrieving Women's History: Changing Perceptions of the Role of Women in Politics and Society.* Oxford: Unesco, 1988.

Koehler, Lyle. *A Search for Power: The "Weaker Sex" in Seventeenth-Century New England.* Urbana: University of Illinois Press, 1980.

Koppedrayer, K. I. "The Making of the First Iroquois Virgin: Early Jesuit Biographies of the Blessed Kateri Tekakwitha." *Ethnohistory* 40 (1993):277–306.

Kulikoff, Allan. *"A Share of Honour": Virginia Women 1600–1945.* Richmond: W. M. Brown and Son for the Virginia Women's Cultural History Project, 1984.

Lacey, Barbara E. "Gender, Piety, and Secularization in Connecticut Religion, 1720–1775." *Journal of Social History* 24, no. 4 (Summer 1991):799–821.

Leacock, Eleanor, ed. *Myths of Male Dominance: Collected Articles on Women Cross-Culturally.* New York: Monthly Review Press, 1981.

Leacock, Eleanor, and Mona Etienne, eds. *Women and Colonization: Anthropological Perspectives.* New York: Preager, 1980.

Lebsock, Suzanne. *The Free Women of Petersburg: Status and Culture in a Southern Town, 1784–1860.* New York: Norton, 1984.

Lee, Jean Butenhoff. "Land and Labor: Parental Bequest Practices in Charles County, Maryland, 1732–1783." In *Colonial Chesapeake Society,* edited by Lois Green Carr, Philip D. Morgan, and Jean B. Russo. Chapel Hill: University of North Carolina Press, 1988.

Leghorn, Lisa, and Katherine Parker. *Woman's Worth: Sexual Economics and the World of Women.* Boston: Routledge and Kegan Paul, 1981.

Leonard, Eudenie Andruss. *The American Woman in Colonial and Revolutionary Times, 1565–1800.* Philadelphia: University of Pennsylvania Press, 1962.

―――. *The Dear-Bought Heritage.* Philadelphia: University of Pennsylvania Press, 1965.

Lerner, Gerda. *The Creation of Patriarchy.* Oxford: Oxford University Press, 1986.

Levin, Carole. *"The Heart and Stomach of a King": Elizabeth I and the Politics of Sex and Power.* Philadelphia: University of Pennsylvania Press, 1994.

Levy, Barry. *Quakers and the American Family: British Settlement in the Delaware Valley.* New York: Oxford University Press, 1988.

Levy, Darline Gay, Harriet Bronson Applewhite, and Mary Durham Johnson. *Women in Revolutionary Paris, 1789–1795: Selected Documents Translated with Notes and Commentary.* Urbana: University of Illinois Press, 1979.

Lewis, Jan. *The Pursuit of Happiness: Family and Values in Jefferson's Virginia.* New York: Cambridge University Press, 1983.

———. "The Republican Wife: Virtue and Seduction in The Early Republic." *William and Mary Quarterly,* 3d ser., 44 (1987):689–721.

Lewis, Johanna Miller. "Women Artisans in Backcountry North Carolina, 1753–1790." *North Carolina Historical Review* 68 (July 1991):214–36.

Linn, John B., and William H. Egle, eds. "Record of Pennsylvania Marriages prior to 1810." In *Pennsylvania Archives.* Philadelphia: Joseph Severns, 1857.

Macdonald, James Ramsay. *Women in the Printing Trades: A Sociological Study.* London: P. S. King and Son, 1904.

MacFarlane, Alan. *Marriage and Love in England: Modes of Reproduction, 1300–1840.* Oxford: Basil Blackwell, 1986.

Mack, Phyllis. *Visionary Women: Ecstatic Prophecy in Seventeenth-Century England.* Berkeley: University of California Press, 1992.

Main, Gloria L. "An Inquiry into When and Why Women Learned to Write in Colonial New England." *Journal of Social History* 24 (1990–91):579–89.

———. "Gender, Work, and Wages in Colonial New England." *William and Mary Quarterly,* 3d ser., 51, no. 1 (1994):39–66.

Manges, Frances May. "Women Shopkeepers, Tavernkeepers, and Artisans in Colonial Philadelphia." Ph.D. diss., University of Pennsylvania, 1958.

Marzolf, Marion. *Up from the Footnote: A History of Women Journalists.* New York: Hastings House, 1977.

Masson, Margaret T. "The Typology of the Female as a Model for the Regenerate: Puritan Preaching, 1690–1740." *Signs* 2 (Winter 1976):304–15.

Matthaei, Julie A. *An Economic History of Women in America.* New York: Schocken Books, 1982.

McCartney, Martha W. "Cockacoeske, Queen of Pamunkey: Diplomat and Suzeraine." In *Powhatan's Mantle: Indians in the Colonial Southeast,* edited by Peter H. Wood, Gregory Waselkov, and M. Thomas Hatley. Lincoln: University of Nebraska Press, 1989.

Meehan, Thomas R. "Not Made out of Levity: Evolution of Divorce in Early Pennsylvania." *Pennsylvania Magazine of History and Biography* 92 (October 1968):441–64.

Meriwether, James B., ed. *South Carolina Women Writers.* Columbia: University of South Carolina Press, 1979.

Morgan, Edmund S. *Virginians at Home: Family Life in the Eighteenth Century.* Williamsburg, Va.: Holt, Rinehart and Winston, 1952.

———. *The Puritan Family: Religion and Domestic Relations in Seventeenth-Century New England.* New York: Harper and Row, 1966.

Morrissey, Marietta. *Slave Women in the New World: Gender Stratification in the Caribbean.* Lawrence: University of Kansas Press, 1989.

Namias, June. *White Captives: Gender and Ethnicity on the American Frontier.* Chapel Hill: University of North Carolina Press, 1993.

———, ed. *A Narrative of the Life of Mrs. Mary Jemison.* Norman: University of Oklahoma Press, 1992.

Norling, Lisa A. "Captain Ahab Had a Wife: Ideology and Experience in the Lives of New England Maritime Women, 1760–1870." Ph.D. diss., Rutgers University, 1992.

Norton, Mary Beth. "Eighteenth-Century Women in Peace and War: The Case of the Loyalists." *William and Mary Quarterly,* 3d ser., 33 (1976):386–409.

———. *Liberty's Daughters: The Revolutionary Experience of American Women, 1750–1800.* Boston: Little, Brown, 1980.

———. "The Evolution of White Women's Experience in Early America." *American Historical Review* 89 (1984):593–619.

———. "Gender and Defamation in Seventeenth-Century Maryland." *William and Mary Quarterly,* 3d ser., 44 (1987):3–39.

———. "Gender, Crime, and Community in Seventeenth-Century Maryland." In *The Transformation of Early American History: Society, Authority and Ideology,* edited by James A. Henretta, Michael Kammen, and Stanley N. Katz. New York: Knopf, 1991.

Nowak, Barbara. "Women's Roles and Status in a Changing Iroquois Society." In *Occasional Papers in Anthropology,* vol. 1, edited by Ann McElroy and Carolyn Matthiasson (Buffalo: Department of Anthropology, State University of New York, 1979), 105–6.

Parish, Debra. "The Power of Female Pietism: Women as Spiritual Authorities and Religious Role Models in Seventeenth-Century England." *Journal of Religious History* 17, no. 1 (June 1992):33–46.

Parramore, Mary Roberts. " 'For Her Sole and Separate Use': *Feme Sole* Trader Status in Early South Carolina." Master's thesis, University of South Carolina, 1991.

Perkins, Elizabeth A. "The Consumer Frontier: Household Consumption in Early Kentucky." *Journal of American History* 78, no. 2 (1991):486–510.

Perlmann, Joel, and Dennis Shirley. "When Did New England Women Acquire Literacy?" *William and Mary Quarterly,* 3d ser., 48, no. 1 (1991):50–67.

Plane, Ann Marie. "Colonizing the Family: Marriage, Household, and Racial Boundaries in Southeastern New England to 1730." Ph.D. diss., Brandeis University, 1994.

Pleck, Elizabeth. *Domestic Tyranny: The Making of American Social Policy against Family Violence from Colonial Times to the Present.* New York: Oxford University Press, 1987.

Porterfield, Amanda. "Beames of Wrath and Brides of Christ: Anger and Female Piety in Puritan New England." *Connecticut Review* 11, no. 2 (Summer 1989): 1–12.

Premo, Terri L. *Winter Friends: Women Growing Old in the New Republic, 1785–1835.* Urbana: University of Illinois Press, 1990.

Prentice, Alison, and Susan M. Trofimenkoff, eds. *The Neglected Majority.* Toronto: McClelland and Stewart, 1985.

Prior, Mary, ed. *Women in English Society, 1500–1800.* New York: Methuen, 1985.

Ramsbottom, Mary McManus. "Religious Society and the Family in Charlestown, Massachusetts, 1630–1740." Ph.D. diss., Yale University, 1987.

Rapley, Elizabeth. *The Dévotes: Women and Church in Seventeenth-Century France.* Montreal: McGill-Queen's Press, 1990.

Reiter, Rayna, ed. *Toward an Anthropology of Women.* New York: Monthly Review Press, 1975.

Riley, Denise. *"Am I That Name?" Feminism and the Category of "Women" in History.* Minneapolis: University of Minnesota Press, 1988.

Robertson, Claire C., and Martin A. Klein, eds. *Women and Slavery in Africa.* Madison: University of Wisconsin Press, 1983.

Ross, Isabel. *Margaret Fell: Mother of Quakerism.* London: Longmans, Green, 1949.

Rowe, Gail Stuart. "The Role of Courthouses in the Lives of Eighteenth-Century Pennsylvania Women." *Western Pennsylvania Historical Magazine* 68 (1985): 5–23.

———. "Women's Crime and Criminal Administration in Pennsylvania." *Pennsylvania Magazine of History and Biography* 109 (1985):335–68.

Ruether, Rosemary Radford, and Rosemary Skinner Keller, eds. *Women and Religion in America: The Colonial and Revolutionary Periods.* San Francisco: Harper and Row, 1983.

Rutman, Darrett B., and Anita H. Rutman. " 'Now-Wives and Sons-in-Law': Parental Death in a Seventeenth-Century Virginia County." In *The Chesapeake in the Seventeenth Century: Essays on Anglo-American Society,* edited by Thad W. Tate and David L. Ammerman. Chapel Hill: University of North Carolina Press, 1979.

Ryan, Mary P. *Womanhood in America: From Colonial Times to the Present.* New York: New Viewpoints, 1975.

———. *Cradle of the Middle Class: The Family in Oneida County, New York, 1790–1865.* New York: Cambridge University Press, 1981.

Salinger, Sharon. " 'Send No More Women': Female Servants in Late Eighteenth-Century Philadelphia." *Pennsylvania Magazine of History and Biography* 107 (January 1983):29–48.

Salmon, Marylynn. "Women and Property in South Carolina: The Evidence from Marriage Settlements, 1730–1830." *William and Mary Quarterly*, 3d ser., 39 (1982):655–85.

———. "The Legal Status of Women in Early America: A Reappraisal." *Law and History Review* 1 (1983):129–51.

———. *Women and the Law of Property in Early America.* Chapel Hill: University of North Carolina Press, 1986.

Scadron, Arlene, ed. *On Their Own: Widows and Widowhood in the American Southwest, 1848–1939.* Urbana: University of Illinois Press, 1988.

Scholten, Catherine M. *Childbearing in American Society: 1650–1850.* New York: New York University Press, 1985.

Schweitzer, Mary M. *Custom and Contract: Household, Government, and the Economy in Colonial Pennsylvania.* New York: Columbia University Press, 1987.

Scott, Anne Firor. *The Southern Lady: From Pedestal to Politics, 1830–1930.* Chicago: University of Chicago Press, 1970.

Scott, Joan Wallach. "Gender: A Useful Category of Historical Analysis." *American Historical Review* 91 (1986):1053–75.

———. *Gender and the Politics of History.* New York: Columbia University Press, 1988.

Shammas, Carole. "The Female Social Structure of Philadelphia in 1775." *Pennsylvania Magazine of History and Biography* 107 (January 1983):69–83.

———. "Black Women's Work and the Evolution of Plantation Society in Virginia." *Labor History* 26 (1985):5–28.

Sharpe, Pamela. "Literally Spinsters: A New Interpretation of Local Economy and Demography in Colyton in the Seventeenth and Eighteenth Centuries." *Economic History Review* 44 (1991):46–65.

Sherry, Suzanna. "Civic Virtue and the Feminine Voice in Constitutional Adjudication." *Virginia Law Review* 72 (1986):543–616.

Shiels, Richard D. "The Feminization of American Congregationalism, 1730–1835." *American Quarterly* 31, no. 1 (Spring 1981):46–62.

Shoemaker, Nancy. "The Rise or Fall of Iroquois Women." *Journal of Women's History* 2 (Winter 1992):39–57.

———, ed. *Negotiators of Change: Historical Perspectives on Native American Women.* New York: Routledge, 1995.

Slotten, Martha C. "Elizabeth Graeme Ferguson: A Poet in the Athens of America." *Pennsylvania Magazine of History and Biography* 108 (July 1984):259–88.

Smith, Daniel Blake. "Mortality and Family in the Colonial Chesapeake." *Journal of Interdisciplinary History* 8 (1978):403–27.

Smith, Daniel Blake. *Inside the Great House: Planter Family Life in Eighteenth-Century Chesapeake Society.* Ithaca, N.Y.: Cornell University Press, 1980.

———. "The Study of the Family in Early America: Trends, Problems, Prospects." *William and Mary Quarterly,* 3d ser., 29 (1982):3–28.

Smith, Daniel Scott. "Parental Power and Marriage Patterns: An Analysis of Historical Trends in Hingham, Massachusetts." *Journal of Marriage and the Family* 35 (1973):419–28.

Smith, Merril D. *Breaking the Bonds: Marital Discord in Pennsylvania, 1730–1830.* New York: New York University Press, 1991.

Smith, Paige. *Daughters of the Promised Land.* Boston: Little, Brown, 1970.

Smith, Ruth L. "Moral Transcendence and Moral Space in the Historical Experiences of Women." *Journal of Feminist Studies in Religion* 4, no. 2 (Fall 1988): 21–37.

Smith-Rosenberg, Carroll. "Domesticating Virtue: Coquettes and Revolutionaries in Young America." In *Literature and the Body: Essays on Populations and Persons,* edited by Elaine Scarry. Baltimore: Johns Hopkins University Press, 1988.

Snydacker, Daniel. "Kinship and Community in Rural Pennsylvania, 1749–1820." *Journal of Interdisciplinary History* 13, no. 1 (1982):41–61.

Sochen, June. *Her Story: A Record of the American Woman's Past.* Palo Alto, Calif.: Mayfield, 1982.

Soderlund, Jean R. "Black Women in Colonial Pennsylvania." *Pennsylvania Magazine of History and Biography* 107 (January 1983):48–68.

———. "Women's Authority in Pennsylvania and New Jersey Quaker Meetings, 1680–1760." *William and Mary Quarterly,* 3d ser., 44, no. 4 (1987):722–49.

———. "Women in Eighteenth-Century Pennsylvania: Toward a Model of Diversity." *Pennsylvania Magazine of History and Biography* 115 (April 1991):163–83.

Somerville, James K. "The Salem (Mass.) Woman in the Home, 1660–1770." *Eighteenth-Century Life* 1 (1974):11–14.

Spector, Janet. *What This Awl Means: Feminist Archaeology at a Wahpeton Dakota Village.* St. Paul: Minnesota Historical Society Press, 1993.

Speth, Linda. "More Than Her 'Thirds': Wives and Widows in Colonial Virginia." *Women and History* 4 (1983):5–41.

Speth, Linda, and Alison Duncan Hirsch. *Women, Family, and Community in Colonial America: Two Perspectives.* New York: Hasworth Press, 1983.

Spittal, William Guy, ed. *Iroquois Women: An Anthology.* Ohsweken, Ont.: Iroqrafts, 1990.

Sprigg, June. *Domestick Beings.* New York: Knopf, 1984.

Spruill, Julia Cherry. *Women's Life and Work in the Southern Colonies.* Chapel Hill: University of North Carolina Press, 1938; reprint, New York: Norton, 1972.

Stansell, Christine. *City of Women: Sex and Class in New York, 1789–1860.* Urbana: University of Illinois Press, 1987.

Staves, Susan. *Married Women's Separate Property in England, 1660–1833.* Cambridge: Harvard University Press, 1990.

Stone, Lawrence. *The Family, Sex, and Marriage in England 1500–1800.* Abridged ed. New York: Harper Torchbooks, 1977.

Sturtz, Linda L. "Law and Women in the Seventeenth-Century Courts of York County, Virginia." Master's thesis, College of William and Mary, 1987.

Tanner, Helen H. "Coocoochee: Mohawk Medicine Woman." *American Indian Culture and Research Journal* 3, no. 3 (1979):23–42.

Terborg-Penn, Rosalyn, Sharon Harley, and Andrea Benton Rushing, eds. *Women in Africa and the African Diaspora.* Washington, D.C.: Howard University Press, 1987.

Thomsett, Christine H. "A Note on the Economic Status of Widows in Colonial New York." *New York History* 55 (1974):319–32.

Tooker, Elisabeth. "Women in Iroquois Society." In *Extending the Rafters: Interdisciplinary Approaches to Iroquoian Studies,* edited by Michael Foster, Jack Campisi, and Marianne Mithun. Albany: State University of New York Press, 1984.

Trumbach, Randolph. *The Rise of the Egalitarian Family: Aristocratic Kinship and Domestic Relations in Eighteenth-Century England.* New York: Academic Press, 1978.

Tryon, Rolla Milton. *Household Manufactures in the United States, 1640–1860.* Chicago: University of Chicago Press, 1917.

Ulrich, Laurel Thatcher. *Good Wives: Image and Reality in the Lives of Women in Northern New England, 1650–1750.* New York: Knopf, 1982.

———. "Martha Ballard and Her Girls: Women's Work in Eighteenth Century Maine." In *Work and Labor in Early America,* edited by Stephen Innes. Chapel Hill: University of North Carolina Press, 1988.

———. "Of Pens and Needles: Sources in Early American Women's History." *Journal of American History* 71 (1990):200–207.

———. *A Midwife's Tale: The Life of Martha Ballard, Based on Her Diary, 1785–1812.* New York: Knopf, 1991.

Underdown, David E. "The Taming of the Scold: The Enforcement of Patriarchal Authority in Early Modern England." In *Order and Disorder in Early Modern England,* edited by Anthony Fletcher and John Stevenson. Cambridge: Cambridge University Press, 1985.

Van Kirk, Sylvia. *"Many Tender Ties": Women in Fur-Trade Society in Western Canada, 1670–1870.* Winnipeg: Watson and Dwyer, 1980.

Walker, Gay. "Women Printers in Early American Printing History." *Yale University Library Gazette* 61 (1987):116–24.

Wall, Helena M. *Fierce Communion: Family and Community in Early America.* Cambridge, Mass.: Harvard University Press, 1990.

Waters, John J. "Patrimony, Succession, and Social Stability: Guilford, Connecticut in the Eighteenth Century." *Perspectives in American History* 10 (1976): 131–60.

Weatherwax, Sarah J. "The Importance of Family in the Community of New Poquoson Parish, York County, Virginia, in the Late Seventeenth Century." Master's thesis, College of William and Mary, 1984.

Wells, Robert V. "Quaker Marriage Patterns in a Colonial Perspective." *William and Mary Quarterly*, 3d ser., 29 (1972):415–42.

———. "Household Size and Composition in the British Colonies in America, 1675–1775." *Journal of Interdisciplinary History* 4 (1974):543–70.

———. "Family History and Demographic Transition." *Journal of Social History* 9 (1975):1–20.

Werner, Raymond C., ed. "Diary of Grace Growden Galloway." *Pennsylvania Magazine of History and Biography* 55 (1931):32–94; 58 (1934):152–89.

Wertheimer, Barbara Mayer. *We Were There: The Story of Working Women in America.* New York: Pantheon Books, 1977.

Westerkamp, Marilyn. "Puritan Patriarchy and the Problem of Revelation." *Journal of Interdisciplinary History* 23, no. 3 (Winter 1993):571–95.

Willen, Diane. "Godly Women in Early Modern England: Puritanism and Gender." *Journal of Ecclesiastical History* 43, no. 4 (October 1992):561–80.

Williams, Selma R. *Demeter's Daughters: The Women Who Founded America, 1587–1787.* New York: Atheneum, 1976.

Wilson, Lisa. "A 'Man of Business': The Widow of Means in Southeastern Pennsylvania, 1750–1850." *William and Mary Quarterly*, 3d ser., 44, no. 1 (1987):40–64.

———. *Life after Death: Widows in Pennsylvania, 1750–1850.* Philadelphia: Temple University Press, 1992.

Withey, Lynne E. "Household Structure in Urban and Rural Areas: The Case of Rhode Island, 1774–1800." *Journal of Family History* 3 (March 1978):37–50.

Woloch, Nancy. *Women and the American Experience.* New York: Knopf, 1984.

Zagarri, Rosemary. "Morals, Manners, and the Republican Mother." *American Quarterly* 44 (June 1992):192–215.

Contributors

LILLIAN ASHCRAFT-EASON is assistant professor of history at Bowling Green State University in Bowling Green, Ohio. She has authored *About My Father's Business: The Life of Elder Michaux* (Greenwood Press, 1981) and several articles related to African American history.

EIRLYS M. BARKER is professor of history at Thomas Nelson Community College in Hampton, Virginia. Her dissertation, "Much Blood and Treasure: South Carolina's Indian Traders, 1670–1755," was directed by James Axtell. Her publications include "Pryce Hughes, Colony Planner, of Charles Town and Wales," *South Carolina Historical Magazine* (1994).

VIVIAN BRUCE CONGER is assistant professor of history at St. Michael's College in Burlington, Vermont. Her dissertation, " 'Being Weak of Body but Firm of Mind and Memory': Widowhood in Colonial America, 1630–1750," was directed by Mary Beth Norton. Conger's professional presentations include "Widowhood in Colonial Maryland" (1990 annual meeting of the Southern Historical Association).

TERRENCE A. CROWLEY is professor of history at the University of Guelph in Guelph, Ontario. He is the editor of four volumes, including *Clio's Craft: A Primer of Historical Methods* (Copp Clark Pitman, 1988), and the author of several others, including *Agnes Macphail and the Politics of Equality* (Lorimer, 1990).

ELIZABETH DALE is assistant professor of history at Clemson University. She is the author of numerous articles on legal history, including "Conflicts of Law: Rethinking the Relation of Law and Religion in Seventeenth-Century Massachusetts Bay," *Numen* (1995).

LARRY D. ELDRIDGE is assistant professor of history and chair of the history department at Widener University in Chester, Pennsylvania.

347

He is the author of *A Distant Heritage: The Growth of Free Speech in Early America* (New York University Press, 1994) and of numerous articles, including " 'Crazy-brained': Mental Illness in Colonial America," *Bulletin of the History of Medicine* (1996).

GRETCHEN L. GREEN is assistant professor of history at Rockhurst College in Kansas City, Missouri. She has numerous publications to her credit, including "Molly Brant, Catharine Brant, and Their Daughters: A Study in Colonial Acculturation," *Ontario History* (1989).

RUTH WALLIS HERNDON is a research fellow at the Philadelphia Center for Early American Studies. Her publications include "On and Off the Record: Town Clerks as Interpreters of Rhode Island History," *Rhode Island History* (1992), and "The Domestic Cost of Seafaring: Town Leaders and Seaman's Families in Rhode Island, 1750–1800," in *Iron Men, Wooden Women: Gender and Atlantic Seafaring, 1700–1920*, edited by Margaret Creighton and Lisa Norling (Johns Hopkins University Press, 1996).

MARTHA J. KING is assistant editor with the Rhode Island Historical Society's "Papers of General Nathaneal Greene" project. She was formerly an assistant editor of the "Thomas A. Edison Papers" at Rutgers University. Her most recent publications include "Clementina Rind," *American National Biography* (1996).

JOHANNA MILLER LEWIS is associate professor of history at the University of Arkansas, Little Rock, and assistant coordinator of the university's Public History Program. Her numerous publications include *Artisans in the North Carolina Backcountry* (University Press of Kentucky, 1995).

JANET MOORE LINDMAN is assistant professor of history at Rowan College of New Jersey. Her more recent professional presentations include "Ritual Practice and the Creation of Baptist Orthodoxy in Eighteenth-Century America" (1995 annual meeting of the American Studies Association) and "The Inner Woman of Anne Emlen: The Construction of a Religious Self and Quaker Spiritual Autobiography" (first annual conference of the Institute of Early American History and Culture, 1995).

JAN V. NOEL is assistant professor of history at the University of Toronto, Erindale. She is the author of *Canada Dry: Temperance Crusades before Confederation* (University of Toronto Press, 1996) and of numerous published essays and articles, including "Women in New France: Further Reflections," *Atlantis* (1982).

JULIE RICHTER is a historian in the department of historical research, Colonial Williamsburg Foundation. Her numerous professional presentations include "In the Community but Not of the Community: Free Blacks in Eighteenth-Century Charles Parish, York County, Virginia" (1990 annual meeting of the Southern Historical Association) and "On Both Sides of the Law: Women and the Investigation of Social Crimes in Seventeenth-Century Charles Parish, York County, Virginia" (1994 Southern Conference on Women's History).

JUDITH A. RIDNER is assistant professor of history at California State University, Northridge. The most recent of her professional presentations include " 'I Am, My Dear Love, Affectionately Yours:' Husbands and Their Wives in the Pennsylvania Backcountry" (1995 annual meeting of the Organization of American Historians).

DEBORAH A. ROSEN is assistant professor of history and chair of the American Studies Program at Lafayette College in Easton, Pennsylvania. She has written "Courts and Commerce in Colonial New York," *American Journal of Legal History* (1992), and with Alden T. Vaughan she is coeditor of *Early American Indian Documents: Treaties and Laws, 1607–1789*, volumes 19 and 20, *Laws, 1607–1789*, forthcoming from University Publications of America.

MERRIL D. SMITH is adjunct professor of history at Temple University in Philadelphia, Pennsylvania. She is the author of *Breaking the Bonds: Marital Discord in Pennsylvania, 1730–1830* (New York University Press, 1991), and her many professional presentations include " 'Unnatural

Mothers': Infanticide, Child Abuse, and Motherhood in the Mid-Atlantic, 1730–1830" (1996 annual meeting of the Organization of American Historians).

KARIN A. WULF is assistant professor of history at American University in Washington, D.C. She is coeditor of *Milcah Martha Moore's Book: The Commonplace Book of an Eighteenth-Century American* (Pennsylvania State University Press, 1996). Her most recent professional presentations include "Gender, Property, and the Formation of Urban Political Culture in Pre-Revolutionary Philadelphia" (1996 Berkshire Conference on the History of Women).

Index

Adultery: examples of, 293, 294–95; punishment of among Baptists, 130; punishment of among southeastern tribes, 52–53. *See also* Bastardy; Fornication

African Americans: destiny as a concept among, 71–72; free community of, in Providence, Rhode Island, 278, 284; free one on New York tax list, 324; one said to be mentally ill, 284; running transient boarding houses, 278; transient profile of, 278–79; two sailors mentioned, 278. *See also* African American women; Race; Slaves

African American women: descriptions of, changed by the American Revolution, 286 n. 7; disadvantages in "warning out" procedures, 282; examples of opposing "warning out" procedures, 282; and freedom in early Virginia, 62–77; free one in Pennsylvania almshouse, 212–13; and literacy, 275; problem of identifying, 286 n. 7; punished for fornication, 67, 76; and trade, 72–73; transients, 269–70, 283–84; widows, 73. *See also* African Americans; Race; Slaves

Age of majority: for English colonists generally, 101, 107 n. 33; in New France, 118–19; in North Carolina, 202

Alimony, in early Pennsylvania, 27. *See also* Divorce; Separations

American Revolution: adds to transient population of New England, 272; changes how women of color are described, 286 n. 7; in Charleston, South Carolina, 158–59; effect on women's roles, 170, 175–76, 178, 180; mentioned, 200, 215; rhetoric of, and women's roles, 101–2; supposed effect on bequeathing patterns, 261

Bastardy: consequences of, and responses to, in early New York, 320; examples of, 296; general concern over, in Virginia,

293, 295–96, 309 n. 5; in North Carolina, 201–2; interracial, 67, 76; prominent in "warning out" cases, 274; punished among Baptists, 130; widows and, 295. *See also* Adultery; Fornication

Begging: women driven to, in Pennsylvania, 221; women seek permission for, in New York, 319–20

Bigamy, and female transiency, 281

Business: gender roles in, in New France, 35–36; operated by women's religious communities, 119–20; women in, 27–28, 147–62, 194–95, 220, 296, 298, 299, 299–300. *See also* Work; Work, gender differences in

Catholic church: effect on Iroquois gender relations, 18; patriarchy in, 113–14, 119, 124; restrictions on women in, 113

Child-raising practices: among Baptist women, 135; among New France nobility, 33–35; among the southeastern tribes, 52; in North Carolina, 201–2, 203; in Pennsylvania, 169, 183, 214, 222; in Virginia, 298

Children: case of binding out, 301; education of, 299, 301–2; discipline of, among the Iroquois, 9; number of, among New France nobles, 31; protection of, 304

Christianity: effect on slaves, 65, 69; effect on the southeastern tribes, 57

Convents: New France women in, 34, 37, 42 n. 31, 109–24. *See also* Dowries

Courts, women and: in New York, 313–27; in Rhode Island, 269–85; in Virginia, 290–309; women rarely settle disputes in, 314

Desertion: and female transiency, 281; in New York, 321–22; in Pennsylvania, 211–24

Disease: ague, 214; fever, 214, measles, 157; rheumatism, 222; smallpox, 112, 150, 151, 213; venereal, 213, 215–16, 226 n. 11

Learning Resources
Centre